Computer Accounting
with
QuickBooks® Online

Third Edition

Donna Kay, MBA, PhD, CPA, CITP

COMPUTER ACCOUNTING WITH QUICKBOOKS® ONLINE, THIRD EDITION

Published by McGraw Hill LLC, 1325 Avenue of the Americas, New York, NY 10019. Copyright ©2023 by McGraw Hill LLC. All rights reserved. Printed in the United States of America. Previous editions ©2021, 2019. No part of this publication may be reproduced or distributed in any form or by any means, or stored in a database or retrieval system, without the prior written consent of McGraw Hill LLC, including, but not limited to, in any network or other electronic storage or transmission, or broadcast for distance learning.

Some ancillaries, including electronic and print components, may not be available to customers outside the United States.

This book is printed on acid-free paper.

1 2 3 4 5 6 7 8 9 LMN 27 26 25 24 23 22

ISBN 978-1-264-12727-6 (bound edition)
MHID 1-264-12727-8 (bound edition)
ISBN 978-1-265-63890-0 (loose-leaf edition)
MHID 1-265-63890-X (loose-leaf edition)

Executive Portfolio Manager: *Steve Schuetz*
Product Developers: *Sarah Sacco, Caira Coleman*
Marketing Manager: *Claire McLemore*
Content Project Managers: *Jill Eccher and Emily Windelborn*
Buyer: *Susan K. Culbertson*
Content Licensing Specialist: *Melissa Homer*
Cover Image: *Sina Ettmer Photography/Shutterstock*
Design Elements: *QuickBooks® and QuickBooks® Online Plus are registered trademarks of Intuit Inc.*
Compositor: *Straive*

All credits appearing on page or at the end of the book are considered to be an extension of the copyright page.

Library of Congress Control Number: 2022901965

mheducation.com/highered

Preface

Computer Accounting with QuickBooks Online

THIRD EDITION   DONNA KAY

Welcome to Learning QuickBooks Online!

Gain a competitive advantage—learn a leading online financial app for entrepreneurs with *Computer Accounting with QuickBooks Online*. Designed using the most effective way to learn QuickBooks Online, this text streamlines learning QuickBooks Online because it focuses on you—the learner.

Proven instructional techniques are incorporated throughout the text to make your mastery of QuickBooks Online as effortless as possible. Using a hands-on approach, this text integrates understanding accounting with mastery of QuickBooks Online. Designed for maximum flexibility to meet your needs, *Computer Accounting with QuickBooks Online* can be used either in a QuickBooks Online course or independently at your own pace.

Good luck with QuickBooks Online and best wishes for your continued success,

Donna Kay

Meet the Author

Donna Kay is a former professor of Accounting and Accounting Systems & Forensics, teaching both undergraduate and graduate accounting. Dr. Kay earned B.S. and MBA degrees from Southern Illinois University at Edwardsville before receiving a Ph.D. from Saint Louis University, where she conducted action research on the perceived effectiveness of instructional techniques for learning technology. Dr. Kay designs her textbooks to incorporate the most effective instructional techniques based on research findings, making your learning journey as effective as possible.

Named to Who's Who Among American Women, Dr. Kay holds certifications as both a Certified Public Accountant (CPA) and Certified Informational Technology Professional (CITP) and is an active member of the American Institute of Certified Public Accountants (AICPA).

Donna Kay is also the author of *Computer Accounting with QuickBooks*, a leading textbook for learning QuickBooks Desktop software for more than 20 years.

Visit Dr. Kay's websites www.my-quickbooks.com and www.my-quickbooksonline.com to learn more about her books and support materials for the texts.

What's New in QBO 3e

Computer Accounting with QuickBooks Online, 3e, continues to offer the features that have made the text a best seller. New, updated, and expanded features in this edition to make learning QuickBooks Online even easier include:

New! QBO Educator Portal Coverage. The new QBO Educator Portal offers instructors the ability to invite students to set up a free full-year student account for QuickBooks Online. Students no longer have to request an account from Intuit. The portal also provides instructors the ability to give each student up to four free QBO companies. See the Instructor Resource Guide for additional information about how to use the QBO Educator Portal and the available Company files in your course.

New! QBO Project Coverage. New QBO Project feature is integrated into this edition. Learn how to link Projects to Customers and track performance.

New! QBO Tag Coverage. New QBO Tag feature permits you to add customized tags to invoices and expenses to provide greater insights for data analytics. This edition covers adding tags and tag groups, tagging transactions, using the tag dashboard, and running tag reports.

New! Expanded Contractors Coverage. This edition offers expanded coverage of contractors, employee versus contractor designation, and additional time-tracking activities for both employees and contractors.

New! Expanded QuickBooks Online Troubleshooting (QT). Chapter 1 includes QBO Troubleshooting. In addition, new Appendix D: QBO Troubleshooting summarizes QBO Help, QBO Troubleshooting (QT) Best Practices, and QBO Troubleshooting Tools and Techniques. Chapter 9, Accounting Essentials, covers how to make correcting entries for an error in QBO. Chapter 10 covers how to use the QBO Audit Log to search for discrepancies and review changed transactions.

New! Expanded Coverage for Aligning the Chart of Accounts with a Tax Return. For most businesses, one of the primary objectives of using QuickBooks is to streamline tax preparation. Additional chapter coverage, exercises, and project activities are offered in this edition to focus on aligning the Chart of Accounts with the company's tax return.

New! Expanded Coverage of Bank Feeds. The new 3rd edition offers expanded bank and credit card matching, including how to load bank and credit card information into QBO.

Updated Chapters and Exercises. Expanded chapter and exercise coverage explores the latest QBO features and functionality.

New Comprehensive Project. A new comprehensive project in Chapter 11 is added in this edition, providing learners with greater opportunity for QBO skill mastery, including Connect grading with interactive student feedback.

QuickBooks Online SatNav

How Do I Streamline Navigating QuickBooks Online?

QBO SatNav is your satellite navigation system for QBO. QBO SatNav breaks navigating QBO into three processes: QBO Settings, QBO Transactions, and QBO Reports. A QBO SatNav is provided with each chapter and project.

 **QBO SatNav**

⚙ QBO Settings

⚙ Company Settings
⚙ Chart of Accounts

**CHAPTERS
1, 2, 11**

💰 QBO Transactions

>>> 💰 Money In 💰 >>>   >>> 💰 Money Out 💰 >>>

💰 Banking
💰 Customers & Sales
💰 Vendors & Expenses
💰 Employees & Payroll

**CHAPTERS
3, 4, 5, 6, 7, 8, 11**

📊 QBO Reports

📊 Reports

**CHAPTERS
9, 10, 11**

The portion of the QBO SatNav that is the focus of the chapter is highlighted. An expanded QBO SatNav gives additional detail about transactions covered in a chapter, such as the following Chapter 4 Banking SatNav.

🌐 QBO SatNav

⚙️ QBO Settings

⚙️ Company Settings
⚙️ Chart of Accounts

💰 QBO Transactions

💰 Banking	*Record Deposits	Write Checks*
💰 Customers & Sales	
💰 Vendors & Expenses	
💰 Employees & Payroll	

📊 QBO Reports

📊 Reports

Faster, Smarter Learning with Smart Dots

How Can I Save Time While Learning QBO?

Make learning QuickBooks Online faster and smarter with Smart Dots. As demonstrated below, step-by-step instructions with coordinating Smart Dots on screen captures make learning QuickBooks Online faster and easier with increased focus.

To use the Navigation Bar to enter sales transactions:

1 From the Navigation Bar, select **Sales**

2 Select **All Sales** tab

3 From the Sales Transactions window, select the drop-down arrow for **New transaction**

4 Select the type of **new transaction** to enter and complete the onscreen form for the new transaction

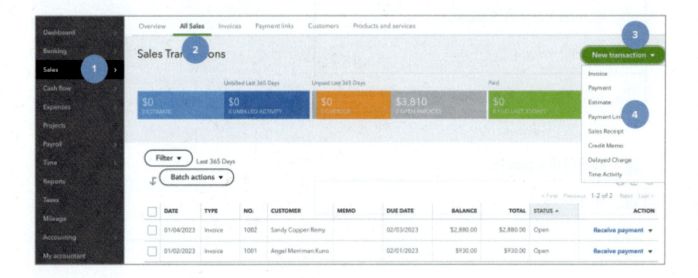

eXplore, Practice, Master (XPM)

What is the most effective way to learn QuickBooks?

Use a highly effective three-step XPM approach to streamline learning QuickBooks Online:

eXplore ➡ Practice ➡ Master

1. eXplore. Providing numerous screenshots and detailed instructions, chapters in *Computer Accounting with Quickbooks Online* are designed as tutorials for you to explore and learn QBO features.

2. Practice. Designed with fewer instructions, the end-of-chapter exercises provide opportunities for you to practice and test your understanding.

3. Master. Virtual company projects provide mastery opportunities for you to apply and integrate your QuickBooks Online skills.

XPM mapping for your text, listing eXplore, Practice, and Master activities, follows.

	1. eXplore ➡	**2.** Practice ➡	**3.** Master
Mookie the Beagle Concierge	Chapter 1	Exercises 1	
	Chapter 2	Exercises 2	
	Chapter 3	Exercises 3	
	Chapter 4	Exercises 4	
	Chapter 5	Exercises 5	
	Chapter 6	Exercises 6	
	Chapter 7	Exercises 7	
	Chapter 8	Exercises 8	
	Chapter 9	Exercises 9	
	Chapter 10	Exercises 10	
QBO Comprehensive Project: Mookie The Beagle Coach			**Chapter 11**

Virtual Activity Mapping

Virtual company cases provide you with a realistic context and business environment to enhance your understanding of QBO. Related learning activities mapping follows.

MOOKIE THE BEAGLE™ CONCIERGE

Mookie The Beagle Concierge is a start-up business that provides pet and vet care services to canine customers. Each chapter and the corresponding exercises focus on exploration and practice in becoming proficient in a specific area of QuickBooks Online, such as Banking, Customers and Sales, and Vendors and Expenses. Your QBO work will carry forward from chapter to chapter, so you will want to check and crosscheck your work to eliminate errors. If you find you have an issue with your QBO company that you are unable to resolve, contact your instructor. If your instructor is unable to assist you in resolving the issue, your instructor can send you another QBO company to restart from the beginning.

- **Chapter 1 and Exercises EM1.1 through EM1.4**
- **Chapter 2 and Exercises EM2.1 through EM2.8**
- **Chapter 3 and Exercises EM3.4 through EM3.12**
- **Chapter 4 and Exercises EM4.2 through EM4.8**
- **Chapter 5 and Exercises EM5.4 through EM5.13**
- **Chapter 6 and Exercises EM6.4 through EM6.13**
- **Chapter 7 and Exercises EM7.4 through EM7.16**
- **Chapter 8 and Exercises EM8.5 through EM8.11**
- **Chapter 9 and Exercises EM9.3 through EM9.12**
- **Chapter 10 and Exercises EM10.4 through EM10.10**

Please note that Exercises that use the QBO Company, Mookie The Beagle Concierge, are designated with an M in the Exercise label, for example, EM1.1.

MOOKIE THE BEAGLE™ COACH

Mookie The Beagle Coach is a merchandising, service company providing pet etiquette and agility training services and selling branded training products. Check and crosscheck your work to eliminate errors. If you find you have an issue with your QBO company that you are unable to resolve, contact your instructor. If your instructor is unable to assist you in resolving the issue, your instructor can send you another QBO company to restart from the beginning.

- **Chapter 11**

QBO Updates

How Do I Stay Up to Date with QBO Updates?

QuickBooks Online is updated on an ongoing basis. So some QBO features may appear slightly different from what is shown in your text due to new rollouts from Intuit.

For your convenience in tracking QBO updates, two sources for update information and how the updates might affect your text are:

1. www.my-quickbooksonline.com, select QBO 3e > QBO 3e Updates
2. If you are using Connect or a digital ebook, you can find updates under Additional Student Resources (ASR). If you do not have access to Connect or the ebook, your instructor can provide you with ASR or use Option 1 above.

QuickBooks Online Certification

How Do I Learn More About QBO Certification?

QuickBooks Online Certification is certification that is obtained by passing the QuickBooks Online Certification Examination. The QBO Certification Exam is updated each year so you are certified for one year. For more information about preparing for QuickBooks Online Certification, see Appendix C: QBO Certification.

Online Learning Resources

Computer Accounting with QuickBooks Online is accompanied by a website that offers additional resources for learning QuickBooks Online.

- www.my-quickbooksonline.com

If you are using Connect or a digital ebook, resources for students can be found under Additional Student Resources (ASR) and include:

- Presentation Slides for each chapter
- QuickBooks Online Updates
- QBO videos

Resources for Instructors include:

- Instructor Resource Guide and Solutions
- Test Bank
- QBO Educator Portal Information for providing students with free QBO access
- Pre-Built Connect Course

Acknowledgments

To make the third edition of the *Computer Accounting with QuickBooks Online* text possible, special thanks to:

- MHE QuickBooks Online team Steve, Kevin and Sarah
- Sandy Roman for her accuracy checking
- Brian Behrens for always being in my corner with greatly appreciated support
- Steve, Sherri, Evan, and Andrea for being there when needed
- Carole and Mimi for putting everything into perspective
- Matt, Grant, and Landon for advice and entertainment
- All the QuickBooks educators who share ideas, comments, and suggestions
  - Cammy Wayne, William Rainey Harper College
  - Emily Corzine, Athens State University
  - Everett Montgomery, Tallahassee Community College
  - Micki Nickla, Ivy Tech Community College
  - Phyllis Gilbert, Baton Rouge Community College

Connect

What kind of study tools does Connect offer?

SmartBook 2.0. A personalized and adaptive learning tool used to maximize the learning experience by helping students study more efficiently and effectively. SmartBook 2.0 highlights where in the chapter to focus, asks review questions on the materials covered and tracks the most challenging content for later review recharge. SmartBook 2.0 is available both online and offline.

Assignment Materials. After completing assignments in *Computer Accounting with QuickBooks Online* students can enter key elements of their solution into Connect for grading. Based on instructor settings, they can receive instant feedback either while working on the assignment or after the assignment is submitted for grade. Assignable materials include: **in-chapter activities, exercises, projects, practice quizzes, and test bank materials.**

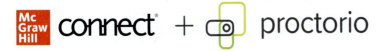

Proctorio. New remote proctoring and browser-locking capabilities, hosted by Proctorio within Connect, provide control of the assessment environment by enabling security options and verifying the identity of the student.

Seamlessly integrated within Connect, these services allow instructors to control students' assessment experience by restricting browser activity, recording students' activity, and verifying students are doing their own work.

Instant and detailed reporting gives instructors an at-a-glance view of potential academic integrity concerns, thereby avoiding personal bias and supporting evidence-based claims.

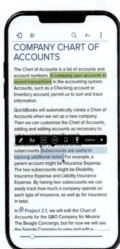

ReadAnywhere App. Using McGraw Hill's app (as shown in the image to the right), you can access the *Computer Accounting with QuickBooks Online* eBook anywhere, both online and offline, data free, by signing in with your Connect login and password. Simply download the entire textbook or only the chapters needed. The app also provides the tools available in the laptop version of the eBook, and any notes or highlights made to the text will sync across platforms so they're available both on the app and in Connect.

Instructors: Student Success Starts with You

Tools to enhance your unique voice

Want to build your own course? No problem. Prefer to use an OLC-aligned, prebuilt course? Easy. Want to make changes throughout the semester? Sure. And you'll save time with Connect's auto-grading too.

65%
Less Time Grading

Laptop: McGraw Hill; Woman/dog: George Doyle/Getty Images

Study made personal

Incorporate adaptive study resources like SmartBook® 2.0 into your course and help your students be better prepared in less time. Learn more about the powerful personalized learning experience available in SmartBook 2.0 at **www.mheducation.com/highered/connect/smartbook**

Affordable solutions, added value

Make technology work for you with LMS integration for single sign-on access, mobile access to the digital textbook, and reports to quickly show you how each of your students is doing. And with our Inclusive Access program you can provide all these tools at a discount to your students. Ask your McGraw Hill representative for more information.

Padlock: Jobalou/Getty Images

Solutions for your challenges

A product isn't a solution. Real solutions are affordable, reliable, and come with training and ongoing support when you need it and how you want it. Visit **www. supportateverystep.com** for videos and resources both you and your students can use throughout the semester.

Checkmark: Jobalou/Getty Images

Students: Get Learning that Fits You

Effective tools for efficient studying

Connect is designed to help you be more productive with simple, flexible, intuitive tools that maximize your study time and meet your individual learning needs. Get learning that works for you with Connect.

Study anytime, anywhere

Download the free ReadAnywhere app and access your online eBook, SmartBook 2.0, or Adaptive Learning Assignments when it's convenient, even if you're offline. And since the app automatically syncs with your Connect account, all of your work is available every time you open it. Find out more at **www.mheducation.com/readanywhere**

"I really liked this app—it made it easy to study when you don't have your text-book in front of you."

- Jordan Cunningham,
Eastern Washington University

Calendar: owattaphotos/Getty Images

Everything you need in one place

Your Connect course has everything you need—whether reading on your digital eBook or completing assignments for class, Connect makes it easy to get your work done.

Learning for everyone

McGraw Hill works directly with Accessibility Services Departments and faculty to meet the learning needs of all students. Please contact your Accessibility Services Office and ask them to email accessibility@mheducation.com, or visit **www.mheducation.com/about/accessibility** for more information.

Top: Jenner Images/Getty Images, Left: Hero Images/Getty Images, Right: Hero Images/Getty Images

Contents

Computer Accounting with QuickBooks Online 3e

Donna Kay

Contents Overview

Designed as hands-on tutorials for learning QuickBooks Online, *Computer Accounting with QuickBooks Online* chapters provide screen captures with step-by-step, detailed instructions. To improve long-term retention of your QuickBooks Online skills, end-of-chapter learning activities are designed with fewer instructions to test your understanding and, when needed, to develop your skills to quickly seek out additional information to complete the task. The ability to find information as needed is an increasingly important skill in a rapidly changing business environment. The design of *Computer Accounting with QuickBooks Online* seamlessly facilitates your development of this crucial skill.

Chapter 1 QuickBooks Online Navigation and Settings

This chapter provides a guided tour of QuickBooks Online using QBO Navigation and QBO tools. In Chapter 1, you learn how to set up a new QBO Company, Mookie the Beagle™ Concierge that will be used throughout the first ten chapters of your text. In addition, Chapter 1 introduces you to the QBO Help feature and QBO troubleshooting.

Chapter 2 QBO Chart of Accounts

This chapter introduces how to customize the QBO Chart of Accounts to meet specific business needs. Chart of Accounts topics include adding accounts, adding subaccounts, editing accounts, and inactivating accounts.

Chapter 3 QBO Transactions

Chapter 3 provides an introduction to the various types of transactions entered in QBO, including banking, customers, vendors, and employees transactions. In addition, Chapter 3 shows how you can use QBO Workspace to enter transactions into QBO.

Chapter 4 Banking

This chapter focuses on the Checking account and Check Register for a small business. Topics include making deposits, writing checks, and matching bank transactions.

Chapter 5 Customers and Sales

Chapter 5 demonstrates how to record customers transactions. Topics include how to create Invoices and record customer payments.

Chapter 6 Vendors and Expenses

Chapter 6 focuses on recording vendors transactions, such as recording expenses for services. Topics include recording vendor services paid by check and credit card.

Chapter 7 Inventory

Chapter 7 focuses on recording vendors transactions related to inventory, including creating purchase orders, entering bills for inventory, and paying bills. In addition, customers transactions related to inventory are also covered.

Chapter 8 Employees and Payroll

Chapter 8 covers tracking time and billing tracked time using QBO employee and payroll features. Chapter 8 also introduces the Contractors List and tracking time for contractors.

Chapter 9 QBO Adjustments

Chapter 9 covers how to create a Trial Balance and enter adjusting entries using QBO.

Chapter 10 QBO Reports

Chapter 10 completes the accounting cycle, covering a variety of QBO reports, including financial statements and management reports.

Chapter 11 QBO Comprehensive Project: Mookie The Beagle Coach

Chapter 11 provides a mastery opportunity in the form of a comprehensive project that covers the entire accounting cycle. The project includes setting up a new QBO company, updating the Chart of Accounts, creating lists and transactions, matching bank and credit card transactions, creating adjusting entries, and generating reports. Both service and inventory transactions are covered.

Appendix A QBO Apps: Mac, Windows, and Mobile

Appendix A summarizes features of the QBO App for Mac and Windows. In addition, QBO Mobile app features are discussed.

Appendix B QuickBooks Online versus QuickBooks Desktop

Appendix B compares the different features of QuickBooks Online and Quickbooks Desktop for both the client versions and the accountant versions of each.

Appendix C QBO Certification

Appendix C summarizes information about two types of QBO Certification: QBO User Certification and QBO Accountant Certification.

Appendix D QBO Troubleshooting

Appendix D summarizes QBO Troubleshooting resources, including QBO Help, QBO troubleshooting (QT) best practices, and QBO tools and techniques. As the last appendix in your text, it's conveniently located for times when you seek insights into QBO troubleshooting.

Chapter 1

QuickBooks Online Navigation and Settings

MOOKIE THE BEAGLE™ CONCIERGE

BACKSTORY

Your smartphone chimes. A message from Cy Walker flashes on your screen.

My wish has come true!

Congrats!

Starting my own business.

That's exciting.

Exciting ... and terrifying at the same time ...

Terrifying? Why?

My new business needs a financial system.

No idea where to start.

Call me...we can work on the details.

When you and Cy connect, Cy shares that he has been searching for a way to meet his demanding work and travel commitments while caring for his pet beagle, Mookie. Cy discovered he was not the only working professional trying to balance pet care and work commitments. Suddenly, he saw an opportunity to launch Mookie The Beagle Concierge.

Cy envisions Mookie The Beagle Concierge employing caring staff who go beyond the typical doggie day care, providing organic and home cooked food, exercising the pet with scheduled walks and playtime, administering required medication, taking the pet to vet visits that often fall during the work day when a professional cannot take time off, and providing other pet wellness services as needed.

Drawing upon a local university veterinarian program, Cy plans to hire vet students with pet care training and flexibility in their schedules. Working as independent contractors, the students are a good fit for providing high-quality, relatively low-cost pet care on a flexible basis.

Cy plans to design and develop a Mookie The Beagle Concierge app which permits clients to schedule pet care service. Mookie The Beagle Concierge app also tracks complicated medication schedules, showing who administered what medication and when. The app permits the client to view and speak to the pet in real time. In addition, the app connects to the vet's office for follow-up questions, provides pet-parent texting to Mookie The Beagle Concierge staff, and offers an on-call button to alert staff of urgent issues.

In short, Mookie The Beagle Concierge elevates pet care to a professional level, providing convenience and advanced pet care support that permits professionals to maintain busy work and travel schedules, while being assured their valued pet is receiving the best of care.

Cy realizes he has many business decisions to make and wants solid information to make those decisions. Building an accounting system that can capture that data and provide information and data analytics for decision making feels overwhelming, yet crucial—if his business is to succeed. Furthermore, Mookie The Beagle Concierge will need a sound financial system that can provide information for preparing business tax returns.

Cy asks if you would research different financial system apps that could meet his business needs, make a recommendation, and then assist him in implementing the new system as soon as possible.

After completing your review of various financial apps, you recommend that for Cy's specific business needs, QuickBooks Online (QBO) would be a good option since it uses accounting in the cloud. This permit both you and Cy to access QBO from different locations and devices. Cy agrees with your recommendation.

Cy gifts you this book for learning QBO fast. Your next step is to learn QuickBooks Online.

Chapter 1
LEARNING OBJECTIVES

Chapter 1 introduces QuickBooks Online. In this chapter, you will learn about the following topics:

- QBO Set Up New Company
- QBO SatNav
  - ‣ QBO Settings
  - ‣ QBO Transactions
  - ‣ QBO Reports
- QBO Navigation
  - ‣ QBO Workspace
  - ‣ QBO Navigation Bar
- QBO Tools
  - ‣ QBO Gear Icon
  - ‣ QBO (+) New Icon
  - ‣ QBO Search Icon
- QBO Help and Troubleshooting
- QBO Settings
  - ‣ Company Settings
  - ‣ QBO Chart of Accounts
- Accounting Essentials: Legal, Tax, and Financial Questions

> 💡**Accounting Essentials** appear at the end of the chapter. Tip: Preview Accounting Essentials <u>before</u> starting the chapter and then review Accounting Essentials <u>after</u> completing the chapter.

WHAT IS QUICKBOOKS ONLINE?

QuickBooks® Online (QBO) is a cloud-based financial system for entrepreneurs. We use a web browser to access QBO instead of using software installed on a computer like QuickBooks® Desktop (QBDT). So the advantage of QBO is that we can access QBO from any desktop or laptop computer that has an Internet connection. QBO also offers an accompanying mobile QBO app for use with smartphones and tablets.

> **QuickBooks Online (QBO)** refers to the QuickBooks system accessed through a web browser with data stored in the cloud. QuickBooks Desktop (QBDT) refers to QuickBooks software that is installed on your desktop or laptop computer.

QBO is updated on an ongoing basis. So some features on your screen may be slightly different from those shown in your text due to new, dynamic QBO updates.

> **QBO updates that affect your text can be viewed as follows:**
> 1. Go to www.My-QuickBooksOnline.com > QBO 3e > QBO 3e Updates, or
> 2. If you are using Connect or a digital ebook, you can find updates under Additional Student Resources (ASR). (If you do not have access to Connect or the ebook, your instructor can provide you with ASR or use Option 1 above.)

QuickBooks® and QuickBooks® Online Plus are registered trademarks of Intuit Inc.

WHAT IS AN EASY WAY TO LEARN QUICKBOOKS ONLINE?

Learning QuickBooks Online (QBO) requires integrating knowledge of accounting, financial systems, and financial technology. Don't become discouraged if you find that you need to go over the same material more than once. That is normal. Learning how accounting and financial technology are interrelated often requires repetition.

To make learning QBO easier, we will use an effective three-step XPM approach:

eXplore → Practice → Master

1. **eXplore** QBO using the chapter with step-by-step walk through screen captures. Don't worry about making mistakes or "breaking" QBO. Instead, focus on learning how to navigate and use QBO.
2. **Practice** entering information and transactions into QBO end-of-chapter exercises.
3. **Master** QBO with a virtual company project. The project covers QuickBooks tasks from setting up a new QBO company and entering transactions to generating QBO reports.

First, we will eXplore using the Chapter illustrations, then we will Practice using Exercises at the end of the chapter, and finally we will Master QBO by completing the QBO Project. XPM mapping, listing eXplore, Practice, and Master activities, follows.

	1. eXplore	→ 2. Practice	→ 3. Master
Mookie The Beagle Concierge	Chapter 1	Exercises 1	
	Chapter 2	Exercises 2	
	Chapter 3	Exercises 3	
	Chapter 4	Exercises 4	
	Chapter 5	Exercises 5	
	Chapter 6	Exercises 6	
	Chapter 7	Exercises 7	
	Chapter 8	Exercises 8	
	Chapter 9	Exercises 9	
	Chapter 10	Exercises 10	↓
QBO Comprehensive Project: Mookie The Beagle Coach			**Chapter 11**

Section 1.1

QBO SET UP NEW COMPANY

As a student enrolled in a QBO course, you can obtain free access to QBO to use with your text. If you were an entrepreneur, you would need to subscribe to QBO, paying a monthly fee for access.

Next, we want to create a new QBO company for Mookie The Beagle Concierge using your free QBO access.

CREATE NEW QBO COMPANY USING INSTRUCTOR INVITATION

To obtain your free QBO access, your instructor will need to send you an email invitation. This invite will permit you to create your own QBO company for Mookie The Beagle Concierge.

> ⚠️ **Important Note: If you have <u>not</u> received an email invitation from your instructor to create your QBO company:**
>
> 1. **Check your email Spam mailbox to verify that the email was not flagged as Junk mail.**
> 2. **Contact your instructor to obtain an email invitation. Your instructor must send you the email invitation in order for you to have free access to create a QBO company.**

> ⚠️ **When setting up a QBO company, if the following steps do not match your QBO screen, then check for QBO 3e Text Updates.**
> - **Go to <u>www.my-quickbooksonline.com</u> > QBO 3e > QBO 3e Updates.**
> - **If you are using Connect or a digital ebook, you can find updates under Additional Student Resources (ASR).**
> - **If you do not have access to Connect or the ebook, contact your instructor who can provide you with ASR and the QBO 3e Text Updates.**

> ⚠️ **Warning! When setting up a QBO company,** it is important to complete the following steps exactly as specified. QBO uses the steps you complete to create a QBO company with specific settings. If the specified steps are not completed, then the QBO company will not have the necessary settings to complete your assignment. Often there is no workaround to fix this later. So the easiest approach is to take your time and stay laser focused while setting up the QBO Company.

Complete the following steps to use the Instructor Invitation for free QBO access:

1   When you receive an email invitation from your instructor to create your own QBO company, select **Accept invitation**. (Note: Intuit recommends using Google Chrome web browser.)

2   To create your account, **enter** the requested information in the appropriate fields. Note: If the Create Account screen doesn't appear automatically, select **Need an account? Sign Up**.

⚠️ *Keep a record of your User ID and Password. You will need this later.*

(If you already have an account established, use your User ID and password to sign in.)

3   Select **Create Account**

4   When Welcome! We're glad you're here. appears, select **Next**

5   When What's your business name? appears, enter the name of your business: **[Last NameFirst Initial] Mookie The Beagle Concierge**. (Example: KayD Mookie The Beagle Concierge.)

⚠️ *Remember to include your name before Mookie The Beagle Concierge. This will assist your instructor in identifying your QBO file.*

6   Uncheck **I'm moving from QuickBooks Desktop™ and want to bring in my data**

7   Select **Next**

8   When What's your industry? appears, leave the field **blank**. This field determines the accounts that will auto-populate the Chart of Accounts. Because we will enter our own Chart of Accounts in Chapter 2, we leave this field blank so that fewer accounts are auto-populated. Otherwise, we would select an industry and QBO would automatically add more accounts to our Chart of Accounts specifically for the industry selected.

9   Select **Skip for now**

10 When What kind of business is this? appears, select **Sole Proprietor**

11 Select **Next**

12 When How does your business make money? appears, select **Provide services**

13 Select **Sells products**

14 Select **Next**

15 When What's your main role? appears, select **Bookkeeper or Accountant**.

⚠️ *This selection determines your view of QBO and the instructions you will see onscreen. Before proceeding, double check that you have selected Bookkeeper or Accountant.*

16 Select **Next**

17 When Who works at this business? appears, select:

- **Contractors**
- **Employees**
- **A few partners and owners**

18 Select **Next**

19 If Ready for a free trial of QuickBooks Payroll? appears, select **Maybe later**.

⚠️ *If payroll is turned on, it may deactivate the time-tracking features used in Chapter 8 of this text and you will be unable to complete those activities. Be sure to select **Maybe later**. If you make the incorrect selection for payroll, please contact your instructor and ask for another QBO company invitation and restart the new QBO company setup.*

20 Select **Next**

21 When What apps do you already use? appears, select **I don't use any apps**

22 Select **Next**

23 When the Link your accounts and see everything in one place screen appears, select **Skip for now**

24 When What is everything you want to set up? appears, select:

- **Invoice customers**
- **Track receipts and bills**
- **Pay employees or contractors**
- **Add sales**
- **Enter and pay bills**
- **Track time**
- **Manage inventory**

⚠️ *These selections determine the settings of your QBO company and it may not be possible to change the settings later. Before proceeding, double-check that you have made the correct selections.*

25 Select **Next**

26 When We're almost ready to dive in! appears, select **Let's go**

27 Your QBO company for Mookie The Beagle Concierge should now appear. If a Welcome To QuickBooks! screen displays, select **Take a quick tour**.

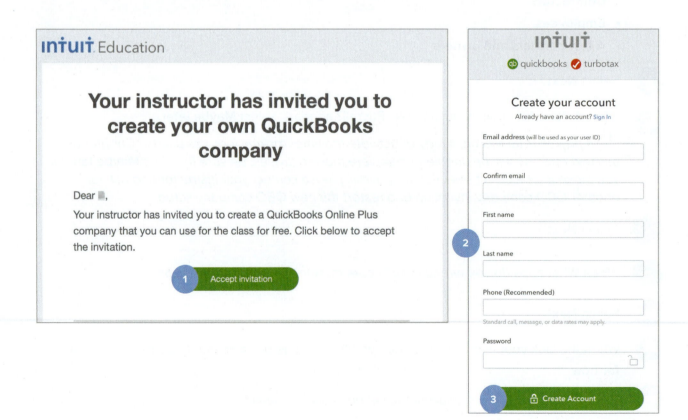

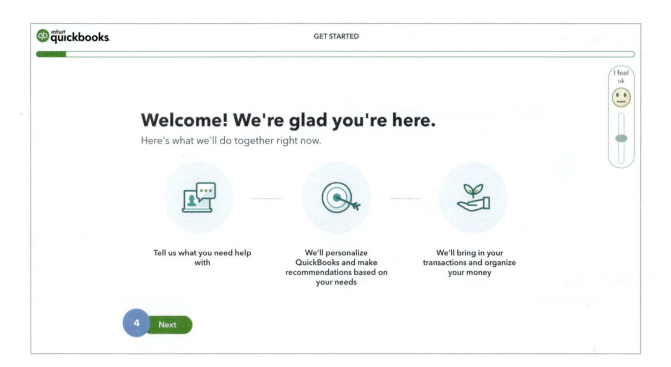

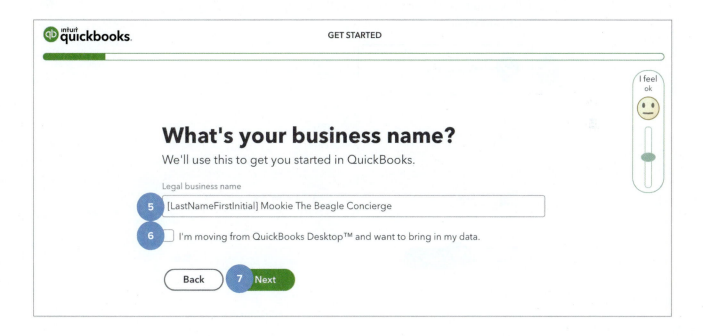

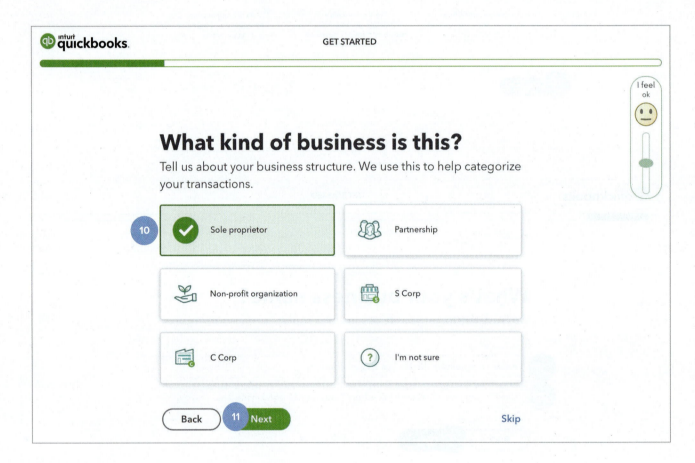

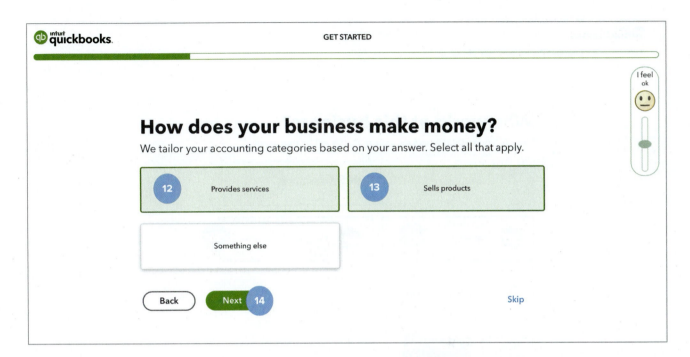

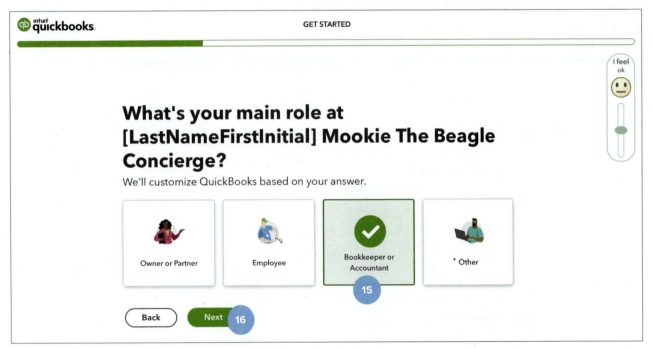

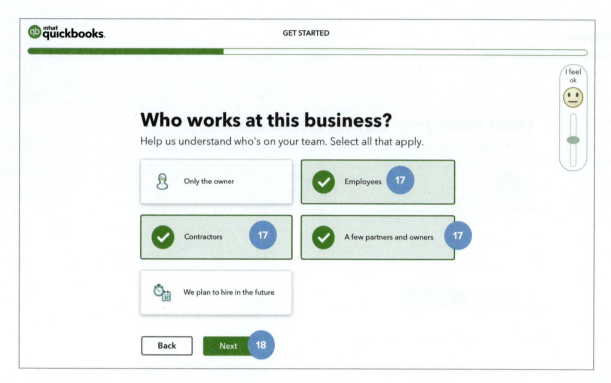

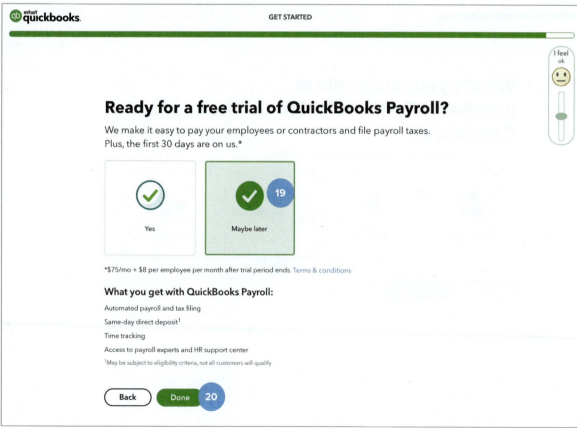

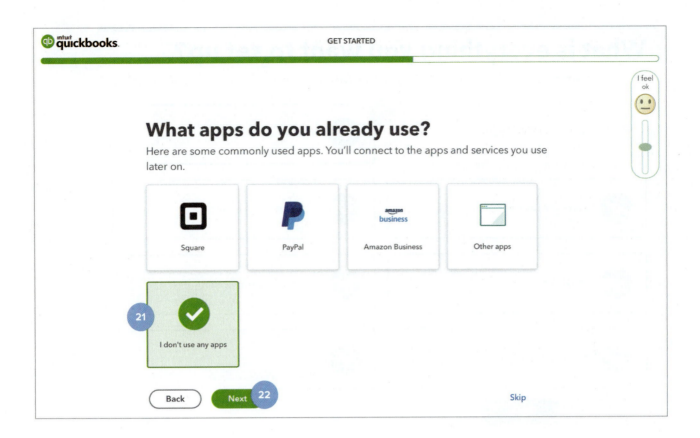

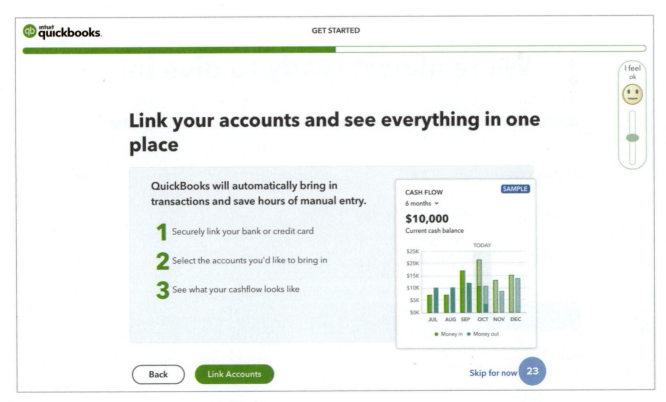

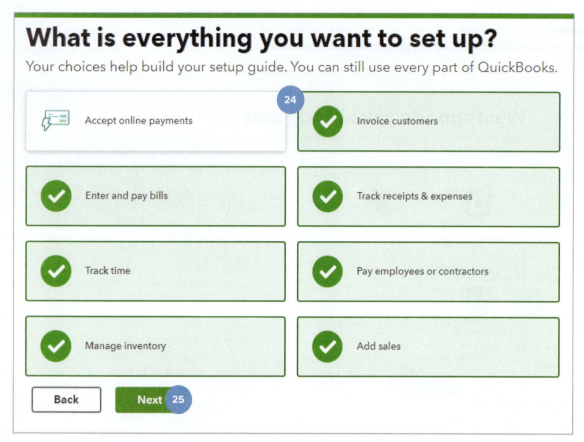

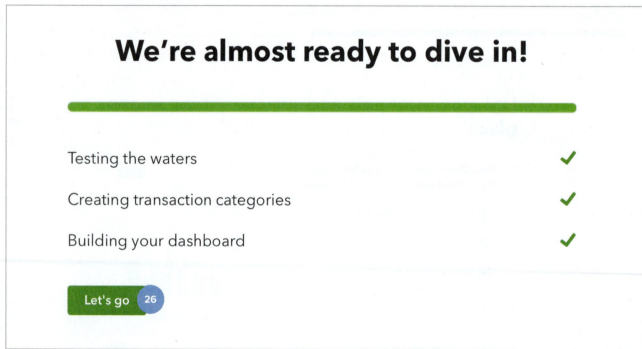

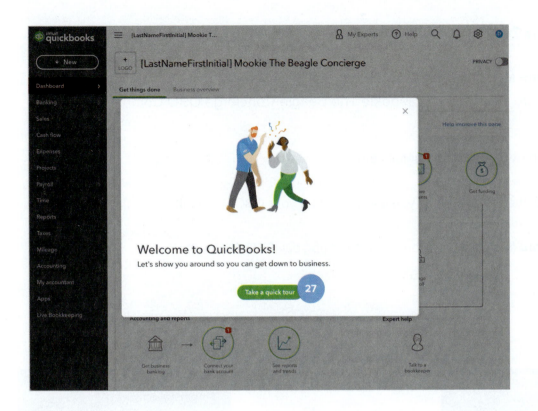

You have now created a QBO Company for Mookie The Beagle Concierge. Later, whenever you need to stop working in your QBO Company, close your browser to log out of the Mookie The Beagle Concierge QBO Company. When you are ready to work again, sign in to QBO using your User ID and Password.

HOW TO SIGN IN TO QBO COMPANY

After completing the steps to create a QBO company using the Instructor Invitation, the next time you are ready to sign in to your Mookie The Beagle Concierge QBO Company, complete the following steps:

1 Using a web browser, go to qbo.intuit.com

2 Enter **User ID** (the email address you used to set up your QBO Account)

3 Enter **Password** (the password you used to set up your QBO Account)

4 Select **Sign in**

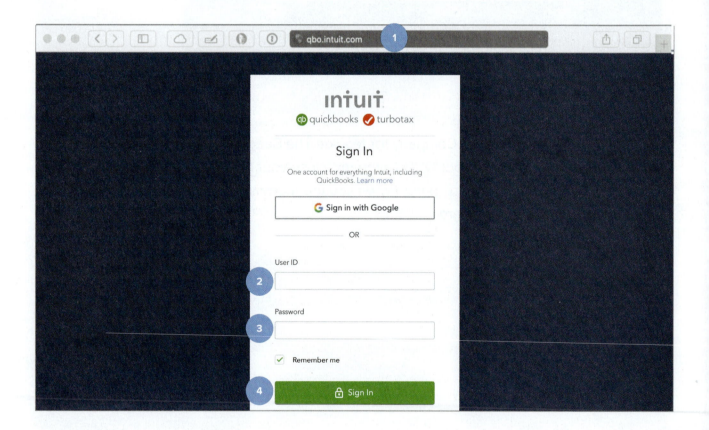

Section 1.2

🌐 QBO SATNAV

QBO SatNav is our satellite navigation for QuickBooks Online, assisting us in navigating QBO

Just like we use a smartphone with satellite mapping to zoom in for detail and zoom out for the big picture, when learning QBO, we may need to adjust our thinking to zoom out to see the big picture of the entire financial system or at other times zoom in to view details.

QBO SatNav is designed to assist us in zooming out and zooming in to successfully navigate QBO. QBO SatNav divides QBO into three main processes:

1. **QBO Settings** include Company Settings and QBO Chart of Accounts.

    *   **Company Settings** involve setting up a new QBO company and selecting company preferences, such as displaying account numbers.

    *   **QBO Chart of Accounts** is a list of all the accounts for a company. Accounts can be used to sort and track accounting information. For example, a business needs one account for cash, another account to track amounts customers owe (Accounts Receivable), and yet another account to track inventory. QBO automatically creates a Chart of Accounts when we set up a new QBO company. QBO then permits us to modify the Chart of Accounts to customize it for specific company needs.

    QBO Settings are covered in Chapters 1, 2, and 11.

2. **QBO Transactions** involve recording transactions as **input** into the financial system. Transaction types can be categorized as Banking, Customers & Sales, Vendors & Expenses, and Employees & Payroll. In basic terms, recording transactions involves recording money in and money out of the company.

    Transactions are exchanges between the QBO company and other parties, such as customers, vendors, and employees. Typically in a transaction, the company gives something and receives something in exchange. QBO is used to keep a record of what is given and what is received in the transaction. We can enter transaction information into QBO using the onscreen Journal or onscreen forms, such as onscreen Invoices and onscreen Checks.

    QBO Transactions are covered in Chapters 3, 4, 5, 6, 7, 8, and 11.

3. **QBO Reports** are the **output** of the system. Reports typically provide information to decision makers. For example, accounting information is used to prepare:

    *   **Financial statements** for external users, such as creditors and investors. Internal users, such as managers, also may use financial statements. Financial statements are standardized financial reports that summarize information about past transactions. The primary financial statements for a business are:

        ▸   **Balance Sheet**: summarizes what a company owns and owes on a particular date.

        ▸   **Profit and Loss Statement** (or **Income Statement**): summarizes what a company has earned and the expenses incurred to earn the income.

        ▸   **Statement of Cash Flows**: summarizes cash inflows and cash outflows for operating, investing, and financing activities of a business.

    *   **Tax returns** for federal and state tax agencies.

    *   **Management reports** for company managers and owners to use when making business decisions. Such decisions include: Are we collecting customer payments when due? An example of such a report is an Accounts Receivable Aging report that summarizes past due customer accounts.

    QBO Reports are covered in Chapters 9, 10, and 11.

💡 **Accounting Essentials** appear at the end of Chapters 1 through 10.
Tip: Preview Accounting Essentials <u>before</u> starting the chapter and then review Accounting Essentials <u>after</u> completing the chapter.

QBO SatNav will be used in each chapter to illustrate which aspect(s) of QBO the chapter will focus on. If you start to feel lost in QBO, return to the QBO SatNav to assist in navigating QBO.

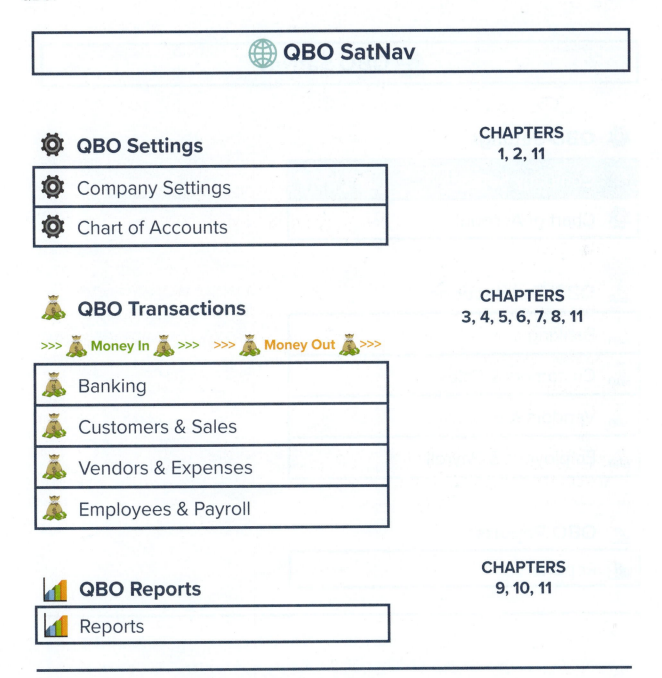

The portion of the QBO SatNav that is the focus of the chapter will be highlighted. For example, in this chapter the focus is on Company Settings, so Company Settings is highlighted in the following QBO SatNav.

QBO SatNav

⚙ QBO Settings

⚙ Company Settings
⚙ Chart of Accounts

💰 QBO Transactions

💰 Banking
💰 Customers & Sales
💰 Vendors & Expenses
💰 Employees & Payroll

📊 QBO Reports

📊 Reports

Section 1.3

QBO NAVIGATION

Taking a few minutes to learn QBO navigation will make learning QBO easier. The primary way to navigate QBO is using the QBO Navigation Bar, located on the left side of the screen. The Navigation Bar permits you to quickly access commonly used QBO screens.

As QBO is updated by Intuit, the items listed on the Navigation Bar may continue to change, so your Navigation Bar may appear slightly different from the following one.

1 **Dashboard** provides on overview and summary of key information for your QuickBooks Online company

2 **Banking** transactions relate to Bank and Credit Card accounts and transactions

3 **Sales** transactions relate to customers and sales transactions (money in)

4 **Cash flow** summarizes money in and money out for the business

5 **Expenses** transactions relate to vendors and expenses transactions (money out)

6 **Projects** is a QBO feature that organizes and tracks the timeline and profitability of projects

7 **Payroll** transactions relate to employees and payroll transactions (money out)

8 **Time** is a QBO feature for tracking time for employees and contractors

9 **Reports** summarize the output of our QBO financial system

10 **Taxes** relate to sales taxes and, if QuickBooks Online payroll is used, payroll taxes

11 **Mileage** is a QBO feature for tracking mileage related to your business

12 **Accounting** displays the Chart of Accounts

13 **My Accountant** is used to connect QBO to your accountant

14 **Apps** summarizes information about apps that work with QBO

DASHBOARD

Dashboard appears when you log into your QBO company. If the dashboard does not appear, click on Dashboard on the Navigation Bar to display it.

Like a car dashboard, this QBO Dashboard provides a digital overview. We can customize the dashboard to display information to meet our specific business needs and requirements. Note that the dashboard appearance may change over time as Intuit rolls out ongoing QBO updates, so your dashboard may appear differently from the dashboard shown here.

Two tabs for the Dashboard are:

1. Getting Things Done
2. Business Overview

Getting Things Done

To view and explore Getting Things Done on the QBO Dashboard:

1 Select **Dashboard** on the Navigation Bar

2 Select **Getting Things Done** tab

3 The Getting Things Done Dashboard displays **Workspace**, a flowchart of various QBO activities and how the activities are related

4 **Money In** displays activities related to bringing money into a business, such as creating customer invoices and receiving customer payments

5 **Money Out** displays activities related to money going out of the business, such as paying bills and managing payroll

6 **Accounting and reports** relates to business banking and reports

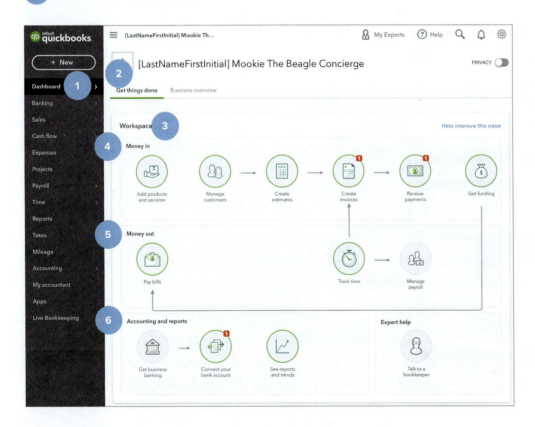

Business Overview

To view and explore Business Overview on the QBO Dashboard:

1 Select **Dashboard** on the Navigation Bar

2 Select **Business Overview** tab. The Business Overview Dashboard displays graphs of useful information in managing a company.

3 The **Profit and Loss** graph displays Net Income, Income (Revenue), and Expenses for tracking profitability

4 The **Invoices** graph shows overdue and not-yet-due amounts from customers. This is useful in focusing attention on collecting overdue customer accounts.

5 The **Expenses** graph reflects the different categories of expenses, focusing attention on how money is spent

6 The **Sales** graph displays how sales vary over the month. Notice that the time period can be changed and the graph updates accordingly.

7 The Dashboard displays a **Bank accounts** summary, listing the company's Bank and Credit Card accounts including the bank balance and the QBO balance

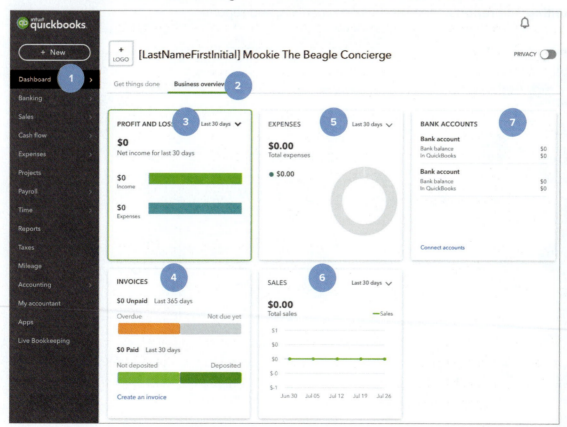

BANKING

Banking transactions relate to Bank and Credit Card accounts and transactions. QBO can be used to record transactions that affect Bank accounts, such as a Checking account, and Credit Card accounts, such as a VISA account.

To facilitate error detection, QBO permits the QBO Bank and Credit Card accounts to be connected directly to the related bank or credit card company. Once connected, you can download transactions from the bank or credit card company automatically and then match the downloaded transactions from the bank to your QBO data.

To explore the QBO Banking features:

1 Select **Banking** on the Navigation Bar

2 Select the **Banking** tab

3 Select **See how it works** to watch a video about QBO Banking features

4 Note the three steps to using QBO Banking.
1. **Connect a bank or credit card to get started.** This step involves connecting the Bank or Credit Card account to QBO so transactions can be downloaded automatically from the bank or credit card company into QBO.
2. **Review and add transactions.** Downloaded transactions can be reviewed for accuracy and to make sure they match what you have entered into QBO.
3. **See how your business is doing.** By connecting a bank or credit card to QBO, it's easier to see if there are any discrepancies between your QBO accounts and the bank or credit card company records. This feature also provides the business with an ongoing view of bank and credit card balances and transactions to better monitor business and cash performance.

5 **Connect account** option walks you through the steps to connect your bank or credit card account to QBO automatically. If your business uses this option, then you search for your financial institution in the list of companies working with QBO.

6 **Upload transactions** option is what your business would have to use if your financial institution is not found in your search. This option involves downloading your transactions from the bank or credit card company and then loading those transactions into QBO. This option requires that you continually download and then load the transactions into QBO to remain up to date.

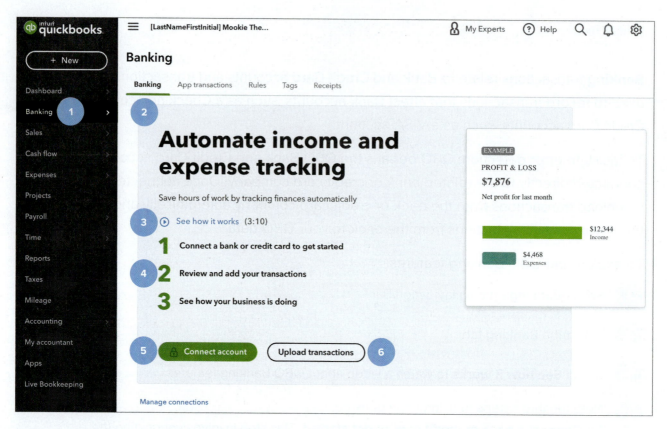

To view an example of how QBO banking appears with connected accounts, see the following banking screen capture.

1 When a bank or credit card has been connected to QBO, from the Banking tab, cards appear at the top of the banking screen for **QBO Bank and Credit Card accounts** that are connected to the related bank accounts

2 The cards at the top summarize key information for the accounts including the **Bank Balance**. This is the balance that the bank shows for the Checking, Savings, or Credit Card account.

3 The card also shows the **Balance in QuickBooks** for the account. When there is a discrepancy between the balance per the bank and the balance per QuickBooks, the discrepancy may be due to an error or a timing difference (the bank has recorded it at a different time than when you recorded it in QBO). With a quick glance at the cards on the banking screen, you can see if there is a discrepancy. Some QBO clients use this approach instead of a monthly bank reconciliation to isolate and track any discrepancies.

4 QBO downloads transactions from the bank account. Then QBO attempts to match the downloaded transactions to transactions previously entered in QBO. In the Action column, **Match** will appear if QBO has found a possible match between the downloaded bank transactions and a transaction already entered in QBO.

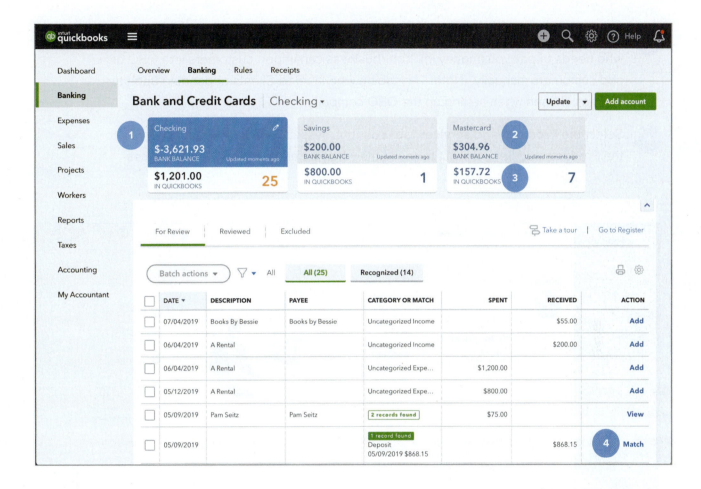

SALES

Sales transactions relate to customers and sales (money in).

To explore the QBO Sales features:

1 Select **Sales** on the Navigation Bar

2 Select the **Overview** tab to view a sales dashboard. The top graphic shows income over time. This provides insight into when sales are occurring. Another graphic shows unpaid and paid invoices. At a glance, you can see if there are overdue amounts from customers.

3 Select the **Invoices** tab. Your business can create invoices using QBO and then get paid. This screen will show the status of invoices as overdue, due, paid (not deposited), or deposited.

4 Select the **Customers** tab. The Customers screen helps your business keep track of who needs to pay you (money in). Your business can import customers into QBO or add customers manually. (Note: This tab may be labeled Clients depending upon the settings chosen when setting up the QBO company.)

5 Select the **Products and services** tab. Your business can add a product or service to the Products and Services List to save time when entering items sold on invoices.

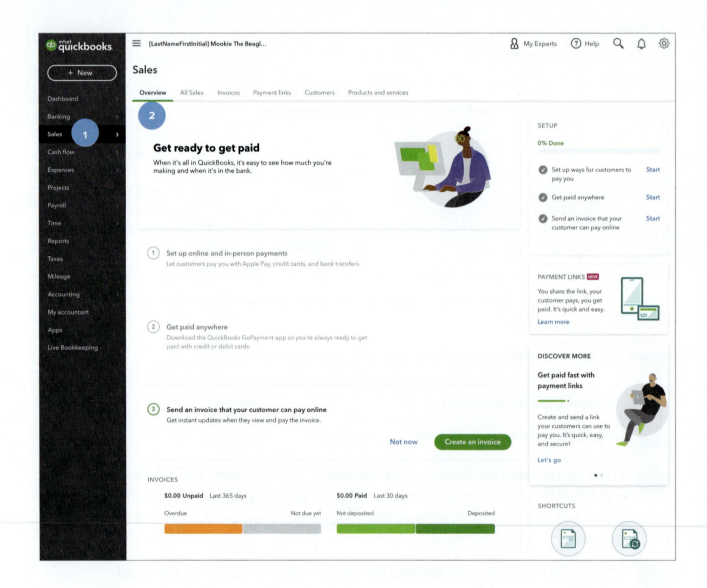

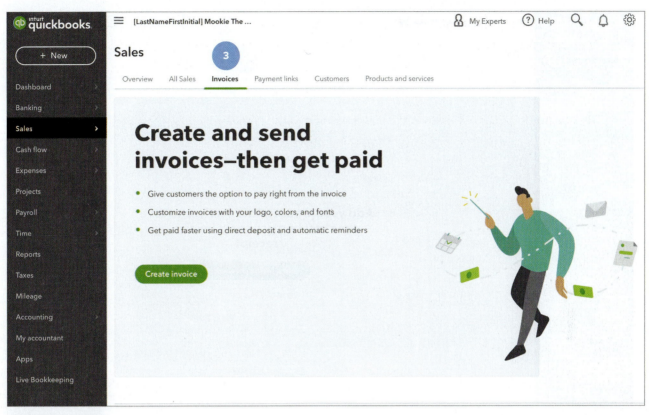

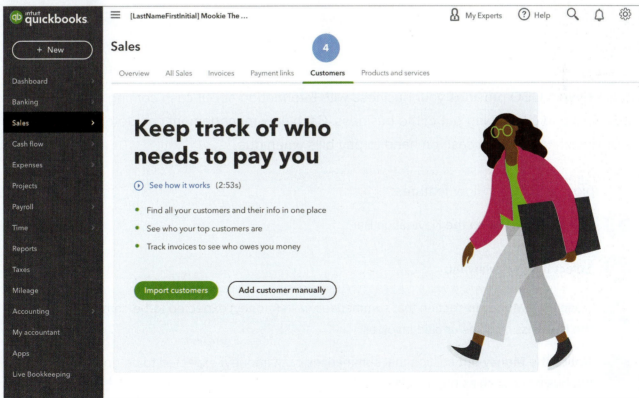

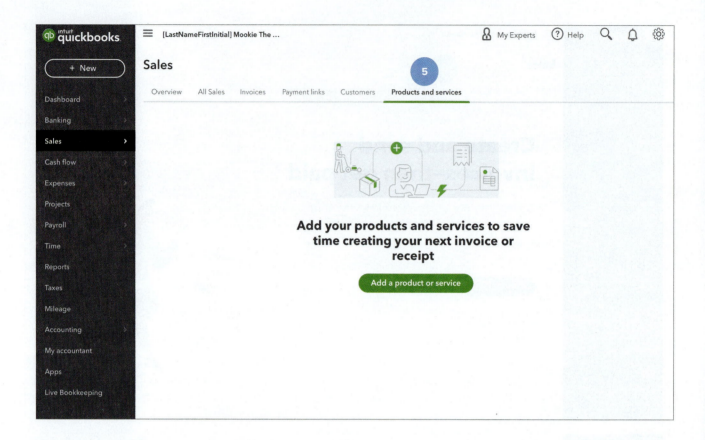

CASH FLOW

Cash flow in QBO provides your business with information about cash coming into the business and cash going out of the business. Cash flow management can determine whether a business has enough cash on hand to pay bills when due.

To explore QBO Cash flow features:

1 Select **Cash flow** on the Navigation Bar

2 Select the **Overview** tab

3 Notice the **Money in** section that summarizes cash (money) expected to be coming into the business, such as unpaid invoices

4 Notice the **Money out** section that summarizes cash (money) expected to be going out of the business, such as unpaid bills

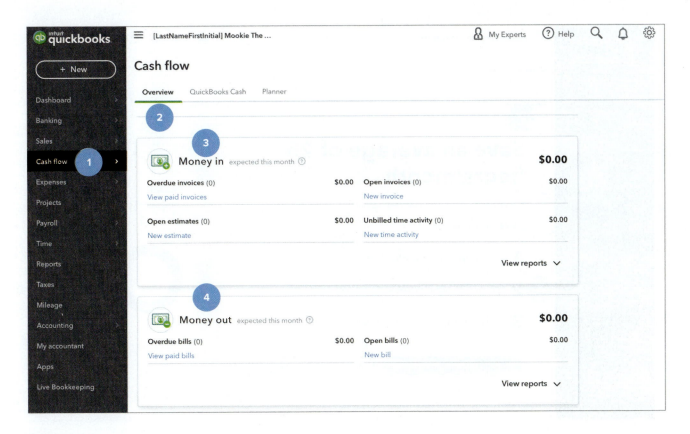

EXPENSES

Expenses transactions relate to vendors and expenses (money out).

To explore QBO Expenses features:

1 Select **Expenses** on the Navigation Bar

2 Select the **Expenses** tab. This screen will list expenses recorded in QBO.

3 Three steps to using QBO with expenses are:
1. **Import expense from your bank and credit cards.** You can save time by connecting your bank and credit card company, or you can add expenses into QBO manually.
2. **Categorize expenses to be ready for tax time.** When expenses are recorded in QBO, it is important to categorize the expenses by identifying which QBO account the expense should be recorded in.
3. **See where you're spending your money.** QBO provides an easy way to keep track of the expenses your business is incurring and on what items money is being spent.

4 Select the **Vendors** tab. The Vendors screen helps your business keep track of who you pay (money out). Your business can import vendors into QBO or add vendors manually.

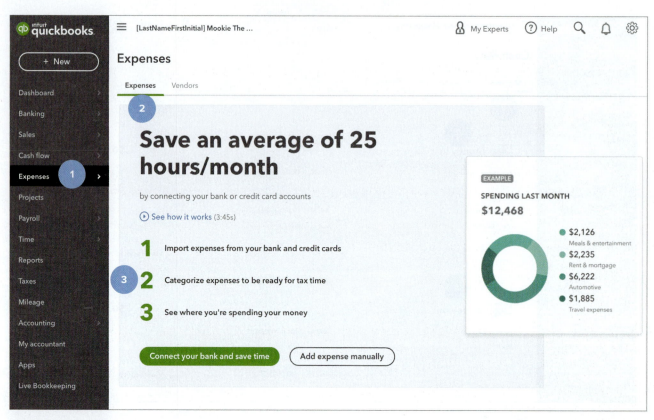

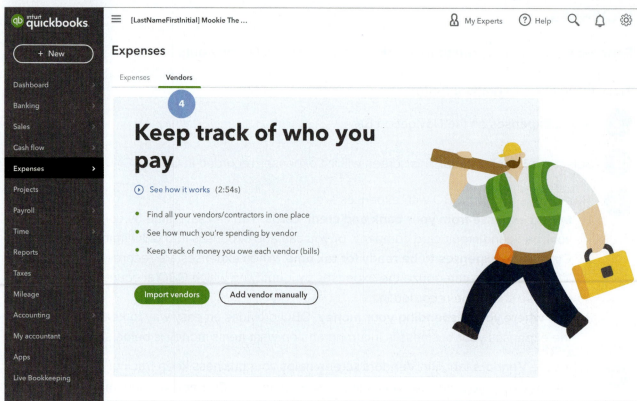

PROJECTS

Projects is a relatively new QBO feature that is useful for organizing project finances to better understand which projects are profitable.

To explore QBO Projects:

1   Select **Projects** on the Navigation Bar

2   Select **See how it works** to view a video on how to use QuickBooks Projects to track project income and costs

3   To set up a QBO project, select **Start a project**

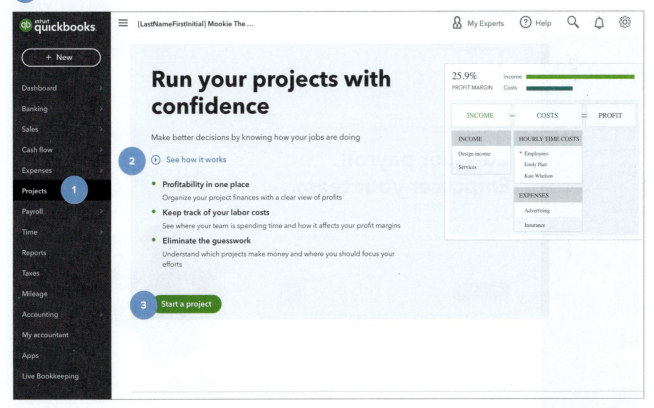

PAYROLL

Payroll transactions relate to employees and contractor transactions (money out). Contractors are not employees, but are vendors that are paid without withholding and other payroll taxes. To be considered a contractor instead of an employee, Internal Revenue Service requirements must be met. For more information about the differences between employee status and contractor status, go to www.irs.gov.

To explore the QBO Payroll feature:

1 Select **Payroll** on the Navigation Bar

2 Select the **Employees** tab. QBO offers QBO payroll services for a fee. The QBO payroll service integrates into your QBO company account. Once QBO payroll is set up, then payroll deductions and paychecks are calculated automatically. In addition, payroll tax forms can be filed and payroll payments can be made electronically through QBO.

3 If your business does not need payroll but wants to use time tracking for employees, you would select **Add an employee**

4 Select the **Contractors** tab. To keep track of information about contractors, you would select **Add your first contractor**.

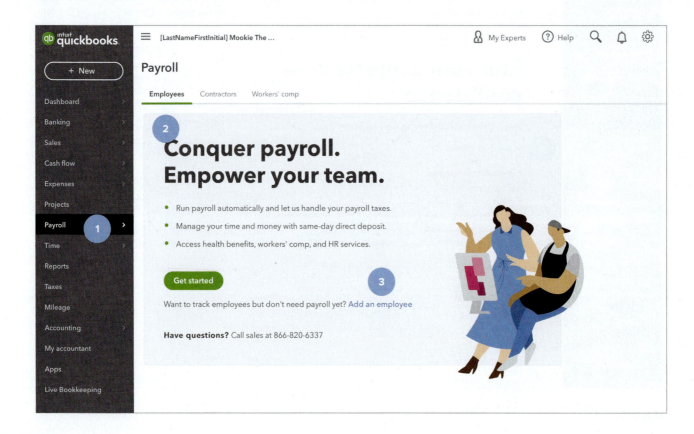

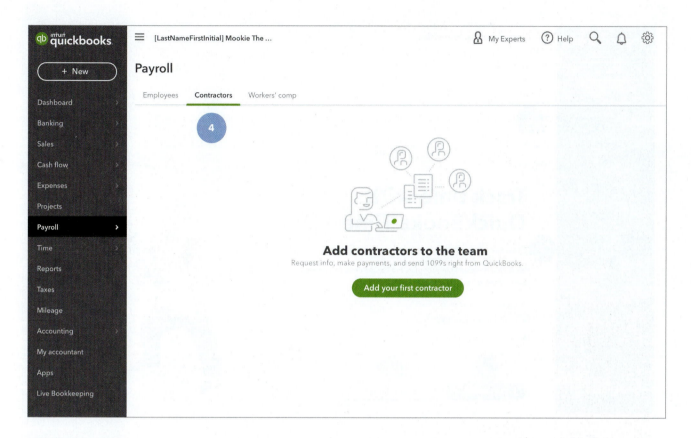

In Chapter 8 you will learn more about QBO payroll and how to use QBO time tracking for tracking employee and contractor time.

TIME

Time is a QBO feature that permits your business to use QBO to track time for employees, owners, and contractors.

To view QBO Time:

1. Select **Time** on the Navigation Bar

2. Select the **Overview** tab

3. Select **See how it works** to view a video on how to use QuickBooks Time

4. Basic time is included with your QBO Plus company. If your business was going to use Basic time, then you would select **Stick with basic time**.

5. QuickBooks Time is available for a fee. If your business wanted to consider using QuickBooks Time for an additional fee, you would select **Compare options**.

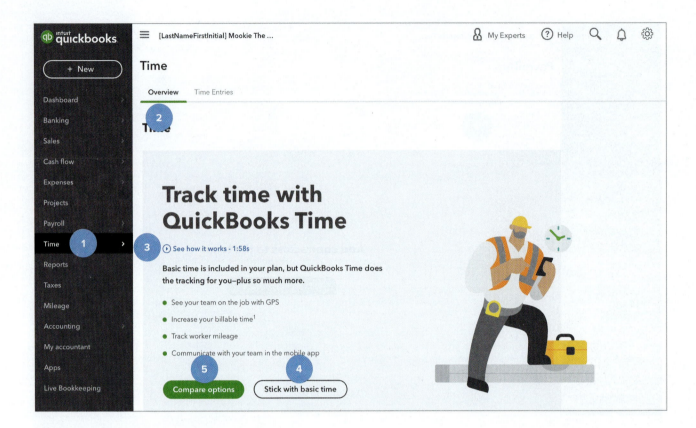

REPORTS

Reports summarize the output of our QBO financial system.

To explore QBO Reports features:

1 Select **Reports** on the Navigation Bar

2 Select the **Standard** tab

3 Notice that you can designate reports as **Favorites** to appear in the section at the top of the screen to save time in the future

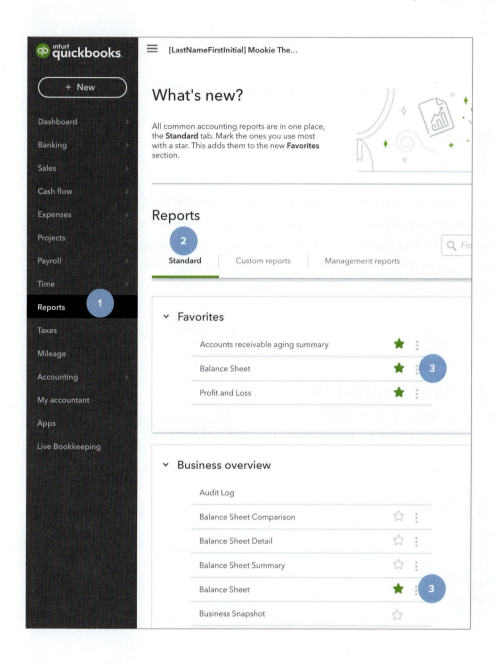

TAXES

Taxes relate to sales taxes and, if QuickBooks Online payroll is used, payroll taxes.

To explore QBO Taxes features:

1 Select **Taxes** on the Navigation Bar

2 If your business was required to charge and collect sales taxes from customers, you could set up sales taxes to streamline the collection and tracking of sales taxes using QBO by selecting **Use Automatic Sales Tax**. Sales tax would then be automatically added to customer invoices for sales that require sales taxes to be collected and remitted to the appropriate tax agency, such as a state department of revenue.

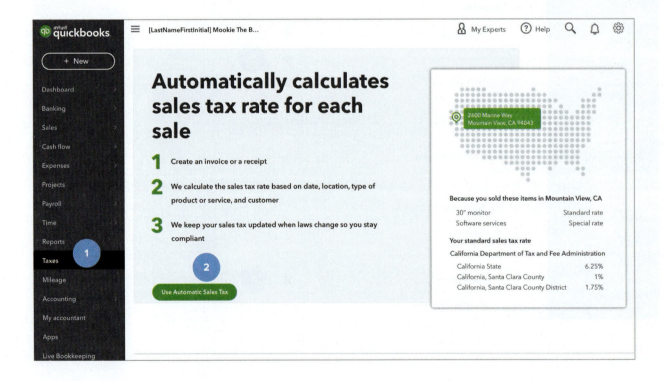

MILEAGE

Mileage can be automatically tracked for employees by QBO. The mileage information includes the purpose of the trip, start location, end location, dates and times, and length of trip. Mileage tracking can improve profitability by tracking mileage billable to specific customers or mileage that may be tax deductible.

To explore the QBO Mileage feature:

1 Select **Mileage** on the Navigation Bar

2 QBO offers a free QuickBooks mobile app for mileage tracking. To access the app, point your device's camera at the **Code** and a link will appear on your device.

3 If your business wanted to add mileage for trips manually, you would select **Or add trips manually**

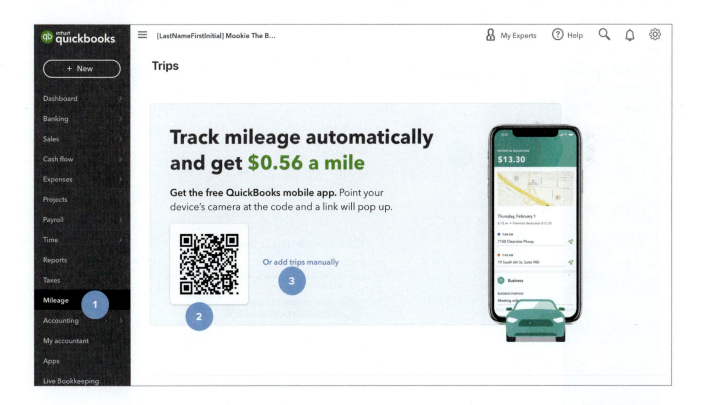

ACCOUNTING

Accounting displays the Chart of Accounts.

To explore the QBO Accounting features:

1 Select **Accounting** on the Navigation Bar

2 Select the **Chart of Accounts** tab

3 Select **See your Chart of Accounts**. From this screen you can add New accounts and Run reports listing the Chart of Accounts.

4 Select the **Reconcile** tab. Some QBO accounts can be connected to Bank accounts or Credit Card accounts, making it easier to match your QBO accounts (your books) to the bank records and reconcile your book balance to the bank balance. It also facilitates finding errors and oversights. In Chapter 4, you will learn more about how to match your bank and credit card QBO accounts to Bank and Credit Card company records.

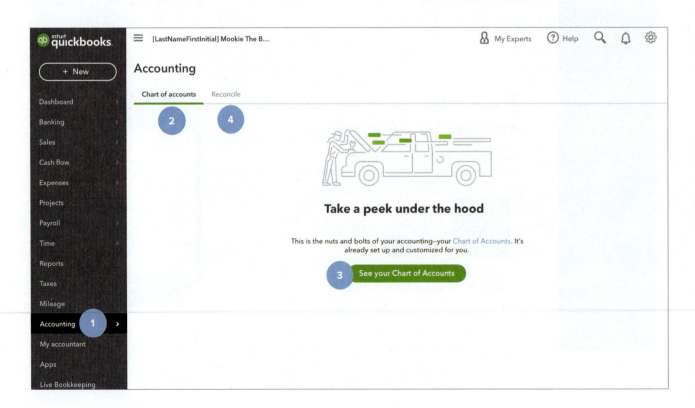

MY ACCOUNTANT

My Accountant is used to connect QBO to your accountant.

To explore the QBO My Accountant feature:

1 Select **My Accountant** on the Navigation Bar

2 If your business wanted to start the process to give your accountant administrative access to your QBO company data, you would enter the **Accountant's email**

3 After entering your accountant's email, you would select **Invite**

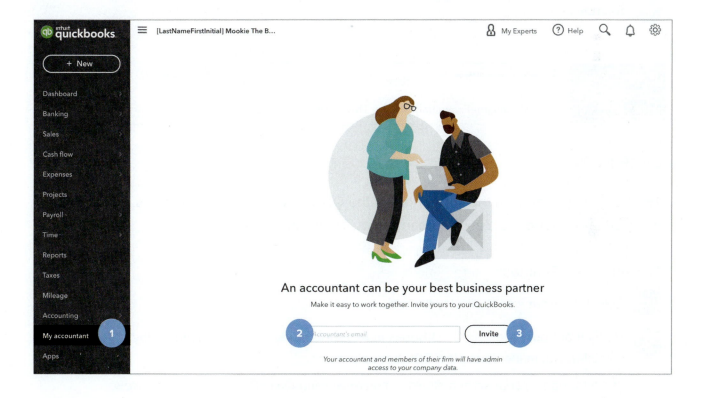

Section 1.4

QBO TOOLS

While the Navigation Bar is the primary way to navigate QBO, we can also access tasks using the following three useful QBO tools:

1 **Gear** icon

2 **(+) New** icon

3 **Search** icon

GEAR ICON

The Gear icon, located in the upper right of the QBO screen, lists various tasks. The tasks are grouped into categories: Your Company, Lists, Tools, and Profile.

To explore the Gear tool:

1 Select the **Gear** icon to display the task options

2 Verify that You're viewing QuickBooks in **Accountant view**. This is based on the selection you made during the QBO set up process.

⚠️ *Important: If your screen displays You're viewing QuickBooks in Business view, select Switch to Accountant view.*

3 Select **Account and settings** to update company settings

4 Select **Chart of accounts** to view and update the list of accounts your company uses

5 Select **All lists** to view lists such as Chart of Accounts, Customers List, and Vendors List

6 Select **Recurring transactions** to view the list of transactions that are saved for future reuse

7 Select **Audit log** to view the list of transactions entered

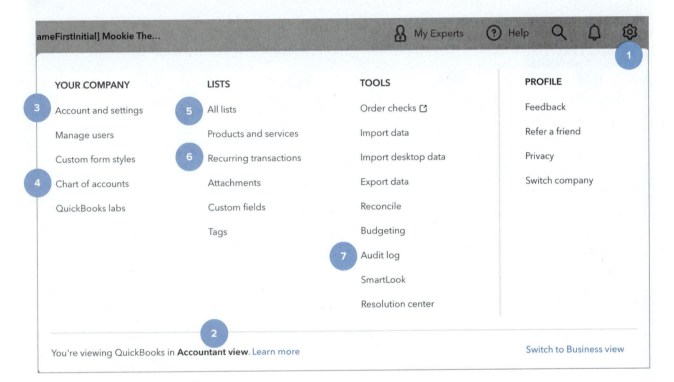

(+) NEW ICON

The (+) New icon, located at the top of the Navigation Bar, lists various new transactions we can create.

To explore the (+) New tool:

1 Select **(+) New** to display options for entering transactions

2 **Customers** transactions include create an invoice, receive payment, create an estimate, create a credit memo, and create a sales receipt

3 **Vendors** transactions include create an expense, enter a check, create a bill, pay bills, create a purchase order, and create a credit card credit

4 **Employees** transactions include entering payroll and time entry for tracking employee time worked

5 **Other** transactions include create a bank deposit, record a bank transfer, create a journal entry, and pay down credit card

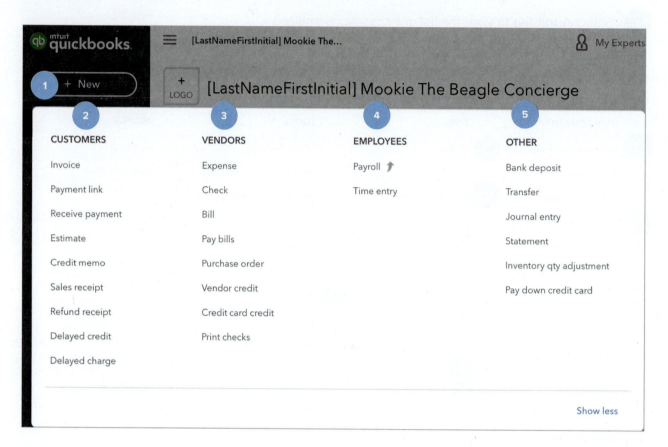

SEARCH ICON

The Search icon located in the upper right of the QBO screen permits us to search for amounts, dates, display names, and more to locate transactions. Advanced Search permits us to further refine our search. The Search feature is useful if we want to review a transaction after it has been entered or we need to update a transaction.

To use the QBO Search feature:

1 Select the **Search** icon

2 Enter **Search** criteria, such as $ Amount, Transaction No., or Date

3 Select **Search**

4 Select **Advanced Search** to enter more detailed search criteria

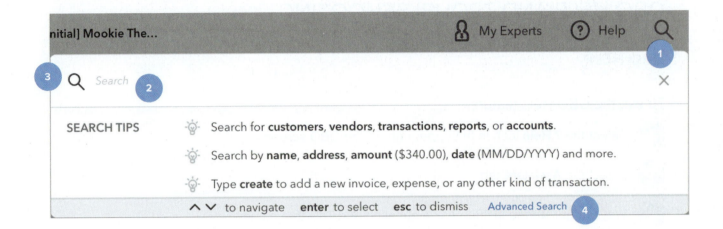

Section 1.5

QBO HELP AND TROUBLESHOOTING

QBO HELP

To use the QBO Help feature:

1 Select the **? Help** icon in the upper right of the QBO screen

2 Select the **Assistant** tab

3 Ways to get started include Ask a question and Talk to a human

4 Enter a question to search

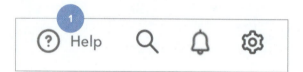

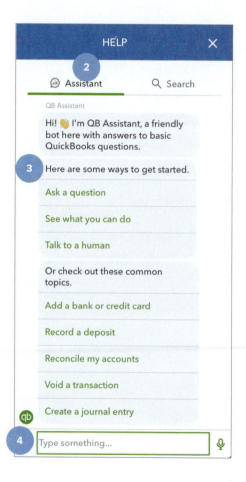

QBO UPDATES

An advantage of using QBO is that QBO is updated automatically on an ongoing basis. However, this may result in your text screen captures looking different than your QBO company screen. In addition, instead of rolling out these updates to all users at the same time, the updates are rolled out to different users at different times.

So if your QBO screen appears differently than your QBO text screen captures and instructions, check for updates to your *Computer Accounting with QuickBooks Online*, 3e, text as follows:

1. Go to www.my-quickbooksonline.com

2. Select **QBO 3E**

3. Select **QBO 3E Updates**

4. Under QBO 3E Updates, there are Text Updates and QBO Application Updates that might affect your text. Review the posted updates to see if the update resolves the issue.

If you are using Connect or a digital ebook, you can find updates under Additional Student Resources (ASR). If you do not have access to Connect or the ebook, your instructor can provide you with ASR.

QBO TROUBLESHOOTING (QT) BEST PRACTICES

QBO Troubleshooting (QT) Best Practices can streamline the troubleshooting process and increase your effectiveness in resolving issues. To learn more about QBO Troubleshooting Best Practices, see Appendix D: QBO Troubleshooting.

BROWSER TROUBLESHOOTING

Chrome Browser

Intuit recommends Google Chrome browser for use with QBO. If you are using a different type of browser and receiving error messages, try switching to a Chrome browser.

Clearing Cookies and Cache

If you receive an error message when using Chrome to access your QBO company, try clearing Cookies and Cache as follows:

1   From the upper right of the Chrome browser, select the **3 dots**

2   Select **More tools**

3   Select **Clear browsing data**

4   Select Time range: **All time**

5   Select **Cookies and other site data**

6   Select **Cached images and files**

7   Select **Clear data**

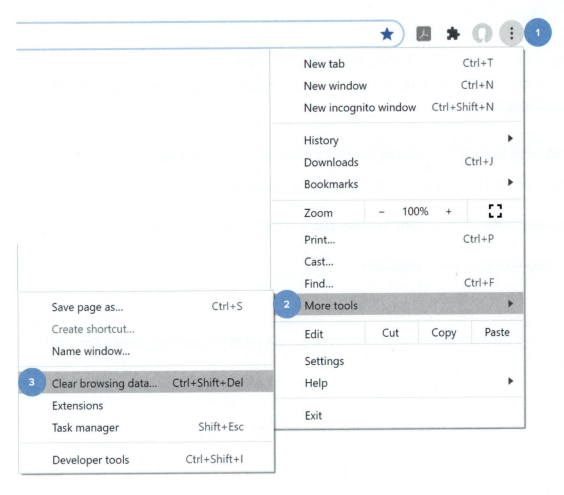

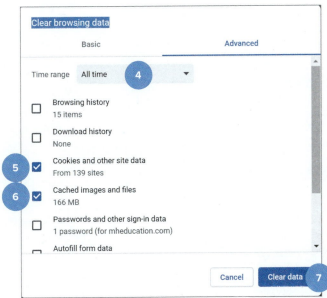

Multiple Browser Windows

When working in QBO, sometimes it is convenient to have more than one QBO window open. This permits you to compare amounts from screen to screen instead of clicking back and forth in the same QBO window.

For example to have two QBO company windows open at the same time:

1 **Sign in** to your QBO Company using Google Chrome browser

2 In the browser, **right-click** the **QBO browser tab** to display a pop-up menu

3 From the pop-up menu, select **Duplicate**

Now you should have two tabs open with two windows for the same Mookie The Beagle Concierge QBO company.

Section 1.6

QBO SETTINGS

When setting up a new QBO company, we want to align QBO with our company's legal and tax information. During setup, we must specify the type of legal entity used by our company, such as sole proprietorship, partnership, LLC, or corporation. In addition, the tax form that our company uses will affect the accounts we need in QBO. For more information about legal entity and tax forms, see Accounting Essentials at the end of this chapter.

Two aspects of QBO settings are:

- Company Settings
- QBO Chart of Accounts

COMPANY SETTINGS

When setting up a new QBO company, you are asked certain questions. Your responses to those questions will determine some of the QBO settings automatically. Some settings can be changed later, but other settings cannot be changed after setup.

After a QBO company has been set up, to access Your Company Settings:

1 Select **Gear** icon

2 Select **Account and Settings**

3 Select **Company** to review Company information, including tax return information

4   Select **Billing & Subscription** to view subscription information for various QBO services. This provides a convenient location to view all subscription information, including:
- QuickBooks Online. Your subscription should be free for one year. To subscribe after one year, select the Subscribe button.
- QuickBooks Online Payroll. To view more information about QuickBooks Online Payroll, select the **Learn more** button.
- QuickBooks Live Full-Service Bookkeeping. QBO offers live support for a fee.
- QuickBooks Time. Basic time tracking is included with your free QBO subscription. For businesses that need more robust time tracking, they can subscribe to QuickBooks Time. To view more information about QuickBooks Time, select **Learn more**.
- QuickBooks Online Payments. QBO offers businesses the ability to accept customer payments by credit card, debit card, Apple Pay, or bank transfer. To view more information about QuickBooks Online Payments, select **Learn more**.
- Checks and Supples. Businesses can shop for QBO supplies, such as checks and tax kits by selecting Shop now.

5   Select **Usage** to view usage limits information for QBO. QuickBooks Online Plus has usage limits. For example, QBO Plus has the following limits:
- Users: limit of 5
- Accounts in the Chart of Accounts: limit of 250
- Tag groups: limit of 40. To learn more about QBO tags, see Chapter 10.

If a QBO user's needs exceed these limitations, Intuit offers QuickBooks Online Advanced. QuickBooks Online Advanced provides for up to 25 users and an unlimited number of accounts in the Chart of Accounts. If you would like to explore QuickBooks Online Advanced, Intuit provides a test drive company at https://qbo.intuit.com/redir/testdrive_us_advanced.

6   Select **Sales** to review Company Sales preferences

7   Select **Expenses** to review Company Expenses preferences

8   Select **Payments** to view more information about QuickBooks Payments, a subscription service that facilitates businesses getting paid, including accepting credit cards and bank transfer payments, accepting payments through QuickBooks emailed invoices and mobile app. QuickBooks Payments also updates QuickBooks automatically when payment is received. Select **Learn more** for more information about QuickBooks Payments.

9   Select **Advanced** to review Advanced preferences for Mookie The Beagle Concierge

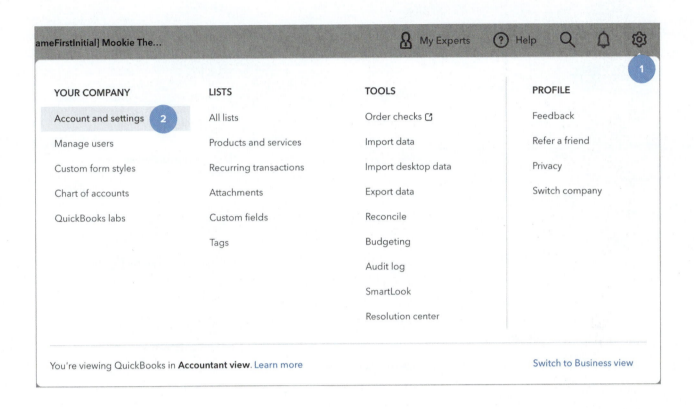

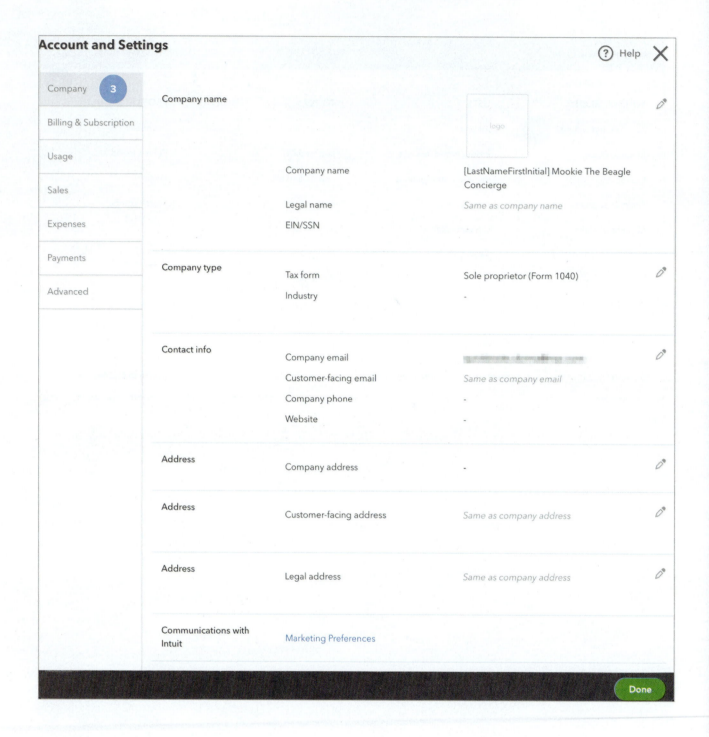

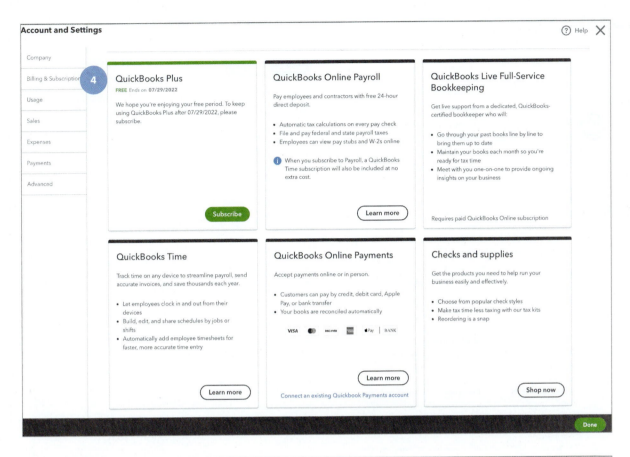

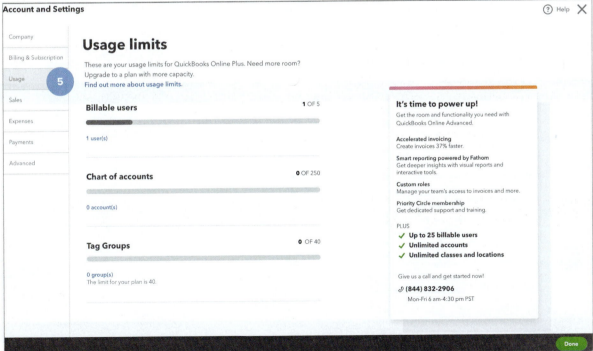

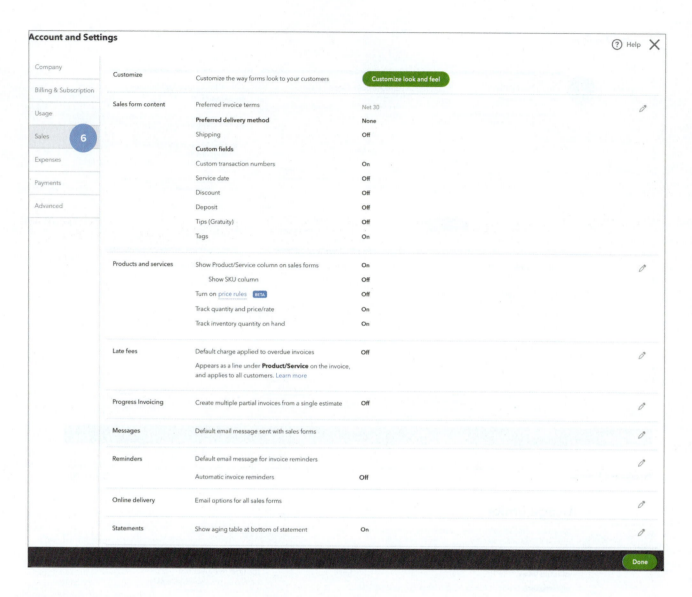

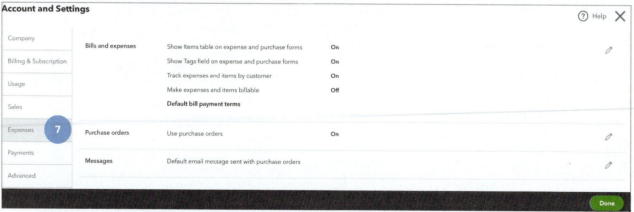

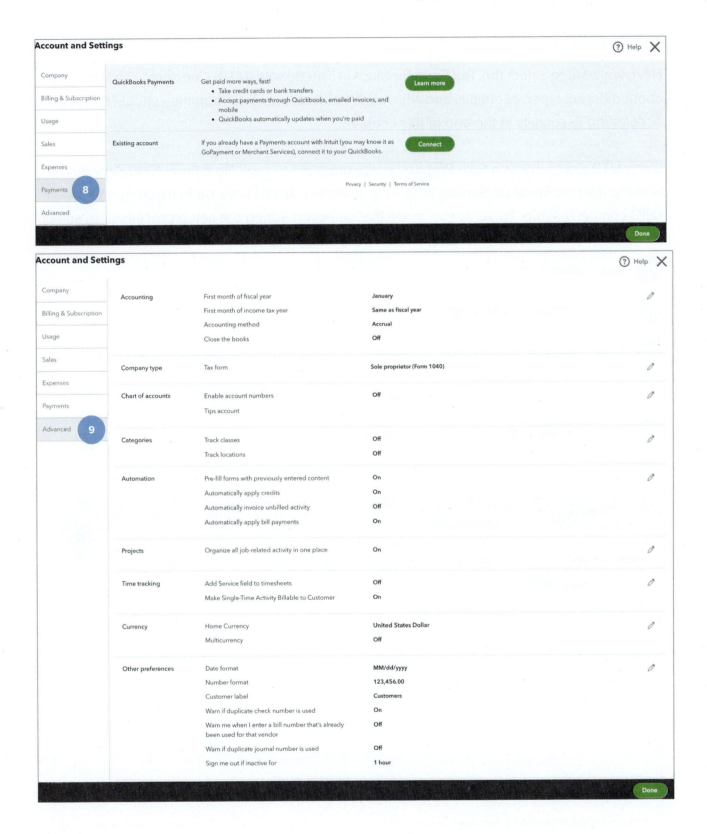

Tax Form

Next, we want to select the Tax Form for Mookie The Beagle (MTB) Concierge. To learn more about different types of entities and which Internal Revenue Tax Form they should file, see Accounting Essentials at the end of this chapter.

Since MTB Concierge is a Sole Proprietorship, the business will file a Form 1040 Schedule C with the Internal Revenue Service (IRS). This selection should have been made during the QBO company setup. To verify you made that selection during the setup process or to select the Form 1040 Tax Form now, complete the following.

1 Select **Gear** icon

2 Select **Account and Settings**

3 Select **Company**. Note that you can also access the tax form preference from Advanced settings.

4 On the right side of the Company Type section, select the **Edit pencil**

5 Select **Tax Form: Sole proprietor (Form 1040)**

6 Select **Save**

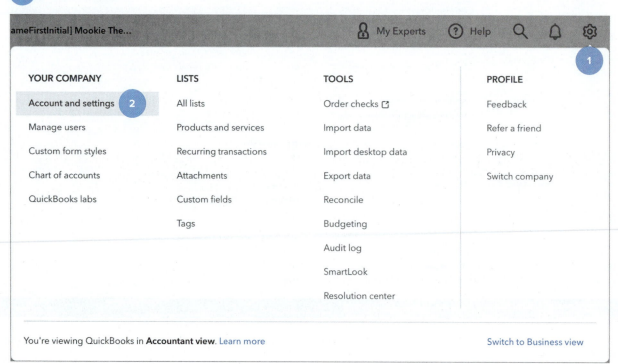

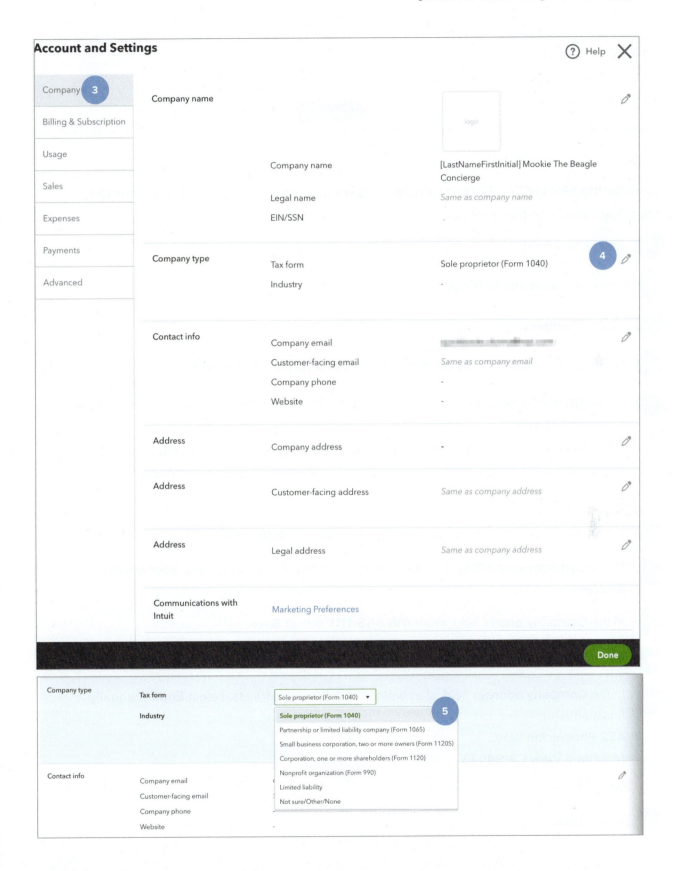

Company type		
	Tax form	Sole proprietor (Form 1040) ▼
	Industry	Enter your industry type
		Cancel Save 6

Company Information

To enter the Mookie The Beagle Concierge company address and email into your QBO company, complete the following.

1 Select **Gear** icon

2 Select **Account and Settings**

3 Select **Company**

4 On the right side of the **Company name** section, select the **Edit pencil**

5 In the **EIN/SSN** (Employer Identification Number/Social Security Number) field, select **SSN** > enter **111-11-1111**.

Note: Since Mookie The Beagle Concierge is a sole proprietorship filing a Schedule C Form 1040, we will use a SSN. EIN is used for Corporations and S Corporations.

Select **Save**.

6 On the right side of the **Contact info** section, select the **Edit pencil**

7 In the **Company email** field, if your email does not already appear, enter **Your email Address**

8 In the **Company phone** field, enter **415-555-1111**. Select **Save**.

9 In the **Address** section, select the **Edit pencil**

10 In the **Company address** field, start typing the following address, select **Enter manually** > finish entering:

432 Phoenician Way
Mountain View CA 94043

Select **Save**.

11 Select **Done**

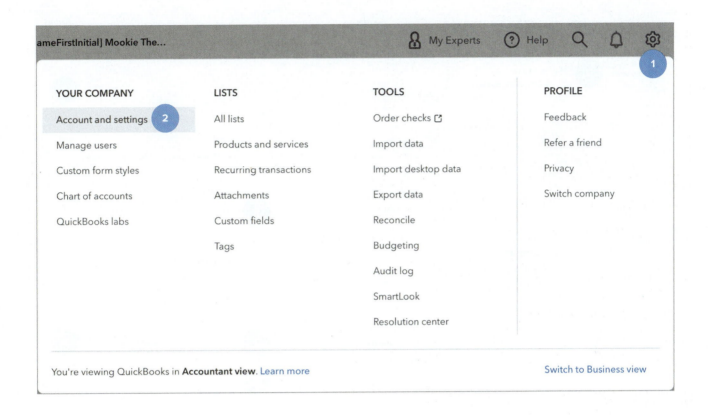

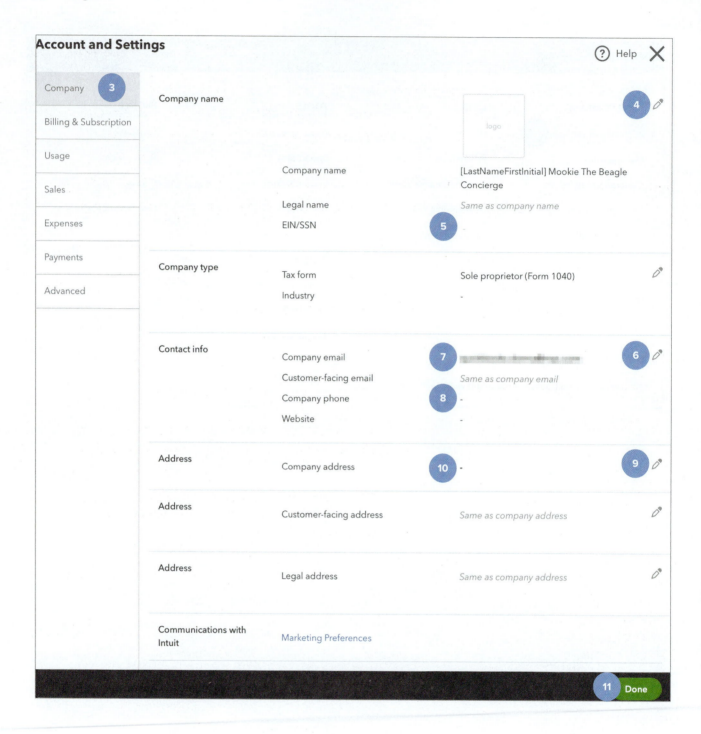

QBO CHART OF ACCOUNTS

The Chart of Accounts is a list of all the accounts for a company. Accounts are used to sort and track information. For example, a business needs one account for cash, another account to track amounts customers owe (Accounts Receivable), and another account to track inventory.

QBO automatically creates a Chart of Accounts (COA) when we set up a new company. Then we may customize the COA, adding and editing accounts as necessary to fit our company's specific needs.

To view the Chart of Accounts:

1 From the Navigation Bar, select **Accounting** to display the COA

2 If necessary, select **See your Chart of Accounts**

3 To run the COA report, from the Chart of Accounts window, select **Run report**

4 To view more detail about a specific account in the COA, from the Chart of Accounts window, select **View register** for the specific account. A register shows every transaction for an account with the running balance.

This completes the chapter activities. If you are ready to proceed to the chapter exercises at this time, leave your browser open with your QBO company displayed. If you will be completing the chapter exercises at a later time, you can close your browser.

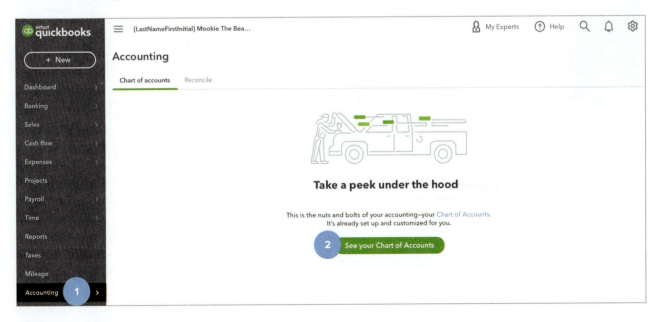

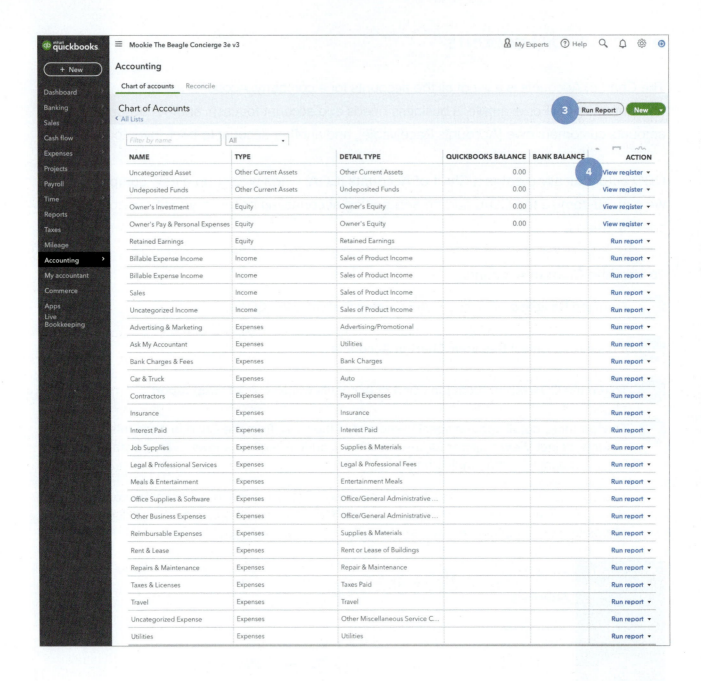

Section 1.7

ACCOUNTING ESSENTIALS
Legal, Tax, and Financial Questions

Accounting Essentials summarize important foundational accounting knowledge that may be useful when using QBO

Why do we care about the legal entity and tax form used by our business when setting up an accounting system?

The type of legal entity a business uses impacts the equity accounts we need and the tax form our business files. The tax form our business must file also impacts the type of financial information we need to track in our financial system. Bottom line: It's all interrelated. If we are going to set up a financial system that meets our business needs, then we need to understand how the legal and tax implications impact the financial system.

What is a legal entity?

How our business legal entity was organized (Sole Proprietorship, Partnership, Limited Liability Partnership (LLP), Limited Liability Company (LLC), C Corporation, S Corporation, or Nonprofit) affects which tax form and tax lines we use. There are advantages and disadvantages to each type of legal entity. Currently, many entrepreneurs use the LLC form to offer tax advantages and also limit liability of the owners.

How does the legal entity affect which business tax return we file?

The legal entity used to organize a business affects which tax return the business files.
- If the legal entity is a sole proprietorship, file Schedule C attached to Form 1040
- If the legal entity is a partnership (LLP), file Form 1065
- If the legal entity is a C corporation, file Form 1120
- If the legal entity is an LLC, then the business chooses how the business wants to be treated for tax purposes

What business tax return does an LLC file?

It depends. If a business is an LLC (Limited Liability Company), then the business has a choice to make regarding how the business wants to be treated for tax purposes. For tax purposes, assuming an LLC meets necessary tax requirements, an LLC can elect to be treated as:
- Sole proprietorship, filing Schedule C attached to owner's Form 1040
- Partnership, filing Form 1065
- S corporation, filing Form 1120S (See irs.gov for more information about requirements to elect the S corporation option for tax purposes.)

How do we know which business tax return needs to be filed?

Business tax returns to file are as follows:
- Sole proprietorships file Schedule C attached to owner's Form 1040
- Partnerships file Form 1065
- C corporations file Form 1120
- S corporations file Form 1120S

Business Type	Tax Form
Sole Proprietorship	Form 1040 Schedule C
Partnership	Form 1065
C Corporation	Form 1120
S Corporation	Form 1120S

How does our business tax return affect our financial system?

When setting up the financial system and accounts for our business, it is often helpful to review the tax form that our business files. Then our company's accounts can be customized to track information needed for our tax form. Basically, we can align our accounts with the tax return, so information in our accounts feeds into the lines on the tax return. This can reduce the amount of extra work needed at year end to obtain information for the business tax return. The tax form used by the type of organization is listed previously, and the forms and tax lines can be viewed at www.irs.gov.

Practice Quiz 1

Q1.1

Which of the following does not appear on the QuickBooks Online Navigation Bar?

a. Accounting
b. Expenses
c. Owners
d. Sales

Q1.2

Which of the following categories does not appear on the QuickBooks (+) New screen?

a. Banking
b. Customers
c. Employees
d. Vendors

Q1.3

How do you access QBO Account and Settings?

a. (+) New icon
b. Gear icon
c. Search icon
d. Help icon

Q1.4

What are two ways that we can access and view the Chart of Accounts in QBO?

a. From the Navigation Bar select Accounting
b. From the (+) New icon select Other > Chart of Accounts
c. From the Gear icon select Chart of Accounts
d. From the Home Page select Chart of Accounts

Q1.5

Which of the following could be considered three main processes of the QBO SatNav for using QuickBooks Online?

a. QBO Settings, QBO Transactions, QBO Reports
b. QBO Sales, QBO Expenses, QBO Reports
c. QBO Chart of Accounts, QBO Exchanges, QBO Settings
d. QBO Sales Transactions, QBO Banking Transactions, QBO Reports

Q1.6

QBO transactions include which of the following?

a. Sales
b. Expenses
c. Banking
d. All of the above

Q1.7

Financial statements include which of the following two?

a. Income statement
b. Statement of cash flows
c. Cash flow forecast
d. Physical inventory worksheet

Q1.8

Which of the following legal entities can use QuickBooks Online?

a. Sole proprietorship
b. Partnership
c. S corporation
d. All of the above

Q1.9

Match the following legal entities with the federal tax return the entity files.

1. Form 1040 Schedule C
2. Form 1120
3. Form 1065
4. Form 1120S

a. Partnership
b. C Corporation
c. S Corporation
d. Sole Proprietorship

Q1.10

Which federal tax return does an LLC (Limited Liability Company) file?

a. Form 1040 Schedule C
b. Form 1065
c. Form 1120S
d. It depends upon how the LLC chooses to be treated for tax purposes

Q1.11

QuickBooks Online Settings to set up a new company include which of the following two?

a.   Chart of Accounts

b.   Reconciliation Settings

c.   Company Settings

d.   Tax Settings

Exercises 1

If necessary, sign in to your Mookie The Beagle Concierge QBO Company as follows:

1   Using a Chrome web browser, go to qbo.intuit.com

2   Enter **User ID** (the email address you used to set up your QBO Account)

3   Enter **Password** (the password you used to set up your QBO Account)

4   Select **Sign in**

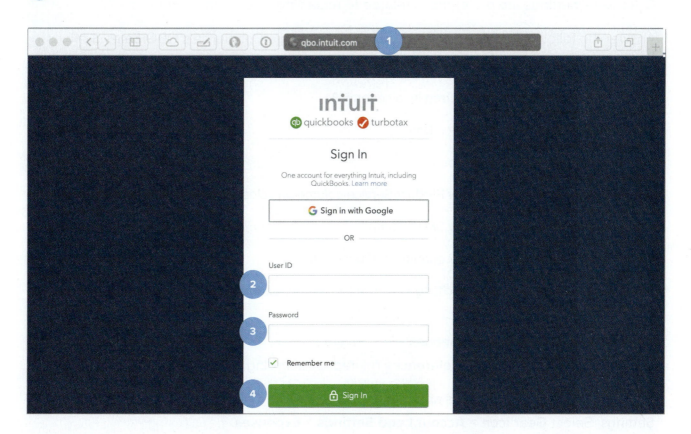

EM1.1 Company Settings: Company

QBO Company Settings are preferences for using QBO. When the QBO company is set up, some of the company settings can be automatically set up at that time. Some company settings can be changed at a later time after company set up.

If you are not signed in to Mookie The Beagle Concierge, sign in to your QBO Company for Mookie The Beagle Concierge. Select **Gear icon** > **Account and Settings** > **Company**.

For Company Settings, complete the following.

1. What is the Tax Form?
   a. Form 1040
   b. Form 1120
   c. Form 1120S
   d. Form K-1

2. What does the Legal name field display?

EM1.2 Company Settings: Sales

QBO Sales Settings are preferences related to recording sales using QBO.

Answer the following questions about Mookie The Beagle Concierge's QBO Sales Settings. Select **Gear icon** > **Account and Settings** > **Sales**.

1. What is the setting for Preferred invoice terms?

2. What is the setting for Service Date?

3. What is the setting for Discount?

4. What is the setting for Show Product/Service column on sales forms?

5. What is the setting for Show SKU column?

6. What is the setting for Track quantity and price/rate?

7. If it does not appear as on, change the Track inventory quantity on hand to **On** > **Save**.

EM1.3 Company Settings: Expenses

QBO Expenses Settings are preferences related to recording expenses using QBO.

Answer the following questions about Mookie The Beagle Concierge's QBO Expenses Settings. Select **Gear icon** > **Account and Settings** > **Expenses**.

1. What is the setting for Show Items table on expense and purchase forms?

2. What is the setting for Track expenses and items by customer?

3. What is the setting for Make expenses and items billable?

4. Change the setting for Make expenses and items billable to **On**.

5. What is the setting for Use purchase orders?

6. Change the setting for Use purchase orders to **On**.

EM1.4 Company Settings: Advanced

QBO Advanced Settings are preferences related to advanced items that are not listed under the other preference settings.

Select **Gear icon** > **Account and Settings** > **Advanced**. Answer the following questions about Mookie The Beagle Concierge's QBO Advanced Settings.

1. First month of fiscal year?

2. First month of income tax year?

3. Accounting method?

4. Close the books?

5. Tax form?

6. Enable account numbers?

7. Pre-fill forms with previously entered content?

8. Automatically apply bill payments?

9. Add Service field to timesheets?

10. Make Single-Time Activity Billable to Customer?

11. Home Currency?

12. Warn if duplicate check number is used?

E1.5 Navigation

Match the following selections from the QBO Navigation Bar with the single best answer for a related activity.

- **Accounting**
- **Expenses**
- **My Accountant**
- **Reports**
- **Sales**

1. View Customers List

2. View Vendors List

3. View Chart of Accounts

4. Create a Balance Sheet

5. Invite Accountant to view QBO company

E1.6 Chart of Accounts

The Chart of Accounts, a list of accounts, contains specific information about each account.

In the following Chart of Accounts, what is the name of each of the columns?

4 _____

5 _____

6 _____

E1.7 Register

A Register contains specific information about transactions for the corresponding account.

From the Navigation Bar select **Accounting** > **View Register** for the Inventory account in the Chart of Accounts. In the following Register, what is the name of each of the columns?

1 _____

2 _____

3 _____

4 _____

5 _____

6 _____

E1.8 Transactions

Transactions can be grouped into different types or categories of transactions.

Match the following categories found on the (+) New window with the following transactions.

- **Customers**
- **Vendors**
- **Employees**
- **Other**

1. Bank deposit

2. Time entry

3. Expense

4. Sales receipt

5. Payroll

6. Journal entry

7. Purchase order

8. Estimate

9. Pay bills

10. Check

11. Receive payment

12. Invoice

E1.9 QBO SatNav

The QBO SatNav provides an overview of QuickBooks Online and the various associated tasks and activities.

Match the three main QBO processes of the QBO SatNav with the following items.

- **QBO Settings**
- **QBO Transactions**
- **QBO Reports**

1. Income Statement

2. Create VISA Credit Card account

3. Exchange of cash for sale of product with customer

4. Statement of Cash Flows

5. Exchange of credit card payment for purchasing of product from vendor

6. Balance Sheet

E1.10 QBO Tools

QBO Tools are used to perform various QBO tasks.

Match the following two QBO tools with the following appropriate items.

- **Gear icon**
- **(+) New icon**

1. Invoice

2. Recurring transactions

3. Purchase order

4. Settings

5. Check

6. All lists

7. Bank deposit

8. Audit log

9. Credit card credit

10. Sales receipt

11. Pay bills

12. Receive payment

13. Chart of Accounts

14. Time entry

15. Manage users

16. Journal entry

QBO Chart of Accounts

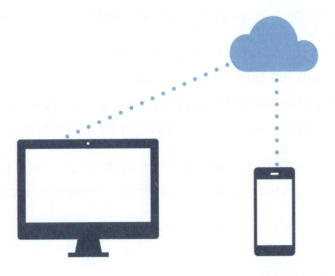

MOOKIE THE BEAGLE™ CONCIERGE

BACKSTORY

Your smartphone chimes with more texts from Cy Walker about his new business, Mookie The Beagle™ Concierge.

> We need to streamline MTB Concierge business as much as possible.

> Understood.

> Could you set up QBO to streamline my business tax prep to save time at year end?

> Ok. Just to confirm, MTB Concierge will file tax form 1040 Schedule C, correct?

> Good question.

> Let's set up a call.

When you call, Cy shares with you that he has observed how chaotic and stressful it can be when a new business waits until it's time to file the tax return to start collecting the data needed. He wants to make running his business more fun and less stressful. Cy would like to use QBO throughout the year to capture data about transactions, so that the information can be easily retrieved from QBO when it is time to file returns.

To streamline the process, Cy has asked you to customize Mookie's QBO Chart of Accounts so it aligns with the business tax return. Cy confirms that Mookie The Beagle Concierge is a sole proprietorship that will be filing a Schedule C, attached to Cy Walker's U.S. Federal Form 1040. Schedule C can be viewed at www.irs.gov.

Your next step is to learn more about the Chart of Accounts and how it can be customized in QBO so it aligns with data needed to complete a business tax return.

Chapter 2

LEARNING OBJECTIVES

Businesses use QuickBooks Online for many reasons, but one of the main reasons is usually to track information for tax return preparation. To provide information the client needs to prepare a tax return requires customizing the QBO Chart of Accounts to align with the tax return.

In this chapter, you will learn about the following topics:

- What is a Chart of Accounts (COA)?
  - View QBO Chart of Accounts
  - View QBO Registers
- QBO COA Account Numbers
  - Display QBO COA Account Numbers
  - Enter QBO COA Account Numbers
- Import QBO Chart of Accounts
- Align QBO Chart of Accounts with Tax Return
- Edit QBO Chart of Accounts
  - Add QBO Accounts
  - Add QBO Subaccounts
  - Edit QBO Accounts
  - Inactivate QBO Accounts
- Accounting Essentials: Chart of Accounts

⚠ **Important Note:** Chapter 2 is a continuation of Chapter 1. You will use the **QBO Company** you created for Chapter 1 to complete Chapter 2. Keep in mind the **QBO Company** for Chapter 2 carries your data forward, including any errors. So it is important to check and cross-check your work to verify it is correct before clicking the Save button.

⚠ **QBO is updated on an ongoing basis. Updates that affect your text** can be viewed as follows:
1. Go to www.My-QuickBooksOnline.com > **QBO 3e** > **QBO 3e Updates**, or
2. If you are using Connect or a digital ebook, you can find updates under Additional Student Resources (ASR). If you do not have access to Connect or the ebook, your instructor can provide you with ASR.

Section 2.1

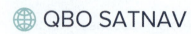 QBO SATNAV

QBO SatNav is our satellite navigation for QuickBooks Online, assisting us in navigating QBO

Chapter 2 focuses on QBO Settings, specifically the QBO Chart of Accounts highlighted in the following QBO SatNav.

QBO SatNav

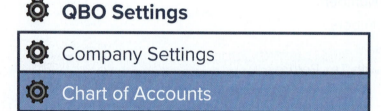

QBO Settings

Company Settings
Chart of Accounts

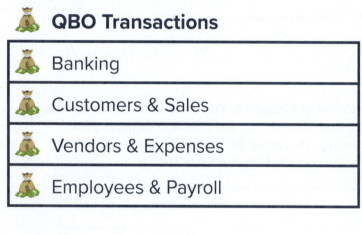

QBO Transactions

Banking
Customers & Sales
Vendors & Expenses
Employees & Payroll

QBO Reports

Reports

Section 2.2

QBO SIGN IN

To sign in to your Mookie The Beagle Concierge QBO Company, complete the following steps.

1 Using a web browser go to qbo.intuit.com

2 Enter **User ID** (the email address you used to set up your QBO Account)

3 Enter **Password** (the password you used to set up your QBO Account)

4 Select **Sign in**

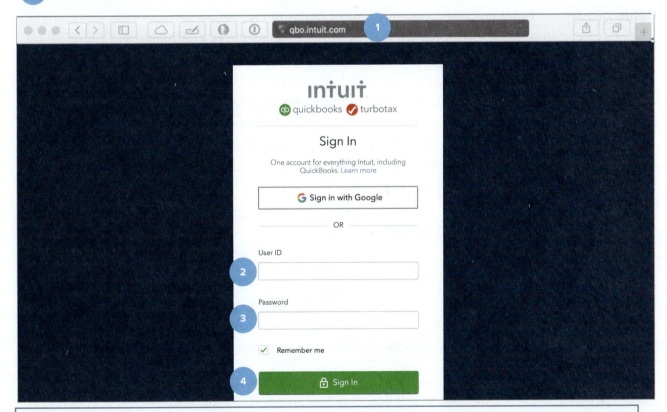

The new **QBO company** we created in Chapter 1 will carry all work forward into future chapters. So it is important to check and cross-check your work to verify it is correct before clicking the Save button. Any uncorrected errors will be carried forward in your **QBO company**.

Section 2.3

WHAT IS A QBO CHART OF ACCOUNTS (COA)?

The Chart of Accounts (COA) is a list of accounts and account numbers. A company uses accounts to record transactions in the accounting system. Accounts, such as a Checking account or Inventory account, permit us to sort and track information.

> 💡 **To refresh your recollection or learn more about the Chart of Accounts,** see **Accounting Essentials: Chart of Accounts at the end of Chapter 2.**

> **Note that QBO sometimes refers to Accounts as Categories.**

QuickBooks will automatically create a Chart of Accounts when we set up a new company. Then we can import our own Chart of Accounts using a csv file or customize the Chart of Accounts, adding and editing accounts as necessary to suit our company's specific needs.

QuickBooks also permits us to use subaccounts. Subaccounts are useful in tracking additional detail. For example, a parent account might be Insurance Expense. The two subaccounts might be Disability Insurance Expense and Liability Insurance Expense. By having two subaccounts we can easily track how much a company spends on each type of insurance, as well as for insurance in total.

VIEW QBO CHART OF ACCOUNTS

To display the Chart of Accounts:

1 Select **Accounting**

2 Select **Chart of accounts** tab and the Chart of Accounts should appear.

3 **Account Name.** In the COA, the Name column displays the name assigned to a specific account. Accounts are used to sort accounting information into the equivalent of accounting buckets. Naming an account or bucket is important since the name should reflect what the account contains to avoid confusion. Also, we want to plan our COA carefully so that we minimize the number of accounts while still meeting our need to track specific information for our company.

4 **Type.** QBO has categories or types of accounts. For example, Checking and Savings accounts are considered Bank accounts. Notice that QBO Account Type can differ from the Account Types we typically use of Assets, Liabilities, Equity, Revenues (Income), and Expenses.

5 **Detail Type.** In addition to the Account Type, QBO uses Detail Type as a subcategory of Account Type. You can think of Detail Type as smaller buckets used to sort inside the larger bucket of Account Type. For example, Other Current Assets is a QBO Account Type, and Accounts Receivable is a Detail Type.

6 **QuickBooks Balance.** QuickBooks Balance is the balance that QBO shows in your accounts. This is based on the transactions and information entered into QBO.

7 **Bank Balance.** Notice that Bank Balance only appears populated for accounts that are connected to a bank. QBO permits you to connect certain bank and credit card accounts to your bank and download the balance that the bank shows you have in your account. This can be very useful information because your QBO balance may show one amount, but the bank displays a different account balance. These differences can be due to timing differences (when you record something in QBO versus when the bank records an item) or it may be due to errors (either the bank's error or your error). Knowing the balance the bank shows for you can assist you in making sure that you do not overdraw a bank account.

8 **Action.** In the Action column, a drop-down arrow menu permits other actions that you can take from the COA screen. For example, if you want to view additional information about the specific account, you can select View Register.

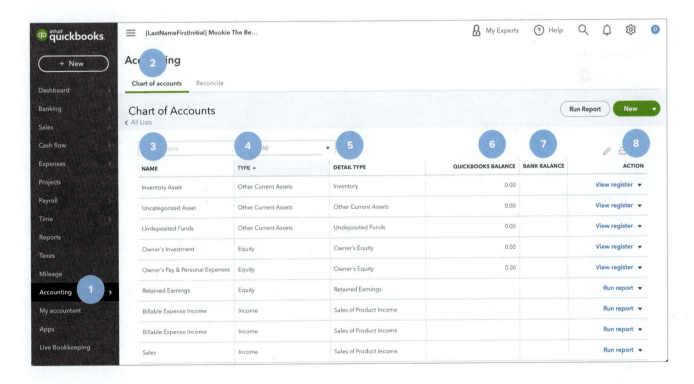

QBO requires certain default accounts in the QBO Chart of Accounts. Such accounts might include Undeposited Funds, Accounts Receivable, and Accounts Payable. If you see some accounts in QBO that you think you will not use, you cannot eliminate those accounts if they are default accounts.

VIEW QBO REGISTERS

Registers display more detailed information about accounts. A register displays all transactions for an account and a running balance.

For example, to view more detail about the Undeposited Funds account, we can view the Undeposited Funds account register. The Undeposited Funds account is an asset account that contains funds our company has received but not yet deposited at a bank. View a register as follows:

1 From the Chart of Accounts window, select **View register** for the specific account. In this case, select **View register** for the Undeposited Funds account.

2 The Undeposited Funds account register would show every transaction in the account, decreases, increases, and a running **Balance** that is displayed on the right

3 Select **Back to Chart of Accounts** to close the Register and return to the Chart of Accounts

Section 2.4

QBO COA ACCOUNT NUMBERS

Account numbers are used to uniquely identify accounts. Using account numbers to identify accounts can reduce errors by eliminating account name misspellings.

Usually account numbers are used as a coding system to also identify the account type. For example, a typical numbering system for accounts might be as follows.

Account Type	Account No.
Asset accounts	10000 - 19999
Liability accounts	20000 - 29999
Equity accounts	30000 - 39999
Revenue (Income) accounts	40000 - 49999
Expense accounts	50000 - 59999

DISPLAY QBO COA ACCOUNT NUMBERS

To display account numbers in the Chart of Accounts:

1 Select the **Gear** icon to display options

2 Select **Account and Settings**

3 Select **Advanced**

4 For Chart of Accounts, select the **Edit Pencil**, then turn on **Enable account numbers**

5 Select **Show account numbers**

6 Select **Save**

7 Select **Done** to close Account and Settings

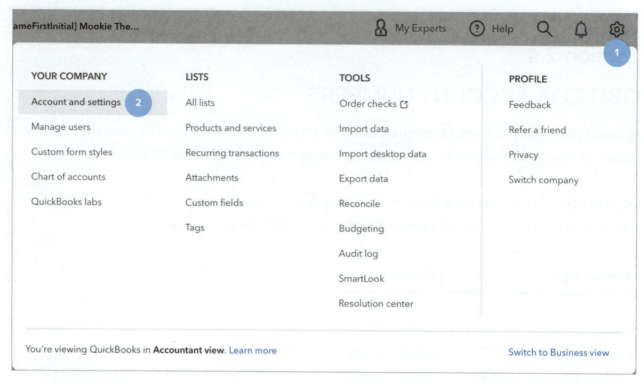

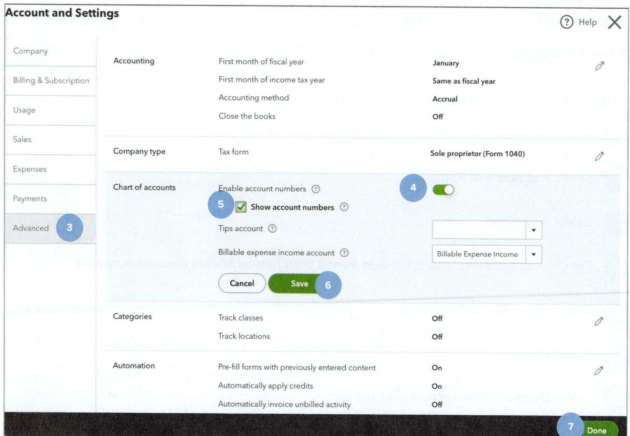

ENTER QBO COA ACCOUNT NUMBERS

After displaying account numbers in the QBO COA, to enter account numbers in the Chart of Accounts:

1 Select **Accounting** in the Navigation Bar

2 Select the **Chart of Accounts** tab. If necessary, select See your Chart of Accounts.

3 Notice that the Chart of Accounts now displays a **Number** column.

4 If necessary, click on **Type** to sort accounts with Other Current Assets appearing at the top of the Chart of Accounts

5 Select the **Edit pencil** icon

6 For the Uncategorized Asset account, enter Account Number **1500** in the Number column

7 Select **Save**

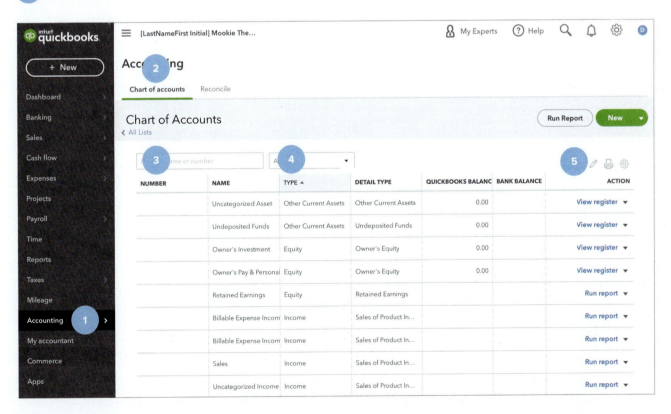

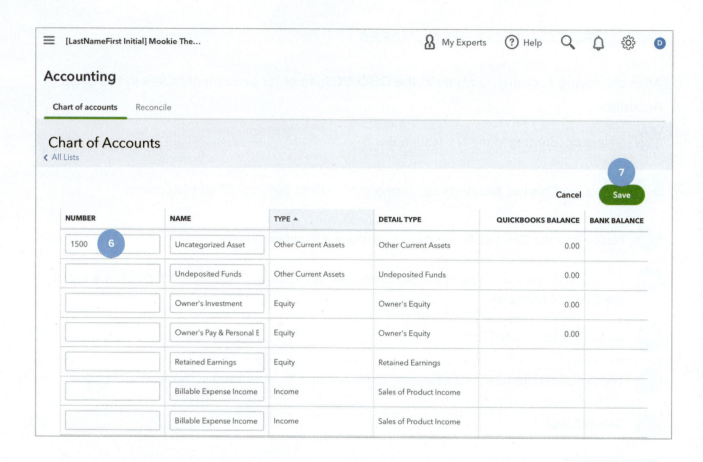

Section 2.5

IMPORT QBO CHART OF ACCOUNTS

Sometimes we already have a Chart of Accounts that is working well for a company. Instead of re-keying all the accounts into QBO, we can import the Chart of Accounts using a csv file. Basically, if we have the COA in a csv file format, then we can import the csv file into QBO.

Two main advantages of importing an existing COA into QBO are:

1. Time savings. Importing a csv file can save a significant amount of time by eliminating the need to re-key each account into QBO.
2. Error reduction. Each time data is re-keyed introduces another opportunity for errors to enter the system. So if we are confident our csv file is error free, then we can import it into QBO to reduce the opportunity for errors entering our system.

There are also a couple of possible disadvantages in importing a COA using a csv file, including:

1. Glitches. Sometimes when importing a csv file, there are glitches that prevent the data from being imported cleanly. This may require significant time to clean up the data that has been imported. Re-keying the data might have been faster and easier.
2. Errors in csv file. If there are existing errors in the csv file that we have imported, then we have just introduced those errors in our new QBO system. This underscores the importance of cross-checking the csv file before importing to ensure we are not carrying forward errors in the imported data.

For Mookie The Beagle Concierge, instead of importing the Chart of Accounts, we will add and edit accounts to customize the Chart of Accounts to meet our business needs.

Section 2.6

ALIGN QBO CHART OF ACCOUNTS WITH TAX RETURN

QBO automatically creates a Chart of Accounts when we set up a new company. Then we can customize the COA, adding and deleting accounts as necessary to fit our company's specific needs. In many cases, we are using QBO to track information for tax return preparation. So to streamline the process, it only makes sense to align the QBO Chart of Accounts with our company's tax return.

When setting up a Chart of Accounts for a business, it is often helpful to review the tax form that the business will use. Then a company's Chart of Accounts can be customized to track information needed for the tax form.

Our goal is to see that the QBO Chart of Accounts feeds into the tax return lines. So first, we need to know which business tax return the company files. For example, if a business is a sole proprietorship, then for federal income taxes the business files Schedule C that is attached to the sole proprietor's Form 1040. If the business is an S corporation, then for federal income taxes the business files Form 1120S. The type of organization and corresponding tax form follow.

Type of Organization	Tax Form
Sole Proprietorship	Form 1040 Schedule C
Partnership	Form 1065
C Corporation	Form 1120
S Corporation	Form 1120S

To view various tax return forms for businesses, go to the Internal Revenue Service (IRS) website: www.irs.gov.

C2.6.1 Aligning COA and Tax Return

Typically when customizing the Chart of Accounts for businesses, we want to verify that the accounts on the Chart of Accounts correspond to expenses shown on the tax return the business files. Mookie The Beagle Concierge files the following IRS Schedule C (Form 1040) for its business operations.

SCHEDULE C
(Form 1040)

Department of the Treasury
Internal Revenue Service (99)

Profit or Loss From Business
(Sole Proprietorship)

▶ Information about Schedule C and its separate instructions is at *www.irs.gov/schedulec*.
▶ Attach to Form 1040, 1040NR, or 1041; partnerships generally must file Form 1065.

Name of proprietor	Social security number (SSN)

A	Principal business or profession, including product or service (see instructions)	B Enter code from instructions ▶

C	Business name. If no separate business name, leave blank.	D Employer ID number (EIN), (see instr.)

E   Business address (including suite or room no.) ▶
    City, town or post office, state, and ZIP code

F   Accounting method: (1) ☐ Cash   (2) ☐ Accrual   (3) ☐ Other (specify) ▶

G   Did you "materially participate" in the operation of this business during 2016? If "No," see instructions for limit on losses . ☐ Yes ☐ No

H   If you started or acquired this business during 2016, check here . . . . ▶ ☐

I   Did you make any payments in 2016 that would require you to file Form(s) 1099? (see instructions) . . . . ☐ Yes ☐ No

J   If "Yes," did you or will you file required Forms 1099? . . . . ☐ Yes ☐ No

Part I Income

1	Gross receipts or sales. See instructions for line 1 and check the box if this income was reported to you on Form W-2 and the "Statutory employee" box on that form was checked . . . . ▶ ☐	1	
2	Returns and allowances	2	
3	Subtract line 2 from line 1	3	
4	Cost of goods sold (from line 42)	4	
5	**Gross profit.** Subtract line 4 from line 3	5	
6	Other income, including federal and state gasoline or fuel tax credit or refund (see instructions)	6	
7	**Gross income.** Add lines 5 and 6 . . . . ▶	7	

Part II Expenses. Enter expenses for business use of your home **only** on line 30.

8	Advertising	8		18	Office expense (see instructions)	18	
9	Car and truck expenses (see instructions).	9		19	Pension and profit-sharing plans .	19	
				20	Rent or lease (see instructions):		
10	Commissions and fees .	10		a	Vehicles, machinery, and equipment	20a	
11	Contract labor (see instructions)	11		b	Other business property . . .	20b	
12	Depletion	12		21	Repairs and maintenance . . .	21	
13	Depreciation and section 179 expense deduction (not included in Part III) (see instructions).	13		22	Supplies (not included in Part III) .	22	
				23	Taxes and licenses	23	
				24	Travel, meals, and entertainment:		
14	Employee benefit programs (other than on line 19) . .	14		a	Travel	24a	
15	Insurance (other than health)	15		b	Deductible meals and entertainment (see instructions) .	24b	
16	Interest:			25	Utilities	25	
a	Mortgage (paid to banks, etc.)	16a		26	Wages (less employment credits) .	26	
b	Other	16b		27a	Other expenses (from line 48) .	27a	
17	Legal and professional services	17		b	**Reserved for future use** . . .	27b	

For the following accounts from Mookie The Beagle Concierge QBO Chart of Accounts, identify the corresponding Line number on Schedule C (Form 1040).

QBO COA	IRS Schedule C (Form 1040)
1. Cost of Goods Sold	Schedule C Line _____
2. Advertising & Marketing	Schedule C Line _____

Section 2.7

EDIT QBO COA

We can customize the Chart of Accounts by adding, editing, and inactivating accounts as needed to meet a company's specific and changing needs.

ADD QBO ACCOUNTS

To add a new account to the Chart of Accounts:

1 From the Navigation Bar, select **Accounting**

2 If necessary, select the **Chart of Accounts** tab

3 From the Chart of Accounts window, select **New**

4 From the Account window, select **Account Type: Bank**

5 Select **Detail Type: Checking**

6 Enter **Name: Checking**

7 Enter **Number: 1001**

8 Since Checking is not a subaccount, uncheck **Is sub-account**

9 Select **Save and Close**

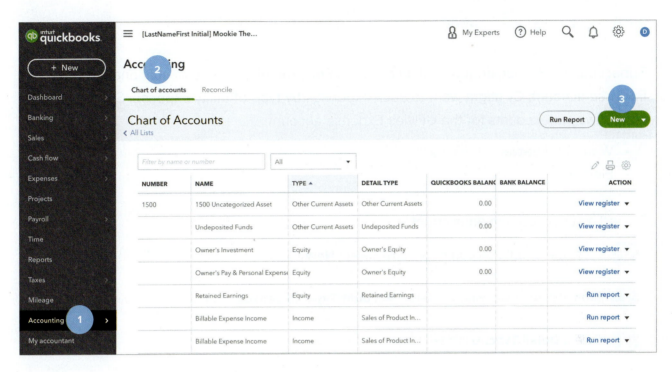

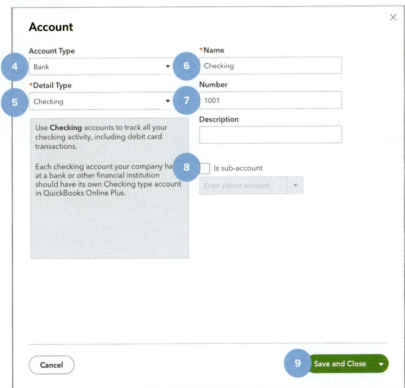

ADD QBO SUBACCOUNTS

Subaccounts are subcategories of an account. For example, instead of only one Utilities Expense account, Cy might want to track expenses by type of utility expense. So you could set up two subaccounts for the Utilities Expense account:

- Water and Sewer
- Electric

To add a subaccount to an account:

1 From the Chart of Accounts window, select **New**

2 From the Account window, select **Account Type: Expenses**

3 Select **Detail Type: Utilities**

4 Enter **Name: Water and Sewer**

5 Enter **Number: 5042**

6 Check **Is sub-account**

7 From the drop-down list, select **Utilities**

8 Select **Save and Close**

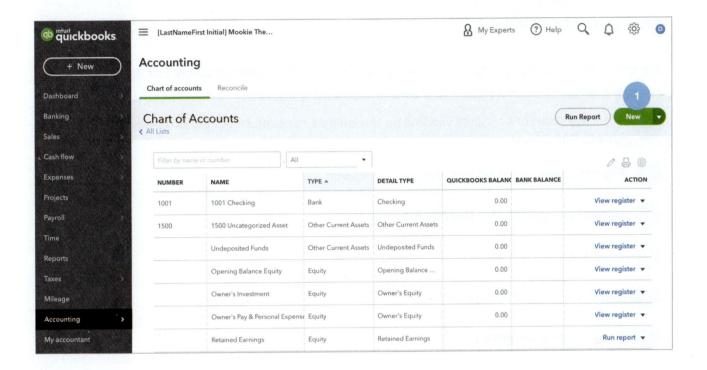

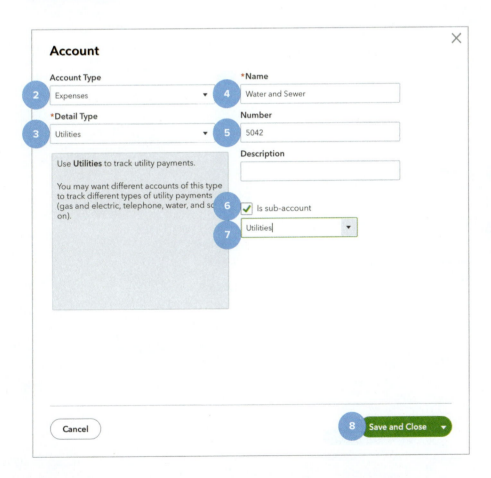

EDIT QBO ACCOUNTS

We can edit an account in QBO to update information about the account. For example, to change the name of an account and add an account number:

1   From the Chart of Accounts window for the Utilities account, select the **drop-down arrow** next to Run Report

2   From the drop-down list that appears, select **Edit**

3   Update **Account Name: Utilities Expense**

4   Enter **Number: 5040**

5   Leave **Description: Blank**

6   Select **Save and Close**

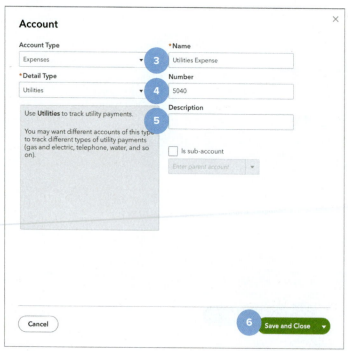

INACTIVATE QBO ACCOUNTS

Sometimes we no longer need to use an account. So QBO permits us to inactivate the account in the Chart of Accounts. If an inactivated account has been used to record transactions, then the transactions are still intact but the account is designated in reports as Inactive. If at a later time, we need to restore an inactive account, QBO will permit us to do so.

To inactivate an account:

1 From the Chart of Accounts window, select the **drop-down arrow** next to Run Report for the Water and Sewer account

2 From the drop-down list that appears, select **Make inactive**

3 When asked Are you sure you want to inactivate this? select **Yes**

4 This completes the chapter activities. If you are ready to proceed to the chapter exercises at this time, leave your browser open with your QBO company displayed. If you will be completing the chapter exercises at a later time, you can close your browser.

NUMBER	NAME	TYPE ▲	DETAIL TYPE	QUICKBOOKS BALANCE	BANK BALANCE	ACTION
5040	5040 Utilities Expense	Expenses	Utilities			Run report ▾
5042	5042 Water and Sewer	Expenses	Utilities			Run report ▾ ① ② Edit / Make inactive (reduces usage)
	Advertising & Marketing	Expenses	Advertising/Promotional			
	Ask My Accountant	Expenses	Utilities			Run report ▾

Chart of accounts   Reconcile

Are you sure you want to inactivate this?

No   **3 Yes**

By adding, editing, and inactivating accounts, we can customize the QBO Chart of Accounts to align with the business tax return. This can save countless hours when preparing tax reports, reduce errors, and streamline tax return preparation.

Section 2.8

ACCOUNTING ESSENTIALS
Chart of Accounts

Accounting Essentials summarize important foundational accounting knowledge you may find useful when using QBO

What is the primary objective of accounting?

- The primary objective of accounting is to provide information for decision making. Businesses use a financial system, such as QuickBooks Online, to capture, track, sort, summarize, and communicate financial information.

How is financial information for decision making provided?

- Financial reports summarize and communicate information about a company's financial position and business operations.

What is the difference between financial reports and financial statements?

- Financial reports include financial statements, in addition to other reports, such as cash-flow forecasts.
- Financial statements are standardized financial reports, typically consisting of a Balance Sheet, Profit and Loss Statement, and a Statement of Cash Flows, that summarize information about past transactions.
- Financial statements are provided to external users and internal users for decision making.
- External users include bankers, creditors, and investors.
- Internal users include managers and employees of the business.

What are the main financial statements for a business?

- The primary financial statements for a business are:
  - **Balance Sheet** summarizes what a company *owns* and *owes* on a particular date.
  - **Profit and Loss Statement** (also referred to as P&L Statement or Income Statement) summarizes the income a company has earned and the expenses incurred to earn the income.
  - **Statement of Cash Flows** summarizes cash inflows and cash outflows for operating, investing, and financing activities of a business.

What is a Chart of Accounts?

- Chart of Accounts (COA) is a list of all the accounts and account numbers for a business. Accounts are used to sort and track accounting information. For example, a business needs one account for cash, another account to track amounts customers owe (Accounts Receivable), and yet another account to track inventory.

Why Use Accounts?

- We use accounts to record transactions in our accounting system. Accounts, such as a Checking account or Insurance Expense account, permit us to sort, organize, summarize, and track information.
- We can add subaccounts for even better tracking. For example, we could add Rental Insurance Expense and Liability Insurance Expense as subaccounts to our Insurance Expense account. The subaccounts, Rental Insurance Expense and Liability Insurance Expense, provide us with additional detail, and the subaccounts roll up into the total for the parent account, Insurance Expense.

What are the Different Types of Accounts?

- We can group accounts into the following different account types:

Balance Sheet Accounts			Profit and Loss Accounts	
Assets	**Liabilities**	**Equity**	**Income**	**Expenses**
Bank account	Accounts Payable	Capital Investment	Sales	Supplies Expense
Accounts Receivable	Credit Cards Payable	Retained Earnings	Consulting Fees	Rent Expense
Equipment	Loans Payable		Interest Income	Utilities Expense

What are Balance Sheet Accounts?

- The Balance Sheet is a financial statement that summarizes what a company owns and what it owes.

- Balance Sheet accounts are accounts that appear on the company's Balance Sheet.

- Three types of accounts appear on the Balance Sheet:
  1. Assets
  2. Liabilities
  3. Owners' (or Stockholders') Equity

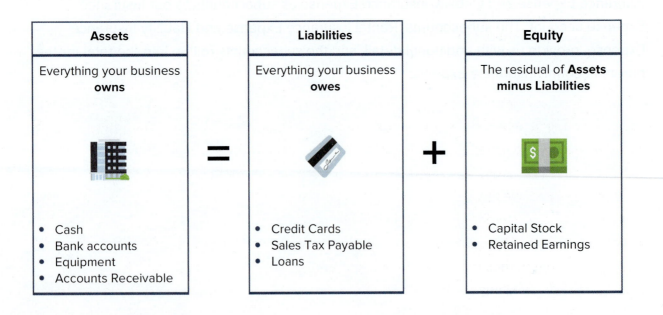

Assets		**Liabilities**		**Equity**
Everything your business **owns**	=	Everything your business **owes**	+	The residual of **Assets minus Liabilities**
• Cash • Bank accounts • Equipment • Accounts Receivable		• Credit Cards • Sales Tax Payable • Loans		• Capital Stock • Retained Earnings

1. Assets are resources that a company owns. These resources are expected to have future benefit.

Asset accounts include:
- Cash
- Accounts receivable (amounts to be received from customers in the future)
- Inventory
- Other current assets (assets likely to be converted to cash or consumed within one year)
- Fixed assets (property used in the operations of the business, such as equipment, buildings, and land)
- Intangible assets (such as copyrights, patents, trademarks, and franchises)

How Do We Know if an Account is an Asset?

Ask:
Will our enterprise receive a *future benefit* from the item?

Answer:
If we will receive *future benefit*, the account is probably an *asset*. For example, prepaid insurance has future benefit.

---

2. Liabilities are amounts a company owes to others. Liabilities are obligations. For example, if a company borrows $10,000 from the bank, the company has an obligation to repay the $10,000 to the bank. Thus, the $10,000 obligation is shown as a liability on the company's Balance Sheet.

Liability accounts include:
- Accounts payable (amounts that are owed and will be paid to suppliers in the future)
- Sales taxes payable (sales tax owed and to be paid in the future)
- Interest payable (interest owed and to be paid in the future)
- Other current liabilities (liabilities due within one year)
- Loan payable (also called notes payable)
- Mortgage payable (The difference between a note payable and a mortgage payable is that a mortgage payable has real estate as collateral.)
- Other long-term liabilities (liabilities due after one year)

How Do We Know if an Account is a Liability?

Ask:
Is our enterprise *obligated* to do something, such as pay a bill or provide a service?

Answer:
If we have an *obligation*, the account is probably a *liability*.

---

3. **Equity accounts** (or stockholders' equity for a corporation) represent the net worth of a business. Equity is calculated as assets (resources owned) minus liabilities (amounts owed).

Different types of business ownership include:
- Sole proprietorship (an unincorporated business with one owner)
- Partnership (an unincorporated business with more than one owner)
- Corporation (an incorporated business with one or more owners)

Owners' equity is increased by:
- Investments by owners. For a corporation, owners invest by buying stock.
- Net profits retained in the business rather than distributed to owners

Owners' equity is decreased by:
- Amounts paid to owners as a return for their investment. For a sole proprietorship or partnership, these are called withdrawals or distributions. For a corporation, they are called dividends.
- Losses incurred by the business

How Do We Calculate Equity?

Equity = Assets – Liabilities

$$
\begin{aligned}
&\ \ Assets\\
-&\ Liabilities\\
=&\ Equity
\end{aligned}
$$

What we *own* minus what we *owe* leaves equity.

What are Profit and Loss Accounts?

- The Profit and Loss Statement (also called the Income Statement or P&L Statement) reports the results of a company's operations, listing income and expenses for a period of time.

- Profit and Loss accounts are accounts that appear on a company's Profit and Loss Statement.

- QBO uses two different types of Profit and Loss accounts:
  1. Income accounts
  2. Expense accounts

1. Income accounts record sales to customers and other revenues earned by the company. Revenues are the prices charged, customers for products and services provided.

Examples of Income accounts include:
- Sales or revenues
- Fees earned
- Interest income
- Rental income
- Gains on sale of assets

2. Expense accounts record costs that have expired or been consumed in the process of generating income. Expenses are the costs of providing products and services to customers.

Examples of Expense accounts include:
- Cost of goods sold (CGS) expense
- Salaries expense
- Insurance expense
- Rent expense
- Interest expense

How Do We Calculate Net Income?

Net Income = Income (Revenue) – Expenses (including CGS)

> *Income (Revenue)*
> *– Expenses (including CGS)*
> *= Net Income (Net Profit or Net Earnings)*

Net income is calculated as income (or revenue) less cost of goods sold and other expenses. Net income is an attempt to match or measure efforts (expenses) against accomplishments (revenues).

Three names for the same thing: Net Income is also referred to as Net Profit or Net Earnings.

What are Permanent Accounts?

- In general, Balance Sheet accounts are considered **permanent** accounts (with the exception of the Withdrawals or Distributions account, which is closed out each year).
- Balances in permanent accounts are carried forward from year to year. Thus, for a Balance Sheet account, such as a Checking account, the balance at December 31 is carried forward and becomes the opening balance on January 1 of the next year.

What are Temporary Accounts?

- Profit and Loss accounts are called **temporary** accounts because they are used to track account data for a temporary period of time, usually one year.
- At the end of each year, temporary accounts are closed (the balance reduced to zero). For example, if a Profit and Loss account, such as Advertising Expense, had a $13,000 balance at December 31, the $13,000 balance would be closed or transferred to owners' equity at year-end. The opening balance on January 1 for the Advertising Expense account would be $0.

Practice Quiz 2

Q2.1

Select two from the following to display the Chart of Accounts (COA):
a. From the Navigation Bar, select Accounting
b. From the Navigation Bar, select Customers > Chart of Accounts
c. From the (+) New icon, select Chart of Accounts
d. From the Gear icon, select Chart of Accounts

Q2.2

In QBO, the Chart of Accounts displays which of the following two columns?
a. QuickBooks Balance
b. Bank Balance
c. All account transactions
d. None of the above

Q2.3

The Chart of Accounts displays:
a. Account Name
b. Type
c. Detail Type
d. All of the above

Q2.4

Why would a company want to use account numbers on its Chart of Accounts?
a. To be able to check the current account balance quickly
b. To uniquely identify each account on the Chart of Accounts
c. To confuse users of the Chart of Accounts
d. None the above

Q2.5

To display account numbers on the Chart of Accounts in QBO:
a. From the Navigation Bar, select Transactions > Chart of Accounts > Enable account numbers > Show account numbers
b. From the (+) New icon, select Other > Chart of Accounts > Account Numbers
c. From the Gear icon, select Chart of Accounts > Account Numbers
d. From the Gear icon, select Account and Settings > Advanced > Enable account numbers > Show account numbers

Q2.6

Registers in QBO:

a.   Display more detailed information about accounts

b.   Display all transactions for the account

c.   Display a running balance for the account

d.   All of the above

Q2.7

To view a register:

a.   Display the Chart of Accounts, then select View Register

b.   From the Navigation Bar, select Register

c.   From the Gear icon, select Register

d.   From the (+) New icon, select Register

Q2.8

Match the following legal entities with the federal tax return the entity files.

1. Schedule C (Form 1040)

2. Form 1120

3. Form 1065

4. Form 1120S

a.   Partnership

b.   C corporation

c.   S corporation

d.   Sole proprietorship

Q2.9

To edit an account in the Chart of Accounts:

a.   Display the Chart of Accounts, then select Edit

b.   Display the Chart of Accounts, then select Run Report drop-down arrow, select Edit

c.   From (+) New icon, select Chart of Accounts, select Edit

d.   None of the above

Q2.10

To inactivate an account in the Chart of Accounts:

a. Display the Chart of Accounts, then select Delete

b. Display the Chart of Accounts, then select Run Report drop-down arrow, select Make Inactive

c. From (+) New icon, select Chart of Accounts, select Delete

d. None of the above

Q2.11

An example of an Asset account is:

a. Mortgage Payable

b. Sales Taxes Payable

c. Equipment

d. None of the above

Q2.12

Income accounts for a company are used to track:

a. Sales to customers and other revenue earned

b. Costs that have expired or been consumed

c. Cost of items sold to customers

d. Purchases from vendors

Q2.13

What are assets?

a. Net worth of a company

b. Amounts paid to owners

c. Resources that a company owns with future benefit

d. Amounts owed to others and are future obligations

Q2.14

Accounts used for only one year are called:

a. Temporary accounts

b. Short-term assets or liabilities

c. Supply accounts

d. Estimate accounts

Exercises 2

If necessary, sign in to your Mookie The Beagle Concierge QBO Company as follows:

1 Using a Chrome web browser, go to qbo.intuit.com

2 Enter **User ID** (the email address you used to set up your QBO Account)

3 Enter **Password** (the password you used to set up your QBO Account)

4 Select **Sign in**

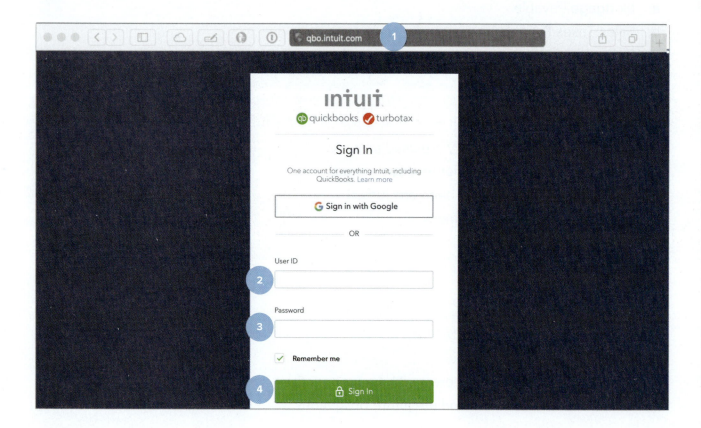

EM2.1 COA: Types of Accounts

The Chart of Accounts is a list of accounts used by a company. The accounts can be grouped into different categories or types.

Using the QBO Company, Mookie The Beagle Concierge, select **Navigation Bar > Accounting > Chart of Accounts**.

Indicate the QBO Account Type for each of the following accounts appearing in Mookie's Chart of Accounts.

QBO Account Types
- **Bank**
- **Other Current Asset**
- **Equity**
- **Income**
- **Cost of Goods Sold**
- **Expenses**

Account	QBO Account Type
1. Bank Charges & Fees	
2. Meals & Entertainment	
3. Undeposited Funds	
4. Repairs & Maintenance	
5. Sales	
6. Rent & Lease	
7. Travel	
8. Retained Earnings	
9. Checking	
10. Advertising & Marketing	
11. Inventory Asset	
12. Opening Balance Equity	
13. Owner's Investment	
14. Insurance	
15. Office Supplies & Software	
16. Legal & Professional Services	
17. Interest Paid	
18. Utilities	

EM2.2 Align COA and Tax Return

Typically when customizing the Chart of Accounts for businesses, we want to verify that the accounts on the Chart of Accounts correspond to expenses shown on the tax return the business files.

Mookie The Beagle Concierge files the following IRS Schedule C (Form 1040) for its business operations.

SCHEDULE C (Form 1040)	**Profit or Loss From Business** (Sole Proprietorship)	
Department of the Treasury Internal Revenue Service (99)	▶ Information about Schedule C and its separate instructions is at *www.irs.gov/schedulec.* ▶ Attach to Form 1040, 1040NR, or 1041; partnerships generally must file Form 1065.	

Name of proprietor | Social security number (SSN)

A Principal business or profession, including product or service (see instructions) | **B** Enter code from instructions ▶

C Business name. If no separate business name, leave blank. | **D** Employer ID number (EIN), (see instr.)

E Business address (including suite or room no.) ▶ ------------------------------------
City, town or post office, state, and ZIP code

F Accounting method: (1) ☐ Cash (2) ☐ Accrual (3) ☐ Other (specify) ▶ ------------------------

G Did you "materially participate" in the operation of this business during 2016? If "No," see instructions for limit on losses . ☐ Yes ☐ No

H If you started or acquired this business during 2016, check here . . . . ▶ ☐

I Did you make any payments in 2016 that would require you to file Form(s) 1099? (see instructions) . . . . ☐ Yes ☐ No

J If "Yes," did you or will you file required Forms 1099? . . . . ☐ Yes ☐ No

Part I Income

1	Gross receipts or sales. See instructions for line 1 and check the box if this income was reported to you on Form W-2 and the "Statutory employee" box on that form was checked . . . . ▶ ☐	1	
2	Returns and allowances	2	
3	Subtract line 2 from line 1	3	
4	Cost of goods sold (from line 42)	4	
5	**Gross profit.** Subtract line 4 from line 3	5	
6	Other income, including federal and state gasoline or fuel tax credit or refund (see instructions)	6	
7	**Gross income.** Add lines 5 and 6 . . . . ▶	7	

Part II Expenses. Enter expenses for business use of your home **only** on line 30.

8	Advertising	8		18	Office expense (see instructions)	18	
9	Car and truck expenses (see instructions)	9		19	Pension and profit-sharing plans .	19	
				20	Rent or lease (see instructions):		
10	Commissions and fees .	10		a	Vehicles, machinery, and equipment	20a	
11	Contract labor (see instructions)	11		b	Other business property . . .	20b	
12	Depletion	12		21	Repairs and maintenance . . .	21	
13	Depreciation and section 179 expense deduction (not included in Part III) (see instructions)	13		22	Supplies (not included in Part III) .	22	
				23	Taxes and licenses	23	
				24	Travel, meals, and entertainment:		
14	Employee benefit programs (other than on line 19) . .	14		a	Travel	24a	
15	Insurance (other than health)	15		b	Deductible meals and entertainment (see instructions) .	24b	
16	Interest:			25	Utilities	25	
a	Mortgage (paid to banks, etc.)	16a		26	Wages (less employment credits) .	26	
b	Other	16b		27a	Other expenses (from line 48) . .	27a	
17	Legal and professional services	17		b	**Reserved for future use** . . .	27b	

For the following accounts from Mookie The Beagle Concierge QBO Chart of Accounts, identify the corresponding Line number on Schedule C (Form 1040).

QBO COA	IRS Schedule C (Form 1040)
1. Legal and Professional Fees	Schedule C Line _____
2. Maintenance and Repair	Schedule C Line _____
3. Office Expenses	Schedule C Line _____
4. Rent or Lease	Schedule C Line _____
5. Taxes and Licenses	Schedule C Line _____
6. Utilities	Schedule C Line _____

EM2.3 Account Numbers

Account numbers are used to uniquely identify accounts. The account number can also be used to identify the type of account.

> **QBO is continually** rolling out new features, so it is possible your Chart of Accounts may not have the same accounts as listed below. If your COA doesn't have the following accounts, add the appropriate accounts to your COA before adding the account numbers. QBO may add some additional accounts that do not appear here, so you can skip adding account numbers for any accounts that do not appear here.

Using the QBO Company, Mookie The Beagle Concierge, complete the following.

1. To confirm that Account Numbers are turned on in your QBO Company, select **Gear icon** > **Account and Settings** > **Advanced** > **Select Enable account numbers** > **Check Show account numbers** > **Save** > **Done**

2. To display COA, from the **Navigation Bar** > select **Accounting** > **Chart of Accounts**

3. On the Chart of Accounts, what is the name of the column displaying the account numbers?

4. Enter Asset Account Numbers.
   a. From the Chart of Accounts window, select **Edit pencil**
   b. Asset accounts will be numbered in the 1000s. If necessary, enter the following accounts numbers for the Asset accounts. If your Chart of Accounts does not display the account, enter the account and the account number into your Chart of Accounts.

      - **1001 Checking**
      - **1500 Uncategorized Asset**
      - **1600 Undeposited Funds**

5. Enter Equity Account Numbers.
   a. If needed, from the COA window, select **Edit pencil**
   b. Equity accounts will be numbered in the 3000s. Enter the following account numbers for the Equity accounts. If your Chart of Accounts does not display the account, enter the account and the account number into your Chart of Accounts.

   - **3001 Opening Balance Equity**
   - **3003 Owner's Investment**
   - **3100 Owner's Pay & Personal Expenses**
   - **3300 Retained Earnings**

6. Enter Income Account Numbers.
   a. If needed, from the COA window, select **Edit pencil**
   b. Income accounts will be numbered in the 4000s. Enter the following account numbers for the Income accounts. If your Chart of Accounts does not display the account, enter the account and the account number into your Chart of Accounts.

   (Note: If your COA displays duplicate Billable Expense Income accounts, inactivate the duplicate accounts by selecting the **drop-down arrow** by Run Report to display the drop-down menu > select **Make Inactive** > when asked, Are you sure you want to inactivate this? select **Yes**.)

   - **4100 Billable Expense Income**
   - **4200 Sales**
   - **4400 Uncategorized Income**

7. Enter Expense Account Numbers.
   a. If needed, from the COA window, select **Edit pencil**
   b. Expense accounts will be numbered in the 5000s. If necessary, enter the following account numbers for the Expense accounts. If your Chart of Accounts does not display the account, enter the account and the account number into your Chart of Accounts.

   - **5001 Advertising and Marketing**
   - **5002 Ask My Accountant**
   - **5003 Bank Charges & Fees**
   - **5004 Car & Truck**
   - **5005 Contractors**
   - **5010 Insurance**
   - **5020 Interest Paid**
   - **5021 Job Supplies**
   - **5022 Legal & Professional Services**
   - **5023 Meals & Entertainment**
   - **5024 Office Supplies & Software**
   - **5025 Other Business Expenses**
   - **5027 Reimbursable Expenses**
   - **5028 Rent & Lease**
   - **5029 Repairs & Maintenance**
   - **5030 Taxes & Licenses**
   - **5031 Travel**
   - **5032 Uncategorized Expense**
   - **5040 Utilities Expense**

EM2.4 COA: Add Asset Accounts

In order to align better with the IRS Schedule C (Form 1040), Cy Walker would like you to add some accounts to the QBO Chart of Accounts. Complete the following steps to add Asset accounts to Mookie The Beagle Concierge's Chart of Accounts.

> **QBO is continually rolling out new features, so it is possible your Chart of Accounts may not appear the same as your text.**

To add accounts to the COA, from the Navigation Bar, select **Accounting > New**.

1. Add Accounts Receivable Account.
   a. Select **Account Type: _____**
   b. Select **Detail Type: _____**
   c. Enter **Name: Accounts Receivable (A/R)**
   d. Enter **Number: 1100**
   e. Leave **Description blank**
   f. Leave **Is sub-account unchecked**
   g. Select **Save and New**

2. Add Prepaid Expenses Account.
   a. Select Account **Type: Other Current Assets**
   b. Select **Detail Type: _____**
   c. Enter **Name: Prepaid Expenses**
   d. Enter **Number: 1200**
   e. Leave **Description blank**
   f. Leave **Is sub-account unchecked**
   g. Select **Save and Close**

EM2.5 COA: Add Liability and Equity Accounts

In order to align better with the IRS Schedule C (Form 1040), Cy Walker would like you to add some accounts to the QBO Chart of Accounts. Complete the following steps to add Liability and Equity accounts to Mookie The Beagle Concierge's Chart of Accounts.

> **QBO is continually rolling out new features, so it is possible your Chart of Accounts may not appear the same as your text.**

To add accounts to the COA, from the Navigation Bar, select **Accounting > New**.

1. Add Accounts Payable Account.
   a. Select **Account Type: _____**
   b. Select **Detail Type: _____**
   c. Enter **Name: Accounts Payable (A/P)**
   d. Enter **Number: 2001**
   e. Leave **Description blank**
   f. Leave **Is sub-account unchecked**
   g. Select **Save and New**

2. Add VISA Credit Card Account.
   a. Select **Account Type: _____**
   b. Select **Detail Type: _____**
   c. Enter **Name: VISA Credit Card**
   d. Enter **Number: 2100**
   e. Leave **Description blank**
   f. Leave **Is sub-account unchecked**
   g. Select **Save and New**

3. Add Unearned Revenue Account.
   a. Select **Account Type: _____**
   b. Select **Detail Type: Other Current Liabilities**
   c. Enter **Name: Unearned Revenue**
   d. Enter **Number: 2200**
   e. Leave **Description blank**
   f. Leave **Is sub-account unchecked**
   g. Select **Save and New**

4. Add Owner Distributions Account.
   a. Select **Account Type: Equity**
   b. Select **Detail Type: _____**
   c. Enter **Name: Owner Distributions**
   d. Enter **Number: 3200**
   e. Leave **Description blank**
   f. Leave **Is sub-account unchecked**
   g. Select **Save and Close**

EM2.6 COA: Add Asset Subaccounts

In order to align better with the IRS Schedule C (Form 1040), Cy Walker would like you to add some accounts to the QBO Chart of Accounts. Complete the following steps to add Asset subaccounts to Mookie The Beagle Concierge's Chart of Accounts.

> **QBO is continually** rolling out new features, so it is possible your Chart of Accounts may not appear the same as your text.

To add accounts to the COA, from the Navigation Bar, select **Accounting > New**.

1. After verifying your COA has a Prepaid Expenses account, add the subaccount: Prepaid Expenses: Supplies.
   a. Select **Account Type: Other Current Assets**
   b. Select **Detail Type: _____**
   c. Enter **Name: Supplies**
   d. Enter **Number: 1210**
   e. Leave **Description blank**
   f. Check: **Is sub-account**
   g. Enter **Parent Account: Prepaid Expenses**
   h. Select **Save and New**

2. Add Subaccount: Prepaid Expenses: Insurance.
   a. Select **Account Type: _____**
   b. Select **Detail Type: _____**
   c. Enter **Name: Insurance**
   d. Enter **Number: 1220**
   e. Leave **Description blank**
   f. Check: **Is sub-account**
   g. Enter **Parent Account: Prepaid Expenses**
   h. Select **Save and New**

3. Add Subaccount: Prepaid Expenses: Rent.
   a. Select **Account Type: _____**
   b. Select **Detail Type: _____**
   c. Enter **Name: Rent**
   d. Enter **Number: 1230**
   e. Leave **Description blank**
   f. Check: **Is sub-account**
   g. Enter **Parent Account: Prepaid Expenses**
   h. Select **Save and Close**

EM2.7 COA: Add Expense Subaccounts

In order to align better with the IRS Schedule C (Form 1040), Cy Walker would like you to add some accounts to the QBO Chart of Accounts. Complete the following steps to add Expense subaccounts to Mookie The Beagle Concierge's Chart of Accounts.

> **QBO is continually** rolling out new features, so it is possible your Chart of Accounts may not appear the same as your text. If your COA doesn't have the following accounts, add them to your COA as follows.

To add accounts to the COA, from the Navigation Bar, select **Accounting > New**.

1. After verifying your COA has an Insurance (Expenses) account, add the subaccount: Insurance: Renter Insurance Expense.
   a. Select **Account Type: _____**
   b. Select **Detail Type: _____**
   c. Enter **Name: Renter Insurance Expense**
   d. Enter **Number: 5011**
   e. Leave **Description blank**
   f. Check: **Is sub-account**
   g. Enter **Parent Account: Insurance (Expenses)**
   h. Select **Save and New**

2. Add Subaccount: Insurance: Liability Insurance Expense.
   a. Select **Account Type: _____**
   b. Select **Detail Type: _____**
   c. Enter **Name: Liability Insurance Expense**
   d. Enter **Number: 5012**
   e. Leave **Description blank**
   f. Check: **Is sub-account**
   g. Enter **Parent Account: Insurance (Expenses)**
   h. Select **Save and Close**

EM2.8 Account Types

For each of the following accounts on Mookie The Beagle Concierge Chart of Accounts, identify the Account Type and Financial Statement on which it appears.

Account Types

- **Asset**
- **Liability**
- **Equity**
- **Income**
- **Expense**

Financial Statements

- **Balance Sheet**
- **Profit and Loss**

Account	Account Type	Financial Statement
1. Sales		
2. Checking		
3. Accounts Receivable (A/R)		
4. Rent & Lease		
5. Prepaid Expenses		
6. Prepaid Expenses: Supplies		
7. Office Supplies & Software		
8. Prepaid Expenses: Insurance		
9. Insurance: Liability Insurance Expense		
10. Undeposited Funds		
11. Accounts Payable (A/P)		
12. VISA Credit Card		
13. Prepaid Insurance: Rent		
14. Interest Paid		
15. Contractors		
16. Legal & Professional Services		
17. Advertising & Marketing		

18. Meals & Entertainment

19. Retained Earnings

20. Owner's Investment

21. Owner Distributions

22. Inventory

23. Utilities

E2.9 Definitions

Match the following Account Types with the appropriate definition.

Account Types

- **Assets**
- **Liabilities**
- **Equity**
- **Revenues**
- **Expenses**

Definitions	Account Type
1. What we own less what we owe equals this	
2. Prices charged customers for products and services	
3. Resources that we own that have future benefit	
4. Obligations or amounts that we owe to others	
5. Costs of providing products and services to customers	

E2.10 Account Types

The Chart of Accounts is a list of accounts a company uses to track accounting information. QBO sets up a Chart of Accounts when setting up a new company. Then accounts can be edited, added, and inactivated as needed.

Answer the following questions about the Chart of Accounts.

Account Types

- **Bank**
- **Accounts Receivable (A/R)**
- **Other Current Assets**
- **Fixed Assets**
- **Accounts Payable (A/P)**
- **Credit Card**
- **Other Current Liabilities**
- **Long-Term Liabilities**
- **Equity**
- **Income**
- **Cost of Goods Sold**
- **Expenses**
- **Other Income**
- **Other Expense**

What is the Account Type for the following accounts?

1. Checking account

2. Visa

3. Accounts Receivable (A/R)

4. Accounts Payable (A/P)

5. Prepaid Expenses

6. Owner Distribution

Chapter 3

QBO Transactions

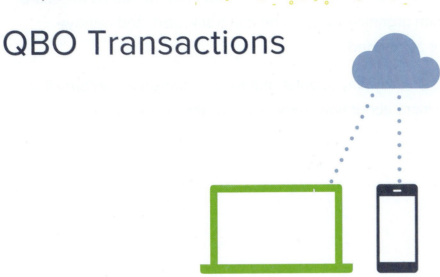

MOOKIE THE BEAGLE™ CONCIERGE

BACKSTORY

You glance at your smartphone and see Cy Walker's text about his new business.

Good news...Mookie The Beagle Concierge business is gaining momentum.

That's great news!

So how do we record all of the business transactions?

We need to get QBO set up to record the transactions ASAP.

Cy, the founder of Mookie The Beagle™ Concierge, needs your assistance with QBO to save time recording transactions for the business. Cy knows that he needs to record all business transactions in an organized way so he can track, sort, and retrieve transaction information later as needed.

QuickBooks Online provides an easy way to enter and retrieve transaction information. So your next step is to learn more about how to record transactions using QBO.

Chapter 3

LEARNING OBJECTIVES

Chapter 3 introduces different types of transactions, and later chapters will look at each type of transaction in greater detail. In this chapter, you will learn about the following topics:

- What are Transactions?
- QBO Lists
  - ‣ Chart of Accounts
  - ‣ Customers List
  - ‣ Vendors List
  - ‣ Employees List
  - ‣ Products and Services List
- Update QBO Lists
  - ‣ Update QBO List Before Entering Transactions
  - ‣ Update QBO List While Entering Transactions
  - ‣ Create QBO Products and Services List
- How Do We Enter Transactions in QBO?
  - ‣ Enter Transaction Using Onscreen Form
  - ‣ Enter Transaction Using Onscreen Journal
- QBO Navigation to Enter Transactions
  - ‣ Navigation Bar
  - ‣ (+) New Icon
  - ‣ Gear Icon and Recurring Transactions
- Types of QBO Transactions
  - ‣ Banking and Credit Card Transactions
  - ‣ Customers and Sales Transactions
  - ‣ Vendors and Expenses Transactions
  - ‣ Employees and Payroll Transactions
  - ‣ Other Transactions
- Banking Transactions
  - ‣ Make Deposit
- Customers and Sales Transactions
  - ‣ Create Invoice
- Vendors and Expenses Transactions
  - ‣ Create Expense
- Employees and Payroll Transactions
- Other Transactions

- Recurring Transactions

- Accounting Essentials: Double-Entry Accounting

> ⚠ **QBO is updated on an ongoing basis. Updates that affect your text** can be viewed as follows:
> 1. **Go to www.My-QuickBooksOnline.com > QBO 3e > QBO 3e Updates, or**
> 2. **If you are using Connect or a digital ebook, you can find updates under Additional Student Resources (ASR). If you do not have access to Connect or the ebook, your instructor can provide you with ASR.**

Section 3.1

 QBO SATNAV

QBO SatNav is your satellite navigation for QuickBooks Online, assisting you in navigating QBO

Chapter 3 provides an overview of QBO transactions, shown in the following QBO SatNav.

 QBO SatNav

 QBO Settings

Company Settings
Chart of Accounts

 **QBO Transactions**

💰 Banking	*Record Deposits | Write Checks*
💰 Customers & Sales	*Create Sales Receipts > Record Deposits*
💰 Vendors & Expenses	*Enter Bills > Pay Bills*
💰 Employees & Payroll	*Enter Time > Pay Employees > Payroll Liabilities*

 QBO Reports

Reports

Section 3.2

QBO CROSSCHECK

As mentioned in Chapter 1, just like we use a smartphone with satellite mapping to zoom in for detail and zoom out for the big picture, when learning QBO, we may need to adjust our thinking to zoom out to see the big picture of the entire financial system or at other times zoom in to view details.

The previous SatNav gives you the big picture overview for Chapter 3. To be successful with QBO we also have to keep the details in focus. Checking and cross-checking for accuracy becomes a crucial habit when working in QBO. Cross-checking refers to checking data or reports against various sources to verify accuracy.

The QBO company we created in Chapter 1, Mookie The Beagle Concierge, carries all work forward to later chapters, including Chapter 3. At this point, cross-checking your QBO Chart of Accounts can make life easier for you later on.

To cross-check your QBO Chart of Accounts:

1. Sign in to your Mookie The Beagle Concierge QBO Company. Using a web browser go to **qbo.intuit.com** > enter **User ID** > enter **Password** > select **Sign in**.

2. Compare your QBO Chart of Accounts with the following COA

3. If necessary, update your QBO COA so that it contains the necessary accounts and account numbers as shown in the following COA

4. Since the QBO company we created in Chapter 1 will carry all work forward into future chapters, while working in Chapter 3 it is important to check and cross-check your work to verify it is correct before clicking the Save button. Any uncorrected errors will be carried forward in your QBO company.

Chart of Accounts
< All Lists

NUMBER	NAME	TYPE ▲	DETAIL TYPE
1001	1001 Checking	Bank	Checking
1100	1100 Accounts Receivable (A/R)	Accounts receivable (A/R)	Accounts Receivable (A/R)
1200	1200 Prepaid Expenses	Other Current Assets	Prepaid Expenses
1210	1210 Supplies	Other Current Assets	Prepaid Expenses
1220	1220 Insurance	Other Current Assets	Prepaid Expenses
1230	1230 Rent	Other Current Assets	Prepaid Expenses
1500	1500 Uncategorized Asset	Other Current Assets	Other Current Assets
1600	1600 Undeposited Funds	Other Current Assets	Undeposited Funds
2001	2001 Accounts Payable (A/P)	Accounts payable (A/P)	Accounts Payable (A/P)
2100	2100 VISA Credit Card	Credit Card	Credit Card
2200	2200 Unearned Revenue	Other Current Liabilities	Other Current Liabilities
3001	3001 Opening Balance Equity	Equity	Opening Balance Equity
3003	3003 Owner's Investment	Equity	Owner's Equity
3100	3100 Owner's Pay & Personal Expenses	Equity	Owner's Equity
3200	3200 Owner Distributions	Equity	Partner Distributions
3300	3300 Retained Earnings	Equity	Retained Earnings
4100	4100 Billable Expense Income	Income	Sales of Product Income
4200	4200 Sales	Income	Sales of Product Income
4400	4400 Uncategorized Income	Income	Sales of Product Income
5001	5001 Advertising & Marketing	Expenses	Advertising/Promotional
5002	5002 Ask My Accountant	Expenses	Utilities
5003	5003 Bank Charges & Fees	Expenses	Bank Charges
5004	5004 Car & Truck	Expenses	Auto
5005	5005 Contractors	Expenses	Payroll Expenses
5010	5010 Insurance	Expenses	Insurance
5011	5011 Renter Insurance Expense	Expenses	Insurance
5012	5012 Liability Insurance Expense	Expenses	Insurance
5020	5020 Interest Paid	Expenses	Interest Paid
5021	5021 Job Supplies	Expenses	Supplies & Materials
5022	5022 Legal & Professional Services	Expenses	Legal & Professional Fees
5023	5023 Meals & Entertainment	Expenses	Entertainment Meals
5024	5024 Office Supplies & Software	Expenses	Office/General Administrative Expenses
5025	5025 Other Business Expenses	Expenses	Office/General Administrative Expenses
5027	5027 Reimbursable Expenses	Expenses	Supplies & Materials
5028	5028 Rent & Lease	Expenses	Rent or Lease of Buildings
5029	5029 Repairs & Maintenance	Expenses	Repair & Maintenance
5030	5030 Taxes & Licenses	Expenses	Taxes Paid
5031	5031 Travel	Expenses	Travel
5032	5032 Uncategorized Expense	Expenses	Other Miscellaneous Service Cost
5040	5040 Utilities Expense	Expenses	Utilities

Section 3.3

WHAT ARE TRANSACTIONS?

One objective of our QBO financial system is to collect information about transactions. Transactions are simply exchanges between our business and other parties, such as customers, vendors, and employees. We need to keep a record of all transactions, and QBO offers us a streamlined way to keep track of those transactions.

After we set up QBO Company Settings and the QBO Chart of Accounts, we are ready to enter transactions into QBO. Transactions increase and decrease accounts so that's why it's important for us to have our Chart of Accounts created before we enter transactions.

When working with QBO companies, such as Mookie The Beagle Concierge, we need to determine the types of transactions that the business will record. Then we plan how to save time and minimize errors when entering those transactions, especially ones that are recurring.

Section 3.4

QBO LISTS

As a company conducts business operations, the company enters into transactions with customers, vendors, and employees. Before recording these transactions in QBO, we typically want to make sure our QBO Lists are up-to-date.

WHAT ARE QBO LISTS?

QBO Lists are a time-saving feature so we don't have to continually re-enter the same information each time we enter a transaction. Lists permit us to collect information that we will reuse, so we do not have to repeatedly re-enter accounts, customers, vendors, and so on.

Some of the lists we might use when entering transactions include:

- Chart of Accounts
- Customers List
- Vendors List
- Employees List
- Products and Services List

To view QBO Lists, select the lists as follows.

1 To display the Chart of Accounts, from the Navigation Bar, select **Accounting** > **Chart of Accounts**.

Chart of Accounts is a list of all the accounts a company uses when recording transactions. Accounts, such as the Checking account, permit us to sort and track accounting information.

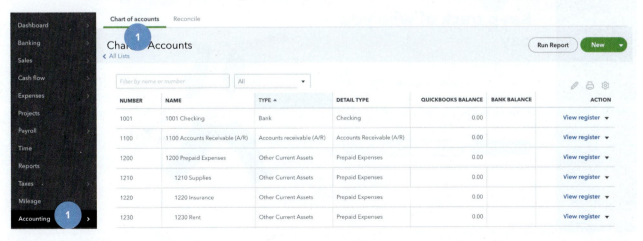

2 To display the Customers List, select **Sales > Customers**.

Customers List, also called the Clients List, collects information about customers, such as customer name, customer number, address, and contact information. Customers can be imported or added manually.

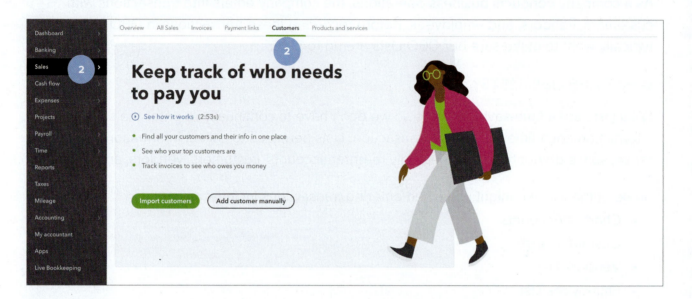

3 To display the Vendors List, select **Expenses > Vendors**.

Vendors List collects information about vendors, such as vendor name, vendor number, and contact information. Vendors can be imported or added manually.

4 To view the Employees List, select **Payroll** > **Employees**.

Employees List collects information about employees for payroll purposes including name, Social Security number, and address.

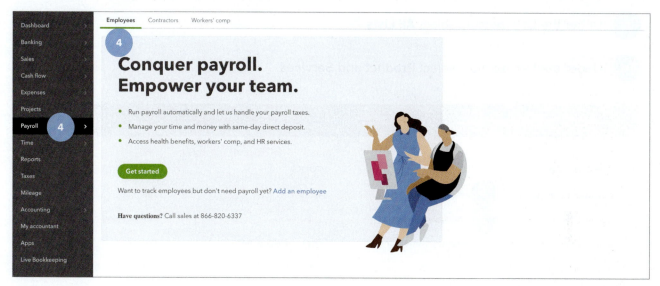

5 To view the Products and Services List, select **Sales** > **Products and Services**.

Products and Services List collects information about the products and services that a company buys from vendors and/or sells to customers. Products and services can be added one at a time or by importing an Excel or csv file.

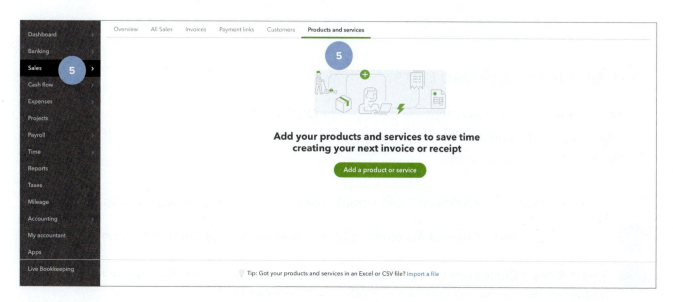

All lists, including the Products and Services List, are also found under the Gear icon as shown below.

1 Select **Gear** icon

2 Under the Lists section, select **All Lists**

3 Under the Lists section, select **Product and Services**

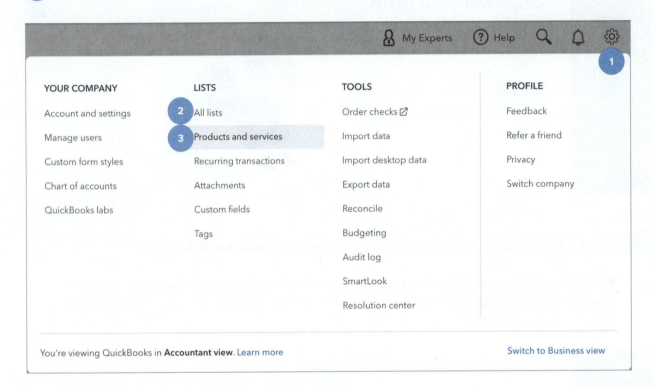

HOW DO WE UPDATE QBO LISTS?

There are basically two ways that we can update QBO Lists.
1. *Before* entering transactions
2. *While* entering transactions

1. *Before* entering transactions, we can update lists from the QBO Navigation Bar as follows.

1 Select **Accounting** > **Chart of Accounts** to display and update the Chart of Accounts

2 Select **Sales** > **Customers** to display and update the Customers List. Select **Sales** > **Products and Services** to view and update the Product and Services List.

3 Select **Expenses** > **Vendors** to display and update the Vendors List

4 Select **Payroll** > **Employees** to view and update the Employees List

2. *While* entering transactions, we can update lists on the fly from the screen where we enter the transaction. If a customer, for example, has not been entered in the Customers List, we can add the customer as follows from an onscreen Invoice form.

1 To view an onscreen Invoice form, select the **(+) New** icon

2 Select **Invoice**

3 On the Invoice form, select **Choose a customer drop-down arrow**

4 To add a new customer, select **+ Add new**

5 In the New Customer window, we would enter the new customer information. In this case, in the Name field, enter **Your Name**.

6 Select **Save** to save the new customer information

7 Select **Cancel** to close the invoice without saving. If asked if you want to leave without saving, select **Yes**.

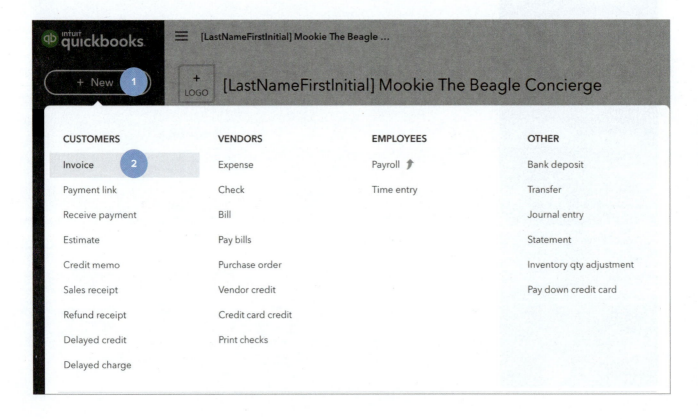

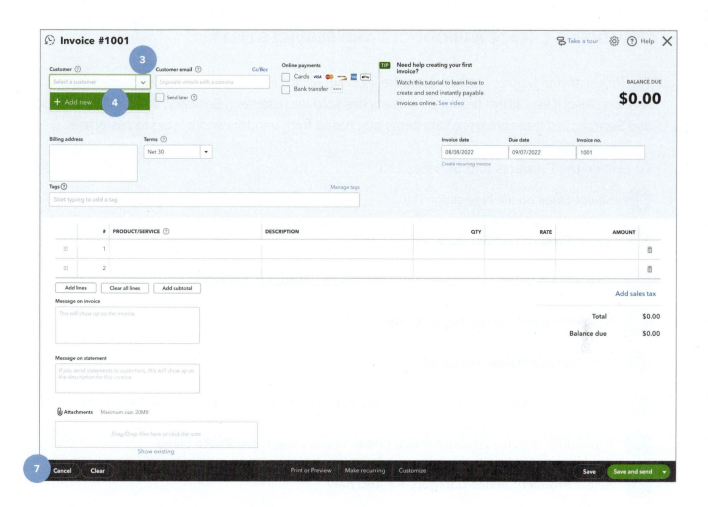

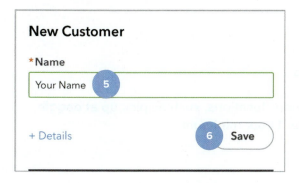

HOW DO WE CREATE A PRODUCTS AND SERVICES LIST?

The Products and Services List contains the listing of all products and services *purchased from vendors*. Also, it lists all the products and services *sold to customers*. Basically, there is one Products and Services List that contains all the items purchased from vendors and/or sold to customers.

To update the Products and Services List:

1. Select **Sales** on the Navigation Bar

2. Select **Product and Services** tab

3. To enter a new product or service, select **Add a product or service**

4. Select **Product/Service Type: Service**

5. Enter **Service Name: Transport**

6. Enter SKU or other product/service identification number. In this case, leave **SKU blank**.

7. If available, attach a product/service photo. In this case, leave **Photo blank**.

8. Select **Product/Service Category > + Add new**

9. Enter New Category **Name: Pet Care**

10. Select **Save**

11. Select **I sell this product/service to my customers**

12. Enter **Description: Pick up and drop off pet at various locations, such as pick up at doggie day care and take home if owner has to work late, 1 hour minimum**

13. Enter **Sales Price/Rate: 80.00**

14. Select **Income Account: 4200 Sales**. This selection connects the service item with the appropriate account in the Chart of Accounts. When this service is recorded on an invoice, then the amount will be recorded in the Sales income account.

15. Under Purchasing information **uncheck I purchase this product/service from a vendor**

16   Select **Save and close**

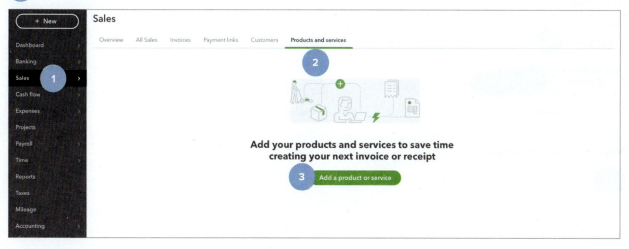

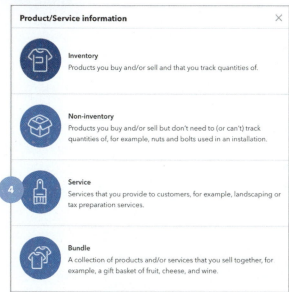

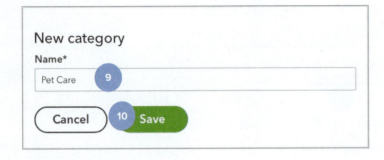

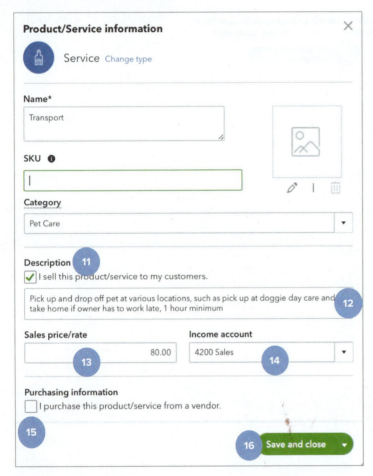

Note: After we begin adding products and services to the Products and Services List, QBO may automatically add some additional accounts to our Chart of Accounts. We can easily identify the added accounts since they do not display account numbers. If desired, account numbers can be entered for these added accounts. For more information about how to enter account numbers, see Chapter 2.

C3.4.1 QBO Lists: Products and Services List

To export the Products and Services List:

1 From the Products and Services screen, select **More** to display the drop-down menu

2 Select **Run Report**

3 After the Product/Service List Report appears, select the **Export** icon to display the drop-down menu

4 Select **Export to PDF**

5 Select **Save as PDF**. The Products and Services List in PDF format should download automatically.

6 Select **Close**

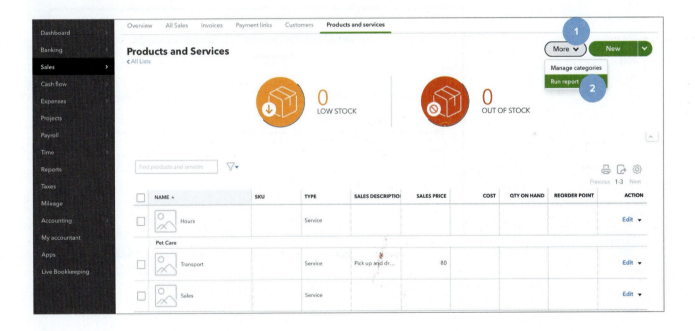

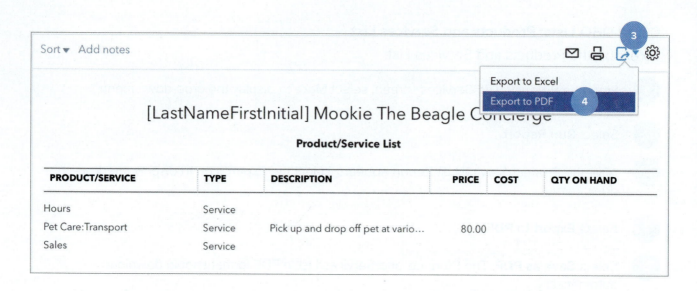

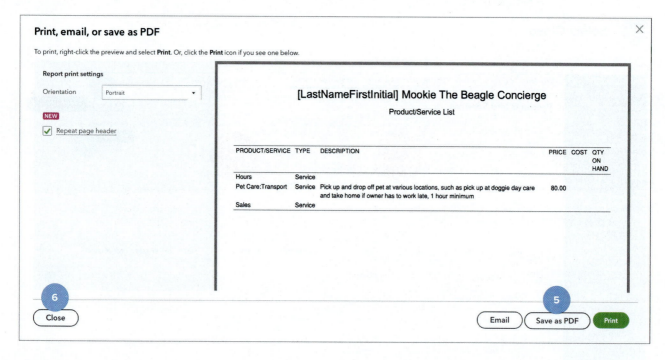

Section 3.5

HOW DO WE ENTER TRANSACTIONS IN QBO?

GIVE AND RECEIVE

Our QBO financial system needs to collect information about transactions. Transactions are exchanges. A business enters into transactions or exchanges between the business and other parties, such as customers, vendors, and employers. The business gives and receives something in an exchange.

A business can exchange services, products, cash, or a promise to pay later (Accounts Payable). A transaction must have two parts to the exchange: something must be given and something must be received.

For example, when Mookie The Beagle Concierge provides 1 hour of pet care services to a customer, the two parts to the transaction are:
1. MTB Concierge gives the customer 1 hour of pet care services.
2. In exchange, MTB Concierge receives cash (or a promise to pay later) from the customer.

When we record transactions in QBO, we need to record what is exchanged: what is given and what is received.

ONSCREEN FORM OR ONSCREEN JOURNAL

QBO offers two different ways to enter transaction information:
1. Onscreen Journal
2. Onscreen forms

Onscreen Journal

We can make debit and credit entries in an onscreen Journal to record transactions. To view the onscreen Journal:

1 Select **(+) New** icon

2 Select **Journal Entry**

3 The onscreen Journal has columns for **Account**, **Debit** amount, and **Credit** amount

4 Select **Cancel** to close the Journal Entry window without saving. If asked if you want to leave without saving, select **Yes**.

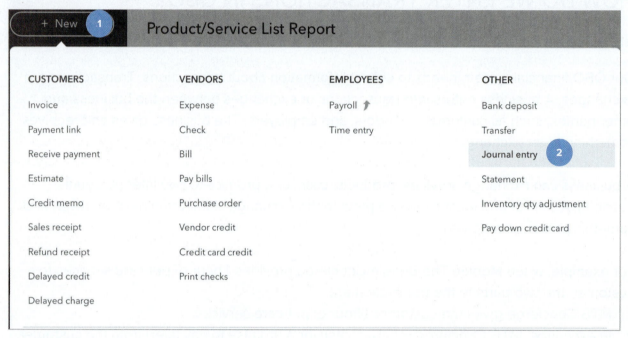

An onscreen Journal is often used to make adjusting entries at year end to bring accounts up to date before preparing financial statements.

Instead of using the onscreen Journal, we can use onscreen forms to enter transaction information in QBO.

Onscreen Forms

We can enter information about transactions using onscreen forms, such as the following Expense form. For example, after using the business credit card to purchase office supplies, we would use the QBO onscreen form for recording the expense and the credit card charge.

When we enter information into an onscreen form, behind the screen QBO automatically converts that information into a journal entry with debits and credits. QBO maintains a list of journal entries for all the transactions entered—whether entered using the onscreen Journal or onscreen forms.

To view the journal entry that QBO created behind the screen for a transaction entered and saved using an onscreen form, complete the following steps.

1 To view the onscreen Expense form, select the **+ New icon**

2 Select **Expense**. The Expense window that appears is an example of an onscreen form. Information about the expense transaction is entered into this onscreen form.

3 Select **Payee**

4 Select **+ Add new**

5 Enter **Name: Bichotte Supplies**

6 Select **Type: Vendor**

7 Select **Save**

8 Select **Payment account: 2100 VISA Credit Card**

9 Select **Date: 01/01/2023**

10 Select **Payment method: Credit Card**

11 Select **Category (Account): 5024 Office Supplies & Software**

12 Enter **Description: Office Supplies**

13 Enter **Amount: 58.00**

14 Enter **Memo: Office Supplies**

15 Select **Save**

16 Notice that after the Expense is saved, the Menu Bar across the bottom of the window changes, adding a new menu option: More. Select **More** at the bottom of the Expense window.

17 Select **Transaction journal**

18 Behind the screen, QBO automatically converted the information in the onscreen Expense form into a journal entry with debits and credits

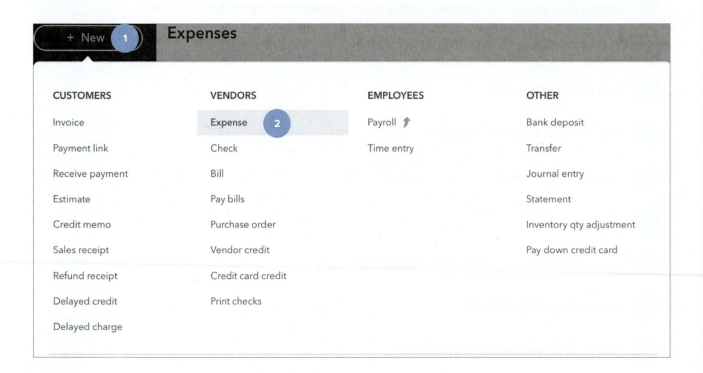

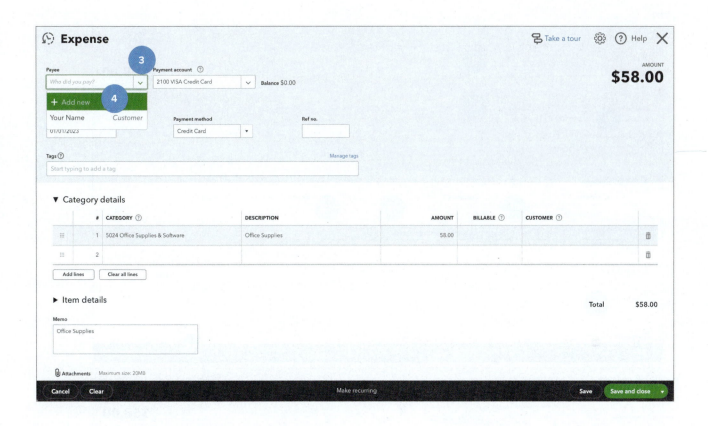

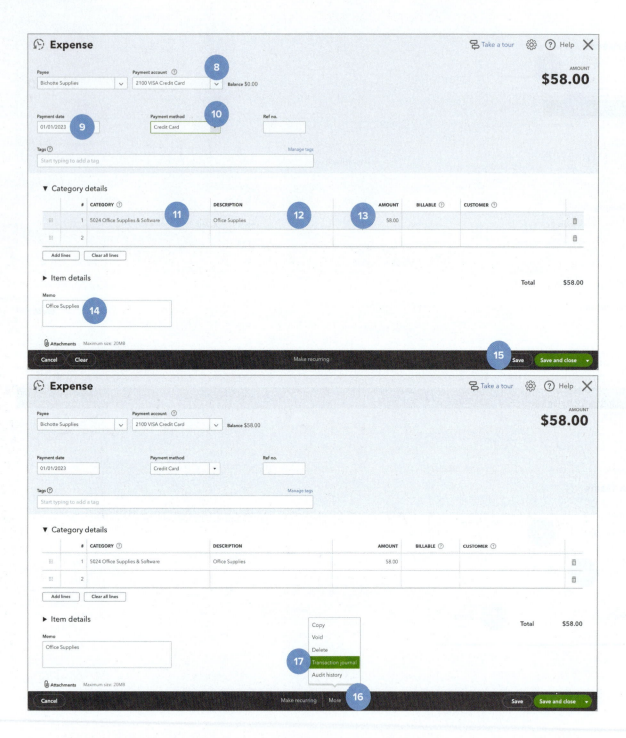

QBO NAVIGATION TO ENTER TRANSACTIONS

QBO offers us three different options to navigate entering transactions using:

1 Navigation Bar

2 (+) New icon

3 Gear icon > Recurring transactions

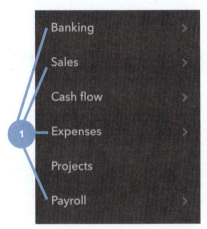

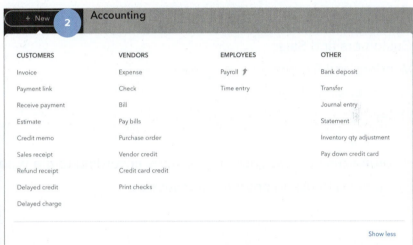

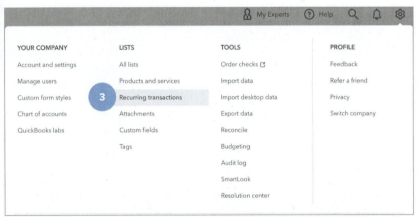

Notice that QBO organizes transactions somewhat differently in the Navigation Bar versus the (+) New icon. In the Navigation Bar, Banking, Sales, and Expenses are the main transactions. In the (+) New icon, banking transactions, such as bank deposit and transfer are shown under the heading Other. In addition, the (+) New icon labels the transactions by parties to the transactions such as Customers, Vendors, and Employees.

Section 3.6

WHAT ARE THE DIFFERENT TYPES OF TRANSACTIONS?

A transaction is simply an exchange between our QBO business and another party, such as a customer, vendor, or employee. Although there are many different types of transactions, generally we can group transactions into the following different types based upon the other party to the transaction:

1. Banking and Credit Card
2. Customers and Sales
3. Vendors and Expenses
4. Employees and Payroll
5. Other

QBO organizes how we enter transactions according to the type of transaction and onscreen form we need to use to enter the transaction.

Section 3.7

BANKING AND CREDIT CARD TRANSACTIONS

🌐 QBO SatNav	

💰 **QBO Transactions**

💰 Banking	*Record Deposits	Write Checks*
💰 Customers & Sales	
💰 Vendors & Expenses	
💰 Employees & Payroll	

Transactions that involve depositing or transferring funds with our bank can be entered using the (+) New icon.

To access Banking transactions through the (+) New icon:

1 Select **(+) New** icon

2 Select **Bank Deposit** to record a bank deposit

3 Select **Transfer** to record a transfer between our company's bank accounts

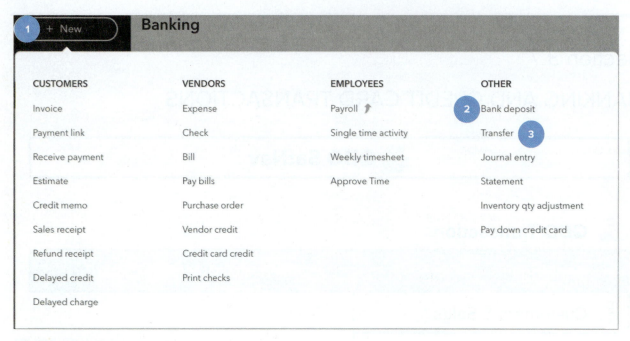

RECORD DEPOSIT

If Mookie The Beagle Concierge needed to record a bank deposit, we would complete the following steps:

1 Select **(+) New** icon

2 Under the Other column, select **Bank Deposit**

3 Select **Account: 1001 Checking**

4 Enter **Date** of deposit: **01/01/2023**

5 In the **Add Funds to This Deposit** section, select **Account: 3003 Owner's Investment**

6 Enter a **Description** of the deposit if desired. The Description field typically displays in reports, but not in the Bank Register. In this case, leave the Description **blank**.

7 Select **Payment Method: Check**

8 Enter **Ref No.: 5000**

9 Enter **Amount: 10000.00**

10 Enter **Memo**. The Memo field typically displays in the Bank Register, making it easier to identify specific transactions in the Register. However, the Memo field does not usually appear in reports. In this case, leave Memo **blank**.

11 Select **Attachments** to add a file or photo of any accompanying document

12 Select **Save and Close**

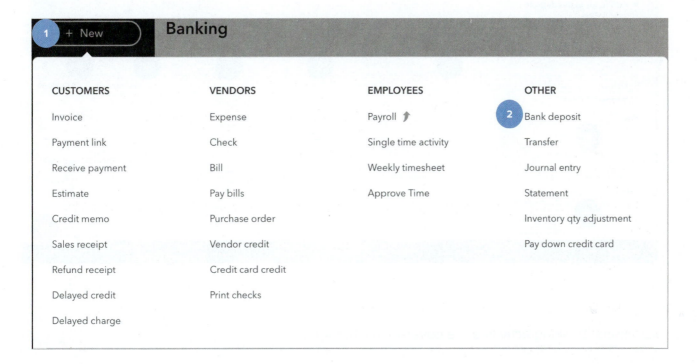

Additional banking activities are covered in Chapter 4.

Section 3.8

CUSTOMERS AND SALES TRANSACTIONS

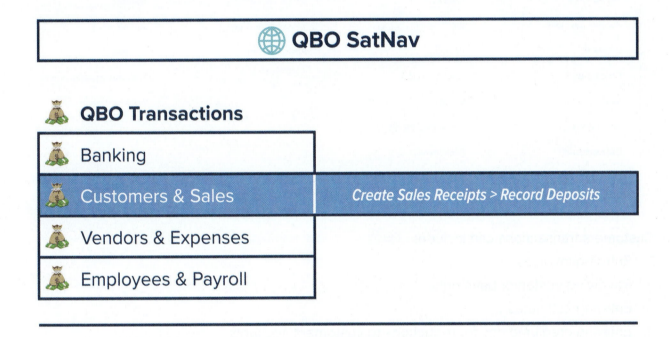

Customers transactions are exchanges between our company and our customers. Typically, these exchanges focus on sales transactions. Customers include parties to whom we sell products or services.

We can enter customers and sales transactions using either the Navigation Bar or the (+) New icon.

To use the (+) New icon to enter Customers transactions:

1 Select **(+) New** icon

2 From the **Customers** column, select the appropriate task

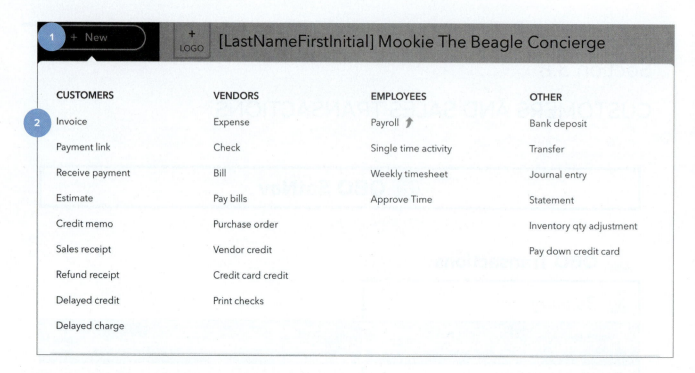

Customers transactions can include:

1. Entering invoices
2. Receiving customer payments
3. Entering estimates
4. Entering credit memos for reductions to customers accounts
5. Entering sales receipts
6. Entering refund receipts

CREATE INVOICE

An Invoice is one of the QBO forms that can be used to record a customer transaction. Typically, an Invoice is used to record sales when the customer will pay later. The Invoice form collects information about the transaction, such as date of the transaction, the item(s) sold, the sales price of the item(s), and the quantity of the item(s) sold.

If Mookie The Beagle Concierge needed to create an invoice to record a sale to a customer, we would complete the following steps:

1 Select **(+) New** icon

2 Select **Invoice**

3 Select **Customer** from the Customer List drop-down menu

4 Enter **Terms**. The terms determine the date when the customer is expected to pay the invoice.

5 Select **Invoice Date**

6 The **Due Date** is automatically calculated by QBO based upon the terms you selected. A best practice is to verify the due date to make certain it is correctly calculated.

7 Select **Product or Service** from the Product/Service List drop-down menu or Add New Product/Service

8 The **Description** of sales transaction should appear automatically using the information entered in the Products and Services List

9 Enter **Quantity (QTY)**

10 The **Rate** should appear automatically based upon the information entered in the Products and Services List

11 The **Amount** should appear automatically. QBO will calculate the amount using the Quantity and Rate.

12 If desired, enter **Message on invoice** describing the sale

13 Add **Attachments**, such as source documents associated with the sale

14 If you wished to email the Invoice to the customer, you would select Save and send or Save and close. In this case, select **Cancel**. If asked if you want to leave without saving, select **Yes**.

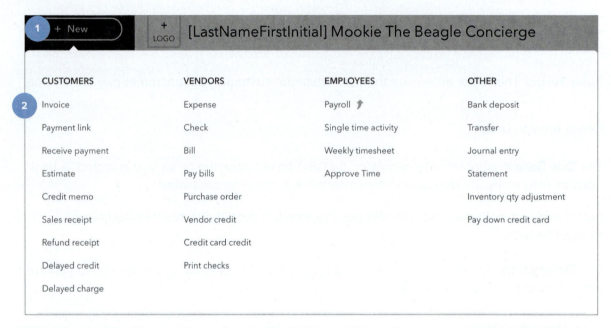

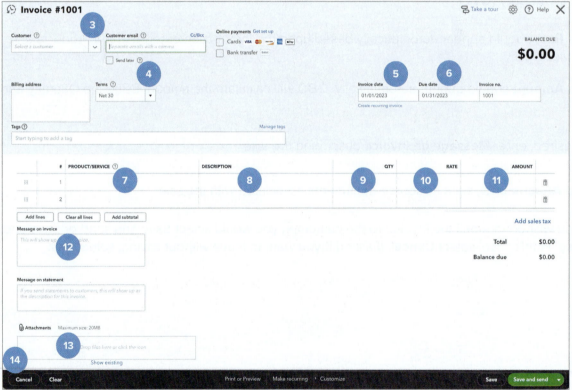

When an invoice is recorded in QBO, behind the screen, the transaction is converted to a journal entry with debits and credits. To record an invoice, the entry should include a debit to the Accounts Receivable account and a credit to a Sales or Income account. Additional customer transactions are covered in Chapter 5.

Section 3.9

VENDORS AND EXPENSES TRANSACTIONS

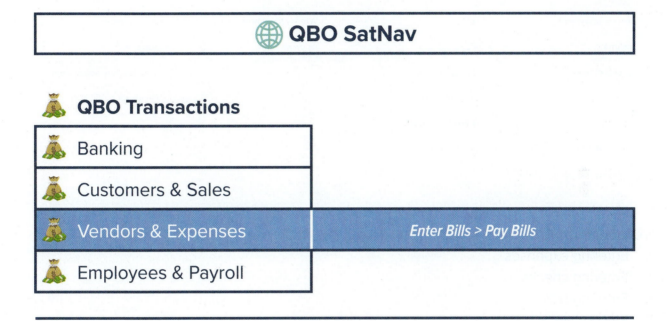

Vendors transactions are exchanges between our company and our vendors. Typically, these exchanges focus on expense transactions. Vendors include suppliers who sell products and professionals who provide services to our company.

We can enter vendors and expenses transactions using either the Navigation Bar or the (+) New icon. To use the (+) New icon to enter Vendors transactions:

1   Select **(+) New** icon

2   From the **Vendors** column, select the appropriate task

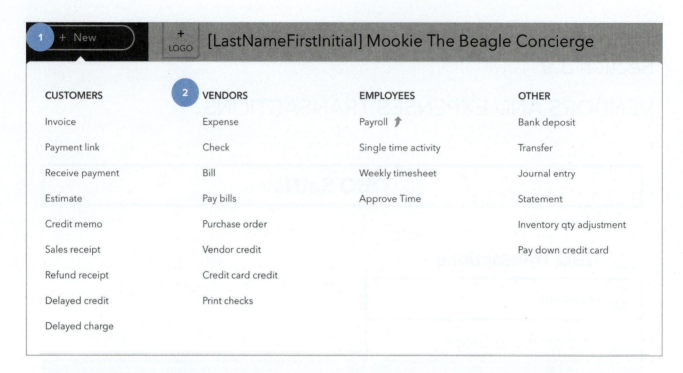

Vendors transactions can include:

1. Entering expenses
2. Entering checks
3. Entering bills
4. Paying bills
5. Entering purchase orders
6. Entering vendor credits
7. Entering credit card credits

CREATE EXPENSE

The Expense form is one of the QBO forms that can be used to record a vendor transaction. If our payment is *made at the same time* we make a purchase, then we can record the purchase using the Expense form. Our payment may consist of cash, check, or credit card. The Expense form collects detailed information about the vendor transaction.

To create an Expense to record a vendor transaction:

1. Select **(+) New** icon

2. Select **Expense** to record the vendor transaction when we make payment at the same time the expense is incurred and we pay with cash, check, or credit card

3 From the Payee drop-down menu, select **Vendor**. If a message appears, asking if you want to autofill the form using prior information, select **Yes**.

4 Using the drop-down menu, select the **Payment Account**

5 Enter **Payment Date**

6 From the Payment Method drop-down menu listing Cash, Check, or various Credit Cards, select **Payment Method**

7 If Payment Method is Check, enter the Check No. in **Reference No.**

8 In the Category Details section, select appropriate **Category** from the drop-down menu. The drop-down Category list contains accounts that can be used to record the expense.

9 Enter **Description**

10 Enter **Amount** of the expense

11 Select **Billable if the expense is billable to a specific customer**

12 If billable, select appropriate **Customer** associated with the expense

13 An expense transaction can be entered using **Item details** instead of Account details, which is covered in Chapter 7

14 If additional detail is needed, enter **Memo** describing the transaction

15 Add **Attachments**, such as source documents associated with the transaction

16 Normally we would select Save and close. In this case, select **Cancel**. If asked if you want to leave without saving, select **Yes**.

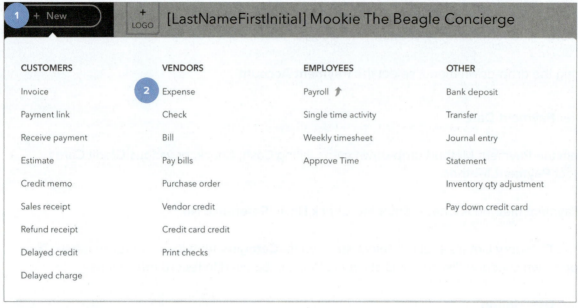

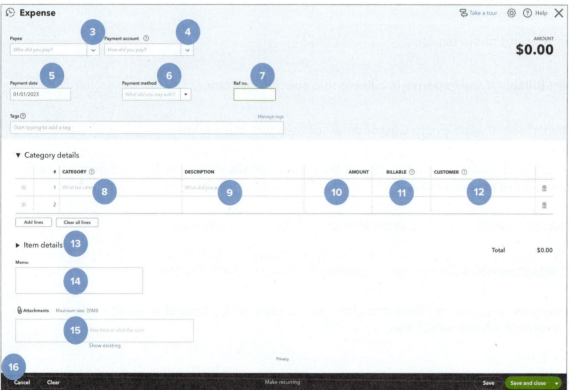

When an expense is recorded in QBO, behind the screen, the transaction is converted to a journal entry with debits and credits. To record an expense, the entry should include a debit to an Expense account and a credit to a Cash or Liability account, such as a credit card account. Additional vendor transactions are covered in Chapters 6 and 7.

Section 3.10

EMPLOYEES AND PAYROLL TRANSACTIONS

 QBO Transactions

Banking	
Customers & Sales	
Vendors & Expenses	
Employees & Payroll	*Enter Time > Pay Employees > Payroll Liabilities*

Employee transactions are exchanges between our company and our employees. Typically, these exchanges focus on payroll transactions, including tracking employee time and paying employees for their services to the company.

We can enter employees and payroll transactions using either the Navigation Bar or the (+) New icon.

To use the (+) New icon to access Employees transactions:

1 Select **(+) New** icon

2 From the **Employees** column, select the appropriate task

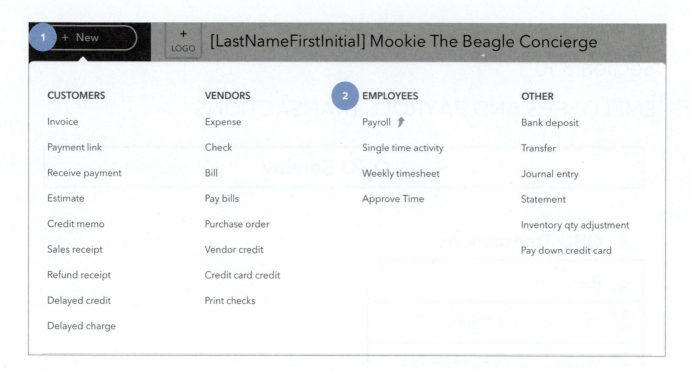

Payroll and employee transactions are covered in Chapter 8.

Section 3.11

OTHER TRANSACTIONS

If a transaction doesn't fall into one of the above categories, then it can be classified as Other. Other transactions might include adjusting entries that are required to bring our accounts up to date at year end before preparing financial reports.

We make adjusting entries using the onscreen Journal accessed as follows.

1 Select **(+) New** icon

2 Select **Journal Entry**

3 In the Journal, we would record the transaction by entering **Accounts**, **Debit** amounts, and **Credit** amounts

4 Select **Cancel** to close the Journal screen. If asked if you wish to leave without saving, select **Yes**.

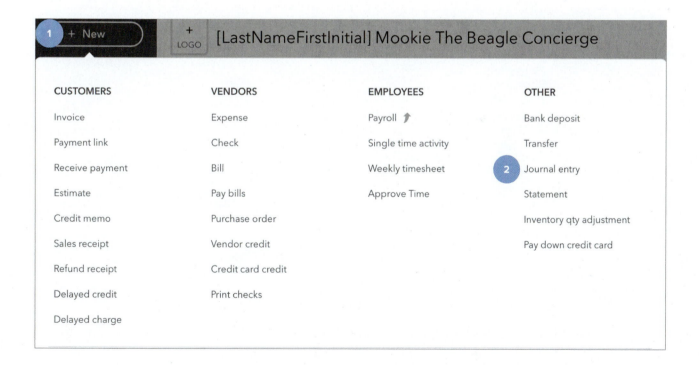

Section 3.12

RECURRING TRANSACTIONS

QBO offers a feature that permits us to save a transaction. One way we reduce errors and save time when entering transactions is to save frequently used transactions as recurring transactions.

Recurring transactions can be classified as one of three types:

1. **Scheduled.** Recurring transactions scheduled for QBO to automatically enter the transaction on a specified date.
2. **Unscheduled.** Transactions appearing in the Recurring Transaction List but QBO does not automatically enter the transaction. Instead, we must go to the Recurring Transaction List and select Use.
3. **Reminder.** Recurring transactions that alert us with a reminder when we should use a recurring transaction to enter a new transaction.

To access the Recurring Transactions List, complete the following steps.

1 Select **Gear** icon

2 Select **Recurring Transactions**

3 If you need to add a new recurring transaction, you would select **New**

4 This completes the chapter activities. If you are ready to proceed to the chapter exercises at this time, leave your browser open with your QBO company displayed. If you will be completing the chapter exercises at a later time, you can close your browser.

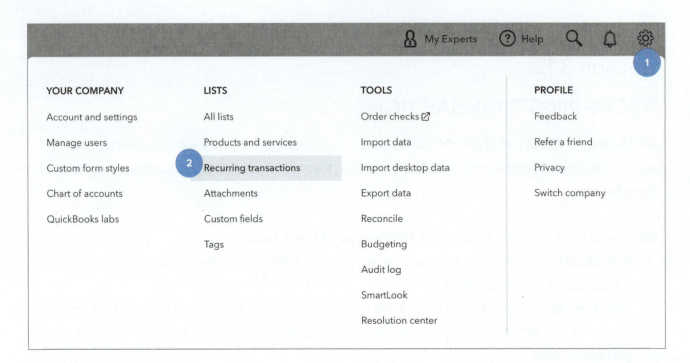

Section 3.13

ACCOUNTING ESSENTIALS
Double-Entry Accounting

Accounting Essentials summarize important foundational accounting knowledge you may find useful when using QBO

What is double-entry accounting?

- Double-entry accounting is used with a journal to record what is exchanged in a transaction:
  1. The amount received, such as equipment purchased, is recorded with a debit
  2. The amount given, such as cash or a promise to pay later, is recorded with a credit

- Each journal entry must balance: debits must equal credits. This is true whether it is a manual accounting system or a cloud-based accounting system, such as QBO.

In double-entry accounting, how do we know if a debit is an increase or a decrease to an account? How do we know if a credit is an increase or a decrease to an account?

- Whether a debit or credit increases or decreases an account depends upon the type of account.

Account Type	Debit	Credit
Assets	Increase	Decrease
Liabilities	Decrease	Increase
Equity	Decrease	Increase
Revenues (Income)	Decrease	Increase
Expenses	Increase	Decrease

What are the different types of accounts and the effect of debits and credits on the accounts?

- Five different types of accounts are listed below along with the normal balance of the account that increases the account balance.

Account Type	Debit/Credit	Effect on Balance
Asset	Debit	Increase
Liabilities	Credit	Increase
Equity	Credit	Increase
Revenues (Income)	Credit	Increase
Expenses	Debit	Increase

- For example, if the transaction is the owner invests $100,000 in the business, the journal entry with debits and credits would be as follows.

Account	Account Type	Debit/Credit	Effect on Balance	Amount
Checking	Asset	Debit	Increase	$100,000
Capital Stock	Equity	Credit	Increase	$100,000

Practice Quiz 3

Q3.1
In QuickBooks Online, information about transactions can be entered in onscreen forms, such as:
a. Check
b. Invoice
c. Purchase Order
d. All of the above

Q3.2
Which of the following two items are displayed in the QBO Navigation Bar:
a. Sales
b. Adjusting Entries
c. Banking
d. Products and Services

Q3.3
Which of the following two transactions are considered Customers and Sales transactions:
a. Invoice
b. Receive Payment
c. Pay Bills
d. Check

Q3.4
Which of the following two transactions are considered Vendors and Expenses transactions:
a. Invoice
b. Receive Payment
c. Pay Bills
d. Check

Q3.5
To enter transactions in QBO:
a. From the Navigation Bar, select Reports
b. From the (+) New icon, select transaction to enter
c. From the Gear icon, select transaction to enter
d. From the Navigation Bar, select Home

Q3.6

QBO Lists include:

a. Chart of Accounts

b. Customers List

c. Vendors List

d. Employees List

e. All of the above are QBO Lists

Q3.7

The Products and Services List can be accessed from the:

a. Navigation Bar > Expenses

b. Gear icon

c. (+) New icon

d. None of the above

Q3.8

Match the following transactions with the type of transaction.

Transaction Types

1. Banking

2. Customers and Sales

3. Vendors and Expenses

4. Employees and Payroll

a. Estimate

b. Deposit

c. Check

d. Weekly Timesheet

Q3.9

Two ways to update QBO Lists are:

a. Before entering transactions

b. While entering transactions

c. After entering transactions

Q3.10

Two different ways to enter transaction information into QBO are:

a. Onscreen forms

b. Chart of Accounts

c. Onscreen Journal

d. QBO Lists

Q3.11

Which of the following QBO features can be used to save a transaction that will be re-used in the future?

a. Saved transactions

b. (+) New icon

c. Recurring transactions

d. None of the above

Q3.12

Access the Recurring Transactions List from the:

a. Navigation Bar

b. Gear icon

c. (+) New icon

d. None of the above

Q3.13

Recurring transactions can be classified as which of the following types?

a. Scheduled

b. Unscheduled

c. Reminder

d. All of the above

Q3.14

Which of the following two are correct when double-entry accounting journal entries are used to record what is exchanged in a transaction?

a. The amount received is recorded with a credit

b. The amount received is recorded with a debit

c. The amount given is recorded with a debit

d. The amount given is recorded with a credit

Exercises 3

If necessary, sign in to your Mookie The Beagle Concierge QBO Company as follows:

1 Using a Chrome web browser, go to qbo.intuit.com

2 Enter **User ID** (the email address you used to set up your QBO Account)

3 Enter **Password** (the password you used to set up your QBO Account)

4 Select **Sign in**

E3.1 Transaction Types

What is the Transaction Type for the following transactions?

Transaction Types

- **Banking**
- **Customers and Sales**
- **Vendors and Expenses**
- **Employees and Payroll**

Transaction	Transaction Type
1. Transfers	
2. Weekly Timesheet	
3. Credit Card Credit	
4. Purchase Order	
5. Estimate	
6. Bill	
7. Invoice	
8. Pay Bills	
9. Receive Payment	
10. Deposit	
11. Sales Receipt	
12. Credit Memo	

E3.2 QBO Lists
Which QBO List would be used with the following transactions?

QBO Lists

- **Customers List**
- **Vendors List**
- **Employees List**
- **Recurring Transactions List**

Transaction	QBO List
1. Weekly Payroll	
2. Expense	
3. Credit Card Credit	
4. Invoice	
5. Estimate	
6. Bill	
7. Purchase Order	
8. Pay Bills	
9. Receive Payment	
10. Saved Deposit Transaction	
11. Sales Receipt	
12. Check	

E3.3 Debits and Credits
Complete the following statements using:

- **Debits**
- **Credits**

1. Assets are increased by _____
2. Liabilities are increased by _____
3. Equity is increased by _____
4. Revenue (Income) is increased by _____
5. Expenses are increased by _____
6. Assets are decreased by _____

7. Liabilities are decreased by _____

8. Equity is decreased by _____

9. Revenue (Income) is decreased by _____

10. Expenses are decreased by _____

EM3.4 COA Debits and Credits

The following accounts are from Mookie The Beagle Concierge Chart of Accounts. For each account indicate:

* If the account is increased by a:
  * **Debit**
  * **Credit**

* Type of account as:
  * **Asset**
  * **Liability**
  * **Equity**
  * **Revenue (Income)**
  * **Expense**

Account	Debit/Credit	Account Type
1. Checking		
2. Inventory		
3. Prepaid Expenses: Insurance		
4. Prepaid Expenses: Supplies		
5. Accounts Payable (A/P)		
6. Unearned Revenue		
7 Owner's Investment		
8. Sales		
9. Bank Charges & Fees		
10. Insurance: Liability Insurance Expense		
11. Legal & Professional Services		
12. Rent & Lease		
13. Utilities		

EM3.5 COA Debits and Credits

The following accounts are from Mookie The Beagle Concierge Chart of Accounts. For each account indicate:

- If the account is increased by a:
  - **Debit**
  - **Credit**
- Type of account as:
  - **Asset**
  - **Liability**
  - **Equity**
  - **Revenue (Income)**
  - **Expense**

Account	Debit/Credit	Account Type
1. Accounts Receivable (A/R)		
2. Prepaid Expenses		
3. Prepaid Expenses: Rent		
4. Undeposited Funds		
5. VISA Credit Card		
6. Owner Distributions		
7. Retained Earnings		
8. Advertising & Marketing		
9. Contractors		
10. Interest Paid		
11. Office Supplies & Software		
12. Repairs & Maintenance		

EM3.6 QBO Products and Services List

Mookie The Beagle Concierge doesn't have a complete list of customers and vendors to enter into a Customers List and Vendors List before we begin entering transactions. So we will enter customer and vendor information at the same time we enter transactions.

We can create a QBO Products and Services List with the following information Cy summarized about the services Mookie The Beagle Concierge will be providing customers. None of the services are subject to sales tax.

To enter the services into the Products and Services List:

1. Select **Navigation Bar > Sales > Products and Services tab > New > Service**. Use the Income account: **4200 Sales**.

2. Enter the following Products and Services Items.

NAME	CATEGORY	TYPE	DESCRIPTION	SALES PRICE
Errand	Pet Care	Service	Pet Personal Shopper, 1 hour minimum	$50
Short Visit	Pet Care	Service	Pet Check to check on status of pet, let pet out, and short walk, 1 hour minimum	$40
Medium Visit	Pet Care	Service	2 to 4 hours	$50
Extended Visit	Pet Care	Service	4 to 8 hours	$60
Intensive	Pet Care	Service	Assume responsibility for pet care while owner is OOT or gone for extended period	$80
Vet Visit	Pet Wellness	Service	Vet services concierge visit or take pet to vet	$130
Medium Wellness	Pet Wellness	Service	1 to 4 hours with administration of medication, home cooked food, wound dressing changes, and other pet healthcare services	$70
Extended Wellness	Pet Wellness	Service	4 to 8 hours providing pet healthcare services	$80
Intensive Wellness	Pet Wellness	Service	Assume responsibility for pet healthcare while owner is OOT or intensive healthcare responsibilities	$90

> **Note:** After we begin adding products and services to the Products and Services List, QBO may automatically add some additional accounts to our Chart of Accounts. We can easily identify the added accounts since they do not display account numbers. If desired, account numbers can be entered for these added accounts. For more information about how to enter account numbers, see Chapter 2.

3. Export the Products and Services List to PDF. From the Products and Services screen, select **More > Run Report > Export icon > Export to PDF**.

EM3.7 Deposit Transaction

Cy Walker invests $20,000 of his personal savings into Mookie The Beagle Concierge. MTB Concierge needs to record the deposit using QBO.

1. Record the Deposit.
   a. Select **(+) New icon > Bank Deposit**
   b. Select **Account: 1001 Checking**
   c. Select **Payment Date: 01/01/2023**
   d. In the Add Funds to This Deposit section, select **Account: 3003 Owner's Investment**
   e. Select **Payment Method: Check**
   f. Enter **Ref No.: 5001**
   g. Enter **Amount: 20000.00**
   h. What type of account is Owner's Investment?
   i. Select **Save and close**

2. View the Transaction Journal for the Deposit.
   a. From the Navigation Bar, select **Accounting**
   b. From the Chart of Accounts, select **Checking > View Register > Deposit > Edit**
   c. From the bottom of the screen, select **More > Transaction Journal**
   d. What are the Account and Amount Debited?
   e. What are the Account and Amount Credited?

EM3.8 Expense Transaction: Check

Mookie The Beagle Concierge hired Carole Design Media to promote Mookie The Beagle Concierge's launch using social media marketing. Mookie The Beagle Concierge paid the bill in full when received. The bill was for 10 hours of service at $100 per hour.

Enter the Expense Transaction as follows.

1. Create an Expense.
   a. Select **(+) New icon > Expense**
   b. Add **Payee: +Add New > Carole Design Media > Vendor Type > Save**
   c. Select **Payment Account: 1001 Checking**
   d. Select **Payment Date: 01/05/2023**
   e. Select **Payment Method: Check**
   f. Enter **Category: 5001 Advertising & Marketing**
   g. Enter **Amount** for **10 hours @ $100.00 per hour**
   h. What is the Total Amount paid to Carole Design Media?
   i. Select **Save**. Leave the Expense window open.

2. View the Transaction Journal for the Expense.
   a. From the bottom of the Carole Design Media Expense window, select **More > Transaction Journal**
   b. What are the Account and Amount Debited?
   c. What are the Account and Amount Credited?

EM3.9 Expense Transaction: Credit Card

Mookie The Beagle Concierge obtained liability insurance from Phoenix Insurance at a cost of $300 for 3 months of insurance coverage. The liability insurance protects Mookie The Beagle Concierge from the risk of legal liability for injury or damages of its business operations in providing pet care and pet wellness services.

1. Create an Expense.
   a. Select **(+) New icon > Expense**
   b. Add **Vendor Payee: Phoenix Insurance**
   c. Select **Payment Account: 2100 VISA Credit Card**
   d. Select **Payment Date: 01/07/2023**
   e. Select **Payment Method: Credit Card**
   f. Select **Category: 5010 Insurance: 5012 Liability Insurance Expense**
   g. Enter **Amount: 300.00**
   h. What is the Total Amount paid to Phoenix Insurance?
   i. Select **Save**. Leave the Expense window open.

2. View the Transaction Journal for the Expense.
   a. From the bottom of the Phoenix Insurance Expense, select **More > Transaction Journal**
   b. What are the Account and Amount Debited?
   c. What are the Account and Amount Credited?

EM3.10 Invoice Transaction

Mookie The Beagle Concierge negotiated an agreement with a local university veterinary program for student interns to work as contractors to provide Mookie The Beagle Concierge services as needed.

One of Mookie The Beagle Concierge's first customers, Angel Merriman, used the Mookie The Beagle Concierge app to schedule care for her black and tan King Shepherd, Kuno, whose paw was injured while playing at a doggie day care. Angel was unable to leave work so she was relieved to be able to schedule the following pet wellness services using the Mookie The Beagle Concierge app:

- Pet Care: Transport 1 hour (pickup at doggie day care)

- Pet Wellness: Vet Visit 2 hours

- Pet Wellness: Intensive 6 hours

- Pet Care: Errand 1 hour to obtain pet supplies

Since you are still learning QBO, you decide that in case a pet parent has more than one pet, the Customer List in QBO will be maintained using the pet parent as the Customer, and the pet will be a sub-customer. For example, one pet parent (customer) could have two pets (sub-customers). This is similar to the treatment we used for accounts and subaccounts in the Chart of Accounts.

1. Complete an Invoice.
    a. From the Navigation Bar, select **Sales > Customers tab > New customer**. Add New **Customer First Name: Angel**. Add **Customer Last Name: Merriman**. Add New **Sub-customer: Kuno**. Select **Bill with parent**.
    b. Select **(+) New icon > Invoice > Customer: Kuno**
    c. Select **Invoice Date: 01/02/2023**
    d. Select **Product/Service: Pet Care: Transport**
    e. Select **QTY: 1**
    f. **Rate** and **Amount** fields should autofill
    g. Select **Product/Service: Pet Wellness: Vet Visit**
    h. Select **QTY: 2**
    i. **Rate** and **Amount** fields should autofill
    j. Select **Product/Service: Pet Wellness: Intensive Wellness**
    k. Select **QTY: 6**
    l. **Rate** and **Amount** fields should autofill
    m. Select **Product/Service: Pet Care: Errand**
    n. Select **QTY: 1**
    o. **Rate** and **Amount** fields should autofill
    p. What is the Balance Due for the Invoice?
    q. Select **Save**. Leave the Invoice window open.

2. View the Transaction Journal for the Invoice.
   a. From the bottom of the Invoice, select **More > Transaction Journal**
   b. What are the Account and Amount Debited?
   c. What are the Accounts and Amounts Credited?

EM3.11 Invoice Transaction

Sandy Copper uses the Mookie The Beagle Concierge app during one of her unplanned business trips to request pet care services for Remy, her rescue dog.

Services provided by Mookie The Beagle Concierge were as follows.

- Pet Care: Intensive (36 hours total)

1. Complete an Invoice.
   a. From the Navigation Bar, select **Sales > Customers tab > New customer**. Add New **Customer First Name: Sandy**. Add **Customer Last Name: Copper**. Add New **Sub-customer: Remy.** Select **Bill with parent**.
   b. Select **(+) New icon > Invoice > Customer: Remy**
   c. Select **Invoice Date: 01/04/2023**
   d. Select **Product/Service: Pet Care: Intensive**
   e. Select **QTY: 36**
   f. **Rate** and **Amount** fields should autofill
   g. What is the Balance Due for the Invoice?
   h. Select **Save**. Leave the Invoice window open.

2. View the Transaction Journal for the Invoice.
   a. From the bottom of the Invoice, select **More > Transaction Journal**
   b. What are the Account and Amount Debited?
   c. What are the Account and Amount Credited?

EM3.12 Recurring Transactions

Mookie The Beagle Concierge will have recurring Contractors Expense to pay the vet students who provide pet care services. Cy asks you to save the Contractors Expense as a QBO Recurring Transaction for ease of future use.

Evan Henry is the contractor who provided the pet care services for both Kuno and Remy. Mookie The Beagle Concierge will pay Evan Henry $20 per hour for those services.

1. Create a Recurring Transaction.
    a. Select **Gear icon** > **Recurring Transactions** > **New**
    b. Select **Transaction Type: Expense** > **OK**
    c. Enter **Template Name: Contractors Expense**
    d. Select **Type: Unscheduled**
    e. Add **Payee: + Add New** > **Vendor Type.** Enter Name: **Evan Henry** > **Save**
    f. Select **Account: 1001 Checking**
    g. Select **Payment Method: Check**
    h. Select **Category: 5005 Contractors (Expense)**
    i. Enter **Amount: based upon the number of hours Evan Henry provided for Kuno and Remy**
    j. What is the Amount for the Recurring Expense?
    k. Select **Save Template**

2. Use a Recurring Transaction.
    a. From the Recurring Transaction List, select **Contractors Expense** > **Use**
    b. Select **Payment Date: 01/10/2023**
    c. Select **Payment Method: Check**
    d. Verify **Amount** is the same as you entered in the Template
    e. Select **Save**
    f. From the bottom of the Contractors Expense window, select **More** > **Transaction Journal**
    g. What are the Account and Amount Debited?
    h. What are the Account and Amount Credited?

Chapter 4

Banking

MOOKIE THE BEAGLE™ CONCIERGE

BACKSTORY

Cy Walker's text flashes across your smartphone screen.

I've heard that cash is king!

Absolutely!

Can QBO help with managing MTB Concierge cash?

Definitely.

Do you have time for a call?

Surely.

Cy Walker realizes that one of the key factors in the long-term success of a business is the ability to pay bills on time. Several of his friends who started businesses had great ideas, fantastic social media marketing, and outstanding employee teams, but didn't survive because the businesses ran out of cash and couldn't pay their bills.

Cy knows that he needs to keep close track of cash flow for Mookie The Beagle™ Concierge to ensure they have adequate cash to pay bills when due. Cy needs a way to track cash going into and out of the business bank accounts, as well as track business credit card charges, payments, and balances.

Your next step is to learn more about how to use QuickBooks Online for banking functions, including Checking accounts and credit cards.

MookieTheBeagle.com © 2017 Carl K. Yazigi. All Rights Reserved. Used with Permission. MookieTheBeagle.com™, Mookie The Beagle™, and the Mookie character, names, and related indicia are trademarks of Carl K. Yazigi and used with permission.

Chapter 4

LEARNING OBJECTIVES

The QBO Banking function encompasses Checking accounts and credit cards. Adequate cash flows determine whether a company can pay its bills on time. So a business needs to track cash going into and cash going out of its bank accounts. QBO provides several banking features to make tracking cash flows easier for businesses.

In Chapter 4 you will learn about the following topics:

- Check Register
  - ‣ View Check Register
  - ‣ Check Register Drill-Down
  - ‣ Use Check Register To Add New Transactions

  Money In
  - ‣ Recording Bank Deposits
- Money Out
  - ‣ Recording Expenses
  - ‣ Recording Checks
- Connecting Bank and Credit Cards with QBO
  - ‣ Add Bank and Credit Card Accounts for Automatic QBO Downloads
  - ‣ Add Bank and Credit Card Transactions
  - ‣ Match Bank and Credit Card Transactions
- Accounting Essentials: Banking for Business

 QBO is updated on an ongoing basis. Updates that affect your text can be viewed as follows:
1. Go to www.My-QuickBooksOnline.com > QBO 3e > QBO 3e Updates, or
2. If you are using Connect or a digital ebook, you can find updates under **Additional Student Resources (ASR).** If you do not have access to Connect or the ebook, your instructor can provide you with **ASR.**

Section 4.1

 ## QBO SatNav

QBO SatNav is your satellite navigation for QuickBooks Online, assisting you in navigating QBO

Chapter 4 focuses on QBO Banking Transactions, shown in the following QBO SatNav.

 QBO SatNav

 QBO Settings

Company Settings
Chart of Accounts

 **QBO Transactions**

Banking	Record Deposits | Write Checks
Customers & Sales	
Vendors & Expenses	
Employees & Payroll	

 QBO Reports

Reports

Section 4.2

CHECK REGISTER

The Check Register is a record of all transactions affecting the Checking account. Typically banking transactions involve money going into and out of our company's bank accounts. Some of the banking activities that we can use QBO to record include the following:

- Bank deposits (money into bank accounts)
- Bank transfers (money into and out of bank accounts)
- Bank checks (money out of bank accounts)
- Enter and pay credit card charges (money out of bank accounts)

VIEW CHECK REGISTER

The QBO Check Register looks similar to a checkbook register used to manually record deposits and checks.

To view the QBO Check Register:

1   From the Navigation Bar, select **Accounting**

2   Select the **Chart of Accounts** tab

3   From the Chart of Accounts window, select **View Register** for the Checking account

4   **Date** column lists the date of the transaction

5   **Ref No. Type** column lists the reference number, such as check number, and type of transaction, such as Deposit

6   **Payee Account** column lists the payee and the account used to record the transaction

7   **Payment** column lists the amount of money out of the Checking account

8   **Deposit** column lists the amount of money into the Checking account

9   ✔ column indicates whether the bank transaction is C (Cleared), R (Reconciled), or blank (Uncleared, Unreconciled)

10   **Balance** column displays the running balance for the Checking account, updating the balance with each new transaction in the account

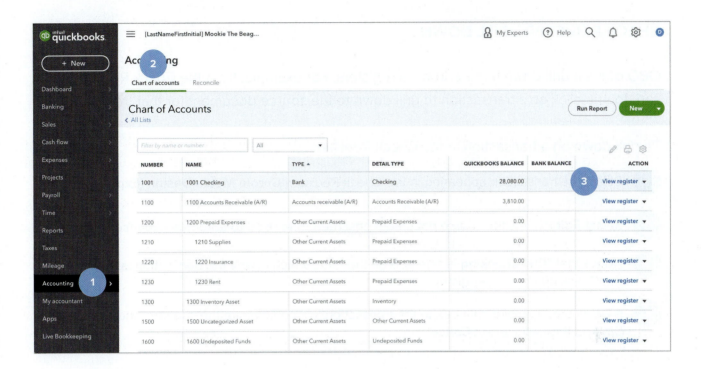

Small enterprises that have strictly cash-based operations sometimes simply use the Check Register to record all transactions. Such enterprises record payments and deposits directly into the Check Register. However, most business enterprises require more advanced features of QBO that are covered in the following chapters.

CHECK REGISTER DRILL DOWN

QBO offers a drill-down feature from its registers. For example, from the Check Register, we can double-click on a transaction to drill down to the source document for that transaction.

To drill down on a transaction in the Check Register:

1   Select the transaction appearing in the Check Register: **Carole Media Design (Expense)**

2   Select **Edit** to view the source document onscreen form used to enter the expense

3   Notice that **1001 Checking** is selected on the form, which is why the transaction appears in the Checking account Register

4   If we wanted to make changes to the transaction, we could make the changes and select Save. In this case, select **Cancel**.

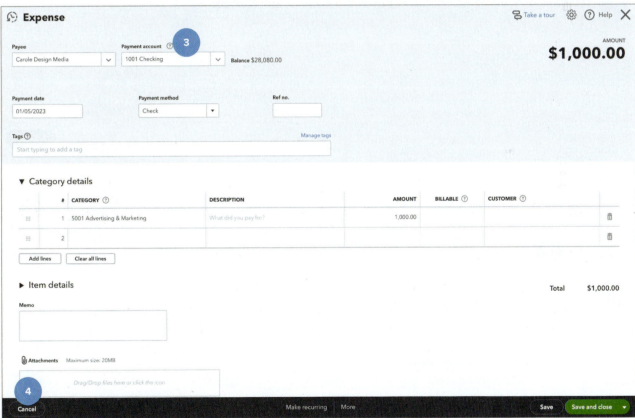

USE CHECK REGISTER TO ADD NEW TRANSACTIONS

We can record deposits and checks directly in the Check Register. The Balance column will update automatically. Another way to enter transactions that will appear in the Check Register is to use the (+) New icon.

To add new transactions from the Check Register window:

1   Select the **drop-down arrow** by Add Check in the Check Register window

2   Select the new type of transaction to enter, such as **Deposit**

3   Enter the new transaction in the Check Register

4   Normally we would select Save, but in this case select **Cancel**

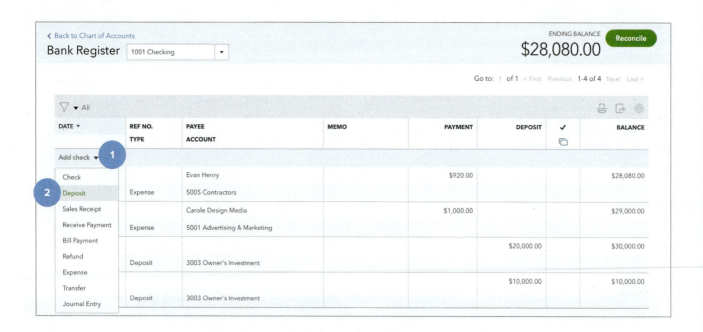

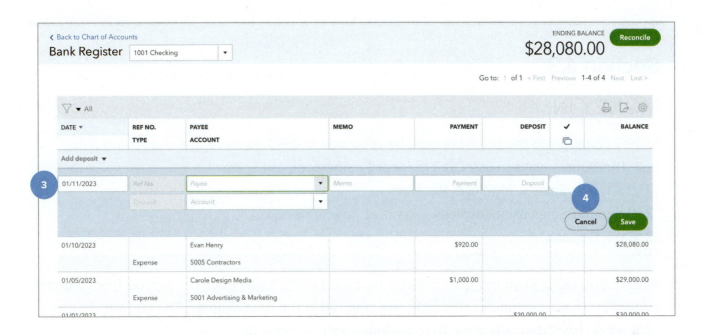

Section 4.3

MONEY IN

Money coming into the business must be recorded in QBO so there is a record and paper trail. Three main ways to use QBO to record money coming in are:

1. Customer Sales using Sales Receipts
2. Customer Sales using Invoices > Receive Payments
3. Bank Deposit

When using QBO, customer sales can be recorded using Sales Receipts (option 1) or Invoices (option 2). These customer sales tasks are covered in the next chapter. The current chapter focuses on bank deposits other than customer sales (option 3).

MONEY IN: BANK DEPOSITS NOT RELATED TO CUSTOMER SALES

If money coming in is not related to customer sales, then we can use a Bank Deposit form to record the money coming in. Examples of money coming in that is not a customer sale include:

- Investments from company owners
- Cash received from loans
- Interest earned
- Other income, such as rental income when our primary business is not a rental business

The above items can be recorded using the Bank Deposit form.

> **Customer sales** should be recorded using only Sales Receipts or Invoices. The Bank Deposit form that is discussed next only should be used for bank deposits not related to customer sales. Recording customer sales is covered in the next chapter.

MONEY IN: RECORDING BANK DEPOSITS

To record a bank deposit not related to a customer sale, we would complete the following:

1 Select **(+) New** icon

2 Under the Other column, select **Bank Deposit**

3 Select **Account: 1001 Checking**

4 Enter **Date** of deposit: **01/11/2023**

5 In the **Add Funds to This Deposit** section, enter **Received From**

6 Select the appropriate **Account**

7 Enter a **Description** of the deposit

8 Enter **Payment Method**

9 Enter **Amount**

10 Enter **Memo**

11 Select **Attachments** to add a file or photo of any accompanying document

12 Normally we would select Save and new or Save and close, but in this case select **Cancel**

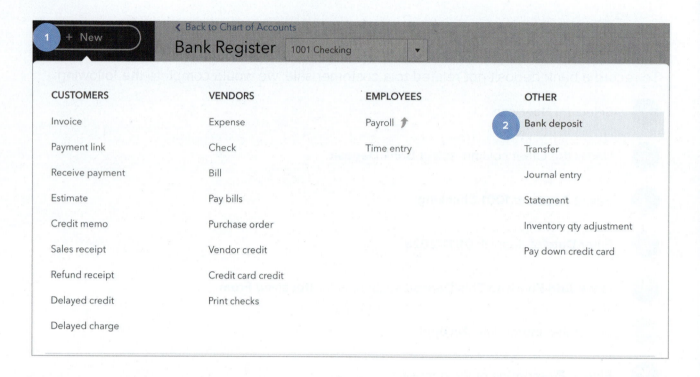

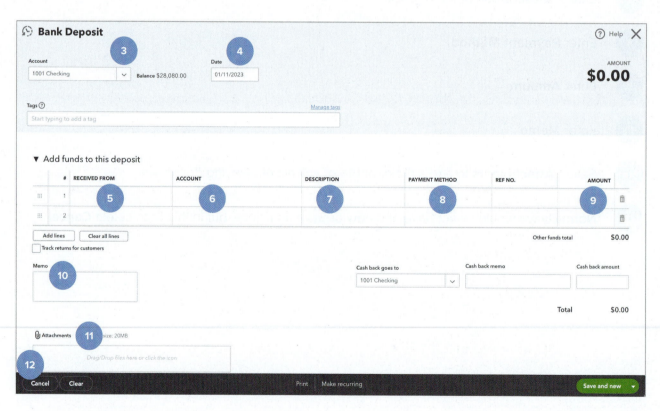

Section 4.4

MONEY OUT

A business needs to track all money out, including all cash paid out of the company's Checking account. Examples of payments include purchases of inventory, office supplies, employee salaries, rent payments, and insurance payments.

Supporting documents (source documents) for payments include canceled checks, receipts, and paid invoices. These source documents provide proof that the transaction occurred; therefore, source documents should be kept on file for tax purposes. QBO permits us to add source documents as attachments.

Four main ways to use QBO to record money out include:

1. Expense
2. Check
3. Bill > Pay Bills
4. Purchase Order > Bill > Pay Bills

The current chapter focuses on using an Expense (option 1) or Check (option 2) to record money out. Recording money out using Bill > Pay Bills (option 3) is covered in Chapter 6. Recording money out using Purchase Order > Bill > Pay Bills (option 4) is covered in Chapter 7.

MONEY OUT: CHECK OR EXPENSE FORM

If money going out is paid at the time the product or service is received (instead of later), it can be recorded using the Expense or Check onscreen form. Examples of money going out that could be recorded using the Expense or Check onscreen form include:

- Rent expense
- Utilities expense
- Insurance expense
- Office supplies expense
- Services expense, such as accounting or legal services

If we are paying for a product or service immediately using cash, check, or credit card, then we can use the Expense onscreen form.

If we are paying for a product or service immediately with a check, then we can use the Check onscreen form to record the check.

Examples of money going out that should not be recorded using a Check or Expense onscreen form include:

- Paychecks to employees for wages and salaries
- Payroll taxes and liabilities
- Sales taxes
- Bills already entered using the Bill onscreen form

MONEY OUT: RECORDING EXPENSES

To record a payment that is made immediately with cash, check, or credit card, use the Expense form as follows:

1 Select **(+) New** icon

2 Under Vendors column, select **Expense**

3 Select **Payee: Bichotte Supplies**

4 Using the drop-down menu, select **Payment Account: 2100 VISA Credit Card**

5 Enter **Payment Date: 01/11/2023**

6 Select **Payment Method: Credit Card**

7 In the Category Details section, select appropriate Category from the drop-down menu. The drop-down Category list contains accounts that can be used to record the expense. If it does not appear automatically, select **Category: 5024 Office Supplies & Software**.

8 Enter a **Description**: **Purchase of software**

9 Enter **Amount** of the expense: **13.00**

10 Select Billable if the expense is billable to a specific customer. In this case since the computer cable does not relate to a specific customer, leave **Billable unchecked**.

11 If billable, select appropriate Customer associated with the expense. In this case, leave **Customer** field **blank**.

12 Enter **Memo** describing the transaction: **Purchase of software**

13 Select **Save**. Leave the Expense form open.

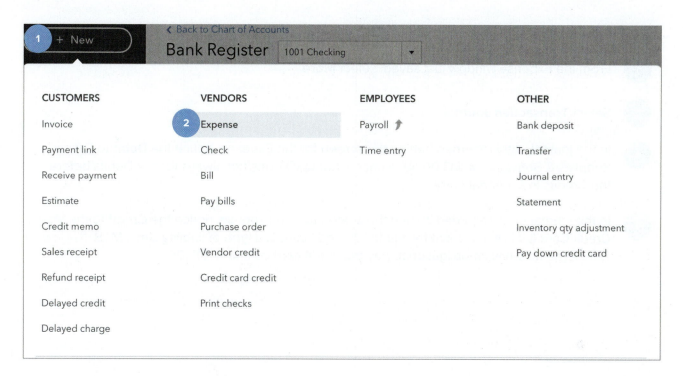

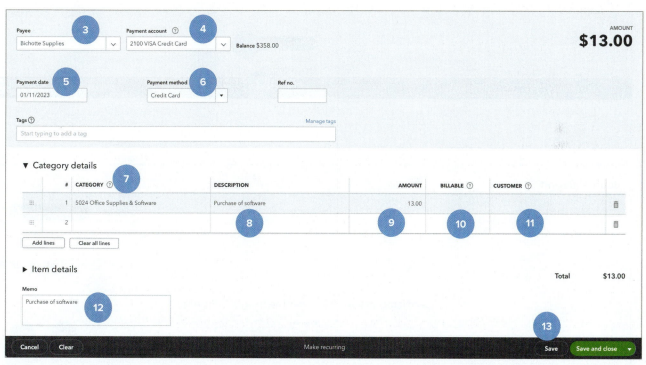

To view the Transaction Journal for the Expense we just created:

1 From the Expense window just saved, select **More**

2 Select **Transaction Journal**

3 In the journal entry recorded behind the screen for the Expense, notice the **Debit** to Office Supplies & Software for $13.00. Also notice that QBO does not always list the Debits before the Credits in a Journal Entry.

4 In the journal entry recorded behind the screen for the Expense, notice the **Credit** to the Visa Credit Card (Liability) account for $13.00. A credit card is a type of liability since MTB Concierge now has an obligation to pay the credit card company $13.00.

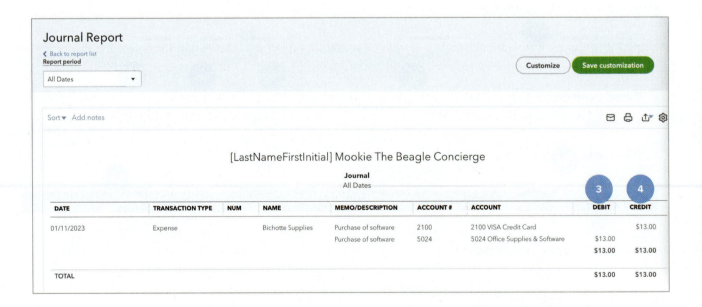

MONEY OUT: RECORDING CHECKS

To record a payment that is made immediately with a check:

1 Select **(+) New** icon

2 Under Vendors column, select **Check**

3 Select **Payee: Bichotte Supplies**

4 Select **Bank Account: 1001 Checking**

5 Enter **Payment Date: 01/13/2023**

6 Notice that the **Check No.** autofills

7 In the Category Details section, select appropriate Category from the drop-down menu. The drop-down Category list contains accounts that can be used to record the expense. Sometimes QBO will autofill this field using information from the last transaction entered for the specific Payee. In this case, if it does not autofill, enter **Category: 5024 Office Supplies & Software (Expenses)**.

8 Enter **Description: Office Supplies**

9 Enter **Amount: 99.00**

10 If the payment was billable to a specific customer, select Billable. In this case since the expense does not relate to a specific customer, leave **Billable unchecked**.

11 If the payment was billable to a specific customer, select that customer in the Customer column from the Customer drop-down list. In this case, leave **Customer** field **blank**.

12 Enter **Memo: Office Supplies**

13 Select **Attachments** to add a file or photo of any accompanying source document, such as a bill

14 Select **Save and close**

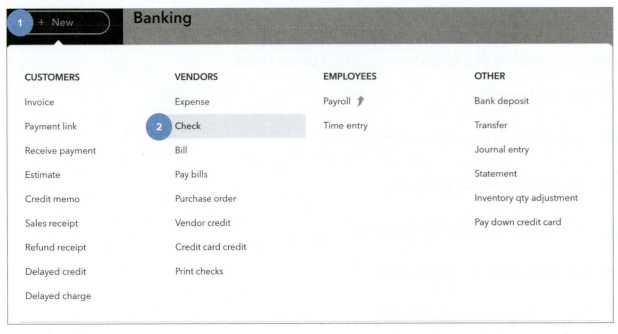

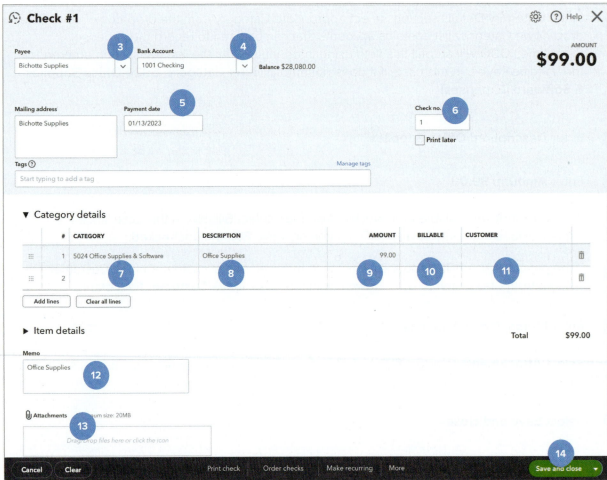

To view the Transaction Journal for the Check we just created:

1 From the Navigation Bar, select **Expenses**

2 Select the **Expenses** tab

3 From the Expense Transactions List, select: **View/Edit** for the Check to **Bichotte Supplies** just entered

4 From the bottom of the Bichotte Supplies Check, select **More**

5 Select **Transaction Journal**

6 In the journal entry recorded behind the screen for the Check, notice the **Debit** to Office Supplies & Software (Expense) for $99.00

7 In the journal entry recorded behind the screen for the Check, notice the **Credit** to Checking for $99.00

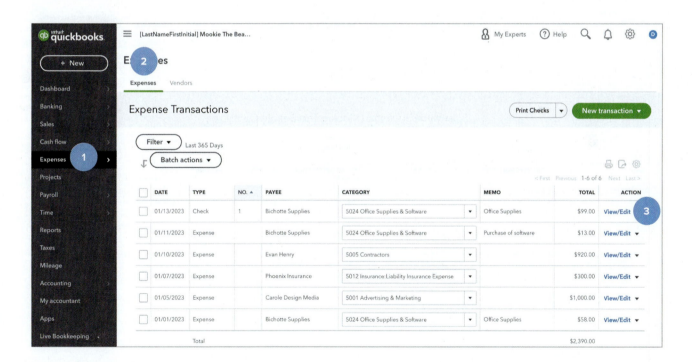

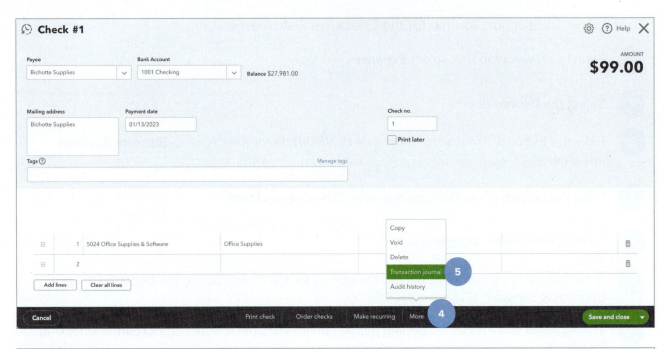

Section 4.5

CONNECT BANK AND CREDIT CARDS WITH QBO

We can connect our bank accounts and our credit card accounts with QBO. This results in the expenses automatically being downloaded from the bank or credit card company into QBO. Then we can Add or Match the downloaded bank and credit card transactions with our QBO entries.

CONNECT BANK AND CREDIT CARD ACCOUNTS FOR AUTOMATIC DOWNLOADS

If your bank or credit card company has connectivity to QBO, then you could connect a bank or credit card account to QBO for automatic downloads as follows:

1 From the Navigation Bar, select **Banking**

2 Select the **Banking** tab

3 To watch a video about connecting a bank account to QBO, select **See how it works**

4 To connect a bank account to QBO, select **Connect account**

5 Then you would follow the onscreen instructions to connect the bank account

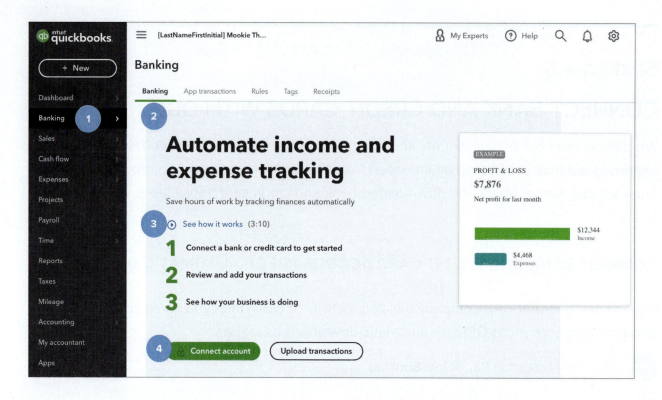

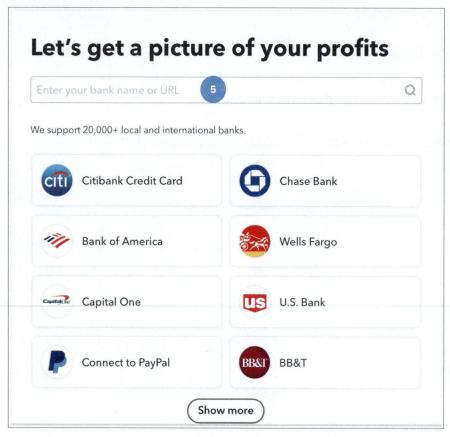

After bank and credit card accounts are connected to QBO, then the transactions download automatically into QBO Bank and Credit Cards window. QBO automatically compares downloaded bank transactions with our QBO entries to identify possible matches.

UPLOAD BANK AND CREDIT CARD TRANSACTIONS

If we are unable to connect a bank or credit card account to QBO, then we can load the bank or credit card transactions into QBO. Mookie The Beagle Concierge is unable to connect QBO to its credit card company, so first we will download the credit card transactions from the credit card company. Then we will load the transactions into QBO.

Mookie The Beagle Concierge has the following transactions for its VISA Credit Card in a spreadsheet form. MTB Concierge needs to upload the credit card transactions into QBO and then match them to QBO transactions previously entered.

VISA CREDIT CARD				
Type	Trans Date	Post Date	Description	Amount
Expense	01/11/2023	01/14/2023	BICHOTTE SUPPLIES	-13.00
Expense	01/07/2023	01/13/2023	PHOENIX INSURANCE	-300.00
Expense	01/01/2023	01/08/2023	BICHOTTE SUPPLIES	-58.00

C4.5.1 Upload Credit Card Transactions

First, download the csv file containing the previous credit card information.
- If you are using Connect, select the link for the data file: **QBO 3E C4.5 Credit Card.csv**.
- If you are not using Connect, go to **www.my-quickbooksonline.com** > select **QBO 3e** > **QBO 3e Data Files** > select link to download **QBO 3E C4.5 Credit Card.csv**.

To load Credit Card Account Transactions into QBO:

1 From the QBO Navigation Bar, select **Banking**

2 Select **Banking** tab

3 Select **Upload transactions**

4 Select **Drag and drop or select files** to select the file to upload > select **File: QBO 3E C4.5 Credit Card.csv**

5   Select **Continue**

6   When Which account are these transactions from? appears, select **QuickBooks Account: 2100 VISA Credit Card**

7   Select **Continue**

8   When Let's set up your file in QuickBooks appears, and the question appears: Is the first row in your file a header?, select **Yes**

9   How many columns show amounts? **One column**

10   What's the date format used in your file? **MM/dd/yyyy**

11   Select **Date: Column 2: Trans Date**

12   Select **Description: Column 4 Description**

13   Select **Amount: Column 5 Amount**

14   Select **Continue**

15   Select **The transactions to import: Select All**

16   Select **Continue**

17   When asked, Do you want to import now?, select **Yes**

18   When Import completed appears, select **Done**

19   To watch a video about your bank connection, select **Get an overview**

20   How many transactions were imported?

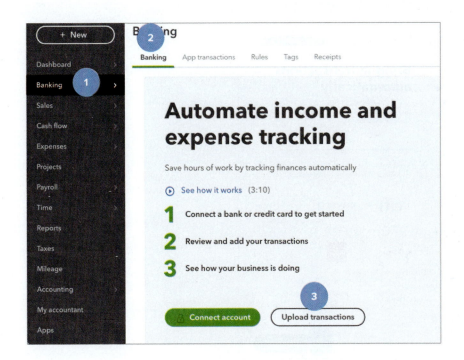

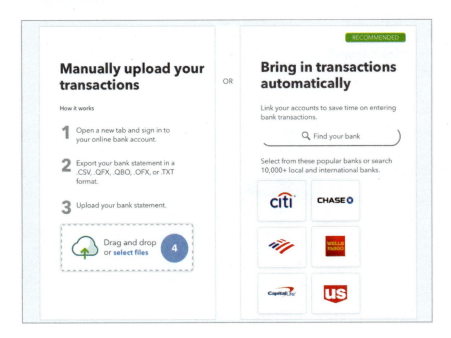

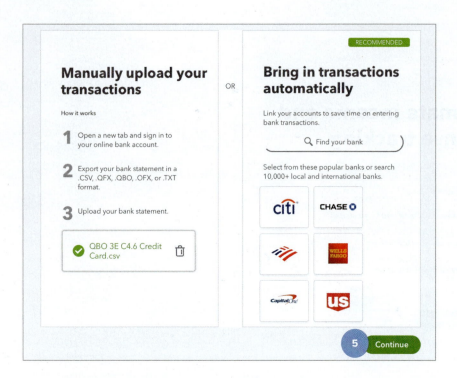

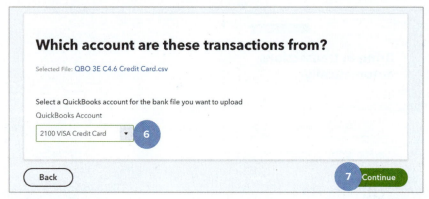

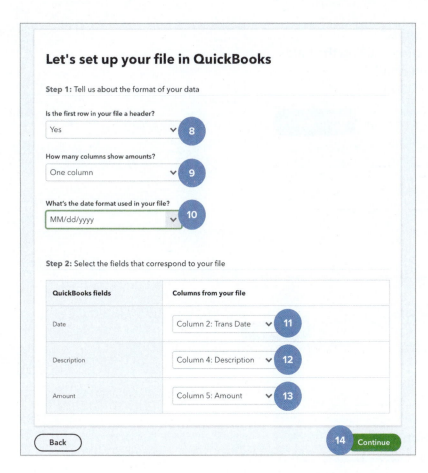

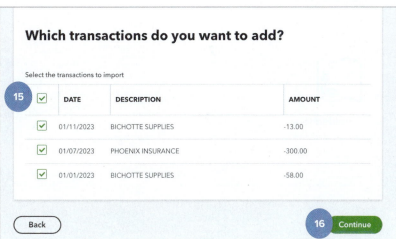

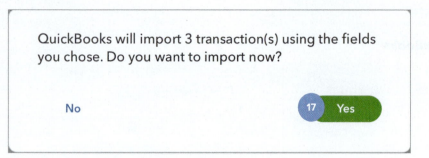

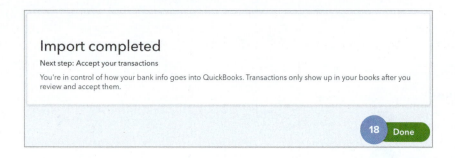

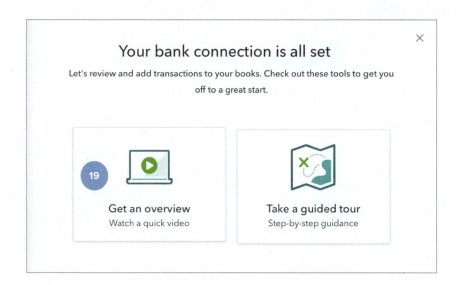

MATCH BANK AND CREDIT CARD TRANSACTIONS

C4.5.2 Match Credit Card Transactions

After loading your credit card transactions into QBO in the prior section, to match uploaded bank or credit card transactions to QBO entries we made previously:

1 From the Navigation Bar, select **Banking**

2 Select **Banking** tab

3 The number of open (unmatched) items appear on the VISA Credit Card at the top of the screen

4 Select **For Review** tab to view the imported transactions

5 The **Action** column may display **Add**, **Match**, or **View**

6 Select **Match** for all Matching items to match the transaction entered in QBO with the uploaded transaction from the credit card company

7 Select **Go to bank register** to view the register for the account: 2100 VISA Credit Card

8 To return to Bank Matching screen, from the Navigation Bar, select **Banking > Banking** tab. Now how many open items appear on the VISA Credit Card at the top of the screen?

9 This completes the chapter activities. If you are ready to proceed to the chapter exercises at this time, leave your browser open with your QBO company displayed. If you will be completing the chapter exercises at a later time, you can close your browser.

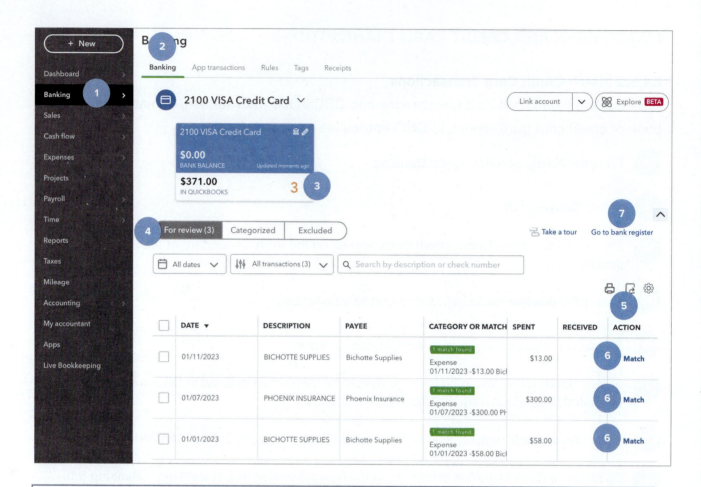

Note that transactions with **Match** in the **Action** column are bank and credit card transactions **entered in QBO** and identified by QBO as a possible **Match** to the uploaded transactions.

Section 4.6

ACCOUNTING ESSENTIALS
Banking for Business

Accounting Essentials summarize important foundational accounting knowledge you may find useful when using QBO

How many checking accounts does a business need?

- A business needs at least one business checking account in the business name. A business should establish a business checking account completely separate from the owner's personal checking account.
- The company's business checking account should be used only for business transactions, such as business insurance and mortgage payments for the company's office building. An owner should maintain a completely separate checking account for personal transactions, such as mortgage payments for the owner's home.
- In addition, a business may need more than one business checking account with one business checking account for operations and a separate business checking account for payroll, for example.

What is a bank reconciliation?

- Typically once a month, the bank sends you a Checking account bank statement. The bank statement lists each deposit, check, and withdrawal from the account during the month. A bank reconciliation is the process of comparing, or reconciling, the bank statement with your accounting records for the Checking account.

What are the objectives of a bank reconciliation?

- The bank reconciliation has two objectives: (1) to detect errors and (2) to update your accounting records for unrecorded items listed on the bank statement (such as service charges). Reconciling bank statements is part of good internal controls that involve comparing the actual asset (what the bank says you have) with your accounting records (QBO Checking account).
- Note that with QBO's ability to match downloaded bank transactions with QBO data on an ongoing basis, some QBO users find that they no longer use a monthly bank reconciliation. Basically, they are comparing the bank balance with their QBO balance on a real time basis instead of a monthly basis, which provides even better internal control since they become aware of discrepancies and potential issues sooner.

Why are there differences between the bank statement and my accounting records?

- Differences between the balance the bank reports on the bank statement and the balance the business shows in its accounting records usually arise for two reasons:
  1. **Errors**. Errors can be either the bank's error(s) or the company's error(s).
  2. **Timing differences**. This occurs when the company records an amount before the bank does or the bank records an amount before the company does. For example, the company may record a deposit in its accounting records, but the bank does not record the deposit before the company's bank statement is prepared.

     Timing differences include:
     - Items the bank has not recorded yet, such as:
       - ✓ **Deposits in transit.** Deposits the company has recorded but the bank has not.
       - ✓ **Outstanding checks.** Checks the company has written and recorded but the bank has not recorded yet.
     - Items the company has not recorded yet, such as:
       - ✓ **Unrecorded charges.** Charges that the bank has recorded on the bank statement but the company has not recorded in its accounting records yet. Unrecorded charges include service charges, loan payments, automatic withdrawals, and ATM withdrawals.
       - ✓ **Interest earned on the account.** Interest the bank has recorded as earned but the company has not recorded yet.

Practice Quiz 4

Q4.1

The Checking Register:

a. Tracks company purchase orders and vendors
b. Tracks company invoices and customers
c. Records all transactions affecting the Checking account
d. Lists all accounts and their account numbers

Q4.2

A company should always use the same checking account for business transactions and for the owner's personal transactions to streamline recording transactions.

a. True
b. False

Q4.3

Deposits other than customer payments are entered using:

a. Receive Payments
b. Pay Bills
c. Bank Deposit
d. All of the above

Q4.4

If we are paying a bill immediately when we receive products or services, we can use the Expenses onscreen form when we pay with:

a. Cash
b. Check
c. Credit Card
d. All of the above

Q4.5

Examples of money going out that can be recorded using the Expense or Check onscreen forms include all of the following except:

a. Rent expense
b. Payroll expense
c. Insurance expense
d. Legal Services expense

Q4.6
Examples of money going out that should *not* be recorded using a Check or Expense onscreen form include:
a. Paychecks to employees
b. Payroll taxes
c. Sales taxes
d. Bills already entered using the Bills onscreen form
e. All of the above

Q4.7
Ways to record money out using QBO include:
a. Enter Bill > Pay Bills
b. Check
c. Expense
d. Purchase Order > Bill > Pay Bills
e. All of the above

Q4.8
Ways to record money coming into QBO include:
a. Customer Sales using Sales Receipts
b. Customer Sales using Invoices and Receive Payments
c. Bank Deposit
d. All of the above

Q4.9
To record a bill payment that is made immediately with a credit card when the product or service is received, use the following onscreen form:
a. Bill
b. Check
c. Pay Bills
d. Expense

Q4.10

Differences between the balance the bank reports on the bank statement and the balance the business shows in its accounting records usually arise for which of the following two reasons:

a. Adjusting entries have been made twice
b. Errors (bank errors or company errors)
c. Timing differences between when the bank records and when the company records an item
d. Closing entries have been made

Q4.11

One of the objectives of reconciling bank statements is:

a. To update the bank's records
b. Update accounting records with unrecorded items
c. To record monthly adjusting entries
d. To update the Chart of Accounts

Q4.12

When reconciling a bank account, which of the following is not considered a timing difference (difference between the bank balance and the book balance)?

a. Interest earned
b. Deposits in transit
c. Errors
d. Unrecorded charges

Exercises 4

If necessary, sign in to your Mookie The Beagle Concierge QBO Company as follows:

1 Using a Chrome web browser, go to qbo.intuit.com

2 Enter **User ID** (the email address you used to set up your QBO Account)

3 Enter **Password** (the password you used to set up your QBO Account)

4 Select **Sign in**

E4.1 Check Register

Match the following items identified in a Checking account Bank Register with the description of the items.

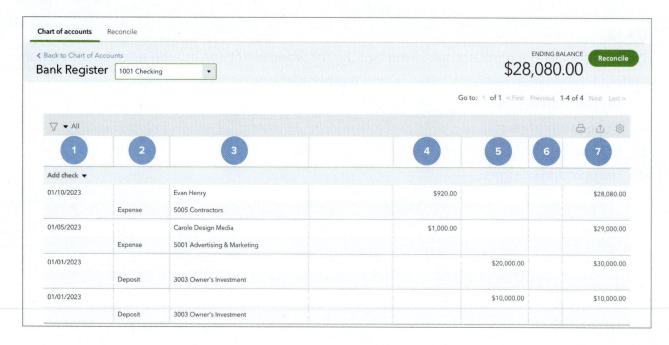

Chart of accounts	Reconcile					
‹ Back to Chart of Accounts					ENDING BALANCE	Reconcile
Bank Register [1001 Checking ▼]					$28,080.00	
				Go to: 1 of 1 ‹ First Previous 1-4 of 4 Next Last ›		
▽ ▼ All						🖨 ⬆ ⚙
1	**2**	**3**		**4**	**5**	**6** **7**
Add check ▼						
01/10/2023		Evan Henry		$920.00		$28,080.00
	Expense	5005 Contractors				
01/05/2023		Carole Design Media		$1,000.00		$29,000.00
	Expense	5001 Advertising & Marketing				
01/01/2023					$20,000.00	$30,000.00
	Deposit	3003 Owner's Investment				
01/01/2023					$10,000.00	$10,000.00
	Deposit	3003 Owner's Investment				

Check Register Item Descriptions

a. Deposit column listing the amount of money going into the Checking account

b. ✔ column indicating whether the bank transaction is Cleared, Reconciled, or blank (Uncleared and Unreconciled)

c. Date column listing the date of the transaction

d. Ref No. and Type lists the type of transaction

e. Balance column displaying the running balance for the Checking account

f. Payee Account column listing the payee and the account used to record the transaction

g. Payment column listing the amount of money going out of the Checking account

Check Register Item

1 _____

2 _____

3 _____

4 _____

5 _____

6 _____

7 _____

EM4.2 Bank Deposit

Cy loans Mookie The Beagle Concierge $1,000 at 6% annual interest. Record the transaction as a loan payable as follows.

1. Complete a Deposit.
   a. Select **(+) New icon > Bank Deposit**
   b. Select **Account: 1001 Checking**
   c. Select **Date: 01/12/2023**
   d. In Add Funds to This Deposit section, select **Account: + Add New > Account Type: Other Current Liabilities > Detail Type: Loan Payable > Name: Loan Payable > Number: 2300 > Save and Close**
   e. Select **Payment Method: Check**
   f. Enter **Ref No.: 5002**
   g. Enter **Amount: 1000.00**
   h. Select **Save and close**
   i. What is the Amount of the Loan Payable?

2. View the Transaction Journal for the Deposit.
   a. From the Navigation Bar, select **Accounting**
   b. From the Chart of Accounts, select **2300 Loan Payable > View Register**
   c. From the Register, select the transaction just recorded > **Edit**
   d. From the bottom of the Loan Payable transaction, select **More > Transaction Journal**
   e. What are the Account and Amount Debited?
   f. What are the Account and Amount Credited?

EM4.3 Expense Credit Card

Complete the following to record Internet services that Mookie The Beagle Concierge incurred.

1. Create an Expense paid with Credit Card.
   a. Select **(+) New icon > Expense**
   b. Add **Vendor Payee + Add new: Luminesse Link**
   c. Select **Payment Account: 2100 VISA Credit Card**
   d. Select **Payment Date: 01/13/2023**
   e. Select **Payment Method: Credit Card**
   f. Enter **Category: 5040 Utilities Expense**
   g. Enter **Description: Internet Service**
   h. Enter **Amount: 200.00**
   i. What is the Total Amount paid to Luminesse Link?
   j. Select **Save** and leave the Expense screen displayed

2. View the Transaction Journal for the Expense.
   a. From the displayed Expense, select **More > Transaction Journal**
   b. What are the Account and Amount Debited?
   c. What are the Account and Amount Credited?

EM4.4 Expense Credit Card

Complete the following to record telephone service that Mookie The Beagle Concierge incurred and paid by credit card.

1. Create an Expense paid with Credit Card.
   a. Select **(+) New icon > Expense**
   b. Select **Payee: Luminesse Link**
   c. Select **Payment Date: 01/15/2023**
   d. Select **Payment Account: VISA Credit Card**
   e. Select **Payment Method: Credit Card**
   f. Enter **Category: 5040 Utilities Expense**
   g. Enter **Description: Telephone Service**
   h. Enter **Amount: 185.00**
   i. What is the Total Amount paid to Luminesse Link?
   j. Select **Save**. Leave the Expense window displayed.

2. View the Transaction Journal for the Expense.
   a. From the displayed Expense, select **More > Transaction Journal**
   b. What are the Account and Amount Debited?
   c. What are the Account and Amount Credited?

EM4.5 Check

Complete the following to record technology accessories that Mookie The Beagle Concierge paid for by check to Merriman Cybersecurity, a firm that specializes in technology supplies and consulting services.

1. Create a Check.
   a. Select **(+) New icon > Check**
   b. Add **Vendor Payee + Add new: Merriman Cybersecurity**
   c. Select **Bank Account: 1001 Checking**
   d. Select **Payment Date: 01/16/2023**
   e. Select **Category: 5024 Office Supplies & Software (Expense)**
   f. Enter **Description: Technology Supplies**
   g. Enter **Amount: 333.00**
   h. What is the Total for the Check?
   i. Select **Save and close**

2. View the Transaction Journal for the Check.
   a. From the Navigation Bar, select **Expenses**
   b. From the Expense Transactions List, select the **Merriman Cybersecurity Check** just entered
   c. From the bottom of the Merriman Cybersecurity Check, select **More > Transaction Journal**
   d. What is the Account and Amount Debited?
   e. What is the Account and Amount Credited?

EM4.6 Match Bank Transactions Credit Card

Mookie The Beagle Concierge has the following transactions for its VISA Credit Card in spreadsheet form (csv file). MTB Concierge needs to upload the credit card transactions into QBO and then match them to QBO transactions previously entered.

VISA CREDIT CARD				
Type	Trans Date	Post Date	Description	Amount
Expense	01/15/2023	01/16/2023	LUMINESSE LINK	-185.00
Expense	01/13/2023	01/15/2023	LUMINESSE LINK	-200.00

1. First, download the csv file containing the credit card transaction information from the credit card company.
   - If you are using Connect, select the link for the data file: **QBO 3E E4.6 Credit Card.csv**.
   - If you are not using Connect, go to **www.my-quickbooksonline.com** > select **QBO 3e link** > scroll down to **QBO Data Files** > select link to download **QBO 3E E4.6 Credit Card.csv**.

2. Upload Credit Card Account Transactions to QBO.
    a. From the Navigation Bar, select **Banking > Banking** tab
    b. Select the Link account drop-down arrow > select **Upload from file**
    c. Select **Drag and drop or select files** to select the file to upload > select **File: QBO 3E E4.6 Credit Card.csv > Continue**
    d. Select **QuickBooks Account: 2100 VISA Credit Card > Continue**
    e. Select **Is the first row in your file a header? Yes**
    f. Select **How many columns show amounts? One column**
    g. Select **What's the date format used in your file? MM/dd/yyyy**
    h. Select **Date: Column 2: Trans Date**
    i. Select **Description: Column 4 Description**
    j. Select **Amount: Column 5 Amount**
    k. Select **Continue**
    l. Select **The transactions to import: Select All > Continue**
    m. When asked, Do you want to import now?, select **Yes**
    n. When Import completed appears, select **Done**
    o. How many transactions were imported?

3. Complete a Credit Card Account Bank Match.
    a. From the Navigation Bar, select **Banking**
    b. How many open items appear on the VISA Credit Card at the top of the screen?
    c. Select **Match** for all Matching items
    d. Now how many open items appear on the VISA Credit Card at the top of the screen?

EM4.7 Match Bank Transactions Checking

Mookie The Beagle Concierge has downloaded the following Checking account transactions in spreadsheet form (csv file). MTB needs to upload these bank transactions into QBO and then match them against QBO transactions previously entered.

CHECKING				
Type	Trans Date	Post Date	Description	Amount
Expense	01/16/2023	01/18/2023	MERRIMAN CYBERSECURITY	-333.00
Expense	01/13/2023	01/14/2023	BICHOTTE SUPPLIES	-99.00
Deposit	01/12/2023	01/13/2023	CY WALKER LOAN	1000.00
Expense	01/10/2023	01/11/2023	EVAN HENRY	-920.00
Expense	01/05/2023	01/06/2023	CAROLE DESIGN MEDIA	-1000.00
Deposit	01/01/2023	01/02/2023	CY WALKER	20000.00
Deposit	01/01/2023	01/02/2023	CY WALKER	10000.00

1. First, download the csv file containing the checking transaction information from the bank.

    -   If you are using Connect, select the link for the data file: **QBO 3E E4.7 Checking.csv**.

    -   If you are not using Connect, go to **www.my-quickbooksonline.com** > select **QBO 3e link** > scroll down to **QBO Data Files** > select link to download **QBO 3E E4.7 Checking.csv**.

2. Upload Checking Account Transactions to QBO.
    a. From the Navigation Bar, select **Banking > Banking** tab
    b. Select the Link account drop-down arrow > select **Upload from file**
    c. Select **Drag and drop or select files** to select the file to upload > select **File: QBO 3E E4.7 Checking.csv > Continue**
    d. Select **QuickBooks Account: 1001 Checking > Continue**
    e. Select **Is the first row in your file a header? Yes**
    f. Select **How many columns show amounts? One column**
    g. Select **What's the date format used in your file? MM/dd/yyyy**
    h. Select **Date: Column 2: Trans Date**
    i. Select **Description: Column 4 Description**
    j. Select **Amount: Column 5 Amount**
    k. Select **Continue**
    l. Select **The transactions to import: Select All > Continue**
    m. When asked, Do you want to import now?, select **Yes**
    n. When Import completed appears, select **Done**
    o. How many transactions were imported?

3. Complete a Checking Account Bank Match.
    a. From the Navigation Bar, select **Banking**
    b. How many open items appear on the Checking card at the top of the screen?
    c. Select **Match** for all Matching items
    d. Now how many open items appear on the Checking card at the top of the screen?

EM4.8 Bank Transfer

Mookie The Beagle Concierge would like to move some cash from the Checking account to a Business Money Market account to ensure funds are available in the future for upcoming expected expenditures and earn a better return on the funds than a Checking account. Complete the following to record the transfer of funds from the Checking account to a Business Money Market account.

1. Record a Transfer.
    a. Select **(+) New icon** > **Transfer**
    b. Select **Transfer Funds From: 1001 Checking**
    c. Select **Transfer Funds To** > select + **Add new** > **Account Type: Bank** > **Detail Type: Money Market** > **Name: Money Market** > **Number: 1010** > **Save and Close**
    d. Enter **Transfer Amount: 10,000.00**
    e. Enter **Date: 01/15/2023**
    f. Enter **Memo: Transfer from Checking to Money Market Account**
    g. Select **Save and close**
    h. After the transfer, what is the balance in the Money Market Account?

2. View the Transaction Journal for the Money Market account transfer.
    a. From the Navigation Bar, select **Banking** > **Banking** tab
    b. At the top of the Bank and Credit Cards screen, select **1001 Checking**
    c. Select **Go to bank register**
    d. Select the entry in the Checking Account Register for the **$10,000 Transfer to Money Market account** > **Edit**
    e. From the bottom of the Transfer form, select **More** > **Transaction Journal**
    f. What are the Account and Amount Debited?
    g. What are the Account and Amount Credited?

Chapter 5

Customers and Sales

MOOKIE THE BEAGLE™ CONCIERGE

BACKSTORY

As sales for Mookie The Beagle™ Concierge ramp up, Cy Walker wants to make certain that all sales to customers are captured and correctly recorded in the financial system. Cy also realizes the importance of collecting and recording customer payments. He knows that collecting customer payments on time is the only way the company will have adequate cash to pay vendor bills when due. So your next step is to learn more about using QuickBooks Online to record customers and sales transactions, including sales to customers and collection of customers' payments.

Chapter 5

LEARNING OBJECTIVES

Chapter 5 focuses on customers and sales transactions for services, such as sales of Mookie The Beagle Concierge pet care services. A later chapter will cover recording customers and sales transactions for products, such as sale of Mookie The Beagle–branded merchandise. In this chapter, you will learn about the following topics:

- Navigating Sales Transactions
  - Navigation Bar
  - (+) New Icon
  - Workspace
- Customers List
  - Update Customers List Before Entering Transactions
  - Update Customers List While Entering Transactions
- Projects
- Products and Services List
  - Inventory
  - Non-inventory
  - Service
  - Bundle
- Record Sales Transactions Using Sales Receipts
  - Create Sales Receipt
  - Create Bank Deposit for Undeposited Funds From Sales Receipt
- Record Sales Transactions Using Invoices
  - Create Invoice
  - Create Receive Payment
  - Create Bank Deposit For Undeposited Funds From Receive Payment
- Accounting Essentials: Customer Sales and Accounts Receivable

⚠️ **QBO is updated on an ongoing basis. Updates that affect your text can be viewed as follows:**
1. **Go to www.My-QuickBooksOnline.com > QBO 3e > QBO 3e Updates, or**
2. **If you are using Connect or a digital ebook, you can find updates under Additional Student Resources (ASR). If you do not have access to Connect or the ebook, your instructor can provide you with ASR.**

Section 5.1

QBO SATNAV

QBO SatNav is your satellite navigation for QuickBooks Online, assisting you in navigating QBO

Chapter 5 focuses on QBO Customers and Sales Transactions, shown in the following QBO SatNav.

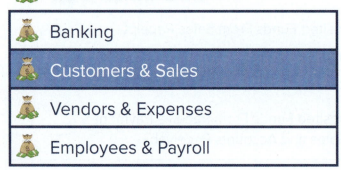

🌐 **QBO SatNav**

⚙ QBO Settings

⚙ Company Settings
⚙ Chart of Accounts

💰 QBO Transactions

💰 Banking
💰 Customers & Sales
💰 Vendors & Expenses
💰 Employees & Payroll

📊 QBO Reports

📊 Reports

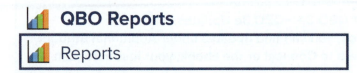

Section 5.2

NAVIGATING SALES TRANSACTIONS

Three different ways to navigate sales transaction entry for QBO are:

1. Navigation Bar
2. (+) New icon
3. Workspace

NAVIGATION BAR

To use the Navigation Bar to enter sales transactions:

1 From the Navigation Bar, select **Sales**

2 Select **All Sales** tab

3 From the Sales Transactions window, select the drop-down arrow for **New transaction**

4 Select the type of **new transaction** to enter and complete the onscreen form for the new transaction

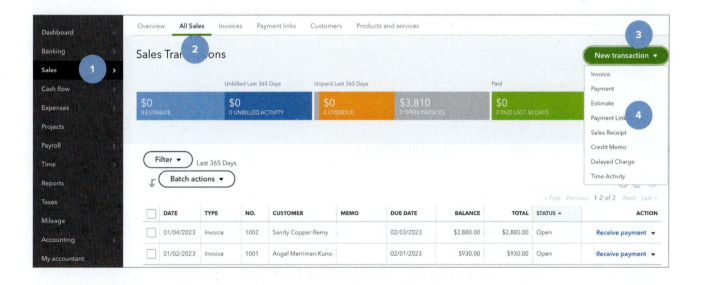

(+) NEW ICON

To use the (+) New icon to enter sales transactions:

1   Select **(+) New** icon

2   Select the **new transaction** from the Customers transactions shown

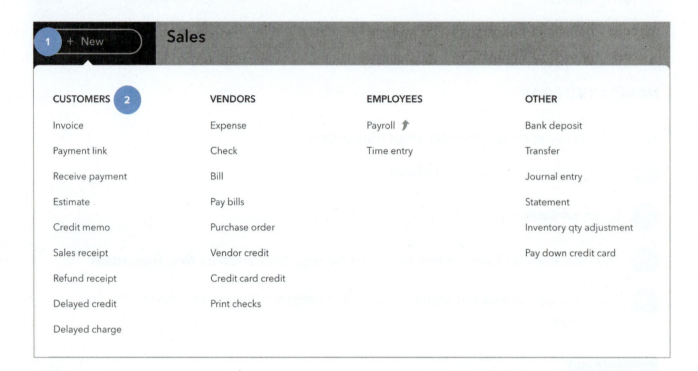

1 + New	Sales		
CUSTOMERS **2**	**VENDORS**	**EMPLOYEES**	**OTHER**
Invoice	Expense	Payroll ↑	Bank deposit
Payment link	Check	Time entry	Transfer
Receive payment	Bill		Journal entry
Estimate	Pay bills		Statement
Credit memo	Purchase order		Inventory qty adjustment
Sales receipt	Vendor credit		Pay down credit card
Refund receipt	Credit card credit		
Delayed credit	Print checks		
Delayed charge			

WORKSPACE

To use Workspace to enter sales transactions:

1   From the Navigation Bar, select **Dashboard**

2   Select **Get things done** tab

3   **Workspace** displays Money in and Money out, including specific QBO tasks for each

4   **Add Products and services** is used to add items to the Products and Services List

5   **Manage Customers** includes adding and editing customers in the Customers List

6   **Send Invoices** is the task to create and send invoices to customers

7   **Receive Payments** records the transaction when payment is received from customers

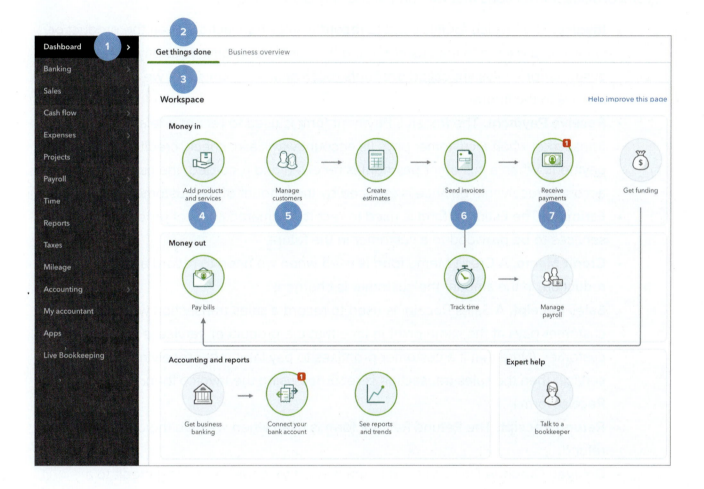

Section 5.3

TYPES OF SALES TRANSACTIONS

Types of sales transactions that we can enter using QBO include:

- **Invoice.** The Invoice form is used to record a sales transaction when the product or service is provided to the customer and the customer promises to pay later. These customer promises are called *accounts receivable*—amounts that we expect to *receive* in the future.
- **Receive Payment.** The Receive Payment form is used to record a related sales transaction when a customer pays its account with cash, check, credit card, or online payment. When a customer payment is received and recorded, the customer's accounts receivable balance is reduced by the amount of the customer payment.
- **Estimate.** The Estimate form is used to record estimated costs of products and services to be provided to a customer in the future.
- **Credit Memo.** A Credit Memo form is used when we need to record a credit, or reduction, in the amount the customer is charged.
- **Sales Receipt.** A Sales Receipt is used to record a sales transaction when the customer pays at the same point in time that the product or service is provided to the customer. (Note that if a customer promises to pay later, after receiving a product or service, then the sales transaction is recorded using the Invoice form, not the Sales Receipt form.)
- **Refund Receipt.** The Refund Receipt form is used when we give the customer a refund.
- **Delayed Credit.** A Delayed Credit form is used to record a pending credit to a customer that will occur at a specified future date.
- **Delayed Charge.** A Delayed Charge form is used to record a pending charge to a customer that will occur at a specified future date.

When we enter the above customers and sales transactions, we need to use two QBO Lists:

1. Customers List
2. Products and Services List

Section 5.4

CUSTOMERS LIST

The QBO Customers List permits us to collect and store information about a customer, such as customer name, address, and mobile number. The Customers List is a time-saving feature. Each time we enter a new transaction for a customer, we can use information from the Customers List instead of continually re-entering the same customer information over and over for each sales transaction.

Two ways that we can update the Customers List are:

1. *Before* entering transactions
2. *While* entering transactions

UPDATE CUSTOMERS LIST BEFORE ENTERING TRANSACTIONS

Before entering transactions, we can update the Customers List from the QBO Navigation Bar as follows.

1 From the Navigation Bar, select **Sales**

2 Select **Customers**

3 To enter new customers, select **New customer**

4 Enter **First Name: Sherry**

5 Enter **Last Name: Byran**

6 Select **Display Name as: Sherry Byran**

7 Enter **Mobile: 415-555-2222**

8 Enter **Billing Address Street: 222 Mure Street**

9 Enter **Billing Address City: Bayshore**

10 Enter **Billing Address State: CA**

11 Enter **Billing Address ZIP: 94326**

12 Enter **Billing Address Country: USA**

13 Select **Shipping Address: Same as billing address**

14 Select **Payment and billing tab**

15 Select **Preferred Payment Method: Credit Card**

16 Select **Terms: Due on receipt**

17 Select **Save**

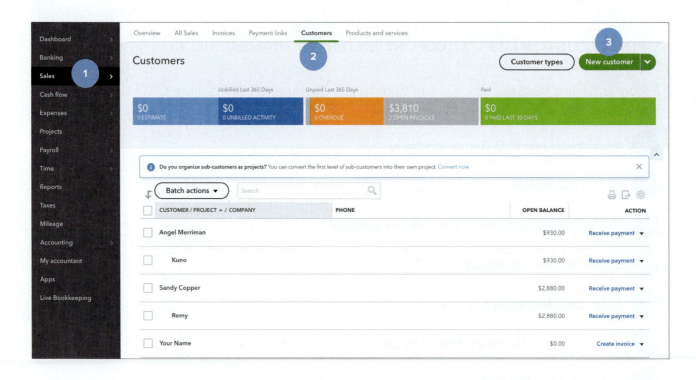

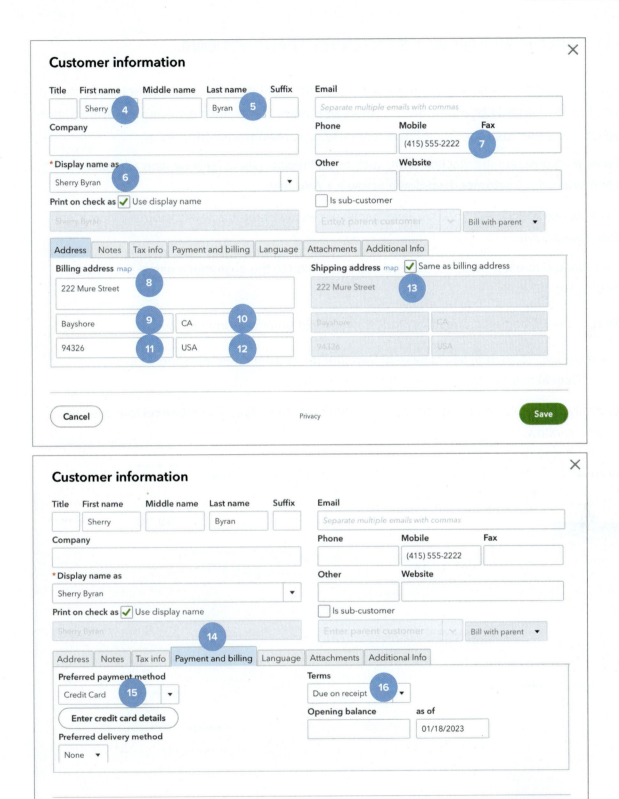

UPDATE CUSTOMERS LIST WHILE ENTERING TRANSACTIONS

While entering transactions, we can update the Customers List from the transaction form. If a customer has not already been entered in the Customers List before entering the transaction, then we can add the customer as follows from the onscreen transaction form.

1. To view an onscreen transaction form, such as an Invoice, select **(+) New icon > Invoice**. Then select the **Customer drop-down arrow > + Add new**.

2. If we only needed to add the customer name, we would enter the new customer's name, and then select Save

3. If we wanted to enter more customer detail in addition to the customer's name, then we would select **Details**

4. Next, in the Customer Information window, we would enter customer details

5. Normally, we would then select Save to save the new customer information. In this case, select **Cancel** to leave the Customer Information window.

6. Typically, we would complete and save the Invoice. In this case, select **Cancel** to leave the Invoice window.

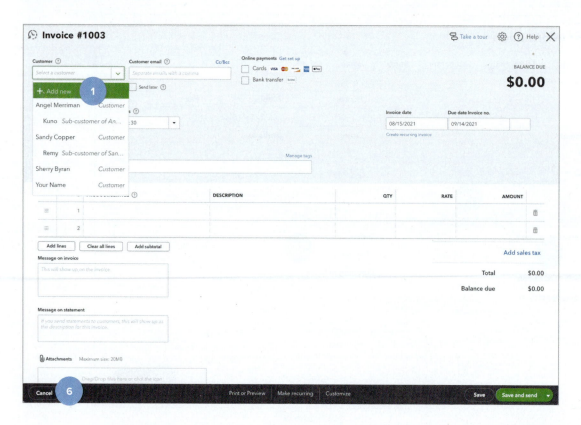

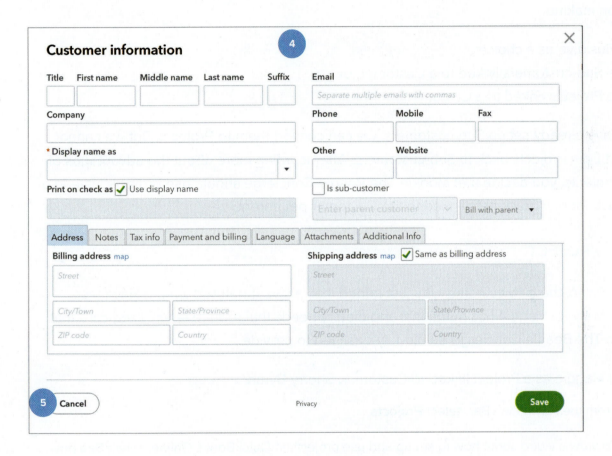

Section 5.5

PROJECTS

Projects is a QBO Plus feature that permits us to set up projects linked to customers. Then we can track transactions and profitability by project, providing us with better information for decision making.

QBO Plus give us a choice:

1. Use Sub-customers linked to a Customer, or
2. Use Projects linked to a Customer

If we have already set up Sub-customers, we can convert them to Projects. But we cannot convert from Projects back to Sub-customers. After learning more about the advantages of QBO Projects, you decide that Mookie The Beagle Concierge should use Projects instead of Sub-customers to track pets linked to the Customer pet parent.

ADD A PROJECT

Sherry Byran, the new customer you just added, has a sweet-natured, cream Havanese named Maggie. Maggie has nutritional and dietary needs that require specialized care that Mookie The Beagle Concierge is uniquely qualified to provide.

To add Maggie as a Project linked to Customer, Sherry Byran:

1 From the Navigation Bar, select **Projects**

2 To view a video about how to set up and use projects in QuickBooks Online, select **See how it works**

3 If this is your first project, select **Start a project**. (If you already have existing projects and would like to add another project, select New project.)

4 In the New project window, enter the **Project name: Maggie**

5 From the Customer drop-down menu, select **Customer: Sherry Byran**

6 To save the new project, select **Save**

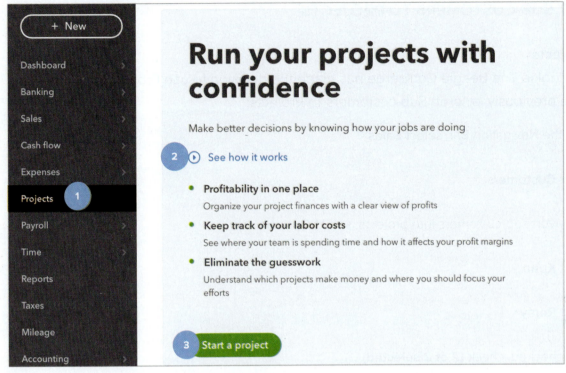

CONVERT SUB-CUSTOMERS TO PROJECTS

C5.5.1 Projects

Now that Mookie The Beagle Concierge has made the decision to use Projects, we need to convert the previously entered Sub-customers to Projects:

1. From the Navigation Bar, select **Sales**

2. Select **Customers**

3. To convert sub-customers into projects, select **Convert now**

4. Select **Kuno**

5. Select **Remy**

6. If not checked, check **(2 of 2 selected)**

7. Select **Convert (2)**

8. When the Ready to convert? window appears, select **Continue**

9. Select **Go to Projects**

10. How many projects are listed for Mookie The Beagle Concierge?

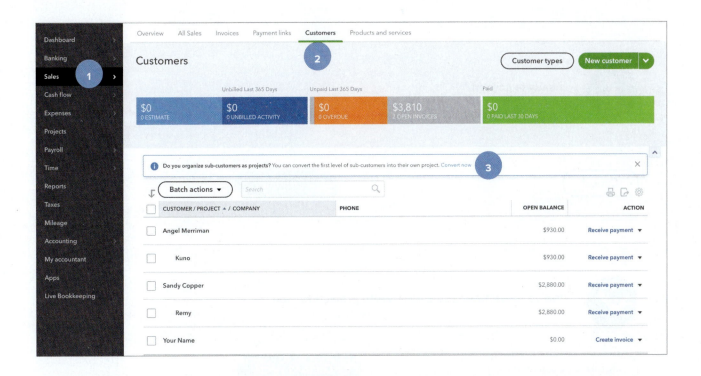

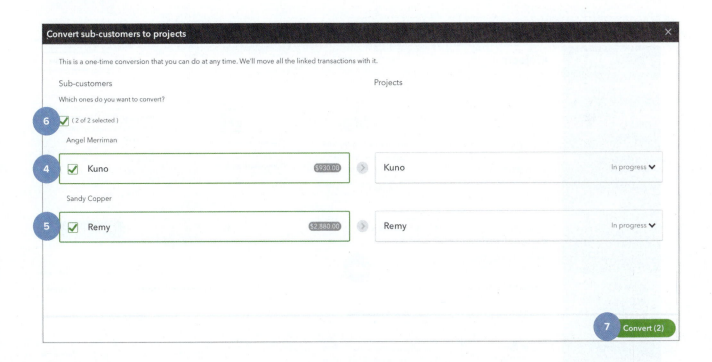

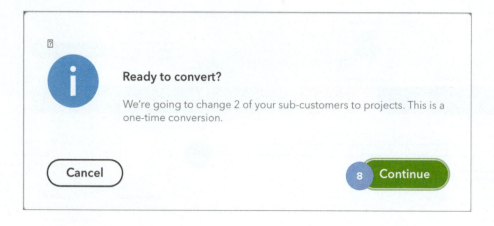

Ready to convert?

We're going to change 2 of your sub-customers to projects. This is a one-time conversion.

Cancel

8 Continue

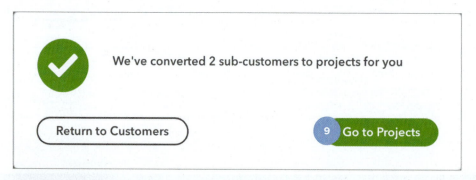

We've converted 2 sub-customers to projects for you

Return to Customers

9 Go to Projects

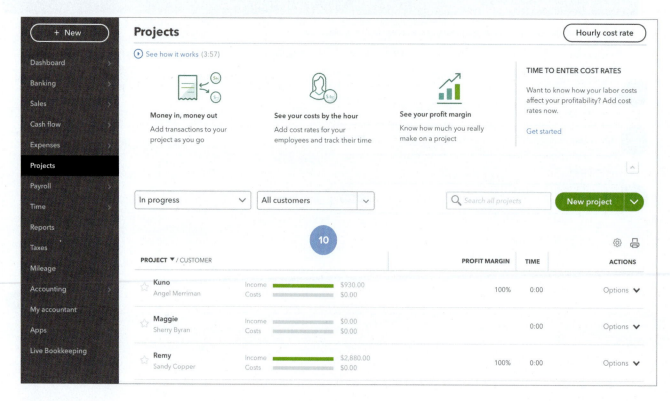

+ New

- Dashboard
- Banking
- Sales
- Cash flow
- Expenses
- Projects
- Payroll
- Time
- Reports
- Taxes
- Mileage
- Accounting
- My accountant
- Apps
- Live Bookkeeping

Projects

Hourly cost rate

⊙ See how it works (3:57)

Money in, money out
Add transactions to your project as you go

See your costs by the hour
Add cost rates for your employees and track their time

See your profit margin
Know how much you really make on a project

TIME TO ENTER COST RATES
Want to know how your labor costs affect your profitability? Add cost rates now.

Get started

In progress | All customers | 🔍 Search all projects | New project ⌄

10

PROJECT ▼ / CUSTOMER			PROFIT MARGIN	TIME	ACTIONS
☆ **Kuno** Angel Merriman	Income Costs	$930.00 $0.00	100%	0:00	Options ⌄
☆ **Maggie** Sherry Byran	Income Costs	$0.00 $0.00		0:00	Options ⌄
☆ **Remy** Sandy Copper	Income Costs	$2,880.00 $0.00	100%	0:00	Options ⌄

From the Projects screen we can:

1 View projects by **status: In progress, Completed, or Canceled**

2 View projects by **customer**

3 Add **New projects**

4 Enter **Hourly cost rate** to be used for time worked on projects

5 Select **Action options** for a project: **Edit this project, Mark as completed, Mark as canceled, Delete**

6 Select **Project: Remy**

7 From the Project screen, we can select **Add to the project** to:
- Create Invoice
- Receive payment
- Enter Expense
- Create Estimate
- Enter Time
- Enter Bill
- Create Purchase Order

8 Select **Overview** tab to view a summary of income, costs, and profit

9 From the Overview, we can add hourly time cost, expenses, or bills by clicking on those selections

10 Select **Transactions** tab to view transactions related to the project. This view can assist businesses in seeing where they are making money and where they are spending money.

11 Select **Time Activity** tab to track time for the project

12 Select **Project Reports** tab to view:
- Project Profitability
- Time cost by employee or vendor
- Unbilled time and expenses

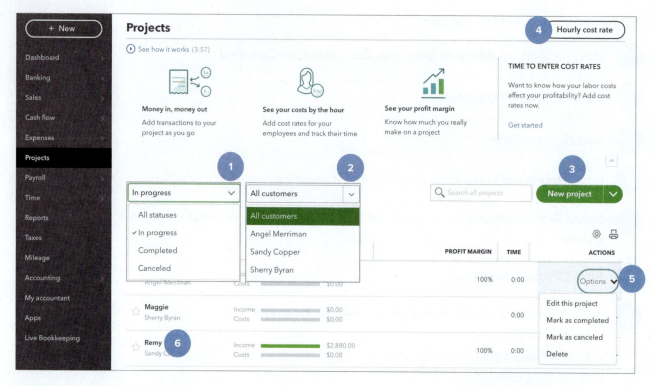

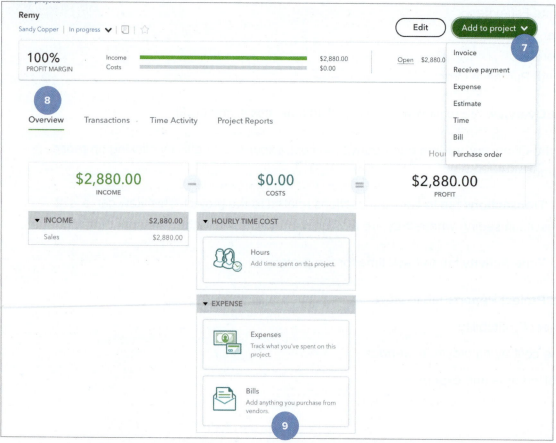

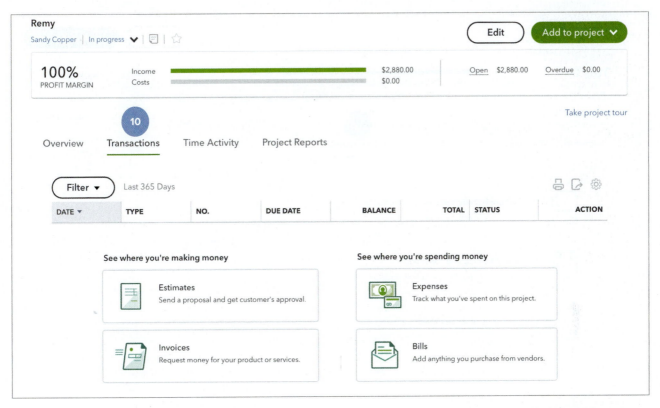

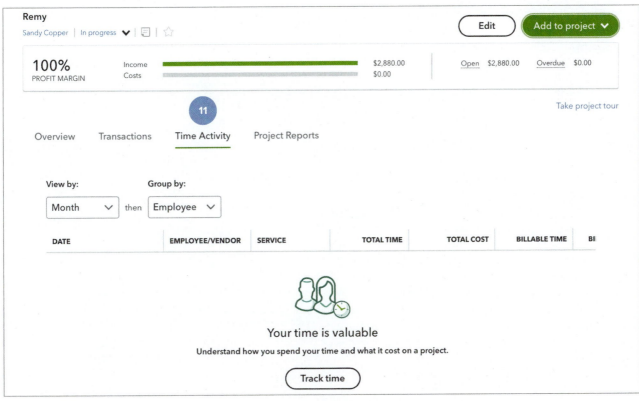

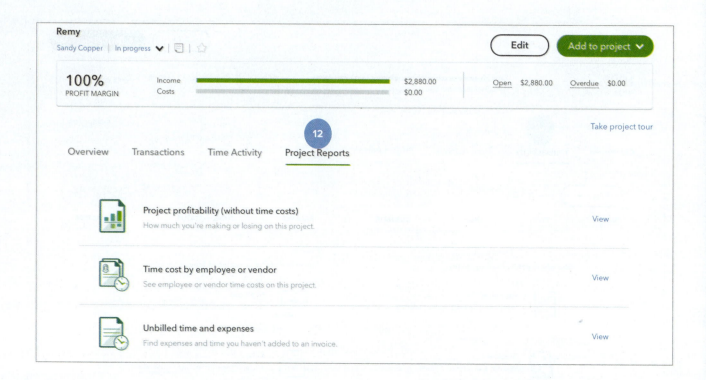

Section 5.6

PRODUCTS AND SERVICES LIST

The Products and Services List collects information about the products and services sold to customers. The Products and Services List is a time-saving feature so that we do not have to continually re-enter the same products and services information each time we enter a new sales transaction.

QBO uses four types of products and services:

1. **Inventory.** Products that we sell for which we track quantities, such as dog hammocks that Mookie The Beagle Concierge sells.
2. **Non-inventory.** Products that we sell but we don't need to track the quantity of the product. An example would be vet supplies that Mookie The Beagle Concierge uses when providing pet care services.
3. **Service.** Services that we provide to customers, such as pet care services that Mookie The Beagle Concierge provides.
4. **Bundle.** A bundle is a collection of products and services that we sell together as a bundle. For example, Mookie The Beagle Concierge might provide a bundle of pet care products and pet care services.

In this chapter we will focus on services, and in Chapter 7 we will focus on products.

Two ways that we can update the Products and Services List are:

1. *Before* entering transactions
2. *While* entering transactions

UPDATE PRODUCTS AND SERVICES LIST BEFORE ENTERING TRANSACTIONS

Before entering transactions, we can update the Products and Services List as follows.

1. Select **Sales** on the Navigation Bar

2. Select **Product and Services** tab

3   To enter new products or services, select **New**

4   Select **Product/Service Type: Service**

5   Enter **Service Name: On Site Vet Service**

6   Enter SKU or other product/service identification number. In this case, leave **SKU blank.**

7   If available, attach a product/service photo. In this case leave **Photo blank.**

8   Select **Product/Service Category: Pet Wellness**

9   Select **I sell this product/service to my customers**

10   Enter **Description: Vet concierge service provided on site**

11   Enter **Sales Price/Rate: 150.00**

12   Select **Income Account: 4200 Sales**. This selection connects the service item with the appropriate account in the Chart of Accounts. When this service is recorded on an Invoice, for example, then the amount will be recorded in the 4200 Sales account.

13   Under Purchasing Information **uncheck I purchase this product/service from a vendor**

14   Select **Save and close**

15   To edit the Vet Visit Description, so it is consistent with the new Service item just added, from the Products and Services List, select **Edit** for **Vet Visit**

16   Update **Description: Pet transport for vet visit**

17   Select **Save and close**

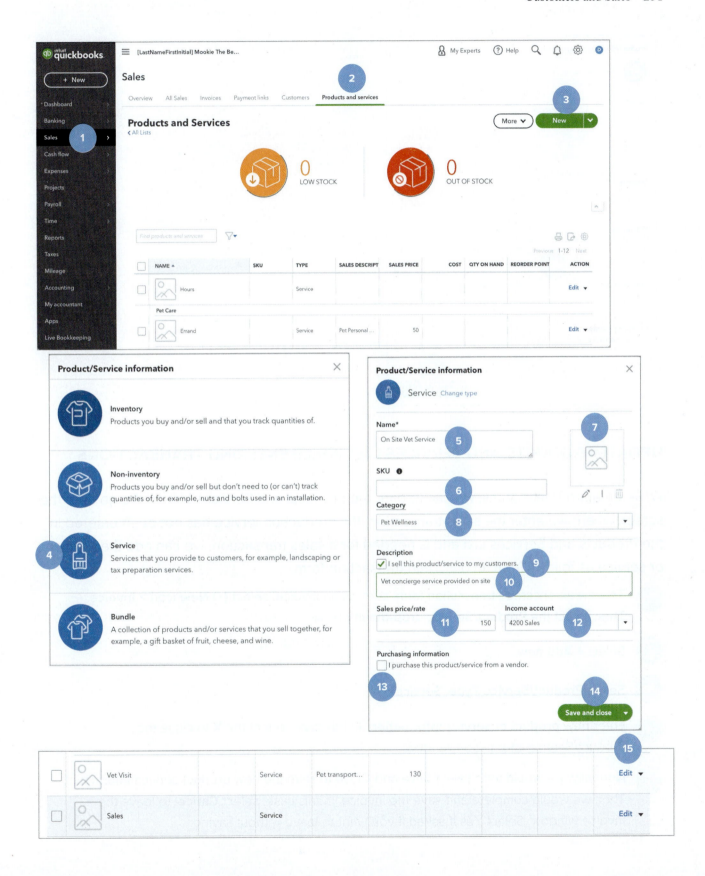

UPDATE PRODUCTS AND SERVICES LIST WHILE ENTERING TRANSACTIONS

While entering transactions, we can update the Products and Services List on the go from the screen where we enter the sales transaction. If a product or service has not been entered in the Products and Services List and is needed for a sales transaction, we can add the product or service as follows from an onscreen transaction form.

1 To view an onscreen transaction form, such as an Invoice, select **(+) New** icon > **Invoice**. Then select the **Product/Service drop-down arrow**.

2 Select **+ Add new**

3 Select **Product/Service Type: Service**

4 Enter **new product or service information**. In this case, select the **X** to close the Product/Service information window.

5 Normally, we would then select Save and Close to save the new product/service information. Then we would complete and save the Invoice. In this case, select **Cancel** to leave the Invoice window. Select Yes if asked if you want to leave without saving.

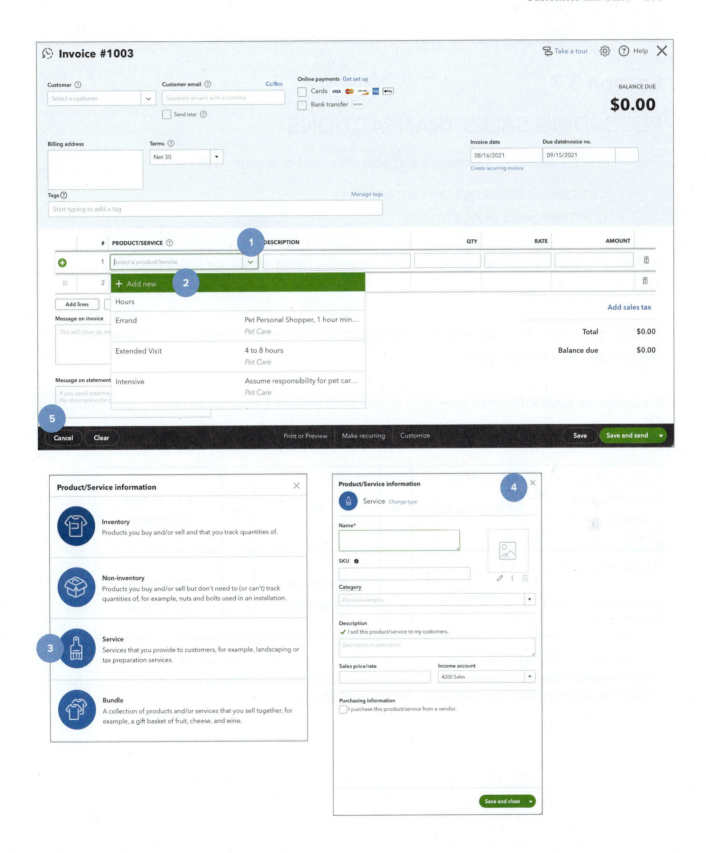

Section 5.7

RECORDING SALES TRANSACTIONS

Two main ways to record customers and sales transactions using QBO are:

- Customer Sales using Sales Receipts
- Customer Sales using Invoices

When using QBO, customer sales must be recorded using either the Sales Receipts form or the Invoice form.

If a customer *pays at the same time* the product or service is provided, then a Sales Receipt can be used to record the sale.

If a customer *pays later after receiving products or services*, then an Invoice is used to record the sale. The customer payment is recorded later using the Receive Payments form.

Customer pays at the same time product or service is provided	**Sales Receipt**	➡		➡		➡	**Checking Account**
Customer pays later after receiving products or services	**Invoice**	➡	**Receive Payment**		➡		**Checking Account**

> **Bank deposits other than customer sales** are recorded using the Bank Deposit form. Bank deposits not related to customer sales were covered in the previous chapter.

Section 5.8

CUSTOMER SALES RECEIPTS

If a customer's payment is *received at the same time* the product or service is provided, we can record the customer sale using the Sales Receipt form. The customer payment may consist of cash, check, or credit card.

When using Sales Receipts to record customer sales:

1 Select **(+) New** icon

2 Create **Sales Receipt** to record the customer sale for the product given and the customer payment received in the form of cash, check, or credit card. If the customer payment is deposited to the Checking account on the Sales Receipt form, this is the last step. If Undeposited Funds is selected on the Sales Receipt, then complete the next step to transfer the customer payment from the Undeposited Funds account to the Checking account.

3 Create **Bank Deposit** to move customer payment from the Undeposited Funds account to the Checking account. This step is required only if Undeposited Funds is selected on the Sales Receipt. Otherwise, this step is not necessary.

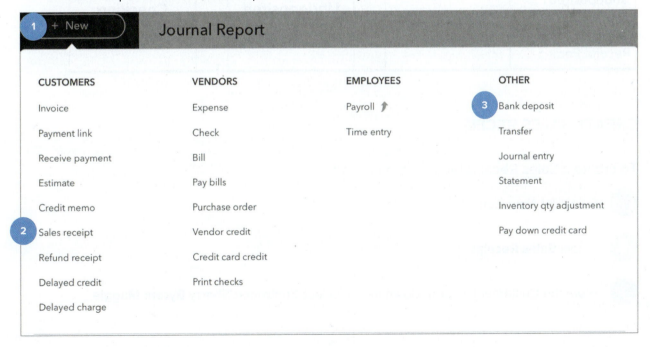

On the Sales Receipt form, we have two options for Deposit to selections as shown on the following diagram.

1. If we select **Deposit to: Checking account**, then the customer payment is recorded directly in the Checking account.
2. If we select **Deposit to: Undeposited Funds account**, the funds are recorded in the Undeposited Funds account. Then the funds must be transferred from the Undeposited Funds account to the Checking account using the Bank Deposit form. This option requires an extra step, transferring the funds from the Undeposited Funds account to the Checking account. The reason that some businesses might use this option is because they may have recorded several sales receipts in one day that are deposited in a single bank deposit. This option permits them to group the sales receipts together into a single bank deposit so their QBO deposit amounts will then match the deposit amounts shown by the bank.

Deposit to: **Checking Account** Selected on Sales Receipt Form	**Sales Receipt**	➡		➡		➡	**Checking Account**
Deposit to: **Undeposited Funds Account** Selected on Sales Receipt Form	**Sales Receipt**	➡	**Undeposited Funds Account**	➡	**Checking Account**		

CREATE SALES RECEIPT

To create a Sales Receipt for a customer sale:

1. Select **(+) New** icon

2. Select **Sales Receipt**

3. From the Customer List drop-down menu, select **Customer: Sherry Byran: Maggie**

4 Enter **Sales Receipt Date: 01/18/2023**

5 Enter **Payment Method: Check**

6 If Payment Method is Check, enter the customer Check No. as Reference No. In this case, enter **Reference No.: 1800**.

7 Select Deposit to account from the drop-down list. If this deposit will be bundled with other deposits, then select Undeposited Funds, and after completing the Sales Receipt, enter a Bank Deposit to move the funds from Undeposited Funds to the Checking account. If this deposit is not bundled with other deposits, then select the appropriate Checking account from the drop-down list. The funds are deposited directly to the Checking account selected and we do not enter a separate Bank Deposit. In this case, since we want to bundle this deposit with other deposits, select **Deposit to: 1600 Undeposited Funds**.

8 From the Product/Service List drop-down menu, select **Product/Service**: **Pet Care: Short Visit**

9 If the Description does not autofill, enter **Description: Pet Check to check on status of pet, let pet out, and short walk, 1 hour minimum**

10 Enter **Quantity (QTY): 2**

11 Rate should autofill as: **Rate: 40.00**

12 **Amount** should calculate automatically

13 Enter **Message displayed on sales receipt**: **Pet care services**

14 Add **Attachments**, such as source documents associated with the sales receipt, if any

15 Select **Save** and leave the Sales Receipt form open

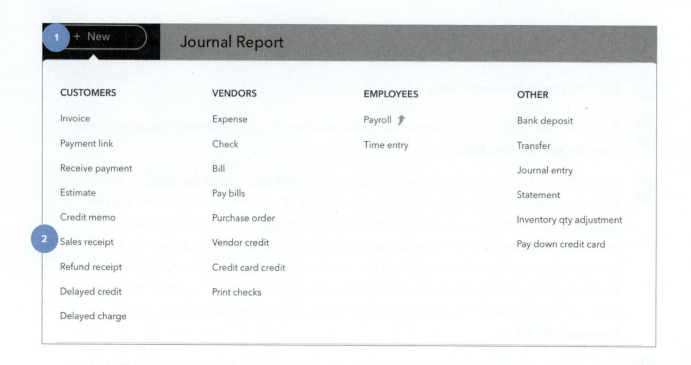

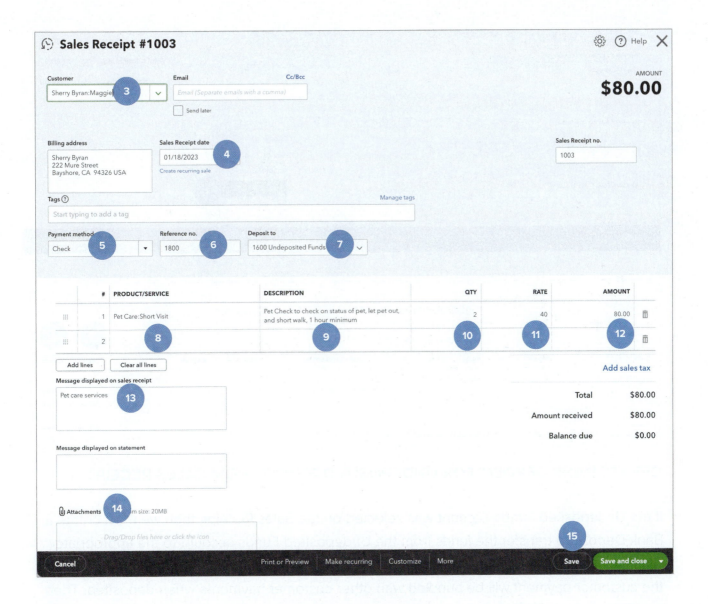

To view the Transaction Journal for the Sales Receipt we just created:

1 From the Sales Receipt window just saved, select **More**

2 Select **Transaction Journal**

3 In the journal entry recorded behind the screen for the Sales Receipt, notice the **Debit** to 1600 Undeposited Funds (Other Current Assets) for $80.00

4 In the journal entry notice the **Credit** to 4200 Sales account for $80.00

CREATE BANK DEPOSIT FOR UNDEPOSITED FUNDS FROM SALES RECEIPT

If the Undeposited Funds account was selected on the Sales Receipt, then we must create a Bank Deposit to transfer the funds from the Undeposited Funds account to the appropriate Checking account. Sometimes the Undeposited Funds account is used on the Sales Receipt if the customer payment will be bundled with other customer payments when deposited. Then our QBO deposit totals will correspond to the deposit total shown by the bank.

> **If we selected Undeposited Funds on the Sales Receipt,** we *must* create a bank deposit to transfer the funds from the Undeposited Funds account to the appropriate bank account. Otherwise, the funds will remain in the Undeposited Funds account and our QBO Checking account will not reflect the correct balance.

> **If we selected a specific bank account, such as Checking account, on the Sales Receipt,** we do *not* need to create a separate bank deposit. We have already recorded the deposit of the customer payment in the bank account.

To record a bank deposit related to a customer sale when Undeposited Funds was selected on the Sales Receipt:

1. Select **(+) New** icon

2. Under Other column, select **Bank Deposit**

3. Select **Account: 1001 Checking**

4. Enter **Date: 01/18/2023**

5. The Select the Payments Included in This Deposit section lists customer payments received but not deposited yet. The customer payments listed are undeposited funds that have been recorded as received but not yet deposited in the bank. **Select the Payments Included in this Deposit: Sherry Byran: Maggie**.

6. Enter **Payment Method: Check**

7. Verify **Amount** is correct

8. If there were additional funds to deposit that had not been recorded using the Sales Receipts form or the Invoice form, then those funds could be listed in the Add Funds to This Deposit section. In this case, leave the **Add Funds to This Deposit** section **blank**.

9. Select **Save and close**

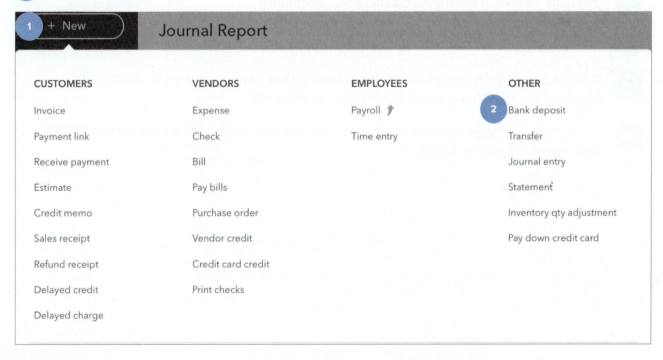

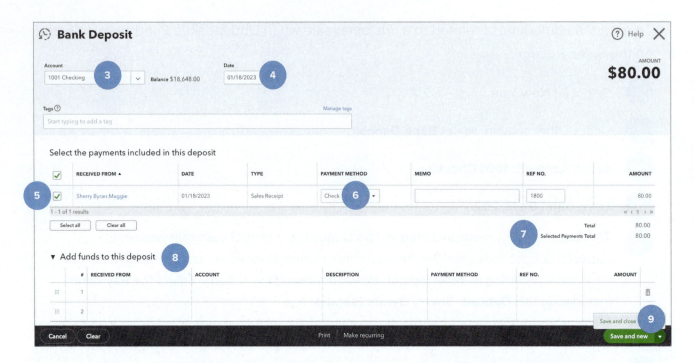

To view the Transaction Journal for the Bank Deposit we just created:

1 From the Tool Bar, select the **Search icon**

2 Under Recent Transactions, select the **Deposit** that we just entered

3 From the bottom of the Bank Deposit form, select **More**

4 Select **Transaction Journal**

5 In the journal entry recorded behind the screen for the Deposit, notice the **Debit** to 1001 Checking account for the total deposit amount of $80.00

6 In the journal entry recorded behind the screen for the Deposit, notice the **Credit** to 1600 Undeposited Funds for $80.00

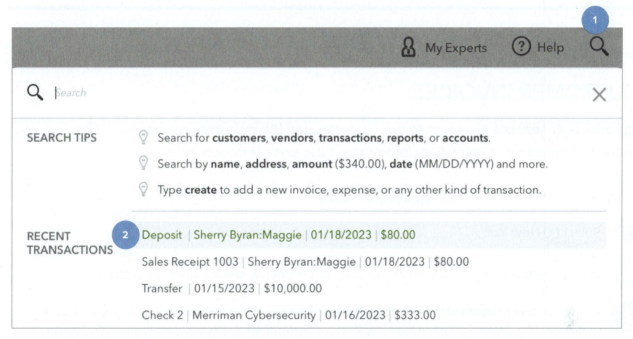

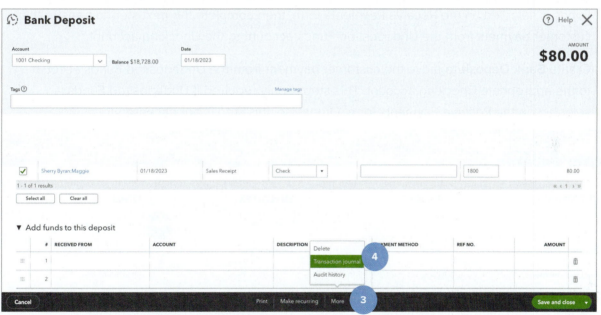

Section 5.9

CUSTOMER INVOICES

If products or services are given to the customer and the customer will pay later, then we use an Invoice instead of a Sales Receipt to record the sales transaction.

When using an Invoice to record customer sales:

1 Select **(+) New** icon

2 Create **Invoice** to record the customer sale for product or service given to customer

3 Create **Receive Payment** to record customer payment. If the customer payment is deposited to the Checking account on the Receive Payment form, this is the last step. If Undeposited Funds is selected on the Receive Payments form, then complete the next step to transfer the customer payment from the Undeposited Funds account to the Checking account.

4 Create **Bank Deposit** to move the customer payment from the Undeposited Funds account to the appropriate Checking account. This step is only required if Undeposited Funds is selected on the Receive Payments form. Otherwise, this step is not necessary.

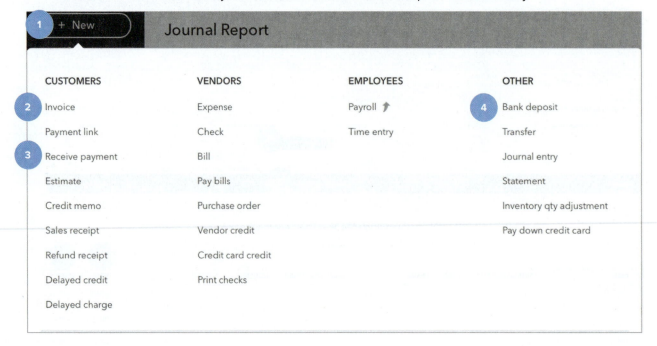

On the Receive Payments form, we have two options for Deposit to selections as shown on the following diagram.

1. If we select **Deposit to: Checking account**, then the customer payment is recorded directly in the Checking account.

2. If we select **Deposit to: Undeposited Funds account**, the funds are recorded in the Undeposited Funds account. Then the funds must be transferred from the Undeposited Funds account to the Checking account using the Bank Deposit form. This option requires an extra step, transferring the funds from the Undeposited Funds account to the Checking account. The reason that some businesses might use this option is because they may have recorded several customer payments that are deposited in a single bank deposit. This option permits them to group the customer payments together into a single bank deposit so their QBO deposit amounts will then match the deposit amounts shown by the bank.

Deposit to: **Checking Account** Selected on Receive Payment Form	Invoice	Receive Payment	➡	➡	➡	Checking Account
Deposit to: **Undeposited Funds Account** Selected on Receive Payment Form	Invoice	Receive Payment	➡	Undeposited Funds Account	➡	Checking Account

CREATE INVOICE

An Invoice is used to record sales when the customer will pay later. An Invoice is a bill that contains detailed information about the products and services provided to a customer.

Sandy Copper needs MTB Concierge to pick up Remy and take her to a follow-up vet visit. To create an Invoice:

1   Select **(+) New** icon

2   Select **Invoice**

3 From the Customer List drop-down menu, select **Customer: Sandy Copper: Remy**

4 Select **Terms: Net 30**

5 Enter **Invoice Date: 01/18/2023**

6 Verify **Due Date**

7 From the Product/Service List drop-down menu, select **Product/Service: Pet Wellness: Vet Visit**

8 If the Description does not autofill, enter **Description: Pet transport for vet visit**

9 Enter **Quantity (QTY): 1**

10 The **Rate** should autofill: **130.00**

11 Verify **Amount** is correct

12 Select **Save** and leave the Invoice form open

1 + New

Journal Report

CUSTOMERS	VENDORS	EMPLOYEES	OTHER
2 Invoice	Expense	Payroll 🔥	Bank deposit
Payment link	Check	Time entry	Transfer
Receive payment	Bill		Journal entry
Estimate	Pay bills		Statement
Credit memo	Purchase order		Inventory qty adjustment
Sales receipt	Vendor credit		Pay down credit card
Refund receipt	Credit card credit		
Delayed credit	Print checks		
Delayed charge			

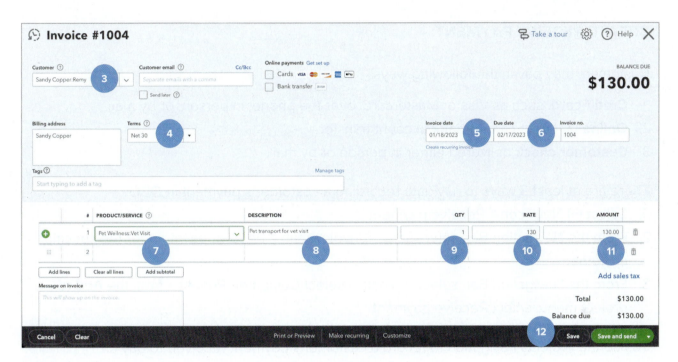

To view the Transaction Journal for the Invoice we just created:

1 From the Invoice window just saved, select **More**

2 Select **Transaction Journal**

3 In the journal entry recorded behind the screen for the Invoice, notice the **Debit** to the 1100 Accounts Receivable account for $130.00

4 In the journal entry notice the **Credit** to the 4200 Sales account for $130.00

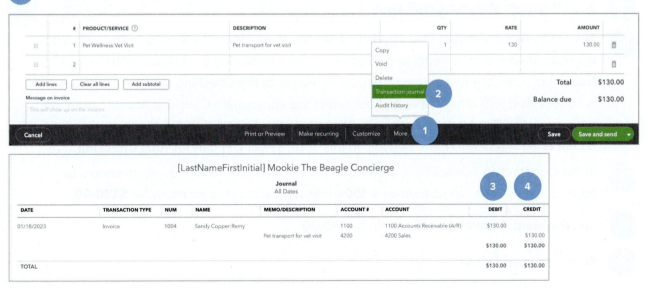

CREATE RECEIVE PAYMENT

Customers may pay in the following ways:

1. **Credit card**, such as Visa or Mastercard, over the phone, in person, or by mail.
2. **Online** by credit card or bank account transfer.
3. **Customer check** delivered either in person or by mail.

There are at least 3 ways to navigate recording a customer's payment in QBO:

1. Select (+) New icon > Receive payment
2. From the Navigation Bar, select Sales > Invoices tab > Receive payment for the specific customer
3. From the Navigation Bar, select Projects > select Customer: Project > from the Add to project menu, select Receive payment

To use the Projects navigation to record a customer's payment received to pay an outstanding Invoice:

1 From the Navigation Bar, select **Projects**

2 Select **Remy**

3 From the Add to project drop-down menu, select **Receive payment**

4 Enter **Payment Date: 01/18/2023**

5 Enter **Payment Method: Credit card**

6 Select Deposit to account from the drop-down list. If this deposit will be bundled with other deposits, then select Undeposited Funds and after completing the Invoice, enter a Bank Deposit to move the funds from Undeposited Funds to the Checking account. If this deposit is not bundled with other deposits, then select the appropriate Checking account from the drop-down list. The funds are deposited directly to the Checking account selected and we do not enter a separate Bank Deposit. In this case, select **Deposit to: 1001 Checking**.

7 In the Outstanding Transactions section, select the Invoice to which payment should be applied. In this case, select **Invoice # 1004** that we just created for Remy for **$130.00**.

8 The **Payment Amount** should autofill for **130.00**

9 Select **Save and close**

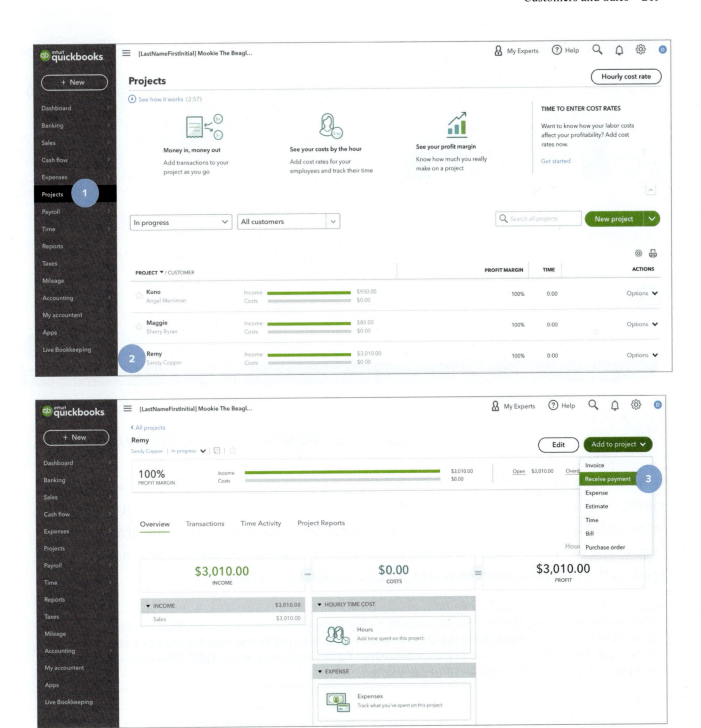

CREATE BANK DEPOSIT FOR UNDEPOSITED FUNDS FROM RECEIVE PAYMENT

If the Undeposited Funds account was selected on the Receive Payment form, then we must create a Bank Deposit to transfer the funds from the Undeposited Funds account to the appropriate Checking account. Sometimes Undeposited Funds is used on the Invoice if the customer payment will be bundled with other customer payments when deposited. Then our totals will correspond to the bank deposit total shown by the bank.

> **If we selected the Undeposited Funds account on the Receive Payment form,** we *must* create a bank deposit to transfer the funds from the Undeposited Funds account to the appropriate bank account. Otherwise, the funds will remain in the Undeposited Funds account and our QBO Checking account will not reflect the correct balance.

> **If we selected a specific bank account, such as Checking account, on the Receive Payment form,** we do *not* need to create a separate bank deposit. We have already recorded the deposit of the customer payment in the bank account.

To record a bank deposit related to a customer sale when the Undeposited Funds account was selected on the Receive Payment form:

1 Select **(+) New** icon

2 Under Other column, select **Bank Deposit**. Complete the steps to record the bank deposit and transfer funds from the Undeposited Funds account to the Checking account as described under the Sales Receipts section of this chapter.

3 This completes the chapter activities. If you are ready to proceed to the chapter exercises at this time, leave your browser open with your QBO company displayed. If you will be completing the chapter exercises at a later time, you can close your browser.

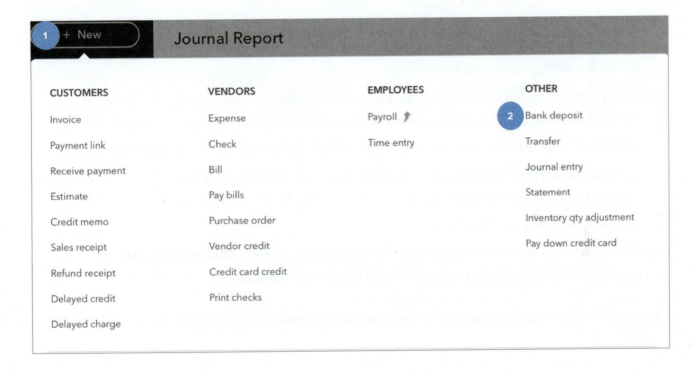

Section 5.10

ACCOUNTING ESSENTIALS
Customer Sales and Accounts Receivable

Accounting Essentials summarize important foundational accounting knowledge you may find useful when using QBO

What are Accounts Receivable?

- Accounts Receivable are amounts that a customer owes our business. When our business makes a credit sale, our business provides goods and services to a customer in exchange for the customer's promise to pay later.

- When a credit sale is recorded on an Invoice, QuickBooks Online increases (debits) Account Receivable—an amount to be received from the customer in the future. When the customer's payment is received, the Account Receivable account is reduced (credited).

- Sometimes the customer breaks the promise and does not pay. So a business should have a credit policy to ensure that credit is extended only to customers who are likely to keep their promise and pay their bills.

- After credit has been extended, a business needs to track accounts receivable to determine if accounts are being collected in a timely manner.

How can a business track accounts receivable to make certain customers are paying on time?

- Accounts Receivable Aging reports provide information about which customers owe our business money, how much the customer owes, and the age of the customer accounts receivable balances.

- In general, the older an account, the less likely the customer will pay the account. So it is important to monitor the age of accounts receivable and take action to collect old accounts.

What happens if a customer does not pay the accounts receivable balance?

- When a customer does not pay the accounts receivable balance, then it is called a bad debt or uncollectible account.

- At the time a credit sale occurs, it is recorded as an increase to sales and an increase to accounts receivable.

- Occasionally a company is unable to collect a customer payment and must write off the customer's account as a bad debt or uncollectible account. When an account is uncollectible, the account receivable is written off or removed from the accounting records.

- There are two different methods that can be used to account for bad debts:
  1. **Direct write-off method.** This method records bad debt expense when it becomes apparent that the customer is not going to pay the amount due. If the direct write-off method is used, the customer's uncollectible account receivable is removed and bad debt expense is recorded at the time a specific customer's account becomes uncollectible. The direct write-off method is used for tax purposes.
  2. **Allowance method.** The allowance method estimates bad debt expense and establishes an allowance or reserve for uncollectible accounts. When using the allowance method, uncollectible accounts expense is estimated in advance of the write-off. The estimate can be calculated as a percentage of sales or as a percentage of accounts receivable. (For example, 2% of credit sales might be estimated to be uncollectible.) This method should be used if uncollectible accounts have a material effect on the company's financial statements used by investors and creditors.

- To record a bad debt, make a journal entry to remove the customer's account receivable (credit Accounts Receivable) and debit either Bad Debt Expense (direct write-off method) or the Allowance for Uncollectible Accounts (allowance method).

Practice Quiz 5

Q5.1

When a sale is recorded on an Invoice, QBO records a:

a. Debit (increase) to cash
b. Credit (increase) to owner's contribution
c. Debit (increase) to accounts receivable
d. Credit (increase) to accounts payable

Q5.2

To enter a sales transaction with payment to be received later:

a. From the Navigation Bar, select Vendors
b. From the Navigation Bar, select Expenses
c. From the (+) New icon, select Invoice
d. From the Gear icon, select Sales Transactions

Q5.3

When a customer pays cash at the time of sale, what do you record?

a. A sales receipt
b. An invoice
c. A purchase order
d. A thank you note

Q5.4

When a customer purchases products or services but does not pay at the point of sale, what do you record?

a. A sales receipt
b. An invoice
c. A purchase order
d. A reminder

Q5.5

We can update the Customers List at which of the following two points?

a. Before entering transactions
b. While entering transactions
c. After entering transactions

Q5.6

Which of the following two are Customers and Sales transactions?

a. Invoice
b. Receive Payment
c. Pay Bills
d. Check

Q5.7

Types of products and services on the Products and Services List include which two of the following?

a. Service
b. Batch
c. Inventory
d. All of the above

Q5.8

Which of the following products and services types track quantities?

a. Service items
b. Inventory items
c. Non-inventory items
d. None of the above

Q5.9

When preparing a Sales Receipt, if we select Deposit to Undeposited Funds, then we must:

a. Create a Bank Deposit to move the customer payment from Undeposited Funds to the Checking account
b. No further action is required
c. Create a second Sales Receipt depositing the amount to the Checking account
d. Create a subsequent Invoice depositing the amount to the Checking account

Q5.10

When preparing a Sales Receipt, if we select Deposit to a Checking account, then we:

a. Create a Bank Deposit to move the customer payment from the Checking account to the Undeposited Funds account
b. No further action is required
c. Create a second Sales Receipt depositing the amount to the Checking account
d. Create a subsequent Invoice depositing the amount to the Checking account

Q5.11

Indicate the order in which the following onscreen customers and sales transaction forms typically should be prepared:

a. Invoice > Bank Deposit > Receive Payment
b. Invoice > Sales Receipt > Bank Deposit
c. Invoice > Receive Payment > Bank Deposit
d. None of the above

Q5.12

Which of the following reports provides information about which customers owe money to a business?

a. Profit & Loss
b. Balance Sheet
c. Statement of Cash Flows
d. Accounts Receivable Aging

Q5.13

Accounts Receivable (A/R) are:

a. Amounts totaling the net worth of a company
b. Amounts paid to owners
c. Amounts that customers owe your business
d. Amounts owed to others and are future obligations

Exercises 5

If necessary, sign in to your Mookie The Beagle Concierge QBO Company as follows:

1 Using a Chrome web browser, go to qbo.intuit.com

2 Enter **User ID** (the email address you used to set up your QBO Account)

3 Enter **Password** (the password you used to set up your QBO Account)

4 Select **Sign in**

E5.1 Customers and Sales Transactions

Match the following customers and sales transactions with the description of the transaction.

Customers and Sales Transaction Descriptions

a. The onscreen form used when we need to record a credit, or reduction, in the amount the customer is charged.

b. An onscreen form used to record a sales transaction when the customer pays at the time of sale when the product or service is provided to the customer.

c. A sales transaction recorded when the product or service is provided to the customer, and the customer promises to pay later.

d. This onscreen form is used when we give the customer a refund.

e. This onscreen form is used to record the transaction when the customer pays its account with cash, check, credit card, or online payment.

f. A form used to record a pending credit to a customer that will occur at a specified future date.

g. This onscreen form is used to record projected costs of products and services to be provided to a customer in the future.

h. An onscreen form used to record a pending charge to a customer that will occur at a specified future date.

Customers and Sales Transaction

1. Invoice
2. Receive Payment
3. Estimate
4. Credit Memo
5. Sales Receipt
6. Refund Receipt
7. Delayed Credit
8. Delayed Charge

E5.2 Sales Receipts Workflow

The Sales Receipts Workflow consists of a series of activities to record the customer transactions. Match the following activities in the Sales Receipts Workflow with the order in which the activities occur. Note: You may use an activity item more than once.

Sales Receipts Workflow Activities

- Bank Deposit
- Sales Receipt
- Undeposited Funds

Sales Receipts Workflow				
Deposit to: **Checking Account** Selected on Sales Receipt Form	1.a. _____	➡ ➡		➡ 1.b. _____
Deposit to: **Undeposited Funds Account** Selected on Sales Receipt Form	2.a. _____	➡ 2.b. _____		➡ 2.c. _____

E5.3 Invoice Workflow

The Invoice Workflow consists of a series of activities to record the customer transactions. Match the following activities in the Invoice Workflow with the order in which the activities occur. Note: You may use an activity item more than once.

Invoice Workflow Activities

- Bank Deposit
- Sales Receipt
- Undeposited Funds
- Receive Payment

Invoice Workflow						
Deposit to: **Checking Account** Selected on Receive Payment Form	1.a. _____	1.b. _____	➡	➡	➡	1.c. _____
Deposit to: **Undeposited Funds Account** Selected on Receive Payment Form	2.a. _____	2.b. _____	➡	2.c. _____	➡	2.d. _____

EM5.4 QBO Project

In appreciation for your efforts with QBO for his new company, Mookie The Beagle Concierge, Cy Walker surprises you with your own puppy, Ozzie, a curly apricot Goldendoodle with a bouncy, fun-loving, cheerful personality. Since you know Ozzie will need pet care, you sign him up as a client of Mookie The Beagle Concierge.

Add Ozzie as a Project linked to Customer: Your Name.

1. Your Name should already be entered in the Customers List, but if not, add Your Name to the Customers List as follows.
   a. From the Navigation Bar, select **Sales**
   b. Select **Customers** tab > **New customer**
   c. Enter **Customer Name: Your Name**

2. Add new project, Ozzie, linked to Customer: Your Name.
   a. From the Navigation Bar, select **Projects > New project**
   b. Enter **Project name: Ozzie**
   c. Select **Customer: Your Name**
   d. Select **Save**
   e. Return to the Projects List. Confirm that Ozzie is listed as a Project linked to Your Name.

3. How many projects now appear for MTB Concierge Projects?

EM5.5 Create Invoice and Receive Payment

Ozzie, your new Goldendoodle puppy, loves everyone, both canine and human. So you were just as surprised as Ozzie, when during his evening walk, an aggressive neighborhood dog gets in a scuffle with Ozzie, biting Ozzie on his backside.

When you see that Ozzie is bleeding, you use the Mookie The Beagle Concierge app urgent care alert for on-site vet care services. MTB Concierge dispatches a vet concierge immediately. After checking thoroughly for injuries, the vet concierge cleans, stitches, and bandages Ozzie's wounds, administering medication. Although happy that MTB Concierge could provide immediate care for Ozzie in his hour of need, when you calculate the cost of the vet visit, you wish you had purchased pet insurance for Ozzie to pay his medical bills.

1. Create an Invoice.
   a. From the Navigation Bar, select **Projects > Ozzie**
   b. From the Add to project menu, select **Invoice**
   c. Select Terms: **Due on receipt**
   d. Select Invoice **Date: 01/19/2023**
   e. Select **Product/Service: Pet Wellness: On Site Vet Service**
   f. Select hours as **QTY: 2**
   g. **Rate** and **Amount** should autofill
   h. What is the Balance Due for the invoice?
   i. Select **Save** and leave the Invoice displayed

2. View the Transaction Journal for the Invoice.
   a. From the bottom of the Invoice, select **More > Transaction Journal**
   b. What are the Account and Amount Debited?
   c. What are the Account and Amount Credited?

3. Create Receive Payment.
   a. From the Navigation Bar, select **Projects > Ozzie**
   b. From the Add to project menu, select **Receive Payment**
   c. Select **Payment Date: 01/20/2023**
   d. Select **Payment Method: Credit Card**
   e. Select **Deposit to: 1001 Checking**
   f. Select **Invoice** previously entered
   g. After selecting the Invoice, what is the Amount Received displayed?
   h. Select **Save and close**

4. View the Transaction Journal for Receive Payment.
   a. From the Navigation Bar, select **Sales > All Sales tab**
   b. From the Sales Transactions List, select the **Your Name: Ozzie Payment** just entered
   c. From the bottom of the Receive Payment, select **More > Transaction Journal**
   d. What are the Account and Amount Debited?
   e. What are the Account and Amount Credited?

EM5.6 Sales Receipt

Angel Merriman used the Mookie The Beagle Concierge app to schedule pet care for Kuno, her King Shepherd. Each Friday from 1 pm until 9 pm, Angel needs pet care for Kuno, starting on 01/14/2023. Kuno requires extra healthcare considerations, including medications, so the 8 hours of service provided would be at the Pet Wellness: Extended Wellness level. Because of the number of hours needed, Cy agrees to a discounted rate for Pet Wellness: Extended Wellness services. Angel paid in advance by check for 9 weeks of pet care services.

Complete the following for Mookie The Beagle Concierge to record a Sales Receipt for Angel.

1. Update customer information in the Customers List.
   a. From the Navigation Bar, select **Sales > Customers** tab
   b. Select **Angel Merriman > Edit**
   c. Enter the following customer information.

Email:	**kuno@www.com**
Mobile:	**415-555-0117**
Billing Address Street:	**86 University Avenue**
Billing Address City:	**Bayshore**
Billing Address State:	**CA**
Billing Address ZIP:	**94326**
Billing Address Country:	**USA**
Shipping Address:	**Same as billing address**

2. Create Sales Receipt.
    a. Select **(+) New icon > Sales Receipt**
    b. Select **Customer: Angel Merriman: Kuno**
    c. Select **Sales Receipt Date: 01/20/2023**
    d. Select **Payment Method: Check**
    e. Enter **Reference No.: 3033**
    f. Select **Deposit to: 1001 Checking**
    g. Select **Product/Service: Pet Wellness: Extended Wellness**
    h. Enter **QTY: 72**
    i. Enter **Rate: 50.00**
    j. What is the Total for the Sales Receipt?
    k. Select **Save** and leave the Sales Receipt displayed

3. View the Transaction Journal for the Sales Receipt.
    a. From the bottom of the Kuno Angel Sales Receipt, select **More > Transaction Journal**
    b. What are the Account and Amount Debited?
    c. What are the Account and Amount Credited?

EM5.7 Sales Receipt

Angel uses the Mookie The Beagle Concierge app to schedule pet care for Kuno, her King Shepherd, for the last weekend in January (01/29/2023 2 pm until 01/30/2023 11 pm) while she is running in a charity marathon. Because Kuno requires extra healthcare considerations, the service will be billed at Pet Wellness: Intensive Wellness rates.

1. Create Sales Receipt.
    a. Select **(+) New icon > Sales Receipt**
    b. Select **Customer: Angel Merriman: Kuno**
    c. Select **Sales Receipt Date: 01/29/2023**
    d. Select **Payment Method: Check**
    e. Enter **Reference No.: 3042**
    f. Select **Deposit to: 1001 Checking**
    g. Select **Product/Service: Pet Wellness: Intensive Wellness**
    h. Enter **QTY: 33**
    i. Enter **Rate: 90.00**
    j. What is the Total for the Sales Receipt?
    k. Select **Save** and leave the Sales Receipt displayed

2. View the Transaction Journal for the Sales Receipt.
   a. From the bottom of the Sales Receipt, select **More** > **Transaction Journal**
   b. What are the Account and Amount Debited?
   c. What are the Account and Amount Credited?

EM5.8 Invoice

Sandy Copper needs to work late at the office, much later than the time that doggie day care closes for her rescue dog, Remy. So Sandy Copper uses the Mookie The Beagle Concierge app to schedule a pickup from doggie day care to take Remy home and pick up dog food, which Sandy hasn't had time to buy because of her demanding work schedule.

So when Sandy is working late, she is pleased to have the Mookie The Beagle Concierge app to schedule the following pet care services.

- Pet Care: Transport 1 hour (pickup at doggie day care)
- Pet Care: Errand 1 hour (minimum) to obtain dog food
- Pet Care: Medium Visit 4 hours

Complete the following to record the Invoice for services provided.

1. Update customer information in the Customers List.
   a. From the Navigation Bar, select **Sales** > **Customers** tab
   b. Select **Sandy Copper** > **Edit**
   c. Enter the following customer information.

Display Name As:	**Sandy Copper**
Email:	**remy@www.com**
Mobile:	**415-555-4320**
Billing Address Street:	**720 Cuivre Drive**
Billing Address City:	**Bayshore**
Billing Address State:	**CA**
Billing Address ZIP:	**94326**
Billing Address Country:	**USA**
Shipping Address:	**Same as billing address**

   d. Select **Save**

2. Create an Invoice.
   a. From the Navigation Bar, select **Projects > Sandy Copper: Remy**
   b. From the Add a project menu, select: **Invoice**
   c. Select **Invoice Date: 01/20/2023**
   d. Select **Product/Service: Pet Care: Transport**
   e. Select **QTY: 1**
   f. **Rate** and **Amount** should autofill
   g. Select **Product/Service: Pet Care: Errand**
   h. Select **QTY: 1**
   i. **Rate** and **Amount** should autofill
   j. Select **Product/Service: Pet Care: Medium Visit**
   k. Select **QTY: 4**
   l. **Rate** and **Amount** should autofill
   m. What is the Balance Due for the invoice?
   n. Select **Save** and leave the Invoice displayed

3. View the Transaction Journal for the Invoice.
   a. From the bottom of the Invoice, select **More > Transaction Journal**
   b. What are the Account and Amount Debited?
   c. What are the Accounts and Amounts Credited?

EM5.9 Invoice

Sandy Copper learns thats she has to work late two evenings, once again much later than the time that doggie day care closes for her pet rescue dog, Remy. So Sandy Copper uses the Mookie The Beagle Concierge app to schedule a pickup from doggie day care to take Remy home and provide pet care services.

Sandy uses the Mookie The Beagle Concierge app to schedule the following pet care services for the next two evenings.

- Pet Care: Transport 1 hour (pickup at doggie day care)
- Pet Care: Medium Visit 4 hours
- Pet Care: Transport 1 hour (pickup at doggie day care)
- Pet Care: Extended Visit 5 hours

Complete the following to record the invoice for services provided.

1. Create an Invoice.
   a. From the Navigation Bar, select **Projects** > **Sandy Copper: Remy**
   b. From the Add a project menu, select: **Invoice**
   c. Select **Customer: Sandy Copper: Remy**
   d. Select **Invoice Date: 01/23/2023**
   e. Select **Product/Service: Pet Care: Transport**
   f. Select **QTY: 1**
   g. **Rate** and **Amount** should autofill
   h. Select **Product/Service: Pet Care: Medium Visit**
   i. Select **QTY: 4**
   j. **Rate** and **Amount** should autofill
   k. Select **Product/Service: Pet Care: Transport**
   l. Select **QTY: 1**
   m. **Rate** and **Amount** should autofill
   n. Select **Product/Service: Pet Care: Extended Visit**
   o. Select **QTY: 5**
   p. **Rate** and **Amount** should autofill
   q. What is the Balance Due for the invoice?
   r. Select **Save** and leave the Invoice displayed

2. View the Transaction Journal for the Invoice.
   a. From the bottom of the Invoice, select **More** > **Transaction Journal**
   b. What are the Account and Amount Debited?
   c. What are the Accounts and Amounts Credited?

EM5.10 Receive Payment

Record the payment that Mookie The Beagle Concierge receives from Sandy Copper in payment for services provided Remy.

1. Create Receive Payment.
   a. From the Navigation Bar, select **Projects** > **Sandy Copper: Remy**
   b. From the Add to project menu, select **Receive payment**
   c. Select **Payment Date: 01/23/2023**
   d. Select **Payment Method: Check**
   e. Select **Deposit to: 1600 Undeposited Funds**
   f. Select **Invoice # 1002**
   g. After selecting the Invoice, what is the Amount Received displayed?
   h. Select **Save and close**

2. View the Transaction Journal for Receive Payment.
    a. From the Navigation Bar, select **Sales** > **All Sales tab**
    b. From the Sales Transactions List, select the **Sandy Copper: Remy** payment just entered
    c. From the bottom of Receive Payment, select **More** > **Transaction Journal**
    d. What are the Account and Amount Debited?
    e. What are the Account and Amount Credited?

EM5.11 Bank Deposit

Record the bank deposit for Mookie The Beagle Concierge related to the Sandy Copper payment for the first services provided Remy.

1. Create Bank Deposit.
    a. Select **(+) New icon** > **Bank Deposit**
    b. Select **Account: 1001 Checking**
    c. Select **Date: 01/23/2023**
    d. **Select The Payments Included in This Deposit: Sandy Copper: Remy**
    e. What is the Selected Payments Total?
    f. Select **Save and close**

2. View the Transaction Journal for the Deposit.
    a. From the Navigation Bar, select **Accounting**
    b. From the Chart of Accounts, select **View Register** for the Checking account
    c. Select **Sandy Copper: Remy deposit** > **Edit**
    d. From the bottom of the Deposit, select **More** > **Transaction Journal**
    e. What are the Account and Amount Debited?
    f. What are the Account and Amount Credited?

EM5.12 Customers: Projects List

Cy requested a copy of Mookie The Beagle Concierge's current QBO Customers List with linked Projects in progress.

To export the Customers: Projects List:

1. From the Navigation Bar, select **Projects** > select **In progress** > select **All customers** > select **Printer icon** > on the Print screen, select **PDF** > **Save as PDF**

EM5.13 Accounts Receivable Aging Summary

Cy requested a copy of Mookie The Beagle Concierge's Accounts Receivable Aging Summary.

To export the Accounts Receivable Aging Summary:

1. From the Navigation Bar, select **Reports** > select **Standard** tab > in the Who owes you section, select **Accounts receivable aging summary**

2. For Report period, select: **Custom** > enter **as of: 01/31/2023**

3. Select **Report date: Days per aging period: 30** > **Number of periods: 4**

4. Select **Run report**

5. Select the **Export icon** > **Export to PDF**

6. What is the total amount of Accounts Receivable that are current?

Chapter 6

Vendors and Expenses

MOOKIE THE BEAGLE™ CONCIERGE

BACKSTORY

In addition to tracking customers and sales transactions, Mookie The Beagle™ Concierge also needs to track vendors and expenses transactions. Cy Walker realizes the importance of all expenses being recorded accurately so MTB Concierge does not miss any tax deductions. Also, Cy needs an efficient way to track when vendor bills are due so the bills are paid on time. Paying bills on time is crucial to building a good credit rating for his new business.

So your next step is to learn more about using QuickBooks Online for vendors and expenses transactions.

Chapter 6

LEARNING OBJECTIVES

Chapter 6 covers using QBO to record vendors and expenses transactions, such as purchasing from vendors, recording expenses, and paying bills. This chapter focuses on expenses and purchasing of services from vendors, such as Mookie The Beagle Concierge purchasing legal services from an attorney. The next chapter will focus on purchasing products that are inventory for resale to customers, such as MTB Concierge purchasing dog hammocks from vendors for resale to customers.

In this chapter, you will learn about the following topics:

- Navigating Vendors and Expenses Transactions
  - ‣ Navigation Bar
  - ‣ (+) New Icon
- Vendors List
  - ‣ Update Vendors List Before Entering Transactions
  - ‣ Update Vendors List While Entering Transactions
- Record Vendors Transactions Using Expense Form
- Record Vendors Transactions Using Check Form
- Record Vendors Transactions Using Bill > Pay Bills
  - ‣ Create Bill
  - ‣ Create Pay Bills
- Accounting Essentials: Vendors Transactions, Accounts Payable, and 1099s

> ⚠️ **QBO is updated on an ongoing basis. Updates that affect your text can be viewed as follows:**
> 1. **Go to www.My-QuickBooksOnline.com > QBO 3e > QBO 3e Updates, or**
> 2. **If you are using Connect or a digital ebook, you can find updates under Additional Student Resources (ASR). If you do not have access to Connect or the ebook, your instructor can provide you with ASR.**

Section 6.1

 ## QBO SATNAV

QBO SatNav is our satellite navigation for QuickBooks Online, assisting us in navigating QBO

Chapter 6 focuses on QBO Vendors and Expenses transactions, shown in the following QBO SatNav.

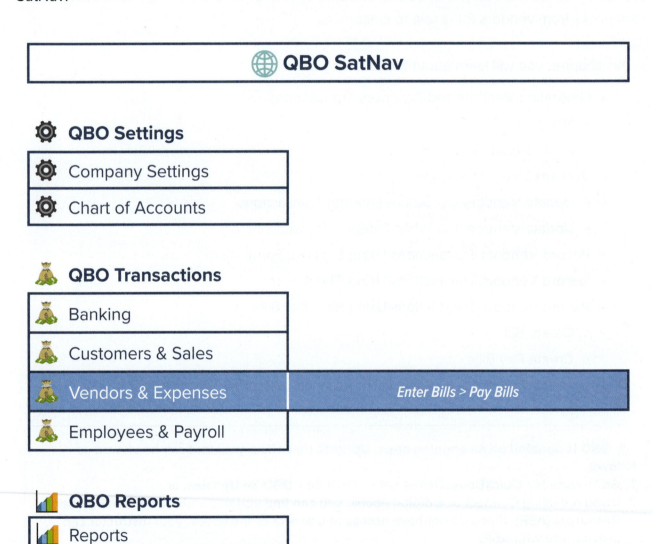

🌐 **QBO SatNav**

⚙ QBO Settings

⚙ Company Settings
⚙ Chart of Accounts

💰 QBO Transactions

💰 Banking	
💰 Customers & Sales	
💰 Vendors & Expenses	*Enter Bills > Pay Bills*
💰 Employees & Payroll	

📊 QBO Reports

📊 Reports

Section 6.2

NAVIGATING VENDORS AND EXPENSES TRANSACTIONS

Two different ways to navigate entering vendors and expenses transactions into QBO are:

1. Navigation Bar
2. (+) New icon

NAVIGATION BAR

To use the Navigation Bar to enter expenses transactions:

1 From the Navigation Bar, select **Expenses**

2 Select **Expenses** tab

3 From the Expenses Transactions window, select the drop-down arrow for **New transaction**

4 Select the type of **new transaction** to enter and complete the onscreen form for the new transaction

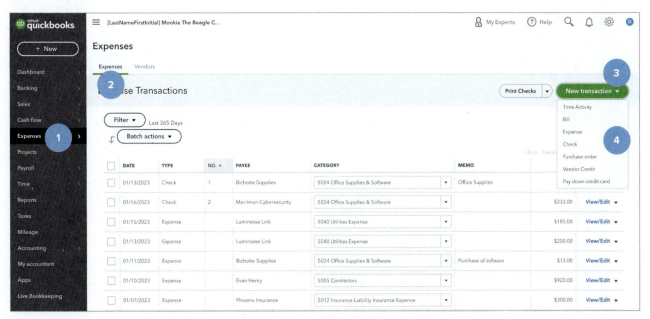

(+) NEW ICON

To use the (+) New icon to enter expenses transactions:

1   Select **(+) New** icon

2   Select the **new transaction** from the Vendors transactions shown

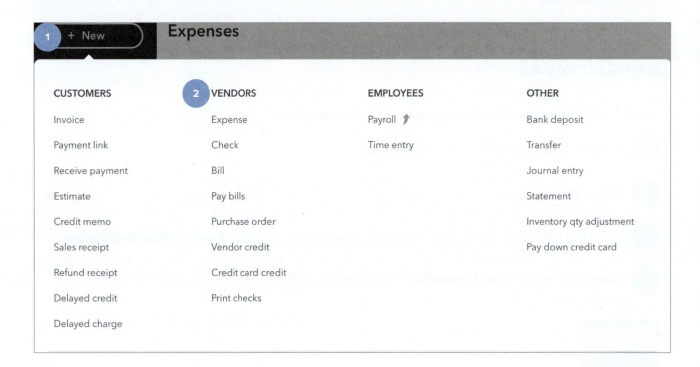

Section 6.3

TYPES OF VENDORS TRANSACTIONS

Types of vendor transactions that we can enter using QBO include:

- **Expense.** The Expense form can be used to record expenses that we pay for at the time we receive the product or service. We can pay using cash, credit card, or check.
- **Check.** The Check form is used when we write a check. Using the Check form was covered in Chapter 4, Banking.
- **Bill.** The Bill form is used to record services, such as utilities or accounting services. We use the Bill form to record a bill received (expense) and our obligation to pay the vendor later (accounts payable).
- **Pay Bills.** The Pay Bills form is used to select bills we want to pay.
- **Purchase Order.** A Purchase Order is used to track products ordered from vendors.
- **Vendor Credit.** The Vendor Credit form is used when a vendor gives us a refund, or reduction in the amount we owe the vendor, to our bill.
- **Credit Card Credit.** A Credit Card Credit form is used to record a credit, or reduction in charges by the vendor, to our credit card.

Section 6.4

VENDORS LIST

The QBO Vendors List permits us to collect and store information about a vendor, such as vendor name, address, and phone number. Then we can reuse the stored vendor information without re-entering it. After vendor information is entered in the Vendors List, when the specific vendor is selected on a vendor transaction form, such as a Check form, QBO automatically transfers the vendor information to the appropriate fields on the transaction form. This feature enables us to enter vendor information one time into QBO instead of re-entering the same vendor information each time a transaction form is created. Not only does this save time, but it also reduces errors.

QBO considers a vendor to be any individual or organization that provides products or services to our company. QBO considers all of the following to be vendors:

- Suppliers from whom we buy inventory or supplies
- Service companies that provide services to our company, such as cleaning services or landscaping services
- Financial institutions, such as banks, that provide financial services including checking accounts and loans
- Tax agencies, such as the IRS. The IRS is considered a vendor because we pay taxes to the IRS.
- Utility and telephone companies

Two ways that we can update the Vendors List are:

1. *Before* entering transactions
2. *While* entering transactions

UPDATE VENDORS LIST BEFORE ENTERING TRANSACTIONS

Before entering transactions, we can update the Vendors List from the QBO Navigation Bar as follows.

1   From the Navigation Bar, select **Expenses**

2   Select **Vendors** tab

3   To enter a new vendor, select **New vendor**

4   In the Vendor Information form, enter **First Name: Joseph**

5   Enter **Last Name: Asher**

6   Enter **Company Name: Joseph Leasing**

7   Select **Display Name as: Joseph Leasing**

8   Enter **Phone: 415-555-0412**

9   Enter **Address Street: 13 Appleton Drive**

10   Enter **Address City: Bayshore**

11   Enter **Address State: CA**

12   Enter **Address ZIP: 94326**

13   Enter **Address Country: USA**

14   Select **Terms: Net 15**

15   Select **Save**

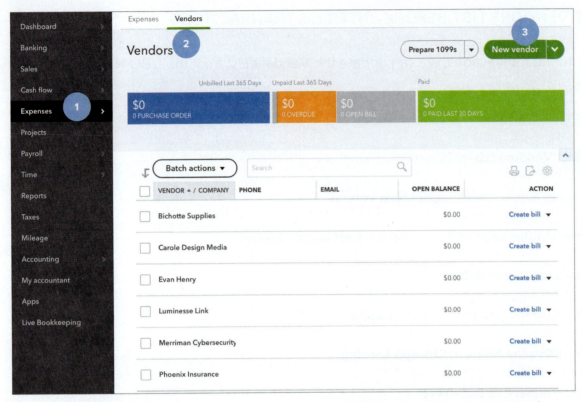

UPDATE VENDORS LIST WHILE ENTERING TRANSACTIONS

While entering transactions, we can update the Vendors List from the transaction form. If a vendor has not already been entered in the Vendors List before entering the transaction, then we can add the vendor as follows from the transaction form.

1 For example, to view an onscreen transaction form, such as an Expense, select **(+) New** icon > **Expense**. Then select **Payee drop-down arrow** > **+ Add new**.

2 In the New Name window, enter **Vendor Name**

3 Select **Type: Vendor**

4 Select **Details**

5 Enter **Vendor Information**

6 Select **Cancel** to close the Vendor Information window, then select **Cancel** again to close the Expense form. Select Yes if asked if you want to leave without saving.

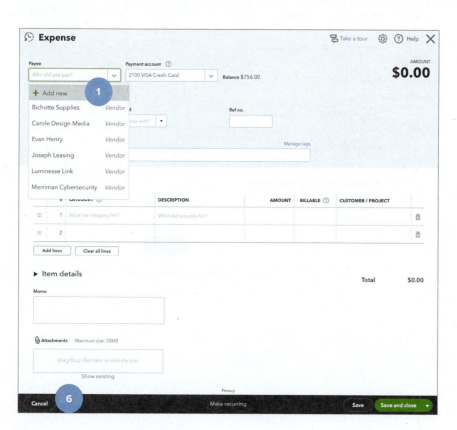

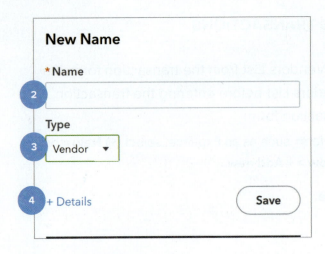

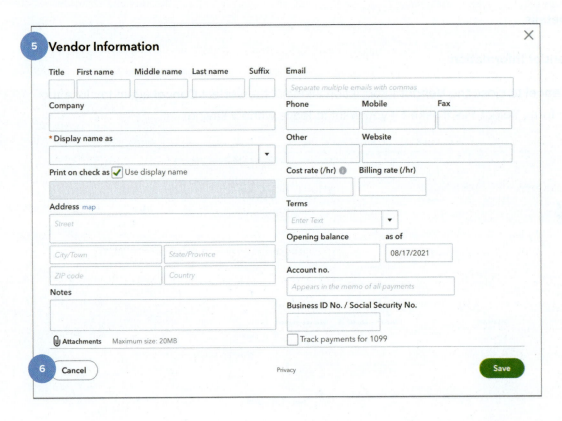

Section 6.5

RECORDING VENDORS TRANSACTIONS

After creating a Vendors List, we are ready to enter vendors and expenses transactions. Ways to record vendors and expenses transactions using QBO include using the following QBO onscreen forms in the following sequences:

- **Expense.** An Expense form can be used to record services purchased when the payment is made at the same time as the purchase. The payment can be by cash, credit card, or check. If the payment is to be made later, then Bill > Pay Bills should be used instead.
- **Check.** A Check form can be used to record services purchased when the payment is made by check at the same time the purchase is made. If the payment is to be made later, then Bill > Pay Bills should be used.
- **Bill > Pay Bills.** This approach is used to record services purchased, such as utilities or legal services when the bill is paid later. Use the Bill form to enter the bill, then use the Pay Bills form when the bill is paid.
- **Purchase Order > Bill > Pay Bills.** This approach is used to record the purchase of inventory items. The purchase order provides a record of the items ordered. After the bill for the items is received, the bill is entered. When the bill is paid, the pay bills form is used to record the bill payment.

This chapter focuses on entering vendor transactions for services using Expense, Check, and Bill forms. The next chapter covers how to record the purchase of inventory items using Purchase Orders, followed by entering bills and paying bills.

The following summary shows whether an Expense, Check, or Bill form should be used for recording various vendors transactions.

QBO Transaction Form For...	Expense Form	Check Form	Bill Form
Services purchased?	Yes	Yes	Yes
Payment made at time of purchase by check?	Yes	Yes	No
Payment made at time of purchase by cash?	Yes	No	No
Payment made at time of purchase by credit card?	Yes	No	No
Payment made later after purchase?	No	No	Yes

Section 6.6

EXPENSE

If our payment is *made at the same time* we make a purchase, then we can record the purchase using the Expense form. When using the Expense form, our payment may consist of cash, check, or credit card.

> **If our purchase is paid by check at the same time as the purchase,** then we can use the Expense form or the Check form to record the transaction.

When using the Expense form to record a vendor transaction:

1 Select **(+) New** icon

2 Select **Expense** to record the vendor transaction when we make payment at the same time the expense is incurred and we use cash, check, or credit card.

3 From the Payee drop-down menu, select **Vendor: Bichotte Supplies**. If a message appears, asking if you want to autofill the form using prior information, select **Yes**.

4 Using the drop-down menu, select the **Payment Account: 2100 VISA Credit Card**

5 Enter **Payment Date: 01/23/2023**

6 From the Payment Method drop-down menu listing Cash, Check, or Credit Card, select **Payment Method: Credit Card**

7 In the Category Details section, select appropriate Category from the drop-down menu. The drop-down Category list contains accounts that can be used to record the expense. If it does not appear automatically, select **Category: 5021 Job Supplies**.

8 Enter **Description** of the transaction: **Supplies for Kuno**. Enter **Memo: Supplies for Kuno**.

9 Enter **Amount** of the expense: **100.00**

10 Select Billable if the expense is billable to a specific customer. In this case select **Billable**.

11 Since the expense is billable to a specific customer, select **Customer: Angel Merriman: Kuno**

12 If you had a receipt, you would want to include it as an **Attachment**

13 Select **Save and close**

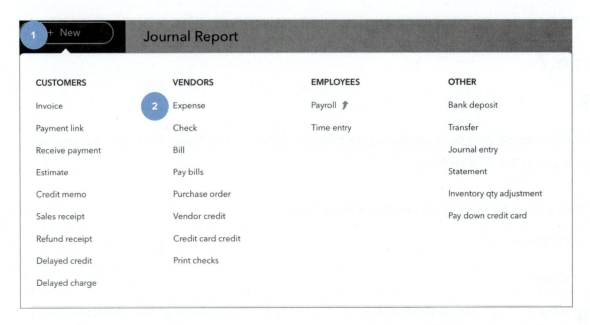

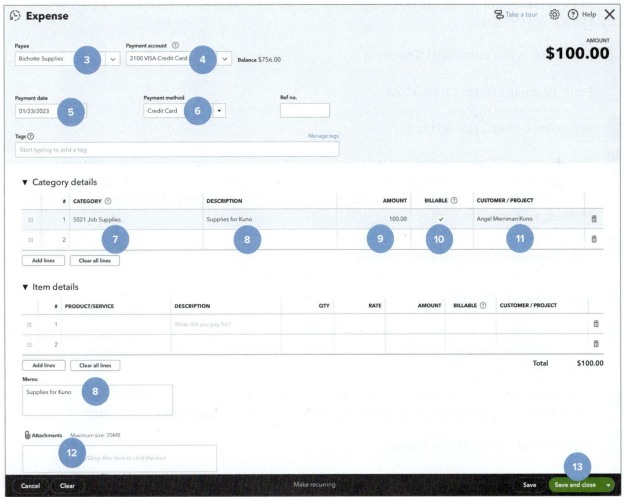

Section 6.7

CHECK

If our payment is *made by check at the same time* we make a purchase, then we can record the purchase using the Check form.

To use a Check form to record the vendor transaction:

1 Select **(+) New** icon

2 Select **Check**

3 Select **Payee: Carole Media Design**. After the Payee is selected, some of the information on the form will autofill, such as Mailing address. This information is pulled from the Vendors List.

4 Select **Bank Account: 1001 Checking**

5 Enter **Payment Date: 01/23/2023**

6 Notice that **Check No.** autofills

7 The drop-down Category List contains accounts that can be used to record the expense. Sometimes QBO will autofill this field using information from the last transaction entered for the specific Payee. In this case, if it does not autofill, enter **Category: 5001 Advertising & Marketing (Expense)**.

8 Enter **Description: Social Media Design**

9 Enter **Amount: 270.00**

10 If the payment was billable to a specific customer, select Billable. In this case since the Computer Repairs (Expenses) does not relate to a specific customer, leave **Billable unchecked**.

11 If the payment was billable to a specific customer, select that customer in the Customer column from the Customer drop-down list. In this case, leave **Customer** field **blank**.

12 Enter **Memo: Social Media Design**

13 Select **Save and close**

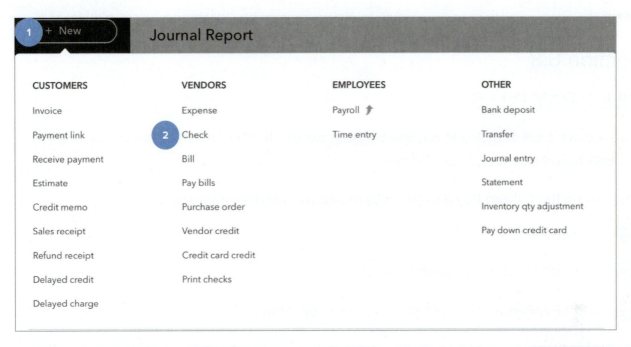

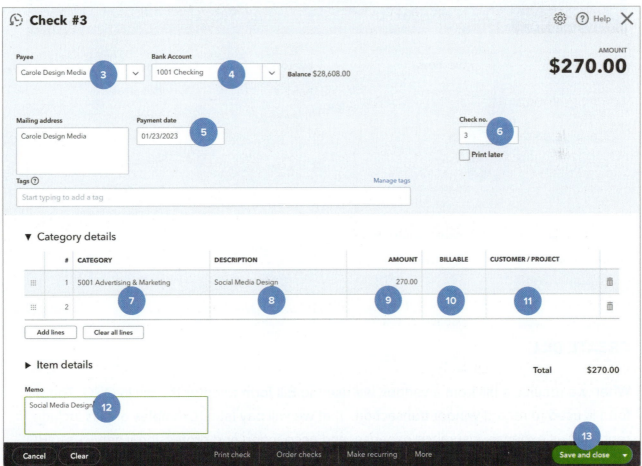

Section 6.8

BILL > PAY BILLS

If we receive a bill and plan to pay the bill later, we use the Bill form to enter the bill and the Pay Bills form when we pay the bill later.

When using the Bill and Pay Bills forms to record the vendors transactions:

1 Select **(+) New** icon

2 Select **Bill** to enter a bill when received

3 Select **Pay Bills** to select bills when we are ready to pay

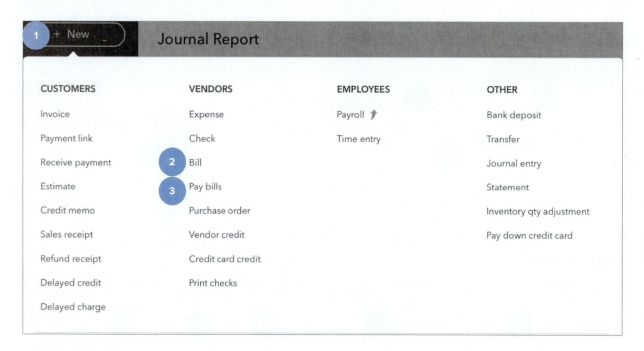

CREATE BILL

When we receive a bill from a vendor, we use the Bill form to enter the bill in QBO. The Bill form is used to record vendor transactions that we will pay later. Examples of bills include rent, utilities expense, insurance expense, and accounting and professional services. QBO will record an obligation (accounts payable liability) to pay the bill later.

> **If we are paying the bill at the time we receive the product or service,** then we can use the Expense form to record the transaction.

To record a bill received that we will pay later:

1   Select **(+) New** icon

2   Select **Bill**

3   From the Vendor drop-down menu, select **Vendor: Joseph Leasing**. If a message appears, asking if you want to autofill the form using prior information, select **Yes**.

4   **Mailing Address** should auto-fill when vendor is selected

5   **Terms** should auto-fill as **Net 15**

6   Select **Bill Date: 01/23/2023**

7   Verify **Due Date** is correct

8   Leave **Bill No. blank**

9   Select **Category: 5028 Rent & Lease**

10   Enter **Description: Equipment rental**

11   Enter **Amount: 420.00**

12   Select Billable if the expense is billable to a specific customer. In this case since Accounting does not relate to a specific customer, leave **Billable unchecked**.

13   If billable, select appropriate Customer associated with the expense. Leave **Customer** field **blank**.

14   If a vendor transaction involved inventory, it can be entered using **Item details** instead of Account details, which is covered in Chapter 7

15   If additional detail is needed, enter a **Memo** describing the transaction

16   Add **Attachments,** such as a copy of the vendor bill received, a source document associated with the transaction

17   Select **Save** and leave the Bill form open

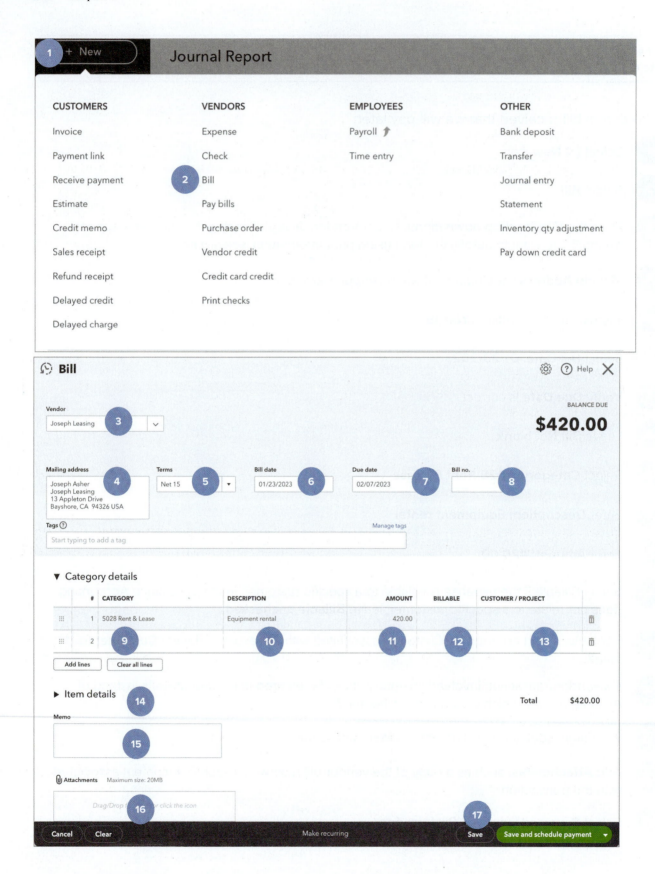

C6.8.1 Bill

To view the Transaction Journal for the Bill we just created:

1 From the Bill window just saved, select **More**

2 Select **Transaction Journal**

3 In the journal entry recorded behind the screen for the Bill, what is the Account and Amount **Debited**?

4 In the journal entry recorded behind the screen for the Bill, what is the Account and Amount **Credited**?

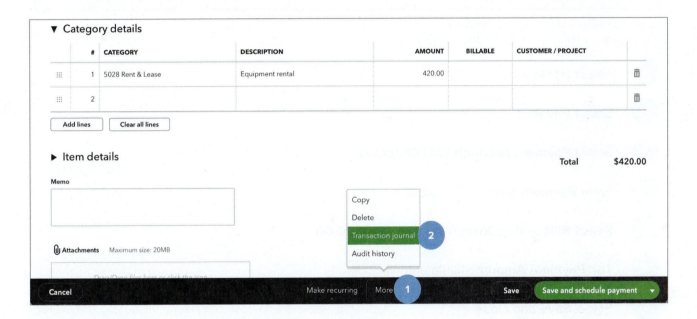

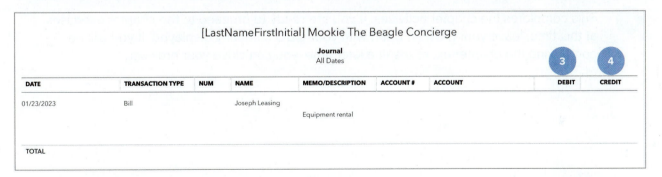

CREATE PAY BILLS

Use the Pay Bills form to select the bills that are due and we are ready to pay. If the bill has been entered using the Bill form, then the bill will automatically appear in the Pay Bills list.

> Use Pay Bills only for bills that have been entered using the Bill forms.

> If the Expense form or the Check form was used to enter the vendor transaction, we do *not* use the Pay Bills form for that item, since it has already been paid at the time the Expense or Check was entered into QBO.

To use Pay Bills to select bills to pay:

1 Select **(+) New** icon

2 Select **Pay Bills**

3 Select **Payment Account: 1001 Checking**

4 Enter **Payment Date: 01/24/2023**

5 Select **Bills to Pay: Joseph Leasing** for **$420.00**

6 The **Payment Amount** should autofill

7 Select **Save and close**

8 This completes the chapter activities. If you are ready to proceed to the chapter exercises at this time, leave your browser open with your QBO company displayed. If you will be completing the chapter exercises at a later time, you can close your browser.

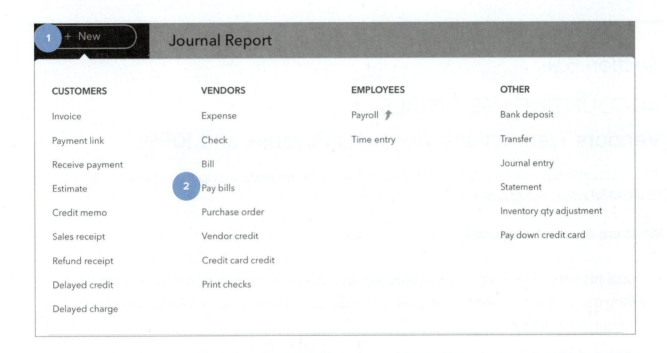

Section 6.9

ACCOUNTING ESSENTIALS
Vendors Transactions, Accounts Payable, and 1099s

Accounting Essentials summarize important foundational accounting knowledge you may find useful when using QBO

What are Accounts Payable?

- Accounts payable consists of amounts that our business is obligated to pay in the future. When our business makes purchases on credit, our business is promising to pay that amount in the future.

- When a purchase is made and recorded as a bill, accounts payable is increased by a credit. When the bill is paid, the accounts payable is decreased by a debit.

How can a business track Accounts Payable to ensure Accounts Payable are paid on time?

- Accounts Payable reports provide information for tracking amounts we owe vendors. An Accounts Payable Aging report summarizes accounts payable balances by the age of the account. This report helps us to track how much we owe vendors and when amounts are due, including the age of past due bills.

What is a 1099 and when does a company need to prepare 1099s?

- IRS Form 1099 must be completed for sole proprietorships and partnerships to which we paid $600 or more for services in a year. The vendor's Tax ID No. is required to complete the 1099. QBO can assist in tracking amounts and preparing 1099s for appropriate vendors. To learn more about preparing 1099s, see the Internal Revenue Service website at www.irs.gov.

Practice Quiz 6

Q6.1
To enter Vendors and Expenses transactions:
a. From the Navigation Bar, select Customers
b. From the Navigation Bar, select Expenses > New Transaction
c. From the Gear icon, select Vendors
d. From the Gear icon, select Expense Transactions

Q6.2
To enter an Expense transaction:
a. From the Navigation Bar, select Customers
b. From the Navigation Bar, select Sales
c. From the (+) New icon, select Expense
d. From the Gear icon, select Vendor Transactions

Q6.3
QuickBooks considers all of the following to be vendors except:
a. Utility companies
b. Suppliers of inventory and supplies
c. Tax agencies such as the IRS
d. Customers purchasing products

Q6.4
Which of the following is not a vendor transaction?
a. Order products
b. Pay bills
c. Make deposits
d. Receive bills

Q6.5
We can update the Vendors List at which of the following two points:
a. Before entering transactions
b. While entering transactions
c. After entering transactions

Q6.6
Which of the following are two Vendors and Expenses transactions?
a. Invoice
b. Receive Payment
c. Pay Bills
d. Check

Q6.7
The Bill form is used to record which one of the following transactions?
a. Owners investment
b. Services received but not yet paid
c. Products sold to customers
d. Cash purchases of supplies

Q6.8
Which of the following activities, and the QBO form used to record it, is incorrect?
a. Receive products, Customers List
b. Order products, Purchase Order
c. Record inventory information, Products and Services List
d. Sell products and bill customers, Invoice

Q6.9
Indicate the order in which the following onscreen Vendors and Expenses transaction forms typically should be prepared:
a. Expense > Pay Bills
b. Check > Pay Bills
c. Bill > Pay Bills
d. Invoice > Pay Bills

Q6.10
Which of the following reports tracks past due bills and bills that are due shortly?
a. Profit & Loss
b. Statement of Cash Flows
c. Accounts Payable Aging
d. Accounts Receivable Aging

Q6.11

Accounts Payable (A/P) are:

a. Amounts totaling the net worth of a company

b. Amounts paid to owners

c. Amounts that customers owe your business

d. Amounts owed to others that are obligations

Q6.12

When a purchase is recorded as a bill, QBO records a:

a. Debit (increase) to cash

b. Credit (increase) to owner's contribution

c. Debit (increase) to accounts receivable

d. Credit (increase) to accounts payable

Exercises 6

If necessary, sign in to your Mookie The Beagle Concierge QBO Company as follows:

1 Using a Chrome web browser, go to qbo.intuit.com

2 Enter **User ID** (the email address you used to set up your QBO Account)

3 Enter **Password** (the password you used to set up your QBO Account)

4 Select **Sign in**

E6.1 Vendors and Expenses Transactions

Match the following vendors and expenses transactions with the description of the transaction.

Vendors and Expenses Transaction Descriptions

a. The form used to select bills we want to pay.

b. The form used to order and track products from vendors.

c. The onscreen form used to record products and services that we pay for at the time we receive the product or service with cash, credit card, or check.

d. The form used when a vendor gives us a refund or reduction in our bill in what we owe the vendor.

e. This form can be used when we pay for products and services at the time of purchase, but cannot be used when we pay with cash or credit card.

f. A form used to record a reduction in charges by the vendor to our credit card.

g. The onscreen form used to record bills we received and the obligation to pay the vendor later (accounts payable).

Vendors and Expenses Transaction

1. Expense
2. Check
3. Bill
4. Pay Bills
5. Purchase Order
6. Vendor Credit
7. Credit Card Credit

E6.2 Vendors Transactions: Expense, Check, or Bill

Complete the following table using Yes and No responses to summarize which QBO form can be used to record vendors transactions.

QBO Transaction Form For...	Expense Form	Check Form	Bill Form
Services purchased?			
Payment made at time of purchase by check?			
Payment made at time of purchase by cash?			
Payment made at time of purchase by credit card?			
Payment made later after purchase?			

E6.3 Bill Pay Workflow

The Bill Pay Workflow consists of a series of activities to record vendor transactions. From the following activities for vendor transactions, complete the Bill Pay Workflow in the order in which the activities should occur for a vendor transaction when the service is received one month before the payment is due. Note: You will not use all activity items listed.

Vendor Transaction Workflow Activities

- Purchase Order

- Check

- Pay Bills

- Expense

- Bill

Bill Pay Workflow			
Service is received one month before payment is due.	1. _____	→	2. _____

EM6.4 Expense Credit Card

Complete the following to record supplies purchased by Mookie The Beagle Concierge from Bichotte Supplies with a credit card.

1. Edit a Vendor in the Vendors List.
   a. From the Navigation Bar, select **Expenses** > **Vendors** tab
   b. From the Vendors List, select **Vendor: Bichotte Supplies** > **Edit**
   c. Update the following vendor information.

Company:	**Bichotte Supplies**
Phone:	**415-555-4567**
Billing Address Street:	**810 Francais Drive**
Billing Address City:	**Bayshore**
Billing Address State:	**CA**
Billing Address ZIP:	**94326**
Billing Address Country:	**USA**

   d. Select **Save**

2. Create Expense paid with Credit Card.
   a. Select **(+) New icon** > **Expense**
   b. Select **Payee: Bichotte Supplies**
   c. Select **Payment Account: 2100 VISA Credit Card**
   d. Select **Payment Date: 01/23/2023**
   e. Select **Payment Method: Credit Card**
   f. Select **Category: 5024 Office Supplies & Software (Expense)**
   g. Enter **Amount: 220.00**
   h. What is the Total on the Expense form?
   i. Select **Save** and leave the Expense displayed

3. View the Transaction Journal for the Expense.
   a. From the bottom of the Expense, select **More** > **Transaction Journal**
   b. What are the Account and Amount Debited?
   c. What are the Account and Amount Credited?

EM6.5 Credit Card Credit

Bichotte Supplies mistakenly overcharged Mookie The Beagle Concierge by $20.00 on the supplies purchases made on 01/23/2023. Complete the following to record the Credit Card Credit when Bichotte Supplies reversed the overcharge.

1. Create Credit Card Credit.
   a. Select **(+) New icon** > **Credit Card Credit**
   b. Select **Payee: Bichotte Supplies**
   c. Select **Bank/Credit Account: 2100 VISA Credit Card**
   d. Select **Payment Date: 01/24/2023**
   e. Select **Category: 5024 Office Supplies & Software (Expense)**
   f. Enter **Description: Refund for overcharge**
   g. Enter **Amount: 20.00**
   h. What is the Total for the Credit Card Credit?
   i. Select **Save and close**

2. View the Transaction Journal for the Credit Card Credit.
   a. From the Navigation Bar, select **Expenses** > select **Expenses** tab
   b. From the Expense Transactions List, select **Bichotte Supplies Credit Card Credit**
   c. From the bottom of the Credit Card Credit, select **More** > **Transaction Journal**
   d. What are the Account and Amount Debited?
   e. What are the Account and Amount Credited?

EM6.6 Expense Checking

Complete the following to record technology supplies purchased by Mookie The Beagle Concierge from Merriman Cybersecurity with a credit card.

1. Edit a Vendor in the Vendors List.
   a. From the Navigation Bar, select **Expenses** > **Vendors** tab
   b. From the Vendors List, select **Vendor: Merriman Cybersecurity** > **Edit**
   c. Update the following vendor information.

First Name:	**Angel**
Last Name:	**Merriman**
Company:	**Merriman Cybersecurity**
Display name as:	**Merriman Cybersecurity**
Phone:	**415-555-7579**
Billing Address Street:	**623 Thorsmork Road**
Billing Address City:	**Bayshore**

Billing Address State:	**CA**
Billing Address ZIP:	**94326**
Billing Address Country:	**USA**

   d. Select **Save**

2. Create Expense Paid with Credit Card.
   a. Select **(+) New icon > Expense**
   b. Select **Payee: Merriman Cybersecurity**
   c. Select **Payment Account: 2100 VISA Credit Card**
   d. Select **Payment Date: 01/24/2023**
   e. Select **Payment Method: Credit Card**
   f. Select **Category: 5024 Office Supplies & Software (Expense)**
   g. Enter **Amount: 432.00**
   h. What is the Total for the Expense?
   i. Select **Save** and leave the Expense displayed on your screen

3. View the Transaction Journal for the Expense.
   a. From the bottom of the Expense, select **More > Transaction Journal**
   b. What are the Account and Amount Debited?
   c. What are the Account and Amount Credited?

EM6.7 Checking Debit Card

Complete the following to record a payment using Mookie The Beagle Concierge's Checking account Debit Card.

1. Create Check with Debit Card.
   a. Select **(+) New icon > Check**
   b. Select **Payee: Bichotte Supplies**
   c. Select **Bank Account: 1001 Checking**
   d. Select **Payment Date: 01/25/2023**
   e. Enter **Check No.: Debit**
   f. Select **Category: 5024 Office Supplies & Software (Expense)**
   g. Enter **Amount: 50.00**
   h. What is the Total for the Check?
   i. Select **Save and close**

2. View the Transaction Journal for the Check.

   a. From the Navigation Bar, select **Accounting**

   b. From the Chart of Accounts, select **View Register** for the Checking account

   c. Select **Bichotte Supplies Debit Check** > **Edit**

   d. From the bottom of the Check, select **More** > **Transaction Journal**

   e. What are the Account and Amount Debited?

   f. What are the Account and Amount Credited?

EM6.8 Recurring Transaction Expense

Use a Recurring Transaction to record paying Evan Henry as a contractor who provided the pet care services for Kuno over the charity run weekend. Mookie The Beagle Concierge pays Evan Henry $20 per hour for those services.

1. Edit a Vendor in the Vendors List.

   a. From the Navigation Bar, select **Expenses** > **Vendors** tab

   b. From the Vendors List, select **Vendor: Evan Henry** > **Edit**

   c. Update the following vendor information.

First Name:	**Evan**
Last Name:	**Henry**
Display Name as:	**Evan Henry**
Mobile:	**415-555-1111**
Billing Address Street:	**99 Andrea Street**
Billing Address City:	**Bayshore**
Billing Address State:	**CA**
Billing Address ZIP:	**94326**
Billing Address Country:	**USA**

   d. Select **Save**

2. Use a Recurring Transaction.

    a. From the Recurring Transaction List, select **Contractors Expense > Use**

    b. Select **Payee: Evan Henry**

    c. Verify **Payment Account: 1001 Checking**

    d. Update **Payment Date: 01/30/2023**

    e. Verify **Category: 5005 Contractors (Expense)**

    f. Enter Amount **based upon 33 hours Evan provided service to Kuno over the charity marathon weekend**

    g. What is the Amount for the Expense?

    h. Select **Save** and leave the Expense displayed

3. View the Transaction Journal for the Expense.

    a. From the bottom of the Expense, select **More > Transaction Journal**

    b. What are the Account and Amount Debited?

    c. What are the Account and Amount Credited?

EM6.9 Bill

Andre LaFortune, a vet student, provided pet care services as a contractor for Remy for a total of 17 hours summarized as follows:

- 6 hours on 01/20/2023
- 5 hours on 01/22/2023
- 6 hours on 01/23/2023

Mookie The Beagle Concierge pays Andre $20 per hour. Complete the following to enter the bill on 01/30/2023. Mookie The Beagle Concierge will pay the contractor bill on 01/31/2023.

1. Add a New Vendor to the Vendors List.

    a. From the Navigation Bar, select **Expenses > Vendors** tab

    b. Select **New vendor**

    c. Enter the following vendor information.

First Name:	**Andre**
Last Name:	**LaFortune**
Display Name as:	**Andre LaFortune**
Phone:	**415-555-1988**
Mobile:	**415-555-1955**
Billing Address Street:	**28 Beach Street**
Billing Address City:	**Bayshore**

Billing Address State:	**CA**
Billing Address ZIP:	**94326**
Billing Address Country:	**USA**

    d. Select **Save**

2. Create Bill.
   a. Select **(+) New icon > Bill**
   b. Select **Vendor: Andre LaFortune**
   c. Select **Bill Date: 01/30/2023**
   d. Select **Category: 5005 Contractors (Expense)**
   e. Enter **Amount based on the 17 hours Andre provided pet care services for Remy**
   f. What is the Total for the Bill?
   g. Select **Save** and leave the Bill displayed

3. View the Transaction Journal for the Bill.
   a. From the bottom of the Bill, select **More > Transaction Journal**
   b. What are the Account and Amount Debited?
   c. What are the Account and Amount Credited?

EM6.10 Pay Bills

Complete the following to pay the contractor bill for Andre LaFortune.

1. Pay Bills.
   a. Select **(+) New icon > Pay Bills**
   b. Select **Payment Account: 1001 Checking**
   c. Select **Payment Date: 01/31/2023**
   d. Select **Starting Check No.: 5**
   e. Select **Payee: Andre LaFortune**
   f. Select **Bill** dated **01/30/2023**
   g. What is the Total Payment Amount?
   h. Select **Save and close**

2. View the Transaction Journal for Paid Bills.
   a. From the Navigation Bar, select **Accounting**
   b. From the Chart of Accounts, select **View Register** for the Checking account
   c. Select **Bill Payment Andre LaFortune $340 > Edit**
   d. From the bottom of the Bill Payment, select **More > Transaction Journal**
   e. What are the Account and Amount Debited?
   f. What are the Account and Amount Credited?

EM6.11 Pay Credit Card

Mookie The Beagle Concierge makes a payment on the VISA credit card on 01/31/2023 in the amount of $800.

To record the payment on the VISA credit card:

1. From the Navigation Bar, select **Expenses** > select **Expenses** tab

2. From the New transaction drop-down menu, select **Pay down credit card**

3. For Which credit card did you pay?, select **2100 VISA Credit Card**

4. For How much did you pay?, enter **800.00**

5. For Date of payment, enter **01/31/2023**

6. For What did you use to make this payment?, select **1001 Checking**

7. Select **Save and close**

8. What is the balance of the VISA Credit Card account after the credit card payment is recorded?

EM6.12 Vendors List

Cy requested a copy of Mookie The Beagle Concierge's current Vendors List.

To export the Vendors List:

1. From the Navigation Bar, select **Reports** > **Standard** tab > **Expenses and Vendors** > **Vendor Contact List** > **Run Report** > **Export icon** > **Export to PDF** > **Save as PDF**.

EM6.13 Accounts Payable Aging Summary

Cy requested a copy of Mookie The Beagle Concierge's Accounts Payable Aging Summary.

To export the Accounts Payable Aging Summary:

1. From the Navigation Bar, select **Reports** > select **Standard** tab > in the **What you owe** section, select **Accounts payable aging summary**

2. For Report period, select: **Custom** > enter **as of: 01/31/2023**

3. Select **Report date: Days per aging period: 30** > **Number of periods: 4**

4. Select **Run report**

5. Select the **Export icon** > **Export to PDF**

6. What is the total amount of Accounts Payable that are currently due?

Chapter 7

Inventory

MOOKIE THE BEAGLE™ CONCIERGE

BACKSTORY

Mookie The Beagle™ Concierge discovers that the young professionals using its pet care services often don't have time to go shopping for pet care items. Cy sees an opportunity to expand and sell Mookie The Beagle Concierge-branded products to customers.

So MTB Concierge starts stocking high-demand items, such as dog hammocks, dog cones, activated charcoal for suspected poisoning, gauze wrap with adhesive tape for wound dressing, gauze nonstick bandages, sterile towels, and oral syringes for administering medications. All the products can be ordered through the MTB Concierge app with delivery scheduled coinciding with a pet care visit or immediately via Mookie The Beagle Concierge delivery service.

With this expansion, Cy realizes that now the accounting system will need to track inventory that is bought from vendors and sold to customers. So your next step is to learn more about using QBO for tracking purchases and sales of inventory.

Chapter 7

LEARNING OBJECTIVES

Chapter 7 focuses on using QBO to record the purchase and sale of product inventory. For example, Mookie The Beagle Concierge purchases dog hammocks from vendors for resale to customers. QBO has the ability to track both the purchase of the hammocks and the subsequent resale to customers.

In this chapter, you will learn about the following topics:

- Navigating Inventory
- Products and Services List
  - Inventory
  - Non-inventory
  - Service
  - Bundle
- Vendors Transaction: Create Purchase Order
- Vendors Transaction: Enter Bill
- Vendors Transaction: Pay Bills
- Customers Transaction: Create Invoice
- Customers Transaction: Receive Payment
- Customers Transaction: Bank Deposit for Undeposited Funds
- Accounting Essentials: Inventory and Internal Control

⚠️ **QBO is updated on an ongoing basis. Updates that affect your text can be viewed as follows:**
1. **Go to www.My-QuickBooksOnline.com > QBO 3e > QBO 3e Updates, or**
2. **If you are using Connect or a digital ebook, you can find updates under Additional Student Resources (ASR). If you do not have access to Connect or the ebook, your instructor can provide you with ASR.**

Section 7.1

 QBO SATNAV

QBO SatNav is our satellite navigation for QuickBooks Online, assisting us in navigating QBO

Chapter 7 focuses on QBO Customers and Sales Transactions and Vendors and Expenses Transactions related to product inventory, as shown in the following QBO SatNav.

 QBO SatNav

 QBO Settings

| Company Settings |
|  Chart of Accounts |

 QBO Transactions

Banking	
Customers & Sales	*Create Invoices > Receive Payments > Record Deposits*
Vendors & Expenses	*PO > Receive Inventory > Enter Bills Inventory > Pay Bills*
Employees & Payroll	

 QBO Reports

| Reports |

Section 7.2

NAVIGATING INVENTORY

If we buy and resell products, then we must maintain inventory records to account for the products we purchase from vendors and resell to customers.

VENDORS	Purchase Products from Vendors ➡	OUR COMPANY	Sell Products to Customers ➡	CUSTOMERS

We can use QBO for inventory to record:

1. **Vendor transactions**, including placing product orders, receiving products, and paying bills
2. **Customer transactions**, including recording sale of product on invoices and receiving customer payments

VENDORS		VENDORS		VENDORS		CUSTOMERS		CUSTOMERS
Purchase Order	➡	Bill	➡	Pay Bills	➡	Invoice	➡	Receive Payment

We can view the order of the QBO tasks we need to complete for inventory from the (+) New screen:

1   **VENDORS: Purchase Order** to record our order of products from vendors. The purchase order is a record of the products and quantities we ordered.

2   **VENDORS: Bill** to record our obligation to pay the vendor for the products (Accounts Payable). Match vendor's bill with our purchase order to verify quantities and amounts are correct.

3   **VENDORS: Pay Bills** to pay vendor bills for products received.

4   **CUSTOMERS: Invoice** to record resale of product to customer and the customer's promise to pay later (Accounts Receivable).

5   **CUSTOMERS: Receive Payment** to record collection of the customer's payment.

6   **CUSTOMERS: Bank Deposit** to record customer's payment in the bank account. (Bank Deposit is used only if Undeposited Funds is selected on the Receive Payment form.)

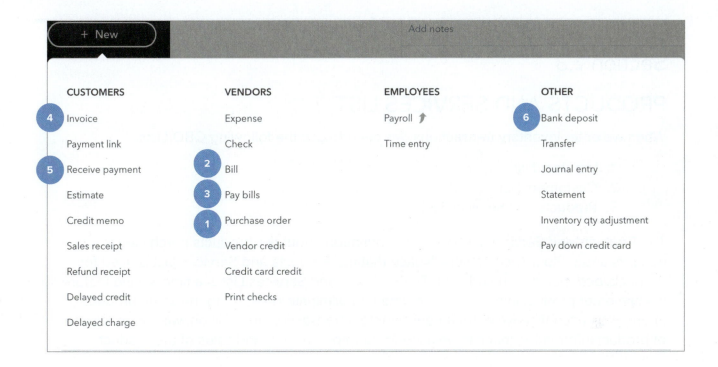

⚠️ **Before continuing, verify** that QBO Inventory Tracking is turned on. Go to Gear icon > **Account and Settings > Sales > Products and Services > Track quantity and price/rate On > Track inventory quantity on hand > On.**

Section 7.3

PRODUCTS AND SERVICES LIST

When we enter inventory transactions, we need to use the following QBO Lists:

1. Vendors List
2. Customers List
3. Products and Services List

The Products and Services List collects information about the products purchased from vendors and/or sold to customers. Notice that the Products and Services List is used for products *both* purchased and sold. The Products and Services List is a time-saving feature so we can enter product information one time and eliminate re-entering the same product information each time we enter a new inventory transaction. In addition, we can enter one set of product information that can be used for both purchasing and sales of the product.

QBO uses four types of products and services:

1. **Inventory.** Products that we buy for which we track quantities, such as dog hammocks that Mookie The Beagle Concierge buys to resell. Inventory items are products that a business purchases, holds as inventory, and then resells to customers. QBO tracks the quantity and cost of inventory items in stock. For consistency, the same inventory item is used when recording sales and purchases. QBO has the capability to track both the cost and the sales price for inventory items. When the product is recorded on a sales invoice, QBO automatically updates our inventory records by reducing the quantity on hand. If we purchased the product, then we would record the product on the purchase order using the same inventory item number that we use on an invoice, except the purchase order uses the product's *cost* while the invoice uses the product's *selling price*.
2. **Non-inventory.** Products that we buy but we don't need to track the quantity of the product, such as pens used for office supplies.
3. **Service.** Services that we buy from vendors, such as legal services.
4. **Bundle.** A bundle is a collection of products and services that we sell together as a bundle. For example, Mookie The Beagle might include charcoal tablets (products) and concierge pet care for pet poisonings (services). Notice that we may buy the products separately, but then bundle the items for resale to customers.

Two ways that we can update the Products and Services List are:

1. *Before* entering transactions
2. *While* entering transactions

UPDATE PRODUCTS AND SERVICES LIST BEFORE ENTERING TRANSACTIONS

Before entering transactions, we can update the Products and Services List as follows.

1. From the Navigation Bar, select **Sales**

2. Select **Product and Services**

3. To enter a new products or services, select **New**

4. Select **Product/Service Type: Inventory**

5. Enter **Name: Mookie The Beagle Bon Appetite Organic Dog Food**

6. Enter SKU or other product identification number. In this case, leave **SKU blank**.

7. Attach a Product/Service photo. In this case, leave **photo blank**.

8. Select an appropriate product/service **Category: <+ Add new> Pet Food Supplies**

9. Enter **Initial Quantity on Hand: 0**

10. Enter **As of Date: 01/01/2023**

11. Enter **Reorder Point** when a new order should be placed to replenish product stock: **1**

12. Select **Inventory Asset Account: Inventory Asset**

13. Enter **Description: Mookie The Beagle Bon Appetite Organic Dog Food**

14. Enter **Sales Price/Rate: 70.00**

15. Select **Income Account: Sales of Product Income**

16. Enter **Purchasing Information: Mookie The Beagle Bon Appetite Organic Dog Food**

17. Enter **Cost: 25.00**

18. Select **Expense Account: Cost of Goods Sold**

19 Select **Preferred Vendor: <+Add new> Only The Best Dog Food**

20 Select **Save and close**

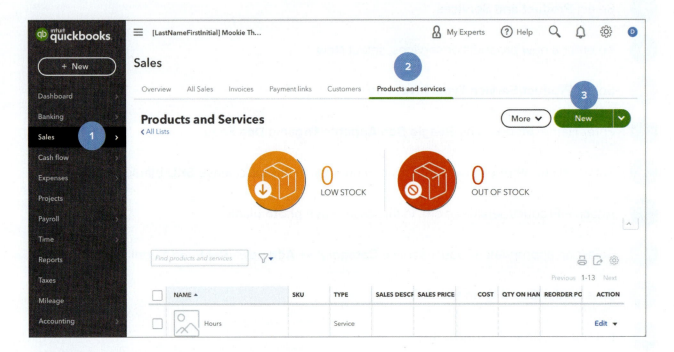

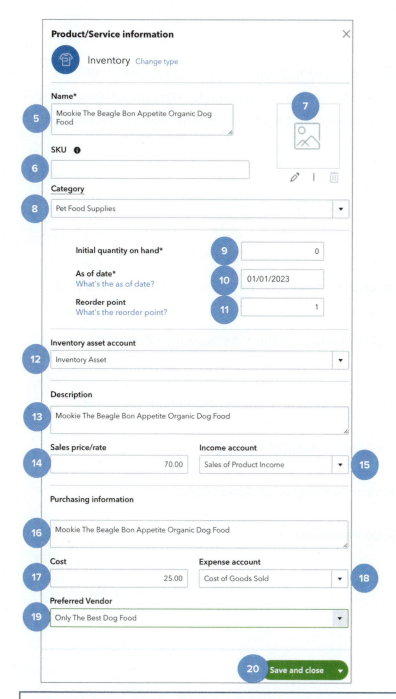

Notice that the **Products and Services List** links the product item to accounts in the Chart of Accounts **for:**

• **Inventory (Asset account)**

• **Sales of Product Income (Income account) and**

• **Cost of Goods Sold (Expense account)**

When we select this product on a QBO transaction form, then the linked accounts are automatically updated also.

UPDATE CHART OF ACCOUNTS

When we add at least one inventory item to the Products and Services List, QBO will automatically add some additional accounts to our Chart of Accounts. We can easily identify the added accounts since they will not display account numbers. Examples of such accounts include:

- Inventory Asset
- Sales of Product Income
- Cost of Goods Sold
- Purchases

To enter account numbers for the new accounts related to inventory items in the Chart of Accounts for Mookie The Beagle Concierge:

1 Display the Chart of Accounts by selecting **Navigation Bar > Accounting > Chart of Accounts**

2 Select the Edit Pencil to enter Inventory Asset Account Number: **1300 Inventory Asset**

3 Enter Sales of Product Income Account Number: **4300 Sales of Product Income**

4 Enter Cost of Goods Sold Account Number: **5000 Cost of Goods Sold**

5 Enter Purchases Account Number: **5050 Purchases**

UPDATE PRODUCTS AND SERVICES LIST WHILE ENTERING TRANSACTIONS

While entering transactions, we can update the Products and Services List from the transaction form. If a product or service has not been entered in the Products and Services List, then we can add the product or service as follows from the onscreen transaction form.

1 To view a transaction form, such as an Invoice, select **(+) New** icon > **Invoice**. Then select the **drop-down arrow** in the Product/Service field to display the menu.

2 Select **+ Add new**

3 Select **Product/Service Type**

4 Enter **new product or service information**

5 If we were adding a new product or service, we would select Save and close. In this case, cancel by selecting the **X** in the upper right corner of the Product/Service Information window.

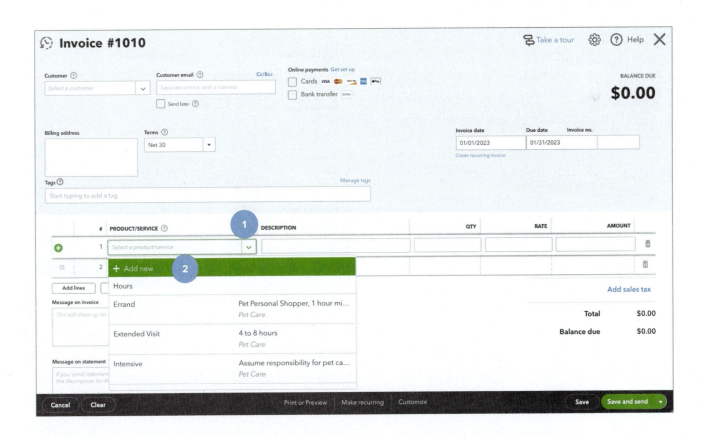

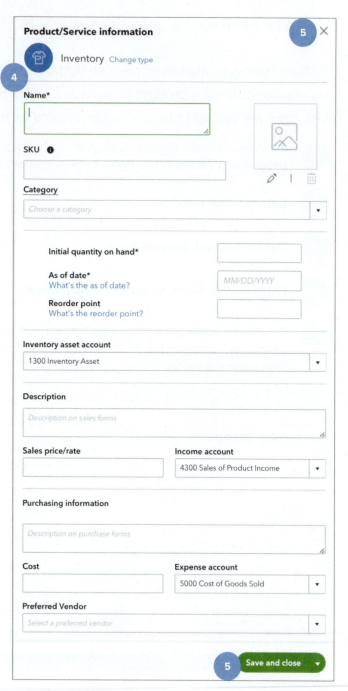

Section 7.4

PURCHASE ORDER

A Purchase Order is a record of an order to purchase products from a vendor. The Purchase Order lists the details of the purchase, such as date, vendor, specific items ordered, and quantity of each item ordered.

To create a Purchase Order:

1 Select **(+) New** icon

2 Select **Purchase Order**

3 From the Vendor drop-down menu, select **Vendor: Only The Best Dog Food**

4 The Purchase Order Status should be **Open**

5 Enter Ship to customer address if the product is to be shipped directly to a customer. In this case, select leave **Ship to: blank**.

6 Enter **Purchase Order Date: 01/02/2023**

7 Leave the **Ship via** field **blank**

8 The Item Details section lists items to order. The product or service selected is linked to an account in the Chart of Accounts, so when we select the product, the linked account is automatically updated. If there are prior POs with the specific vendor, then the prior items ordered may autofill. In this case, select the product to order from the **Product/Service** drop-down list: **Mookie The Beagle Bon Appetite Dog Food**.

9 The **Description** should autofill: **Mookie The Beagle Bon Appetite Organic Dog Food**

10 Enter **QTY** to order: **4**

11 The **Rate** should autofill: **25.00**

12 Verify **Amount** is calculated correctly

13 If associated with a specific customer, select appropriate Customer. In this case, leave **Customer/Project: blank**.

14 To add lines for additional products, select Add lines. To delete extra items, select the Trash Can.

15 Enter **Your Message to Vendor** with additional instructions. In this case, leave the field **blank**.

16 Enter **Memo: Mookie The Beagle Bon Appetite Organic Dog Food**

17 Add **Attachments**, such as source documents associated with the transaction. For example, attach written authorization for the purchase order.

18 Select **Save and close**

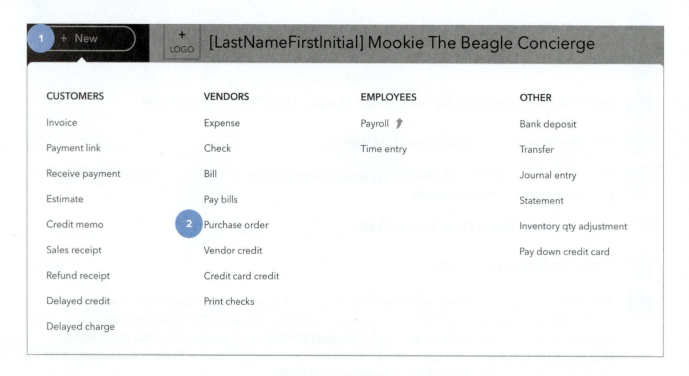

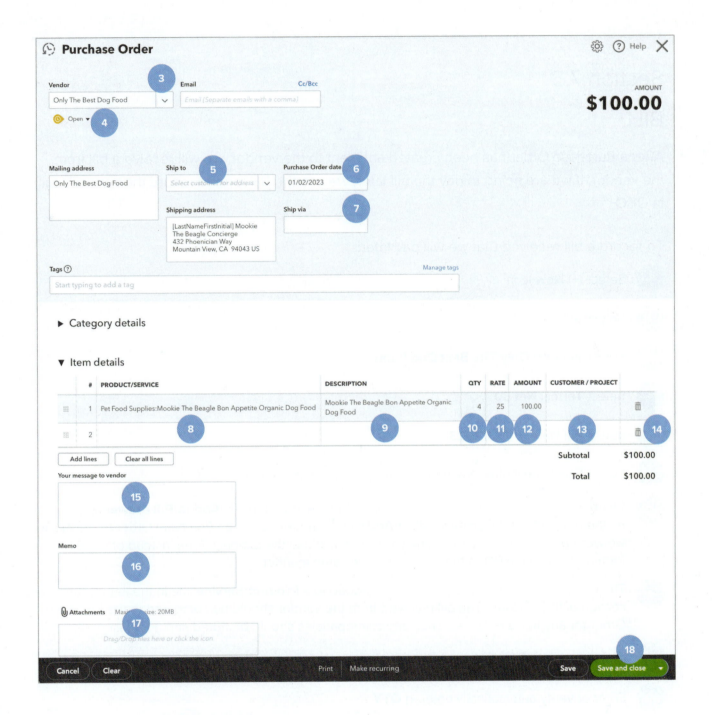

Section 7.5

BILL

After a Purchase Order has been created and sent to the vendor, we will receive a bill from the vendor. If we are going to pay the bill later, we use the Bill form to record the vendor's bill in QBO.

To record a bill received that we will pay later:

1 Select **(+) New** icon

2 Select **Bill**

3 Select **Vendor: Only The Best Dog Food**

4 Select **Terms: Net 30**

5 Select **Bill Date: 01/03/2023**

6 Select **Due Date** if different than the due date automatically displayed

7 When a vendor is selected, if there are open Purchase Orders, an **Add to Bill drawer** appears on the right side of the screen. Select **Add** to add the related open Purchase Order to the bill. If we were paying the bill at the same time, we could use the Expense form instead of the Bill form and attach the PO to the Expense in the same manner.

8 The information on the Purchase Order is added to a **Product/Service** line in the Item Detail section of the Bill form. The bill received from the vendor should be compared to the Purchase Order for any items received. Then any discrepancies should be noted and addressed.

9 Enter or update **Description**

10 Enter or verify automatically entered **QTY**

11 Enter or verify automatically entered **Rate**

12 Enter or verify automatically entered **Amount**

13 Select Billable if the item is billable to a specific customer. In this case, leave **Billable unchecked**.

14 If billable, select appropriate Customer associated with the item. Leave the **Customer** field **blank**.

15 Select the **Link** icon to display information about the linked Purchase Order

16 Enter **Memo** describing the transaction: **Purchase of Mookie The Beagle Bon Appetite Organic Dog Food**

17 Select **Save and close**

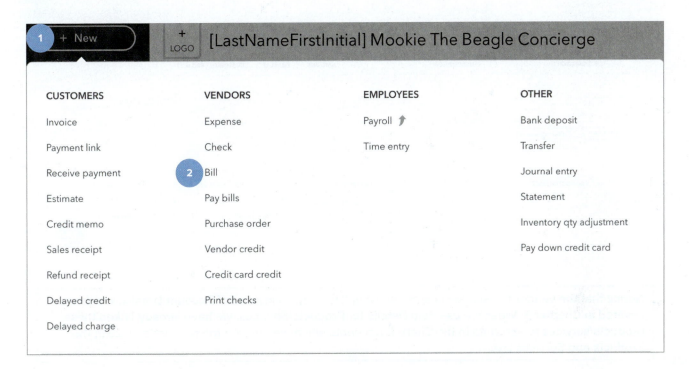

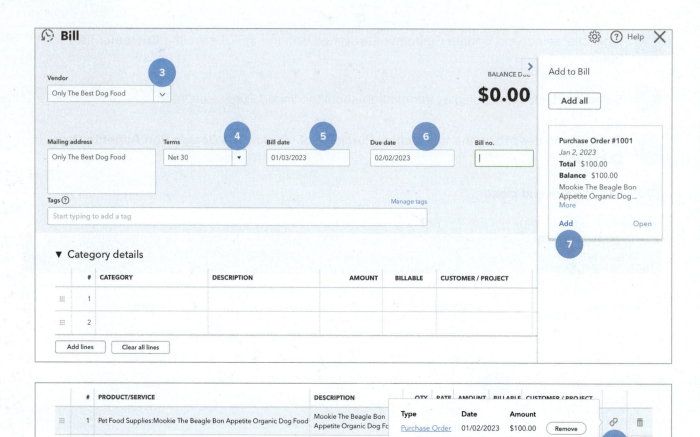

Notice that the vendor transaction is entered using **Item Details** instead of **Account Details**, which was covered in Chapter 6. When we use **Item Details** for Products/Services, we have already linked these products/services to accounts in the Chart of Accounts when we entered the product/service in the Products and Services List.

Section 7.6

PAY BILLS

Use Pay Bills to select the bills that are due and we are ready to pay. If the bill has been entered using the Bill form, then the bill will automatically appear in the Pay Bills list.

> **Use Pay Bills only** for bills that have been entered using the Bill form.

> **If the Expense form or the Check form** was used to enter the vendor transaction, we do *not* use the Pay Bills form for that item, since it has already been paid at the time the Expense or Check was entered into QBO.

To use Pay Bills to select bills to pay:

1 Select **(+) New** icon

2 Select **Pay Bills**

3 Select **Payment Account: 2100 VISA Credit Card**

4 Enter **Payment Date: 01/05/2023**

5 Select **Bills to Pay: Only The Best Dog Food with an Open Balance of $100.00**

6 If the Payment field autofills, verify the **Payment Amount**

7 Select **Save and close**

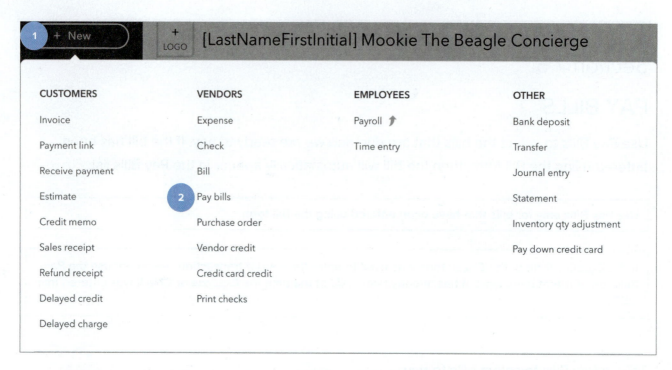

Section 7.7

INVOICE

An Invoice is used to record sales when the customer will pay later. An Invoice contains detailed information about the products and services provided to a customer.

C7.7.1 Customers: Invoice

To create an Invoice:

1 Select **(+) New** icon

2 Select **Invoice**

3 Select **Customer: Sandy Copper: Remy**

4 Enter **Terms: Net 30**

5 Enter **Invoice Date: 01/08/2023**

6 Verify **Due Date**

7 Select **Product/Service: Mookie The Beagle Bon Appetite Organic Dog Food**

8 If the Description field does not autofill, enter **Description: Mookie The Beagle Bon Appetite Organic Dog Food**

9 Enter **Quantity (QTY): 2**

10 If inventory tracking is turned on for an item, hover the cursor over QTY to see quantity of the inventory item on hand. Note: After saving this invoice, the Quantity on hand will be 2, the Reorder point will be 1, and the Quantity on Purchase Order will be 0.

11 Verify **Rate**

12 Verify **Amount**

13 Select **Save > More > Transaction Journal**. What are the accounts and amounts debited? What are the accounts and amounts credited?

14 Select **Save and close**

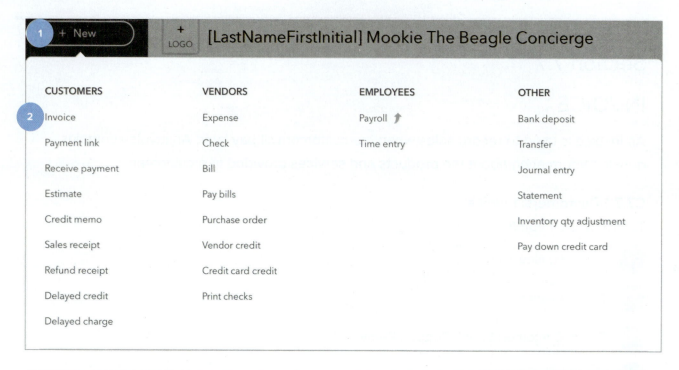

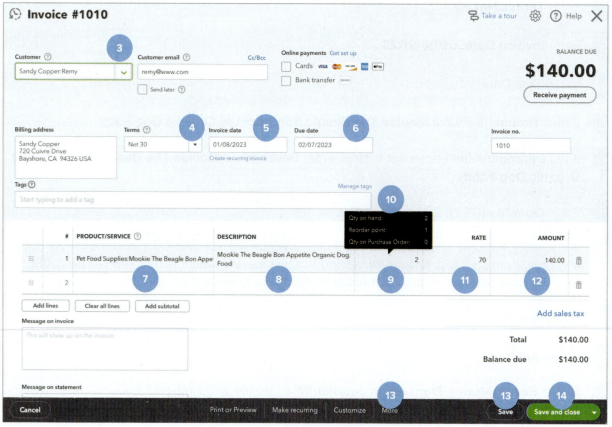

Section 7.8

RECEIVE PAYMENT

Customers may pay in the following ways:

1. **Credit card**, such as Visa or Mastercard, over the phone, in person, or by mail. Using QuickBooks' Merchant Account Service, you can obtain online authorization and then download payments directly into QuickBooks.
2. **Online** by credit card or bank account transfer.
3. **Customer check** delivered either in person or by mail.

To record a customer's payment received to pay an outstanding Invoice:

1 Select **(+) New** icon

2 Select **Receive Payment**

3 Select **Customer**: **Sandy Copper: Remy**

4 Enter **Payment Date: 01/010/2023**

5 Enter **Payment Method: Credit Card**

6 If this deposit will be bundled with other deposits, then select Undeposited Funds and after completing the Invoice, enter a Bank Deposit to move the funds from Undeposited Funds to the Checking account. If this deposit is not bundled with other deposits, then select the appropriate Checking account from the drop-down list. The funds are deposited directly to the Checking account selected and we do not enter a separate Bank Deposit. In this case, select **Deposit to: 1001 Checking**.

7 In the Outstanding Transactions section, select the Invoice to which payment should be applied. Select the Invoice you just entered with an **Open Balance of 140.00**.

8 Verify the **Payment Amount**

9 Select **Save and close**

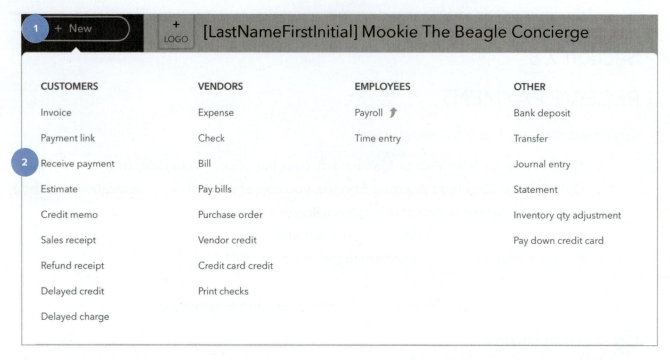

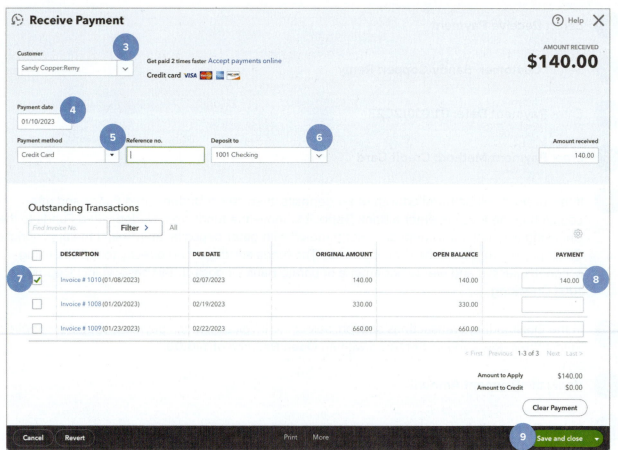

Section 7.9

BANK DEPOSIT FOR UNDEPOSITED FUNDS

If Undeposited Funds was selected on the Receive Payment form, then we must create a Bank Deposit to transfer the funds from the Undeposited Funds account to the appropriate Checking account. Sometimes Undeposited Funds is used on the Receive Payment form if the customer payment will be bundled with other customer payments when deposited. Then our totals will correspond to the bank deposit total shown by the bank.

> **If we selected Undeposited Funds on the Receive Payment form, we *must* create a bank deposit to transfer the funds from the Undeposited Funds account to the appropriate bank account. Otherwise, the funds will remain in the Undeposited Funds account and our Checking account balance will be incorrect.**

> **If we selected a specific bank account, such as Checking account on the Receive Payment form, then we do *not* need to create a bank deposit. We have already recorded the deposit of the customer payment in the bank account.**

To record a bank deposit related to a customer sale when Undeposited Funds was selected on the Receive Payment form:

1. Select **(+) New** icon

2. Under Other column, select **Bank Deposit**

3. Select **Bank** account

4. Enter **Date** of deposit

5. The Select Existing Payments section will list customer payments received but not deposited yet

6. Enter appropriate **Payment Method**

7. If appropriate, enter **Memo** describing the deposit

8. Verify **Amount** is correct

9. Select **Attachments** to add a file or photo of any accompanying document

10   Select Save and close. In this case, select **Cancel**.

11   This completes the chapter activities. If you are ready to proceed to the chapter exercises at this time, leave your browser open with your QBO company displayed. If you will be completing the chapter exercises at a later time, you can close your browser.

Section 7.10

ACCOUNTING ESSENTIALS
Inventory and Internal Control

Accounting Essentials summarize important foundational accounting knowledge you may find useful when using QBO

How do we improve internal control over inventory?

- Internal control is a set of processes and procedures to safeguard assets and detect errors. Since inventory is one of the main targets of fraud and theft, we want to have a good system of internal control to safeguard inventory.

- One principle of internal control is periodically to compare and reconcile the actual asset with the accounting records to identify and track any discrepancies. So at least once a year, businesses typically reconcile:
  1. Inventory on hand confirmed by a physical count of inventory assets on hand with
  2. Inventory recorded in the accounting records

- The process of taking a physical inventory count and comparing it to the inventory amounts recorded in the accounting system identifies discrepancies between the actual asset Inventory and what is reflected in the Inventory asset account in the company records. Discrepancies can then be investigated to determine whether it is an error in the accounting system or missing inventory.

What is a 3-way match?

- Another principle of internal control is to use a 3-way match when ordering, receiving, and paying for inventory.

- 3-way match compares:
  1. What was *ordered*?
  2. What was *received*?
  3. What was *billed*?

- Basically, we want to compare what we *ordered* with what we *received*, and what we were *billed*. These three amounts should agree so that we are not paying for more than what we ordered or received.

Practice Quiz 7

Q7.1

To enter Customers and Sales transactions:

a. From the Navigation Bar, select Transactions > Customers
b. From the Navigation Bar, select Transactions > Expenses > New Transaction
c. From the (+) New icon, select the appropriate customer transaction
d. From the Gear icon, select Expense Transactions

Q7.2

To enter Vendors and Expenses transactions:

a. From the Navigation Bar, select Transactions > Customers
b. From the Navigation Bar, select Transactions > Sales
c. From the (+) New icon, select the appropriate vendor transaction
d. From the Gear icon, select Vendor transactions

Q7.3

QuickBooks considers all of the following to be vendors except:

a. Utility companies
b. Suppliers of inventory and supplies
c. Tax agencies such as the IRS
d. Customers purchasing products

Q7.4

Which of the following is a vendors transaction?

a. Purchase Order
b. Invoice
c. Make deposit
d. Receive Payment

Q7.5

We can update the Products and Services List at which of the following two points:

a. Before entering transactions
b. While entering transactions
c. After entering transactions

Q7.6

Which of the following is a Customers transaction?

a. Invoice
b. Purchase Order
c. Pay Bills
d. Bill

Q7.7

Types of products and services on the Products and Services List include:

a. Service
b. Non-inventory
c. Inventory
d. All of the above

Q7.8

Which of the following products and services types track quantities?

a. Service items
b. Inventory items
c. Non-inventory items
d. None of the above

Q7.9

The Purchase Order form is used to record which one of the following transactions?

a. Owner's investment
b. Services received but not yet paid
c. Products sold to customers
d. Products ordered from vendors

Q7.10

Which of the following activities, and the QBO form used to record it, is incorrect?

a. Receive customer payment, Pay Bills
b. Order products, Purchase Order
c. Receive bill to be paid later, Bill
d. Sell products and bill customers, Invoice

Q7.11

Indicate two of the following that show the order in which the following onscreen vendor transaction forms typically should be prepared.

a. Expense > Pay Bills

b. Purchase Order > Bill > Pay Bills

c. Bill > Pay Bills

d. Invoice > Pay Bills

Q7.12

Recording a purchase of products using QBO involves all of the following steps except:

a. Create invoice to bill vendors for purchases

b. Create purchase order to order items from vendors

c. Receive bill and record obligation to pay vendor later

d. Pay bill entered previously

Q7.13

To record a bill received that we will pay later, we use which of the following QBO forms?

a. Purchase Order

b. Pay Bills

c. Expense

d. Bill

Q7.14

Use the Pay Bills form only for:

a. Bills that have been entered using the Bill form

b. Bills that have been entered using the Expense form

c. Bills that have been entered using the Check form

d. Bills that have never been entered in QBO

Exercises 7

If necessary, sign in to your Mookie The Beagle Concierge QBO Company as follows:

1 Using a Chrome web browser, go to qbo.intuit.com

2 Enter **User ID** (the email address you used to set up your QBO Account)

3 Enter **Password** (the password you used to set up your QBO Account)

4 Select **Sign in**

E7.1 Vendors and Expenses Transactions
Match the following vendors and expenses transactions with the description of the transaction.

Vendors and Expenses Transaction Descriptions

a. The form used to select bills we want to pay.

b. The form used to order and track products from vendors.

c. The onscreen form used to record products and services that we pay for at the time we receive the product or service with cash, credit card, or check.

d. The form used when a vendor gives us a refund or reduction in our bill.

e. This form can be used when we pay for products and services at the time of purchase, but cannot be used when we pay with cash or credit card.

f. A form used to record a reduction in charges by the vendor to our credit card.

g. The form used to record bills we receive and our obligation to pay the vendor later (accounts payable).

Vendors and Expenses Transaction

1. Expense
2. Check
3. Bill
4. Pay Bills
5. Purchase Order
6. Vendor Credit
7. Credit Card Credit

E7.2 Inventory Flow

Match the following items with the appropriate diagram number.

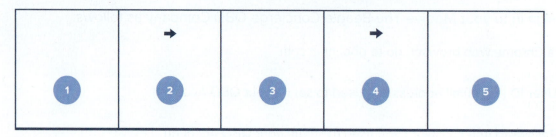

a. Sell Products to Customers

b. Purchase Products from Vendors

c. Customers

d. Vendors

e. Our Company

Item

1 _____

2 _____

3 _____

4 _____

5 _____

E7.3 Inventory and Transactions

Match the following transaction descriptions with the order in which the transactions typically would be recorded.

Transaction Descriptions

a. Records our obligation to pay the vendor for the products (Accounts Payable).

b. Records our order of products from vendors.

c. Records resale of product to customer and the customer's promise to pay later (Accounts Receivable).

d. Records customer's payment in the bank account, used only if Undeposited Funds is selected on the Receive Payment form.

e. Records collection of the customer's payment.

f. Pays vendors for products received.

Transaction Order

1. _____
2. _____
3. _____
4. _____
5. _____
6. _____

EM7.4 Products and Services List

Before starting EM7.4, verify that QBO Inventory Tracking is turned on. Go to Gear icon > Account and Settings > Sales > Products and Services > Track quantity and price/rate On > Track inventory quantity on hand > On.

To enter products into the Products and Services List:

1. From the Navigation Bar, select **Sales > Products and Services > New > Inventory**

2. Enter the following information about Mookie The Beagle Concierge branded products.

Use the following when entering inventory:

- **Inventory Asset Account: 1300 Inventory Asset**
- **Income Account: 4300 Sales of Product Income**
- **Expense Account: 5000 Cost of Goods Sold**
- **Initial Quantity on Hand: -0-**
- **As of Date: 01/01/2023**. (Note: If you receive an error message when saving, try selecting the calendar and selecting the date from the calendar even if the date autopopulates.)
- **Reorder Point: -0-**

CATEGORY	NAME	TYPE	DESCRIPTION	SALES PRICE	COST
Pet Hammocks	Mookie The Beagle Hammock Small	Inventory	Mookie The Beagle Pet Hammock Small	$ 300	$ 90
Pet Hammocks	Mookie The Beagle Hammock Medium	Inventory	Mookie The Beagle Pet Hammock Medium	$ 400	$ 160
Pet Hammocks	Mookie The Beagle Hammock Large	Inventory	Mookie The Beagle Pet Hammock Large	$ 500	$200
Pet Wellness Supplies	E-Collar Cone	Inventory	E-Collar Cone Adjustable (Fits Various Size Doggie Necks for Wound Healing)	$ 50	$ 16
Pet Wellness Supplies	Activated Charcoal	Inventory	Activated Charcoal for Suspected Poisoning	$ 36	$ 10
Pet Wellness Supplies	Gauze Bandages	Inventory	Gauze Bandages for Wound Dressing	$ 24	$ 6
Pet Wellness Supplies	Sterile Wipes	Inventory	Sterile Wipes for Wound Cleaning	$ 30	$ 8
Pet Wellness Supplies	Oral Syringes	Inventory	Oral Syringes for Medication Administration (10 pack)	$ 20	$ 4
Pet Wellness Supplies	Sterile Latex Gloves	Inventory	Sterile Latex Gloves (50 pack)	$ 72	$ 22

3. Export the Products and Services List to PDF.
   a. From the Products and Services List screen, select **More** > **Run Report**
   b. To sort the Products and Services List, select **Sort** > **Sort by: Type** > **Sort in: Ascending order**. Service items should at the top of the Products and Services List followed by Inventory items.
   c. Select **Export drop-down arrow** > **Export to PDF** > **Save as PDF**

4. Verify or enter Mookie The Beagle Concierge Address.
   a. Select **Gear icon** > **Account and Settings** > **Company** > **Address** > **Company Address**
   b. Enter **Address: 432 Phoenician Way**. (Note: Start typing, then select Enter manually.)
   c. Enter **City: Mountain View**
   d. Enter **State: California**
   e. Enter **Zip: 94043**
   f. Select **Customer-facing Address: Same as company address**
   g. Select **Legal Address: Same as company address**
   h. Select **Save** > **Done**

EM7.5 Vendors Transaction: Purchase Order

Complete the following Mookie The Beagle Concierge Purchase Order to order Mookie The Beagle hammocks.

1. Add a new Vendor to the Vendors List.
   a. From the Navigation Bar, select **Expenses** > **Vendors** tab
   b. Select **New vendor**
   c. Enter the following vendor information.

First Name:	**Maddy**
Company:	**Maddy's Marvels**
Display Name As:	**Maddy's Marvels**
Phone:	**415-555-2727**
Billing Address Street:	**27 Aquarian Rue**
Billing Address City:	**Bayshore**
Billing Address State:	**CA**
Billing Address ZIP:	**94326**
Billing Address Country:	**USA**

   d. Select **Save**

2. Create Purchase Order.
   a. Select **(+) New icon > Purchase Order**
   b. Select **Vendor: Maddy's Marvels**
   c. Select **Purchase Order Date: 01/18/2023**
   d. Verify **Shipping Address: Mookie The Beagle Concierge, 432 Phoenician Way, Mountain View, CA 94043**
   e. Select Item Details Line 1: **Product/Service: Pet Hammocks: Mookie The Beagle Hammock Small**
   f. Enter **QTY: 2**
   g. **Rate** and **Amount** fields should autofill
   h. What is the Rate that autofills?
   i. What is the Total Amount for Line 1?

3. Enter PO Line 2.
   a. Select Item Details Line 2: **Product/Service: Pet Hammocks: Mookie The Beagle Hammock Medium**
   b. Enter **QTY: 3**
   c. **Rate** and **Amount** fields should autofill
   d. What is the Rate that autofills?
   e. What is the Total Amount for Line 2?

4. Enter PO Line 3.
   a. Select Item Details Line 3: **Product/Service: Pet Hammocks: Mookie The Beagle Hammock Large**
   b. Enter **QTY: 1**
   c. **Rate** and **Amount** fields should autofill
   d. What is the Rate that autofills?
   e. What is the Total Amount for Line 3?

5. Total PO.
   a. What is the Total Amount for the Purchase Order?
   b. Select **Save and close**

EM7.6 Vendors Transaction: Purchase Order

Complete the following Mookie The Beagle Concierge Purchase Order to order Mookie The Beagle Concierge pet wellness inventory.

1. Add a new Vendor to the Vendors List.
   a. From the Navigation Bar, select **Expenses > Vendors** tab
   b. Select **New vendor**
   c. Enter the following vendor information.

Company:	**Meta Pet Supply**
Phone:	**415-555-8866**
Billing Address Street:	**86 Tron Boulevard**
Billing Address City:	**Bayshore**
Billing Address State:	**CA**
Billing Address ZIP:	**94326**
Billing Address Country:	**USA**

    d.   Select **Save**

2. Create Purchase Order.
    a.   Select **(+) New icon > Purchase Order**
    b.   Select **Vendor: Meta Pet Supply**
    c.   Select **Purchase Order Date: 01/18/2023**
    d.   Select Item Details Line 1: **Product/Service: Pet Wellness Supplies: E-Collar Cone**
    e.   Enter **QTY: 1**
    f.   **Rate** and **Amount** fields should autofill
    g.   What is the Rate that autofills?
    h.   What is the Total Amount for Line 1?

3. Enter PO Line 2.
    a.   Select Item Details Line 2: **Product/Service: Pet Wellness Supplies: Activated Charcoal**
    b.   Enter **QTY: 5**
    c.   **Rate** and **Amount** fields should autofill
    d.   What is the Rate that autofills?
    e.   What is the Total Amount for Line 2?

4. Enter PO Line 3.
    a.   Select Item Details Line 3: **Product/Service: Pet Wellness Supplies: Gauze Bandages**
    b.   Enter **QTY: 4**
    c.   **Rate** and **Amount** fields should autofill
    d.   What is the Rate that autofills?
    e.   What is the Total Amount for Line 3?

5. Enter PO Line 4.
    a.   Select Item Details Line 4: **Product/Service: Pet Wellness Supplies: Sterile Wipes**
    b.   Enter **QTY: 6**
    c.   **Rate** and **Amount** fields should autofill
    d.   What is the Rate that autofills?
    e.   What is the Total Amount for Line 4?

6. Enter PO Line 5.
   a. Select Item Details Line 4: Product/Service: Pet Wellness Supplies: Oral Syringes
   b. Enter **QTY: 2**
   c. **Rate** and **Amount** fields should autofill
   d. What is the Rate that autofills?
   e. What is the Total Amount for Line 5?

7. Enter PO Line 6.
   a. Select Item Details Line 4: **Product/Service: Pet Wellness Supplies: Sterile Latex Gloves**
   b. Enter **QTY: 6**
   c. **Rate** and **Amount** fields should autofill
   d. What is the Rate that autofills?
   e. What is the Total Amount for Line 6?

8. Total PO.
   a. What is the Total Amount for the Purchase Order?
   b. Select **Save and close**

EM7.7 Vendors Transaction: Purchase Order

Complete the following Purchase Order to order Mookie The Beagle Bon Appetite Organic Dog Food.

1. Update Vendor information in the Vendors List.
   a. From the Navigation Bar, select **Expenses** > **Vendors** tab
   b. Select **Vendor: Only The Best Dog Food**
   c. Update the following vendor information.

Company:	Only The Best Dog Food
Phone:	415-555-6354
Billing Address Street:	91 Elsker Avenue
Billing Address City:	Bayshore
Billing Address State:	CA
Billing Address ZIP:	94326
Billing Address Country:	USA

   d. Select **Save**

2. Create Purchase Order.
   a. Select **(+) New icon > Purchase Order**
   b. Select **Vendor: Only The Best Dog Food**
   c. Select **Purchase Order Date: 01/18/2023**
   d. Select Item Details Line 1: **Product/Service: Pet Food Supplies: Mookie The Beagle Bon Appetite Organic Dog Food**
   e. Enter **QTY: 10**
   f. **Rate** and **Amount** fields should autofill
   g. What is the Rate that autofills?
   h. What is the Total Amount for Line 1?

3. Total PO.
   a. What is the Total Amount for the Purchase Order?
   b. Select **Save and close**

EM7.8 Vendors Transaction: Bill

Complete the following to record a bill received for the Mookie The Beagle Dog Hammocks ordered.

1. Create Bill.
   a. Select **(+) New icon > Bill**
   b. Select **Vendor: Maddy's Marvels**
   c. Select **Bill Date: 01/21/2023**
   d. The Purchase Order entered previously should appear in the Add to Bill drawer on the right side of the screen. Select **Add** to add the PO to the bill. Item Details should now show the items from the PO.
   e. What is the Total for the Bill?
   f. Select **Save**

2. View the Transaction Journal for the Bill.
   a. From the bottom of the Maddy's Marvels Bill, select **More > Transaction Journal**
   b. What are the Accounts and Amounts Debited?
   c. What are the Account and Amount Credited?

EM7.9 Vendors Transaction: Bill

Complete the following to record a bill received for the Mookie The Beagle Concierge pet wellness supplies ordered.

1. Create Bill.
   a. Select **(+) New icon > Bill**
   b. Select **Vendor: Meta Pet Supply**
   c. Select **Bill Date: 01/23/2023**
   d. The Purchase Order entered previously should appear in the Add to Bill drawer. Select **Add** to add the PO to the bill. Item Details should now show the items from the PO.
   e. What is the Total for the Bill?
   f. Select **Save**

2. View the Transaction Journal for the Bill.
   a. From the bottom of the Meta Pet Supply Bill, select **More > Transaction Journal**
   b. What are the Accounts and Amounts Debited?
   c. What are the Account and Amount Credited?

EM7.10 Vendors Transaction: Bill

Complete the following to record a bill received for the Mookie The Beagle Organic Dog Food ordered.

1. Create Bill.
   a. Select **(+) New icon > Bill**
   b. Select **Vendor: Only the Best Dog Food**
   c. Select **Bill Date: 01/23/2023**
   d. The Purchase Order entered previously should appear in the Add to Bill drawer. *Before adding, if the Bill autofilled with prior bill Item Details, select the trash can to delete the prior bill Item Details.* Then select **Add** to add the PO to the bill. Item Details should now show the items from the PO.
   e. What is the Total for the Bill?
   f. Select **Save**

2. View the Transaction Journal for the Bill.
   a. From the bottom of the Bill, select **More > Transaction Journal**
   b. What are the Account and Amount Debited?
   c. What are the Account and Amount Credited?

EM7.11 Vendors Transaction: Pay Bills

Complete the following to pay Mookie The Beagle Concierge bills.

1. Pay Bills.
    a. Select **(+) New icon** > **Pay Bills**
    b. Select **Payment Account: 1001 Checking**
    c. Select **Payment Date: 01/24/2023**
    d. Select **Payee: Maddy's Marvels**
    e. Select **Payee: Only the Best Dog Food**
    f. What is the Total Payment Amount?
    g. Select **Save and close**

2. View the Transaction Journal for Pay Bills.
    a. From the Navigation Bar, select **Expenses** > **Expenses** tab
    b. From the Expense Transactions List, select **Bill Payment to Maddy's Marvels**
    c. From the bottom of Maddy's Marvels Bill Payment, select **More** > **Transaction Journal**
    d. What are the Account and Amount Debited?
    e. What are the Account and Amount Credited?

3. View the Transaction Journal for Pay Bills.
    a. From the Navigation Bar, select **Expenses**
    b. From the Expense Transactions List, select **Bill Payment to Only the Best Dog Food**
    c. From the bottom of Only the Best Dog Food Bill Payment, select **More** > **Transaction Journal**
    d. What are the Account and Amount Debited?
    e. What are the Account and Amount Credited?

EM7.12 Customers Transaction: Invoice

Complete the following to record the sale of a Mookie The Beagle Dog Hammock to Sandy Copper for Remy, her rescue dog.

1. Set up Sales Tax.
    a. From the Navigation Bar, select **Taxes** > **Use Automatic Sales Tax**
    b. Verify **Business Address** for **Mookie The Beagle Concierge** > select **Next**
    c. Do you need to collect sales tax outside of California? Select **No** > **Next**
    d. Select **Create Invoice** from the Automatic Sales Tax is All Set Up window

2 Create Invoice.

   a. If the Invoice does not automatically appear on your screen, select **(+) New icon >
Invoice**

   b. Select **Customer: Sandy Copper: Remy**

   c. Select **Invoice Date: 01/25/2023**

   d. Select Item Details Line 1: **Product/Service: Pet Hammocks: Mookie The Beagle
Hammock Medium**

   e. Enter **QTY: 1**

   f. **Rate** and **Amount** fields should autofill

   g. What is the Amount?

   h. Check **Tax**

   i. Select **Sales Tax Rate** > select **Add rate** > select **Single** > enter **Name: Sales Tax** >
select **Agency: California Department of Tax and Fee Administration** > enter **Rate: 9%**
> select **Save**

   j. What is the Total for the Invoice?

   k. Select **Save** and leave the Invoice displayed

3 View the Transaction Journal for the Invoice.

   a. From the bottom of the Invoice, select **More > Transaction Journal**

   b. What are the Accounts and Amounts Debited?

   c. What are the Accounts and Amounts Credited?

EM7.13 Customers Transaction: Invoice

While your pet Goldendoodle, Ozzie, is recovering from being bitten by another dog, Ozzie
needs in home care. So you order the following products and services using the Mookie The
Beagle Concierge app.

- 1 Mookie The Beagle Dog Hammock Medium
- 1 Mookie The Beagle E-Collar Cone
- 3 Gauze Bandages
- 2 Sterile Wipes
- 1 Oral Syringes (10 pack)
- 1 Sterile Latex Gloves (50 pack)
- 1 Pet Care Errand Service (to deliver the Mookie The Beagle Concierge supplies
ordered)
- 2 Pet Wellness Medium Wellness Service (to administer medication and change wound
dressings)

1. Create Invoice.
   a. Select **(+) New icon** > **Invoice**
   b. Select **Customer: Your Name: Ozzie**
   c. Select **Invoice Date: 01/27/2023**
   d. Select Item Details Line 1: **Product/Service: Pet Hammocks: Mookie The Beagle Hammock Medium**
   e. Enter **QTY: 1**
   f. **Rate** and **Amount** fields should autofill
   g. What is the Amount on Line 1?
   h. Check **Tax** > select **Tax Rate: 9%**

2. Enter Invoice Line 2.
   a. Select Item Details Line 2: **Product/Service: Pet Wellness Supplies: E-Collar Cone**
   b. Enter **QTY: 1**
   c. **Rate** and **Amount** fields should autofill
   d. What is the Amount on Line 2?
   e. Check **Tax**

3. Enter Invoice Line 3.
   a. Select Item Details Line 3: **Product/Service: Pet Wellness Supplies: Gauze Bandages**
   b. Enter **QTY: 3**
   c. **Rate** and **Amount** fields should autofill
   d. What is the Amount on Line 3?
   e. Check **Tax**

4. Enter Invoice Line 4.
   a. Select Item Details Line 4: **Product/Service: Pet Wellness Supplies: Sterile Wipes**
   b. Enter **QTY: 2**
   c. **Rate** and **Amount** fields should autofill
   d. What is the Amount on Line 4?
   e. Check **Tax**

5. Enter Invoice Line 5.
   a. Select Item Details Line 5: **Product/Service: Pet Wellness Supplies: Oral Syringes**
   b. Enter **QTY: 1**
   c. **Rate** and **Amount** fields should autofill
   d. What is the Amount on Line 5?
   e. Check **Tax**

6. Enter Invoice Line 6.
   a. Select Item Details Line 6: **Product/Service: Pet Wellness Supplies: Sterile Latex Gloves**
   b. Enter **QTY: 1**
   c. **Rate** and **Amount** fields should autofill
   d. What is the Amount on Line 6?
   e. Check **Tax**

7. Enter Invoice Line 7.
    a. Select Item Details Line 7: **Product/Service: Pet Care: Errand**
    b. Enter **QTY: 1**
    c. **Rate** and **Amount** fields should autofill
    d. What is the Amount on Line 7?
    e. Uncheck **Tax**

8. Enter Invoice Line 8.
    a. Select Item Details Line 8: **Product/Service: Pet Wellness: Medium Wellness**
    b. Enter **QTY: 2**
    c. **Rate** and **Amount** fields should autofill
    d. What is the Amount on Line 8?
    e. Uncheck **Tax**

9. Sales Tax.
    a. What is the Subtotal for the Invoice?
    b. What is the Amount of Sales Tax?
    c. What is the Total for the Invoice?
    d. Select **Save** and leave the Invoice displayed

10. View the Transaction Journal for the Invoice.
    a. From the bottom of the Invoice, select **More > Transaction Journal**
    b. What are the Accounts and Amounts Debited?
    c. What are the Accounts and Amounts Credited?

EM7.14 Customers Transaction: Invoice

Angel Merriman used the Mookie The Beagle Concierge app to purchase the following products and services for her pet King Shepherd, Kuno, when Angel was detained for hours longer than planned working on a client cybersecurity project gone awry.

- 1 Mookie The Beagle Dog Hammock Large
- 2 bags of Mookie The Beagle Bon Appetite Organic Dog Food
- 1 Pet Care Errand Service (to deliver the Mookie The Beagle Concierge supplies ordered)
- 2 Pet Care Short Visit Service (to feed and take Kuno on a couple of short walks)

Complete the following for Mookie The Beagle Concierge to record an Invoice.

1. Update Customer information in the Customers List.
    a. From the Navigation Bar, select **Sales > Customers** tab
    b. Select **Customer: Angel Merriman**
    c. Enter the following updated customer information.

Phone	415-555-9999

    d. Select **Save**

2. Create Invoice and Enter Products Purchased.
   a. Select **(+) New icon > Invoice**
   b. Select **Customer: Angel Merriman: Kuno**
   c. Select **Invoice Date: 01/28/2023**
   d. Select Item Details Line 1: **Product/Service: Pet Hammocks: Mookie The Beagle Hammock Large**
   e. Enter **QTY: 1**
   f. **Rate** and **Amount** fields should autofill
   g. What is the Amount for Line 1?
   h. Check **Tax** > select **Tax Rate: 9%**
   i. Select Item Details Line 2: **Product/Service: Pet Food Supplies: Mookie Bon Appetite Organic Dog Food**
   j. Enter **QTY: 2**
   k. **Rate** and **Amount** fields should autofill
   l. What is the Amount for Line 2?
   m. Check **Tax**
   n. Select **Save** and leave the Invoice displayed

3. Enter Services Purchased on Invoice.
   a. Select Item Details Line 3: **Product/Service: Pet Care: Errand**
   b. Enter **QTY: 1**
   c. **Rate** and **Amount** fields should autofill
   d. What is the Amount for Line 3?
   e. Uncheck **Tax**
   f. Select Item Details Line 4: **Product/Service: Pet Care: Short Visit**
   g. Enter **QTY: 2**
   h. **Rate** and **Amount** fields should autofill
   i. What is the Amount for Line 4?
   j. Uncheck **Tax**
   k. Select **California Sales Tax Rate: 9%**
   l. What is the Subtotal for the Invoice?
   m. What is the Taxable Subtotal for the Invoice?
   n. What is the Amount of Sales Tax on the Invoice?
   o. What is the Total for the Invoice?
   p. Select **Save** and leave the Invoice displayed

4. View the Transaction Journal for the Invoice.
   a. From the bottom of the Invoice, select **More > Transaction Journal**
   b. What are the Accounts and Amounts Debited?
   c. What are the Accounts and Amounts Credited?

EM7.15 Customers Transaction: Receive Payment

Complete the following to record a customer payment from Angel Merriman.

1. Create Receive Payment.
   a. Select **(+) New icon > Receive Payment**
   b. Select **Customer: Angel Merriman: Kuno**
   c. Select **Payment Date: 01/30/2023**
   d. Select **Payment Method: Credit Card**
   e. Select **Deposit to: 1001 Checking**
   f. Select the **Angel Merriman: Kuno Invoice** just entered
   g. What is the Amount Received?
   h. Select **Save and close**

2. View the Transaction Journal for Receive Payments.
   a. From the Navigation Bar, select **Sales > All Sales** tab
   b. From the Sales Transactions List, select **Angel Merriman: Kuno Payment** just entered
   c. From the bottom of Receive Payment, select **More > Transaction Journal**
   d. What are the Account and Amount Debited?
   e. What are the Account and Amount Credited?

EM7.16 Customers Transaction: Refund Receipt

There was an error when delivering the order for Kuno's dog food. Angel Merriman received only one bag of dog food instead of the two she was billed for. Complete the following to record a refund receipt to Angel Merriman for the extra bag of dog food that she did not receive.

1. Create Refund Receipt.
   a. Select **(+) New icon > Refund Receipt**
   b. Select **Customer: Angel Merriman: Kuno**
   c. Select **Refund Receipt Date: 01/31/2023**
   d. Select **Payment Method: Credit Card**
   e. Select **Refund from: 1001 Checking**
   f. Select **Product/Service: Mookie The Beagle Bon Appetite Organic Dog Food**
   g. Select **Tax > select Tax Rate: 9%**
   h. What is the Subtotal of the Refund Receipt?
   i. What is the Total Amount Refunded?
   j. Select **Save and close**

2. View the Transaction Journal for Receive Payments.
   a. From the Navigation Bar, select **Sales > All Sales** tab
   b. From the Sales Transactions List, select **Angel Merriman: Kuno Refund** just entered
   c. From the bottom of Refund Receipt, select **More > Transaction Journal**
   d. What are the Account and Amount Debited?
   e. What are the Account and Amount Credited?

Chapter 8

Employees and Payroll

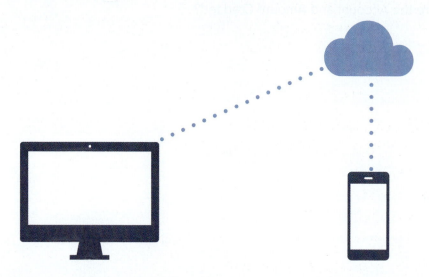

MOOKIE THE BEAGLE™ CONCIERGE

BACKSTORY

Mookie The Beagle™ Concierge, a business offering high-quality pet care on demand, has only one employee, Cy Walker. Cy is also the founder and owner of MTB Concierge. Other MTB Concierge pet care service providers are hired as independent contractors, meeting all IRS requirements to be classified as such.

Mookie The Beagle Concierge would like your assistance in using the QBO time-tracking feature to track time for specific contractors providing pet care to customer pets. Cy plans to use the tracked time to pay contractors he hires to provide pet services. Also, he can use the tracked time to invoice customers for services provided. So your next task is to learn more about using QuickBooks Online for tracking time.

Chapter 8

LEARNING OBJECTIVES

Chapter 8 focuses on recording employees and payroll transactions. Payroll involves preparing employee paychecks, withholding the appropriate amount in taxes, and paying the company's share of payroll taxes. To assist in processing payroll, QBO offers a time-tracking feature that permits us to track the amount of time worked.

In Chapter 8, you will learn about the following topics:

- Navigating Employees Transactions
  - ▸ Payroll Setup
  - ▸ Payroll Processing
- Employees List
- Contractors List
- Time Tracking
  - ▸ Turn on Time Tracking Preferences
  - ▸ Enter Time Tracking
- Invoice Tracked Time
- QBO Payroll Options
- Pay Employees
- Pay Payroll Liabilities
- File Payroll Forms
- Accounting Essentials: Payroll Liabilities and Payroll Taxes

---

⚠ **QBO is updated on an ongoing basis. Updates that affect your text can be viewed as follows:**

1. **Go to www.My-QuickBooksOnline.com > QBO 3e > QBO 3e Updates, or**
2. **If you are using Connect or a digital ebook, you can find updates under Additional Student Resources (ASR). If you do not have access to Connect or the ebook, your instructor can provide you with ASR.**

Section 8.1

 ## QBO SATNAV

QBO SatNav is our satellite navigation for QuickBooks Online, assisting us in navigating QBO

Chapter 8 focuses on QBO Employees & Payroll Transactions as shown in the following QBO SatNav.

 QBO SatNav

 QBO Settings

Company Settings
Chart of Accounts

 QBO Transactions

Banking	
Customers & Sales	
Vendors & Expenses	
 Employees & Payroll	*Enter Time > Pay Employees > Payroll Liabilities*

 QBO Reports

Reports

Section 8.2

NAVIGATING EMPLOYEES TRANSACTIONS

There are two main aspects to using QBO for Employees and Payroll Transaction purposes:

- Setting up payroll
- Processing payroll

PAYROLL SETUP

Payroll setup requires:

1. Set up **Employees List**
2. Turn on **Time Tracking** preference
3. Turn on **QBO Payroll**

PAYROLL PROCESSING

Payroll processing consists of the following four main types of tasks:

1. **Enter Time.** QBO permits us to track employee time worked to use in processing payroll and billing customers.
2. **Pay Employees.** Select employees to pay and create their paychecks.
3. **Pay Payroll Liabilities.** Pay payroll tax liabilities due governmental agencies, such as the IRS. Payroll tax liabilities include federal income taxes withheld, state income taxes withheld, FICA (Social Security and Medicare), and unemployment taxes.
4. **Process Payroll Forms.** Process payroll forms including Forms 940, 941, W-2, and W-3 that must be submitted to governmental agencies.

Section 8.3

EMPLOYEES LIST

The Employees List contains employee information such as address, telephone, salary or wage rate, and Social Security number.

Intuit QBO Payroll is changing rapidly. So your QBO screens may differ from your text instructions. For your convenience, there are two options presented here. If neither option matches your QBO screens, check the text updates in Connect or at www.my-quickbooksonline.com and contact your instructor.

OPTION 1. ADD NAME TO EMPLOYEES LIST FOR TIME TRACKING

To add employees to the Employees list, QBO may require that we turn on Time Tracking first.

To turn on the QBO time entry feature:

1 From the Navigation Bar, select **Time**

2 Select **Overview** tab

3 Select **Stick with basic time**.
⚠ If **Stick with basic time** does not appear as an option on your screen, see the following section, **Option 2. Add Name to Contractors List for Time Tracking**.

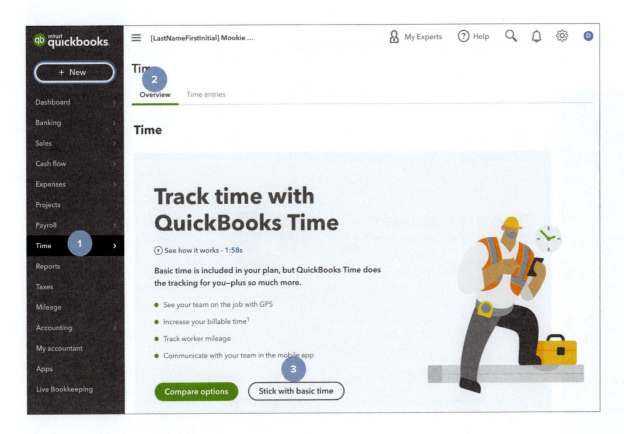

To add an Employee to the Employees List:

1 From the Navigation Bar, select **Time**

2 Select **Add an employee**

3 When the Employee Information window appears, enter **First name: Cy**

4 Enter **Last name: Walker**

5 Enter **Display name as: Cy Walker**

6 Enter **Employee ID: 111-11-1111**

7 Select **Save**

8 Select **Payroll > Employees** tab. Now Cy Walker's name appears in the Employees List.

9 To update Cy Walker's employee information, select **Edit**

10 To add another employee, select **Add an employee**

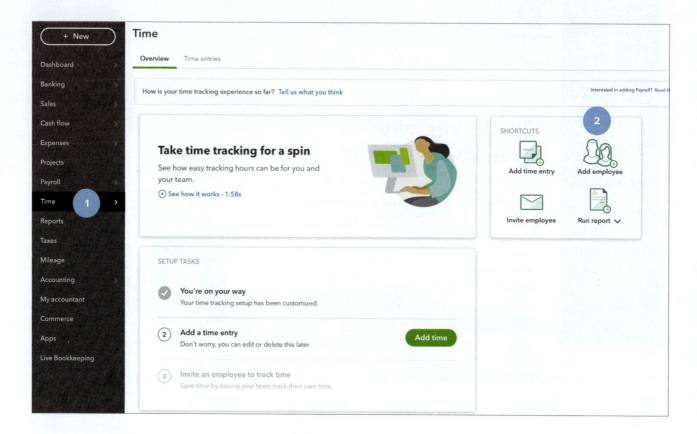

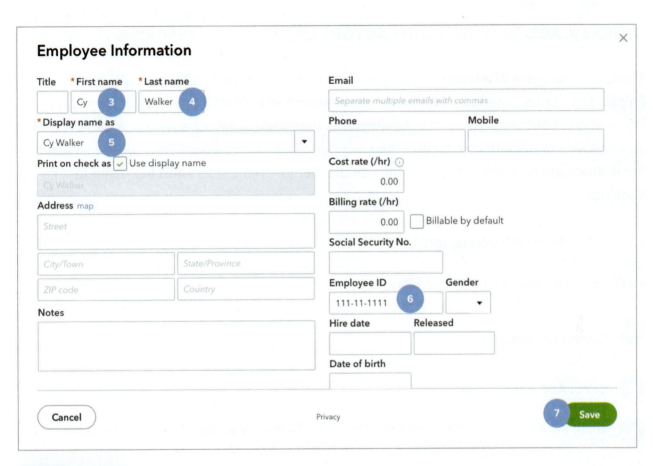

Employee Information   ✕

Title	*First name	*Last name		Email

Title [ ] *First name [Cy] ③   *Last name [Walker] ④

Email [Separate multiple emails with commas]

*Display name as
[Cy Walker] ⑤   ▾

Phone [   ]   Mobile [   ]

Print on check as ✓ Use display name

Cost rate (/hr) ⓘ
[0.00]

[Cy Walker]

Billing rate (/hr)
[0.00]   ☐ Billable by default

Address map

[Street   ]

Social Security No.
[   ]

[City/Town   ] [State/Province   ]

[ZIP code   ] [Country   ]

Employee ID   Gender
[111-11-1111] ⑥   [▾]

Notes

[   ]

Hire date   Released
[   ]   [   ]

Date of birth
[   ]

Cancel   Privacy   ⑦ Save

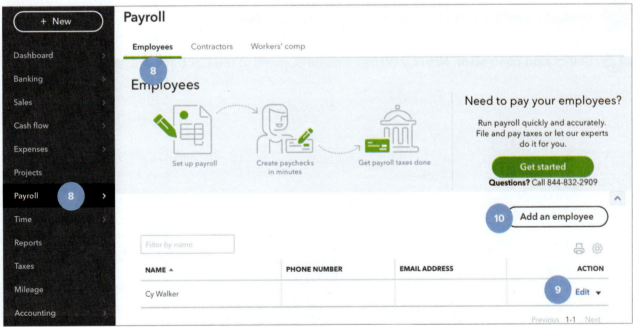

+ New

Payroll

Dashboard
Banking
Sales
Cash flow
Expenses
Projects
Payroll   ⑧
Time
Reports
Taxes
Mileage
Accounting

Employees   Contractors   Workers' comp
⑧
Employees

Set up payroll   →   Create paychecks in minutes   →   Get payroll taxes done

Need to pay your employees?
Run payroll quickly and accurately. File and pay taxes or let our experts do it for you.

Get started

Questions? Call 844-832-2909

⑩ Add an employee

Filter by name   🖨 ⚙

NAME ▲	PHONE NUMBER	EMAIL ADDRESS	ACTION
Cy Walker			⑨ Edit ▾

Previous 1-1 Next

OPTION 2. ADD NAME TO CONTRACTORS LIST FOR TIME TRACKING

There are two types of workers: employees and contractors. QBO features both an Employees List for organizing employee information and a Contractors List for organizing information about contractors. IRS requirements determine whether a worker is classified as an employee or a contractor. If QBO does not permit you to create an Employees List using the instructions in Option 1, then we can use the Contractors List to enter the name for time tracking.

To add a name to the Contractors List:

1 From the Navigation Bar, select **Payroll**

2 Select **Contractors** tab

3 Select **Add a contractor**

4 When the Add a contractor screen appears, enter **Name: Cy Walker**. Note: If you receive an error message, modify Cy Walker's name so QBO will accept it.

5 **Uncheck: Email this contractor to complete their profile.**

6 Select **Add contractor**. Now Cy Walker's name appears in the Contractors List.

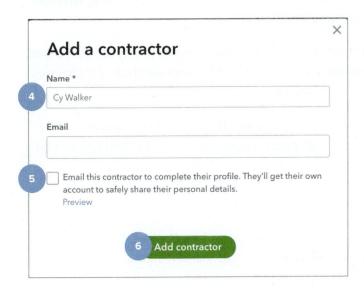

Section 8.4

CONTRACTORS LIST

A company's workers can be either:

- Employees or
- Contractors

IRS rules determine if a worker is classified as an employee or an independent contractor. See www.irs.gov for more information about specific IRS requirements to determine whether a worker should be classified as an employee or a contractor.

Employees are hired by a business with the business paying wages, salary, payroll taxes and employee benefits, such as health insurance. As you learned in the prior section, employees can be added to the Employees List by selecting Payroll > Employees.

Contractors are paid a contracted fee, a fee specified by a contract. The business does not pay payroll taxes or additional benefits. Instead, the contractor is responsible for paying self-employment taxes. Contractors are vendors.

FLAG VENDORS WHO ARE CONTRACTORS

Andre LaFortune and Evan Henry work as contractors for Mookie The Beagle Concierge. Both have been previously added as vendors to MBT Concierge Vendors List.

To flag Andre LaFortune and Evan Henry as vendors who are contractors:

1. From the Navigation Bar, select **Expenses**

2. Select **Vendors** tab

3. Notice that **Andre LaFortune** and **Evan Henry** appear in the Vendors List

4. Select **Andre LaFortune**

5. Select **Edit**

6. Enter **Social Security No.: 987-65-4321**

7   Check **Track payments for 1099**

8   Select **Save**

9   From the Vendors List, select **Evan Henry**

10   Select **Edit**

11   Enter **Social Security No.: 987-65-4320**

12   Check **Track payments for 1099**

13   Select **Save**

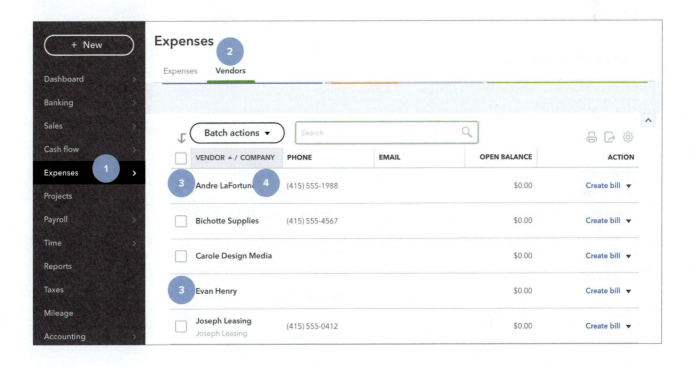

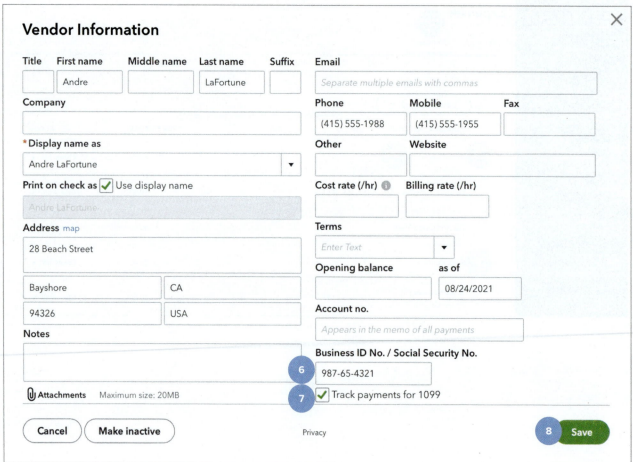

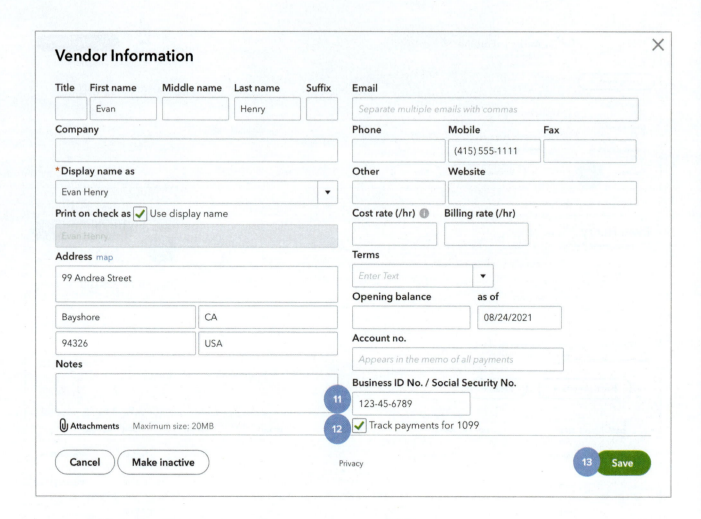

VIEW CONTRACTORS LIST USING PAYROLL MENU

Vendors who are flagged as contractors will appear in the Contractors List that can be viewed from the Payroll menu. After selecting Track payments for 1099 for the vendors, Andre LaFortune and Evan Henry, those vendors should now appear in the Contractors List.

To view the Contractors List:

1. From the Navigation Bar, select **Payroll**

2. Select **Contractors** tab. Andre LaFortune and Evan Henry should now appear in the Contractors List.

3. If we wanted to add another contractor, we would select **Add a contractor**

4. If it was year end and we needed to prepare Form 1099s for contractors, we would select **Prepare 1099s**

5   Select **Evan Henry**

6   From the contractor screen, we can **Write check**, **Create expense**, or **Create bill**

7   Select the **Details** tab to view or edit personal details

8   Select **Payments** tab to view payments made to the contractor

9   Select **Documents** tab to view information about W-9, a tax form used to collect information about contractors

10   Select the **Contractors** link to return to the Contractors List

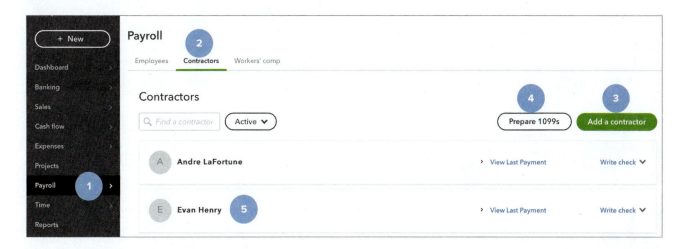

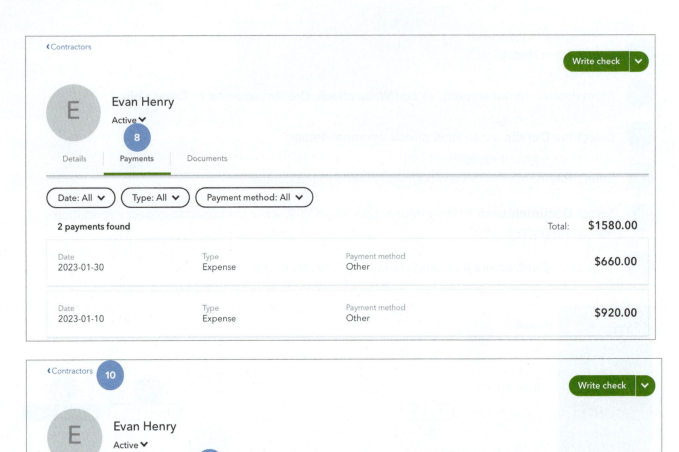

If Contractors are not Employees, why are Contractors under the Payroll menu? **Are you wondering why the Contractors List is located in the Payroll menu when Contractors are Vendors (Expenses menu), not Employees (Payroll menu)? QBO, like other applications, evolves over time. At one time, the Payroll menu was called the Workers menu. Workers consist of Employees and Contractors. The Workers menu was renamed to Payroll menu, but the Contractors List was left in the same location.**

Section 8.5

TIME TRACKING

QBO time tracking permits us to track the amount of time worked. QBO uses time tracked to:

1. Calculate employee paychecks
2. Calculate contractor payments
3. Transfer time to sales invoices to bill customers for work performed

Work can be performed by employees, contractors, or owners. The time-tracking feature can be used to track time worked by any of the three. How we record the payment, however, depends upon the status of the individual who performs the work: employee, contractor, or business owner.

So it's important that we determine the status of the individual performing the work. The status determines whether we record payments to the individual as an employee paycheck, vendor payment, or owner distribution.

Status	QBO Payment	Tax Form
Employee	Employee Paycheck	Form W-2
Contractor	Vendor Payment	Form 1099
Owner	Owner Distribution	Owner's Tax Return

TURN ON TIME-TRACKING PREFERENCES

To turn on QBO time-tracking preferences:

1 Select **Gear** icon

2 Under Your Company column, select **Account and Settings**

3 From the Account and Settings screen, select **Time**

4 Select the **Edit Pencil**

5 Select First day of work week: **Monday**

6   Select **Save**

7   Select **Edit Pencil**, then select **Show service field** to display **On**

8   Select **Allow time to be billable** to display **On**

9   Select **Save**

10   Select **Done**

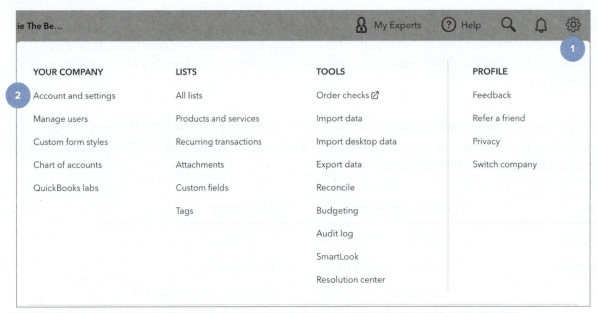

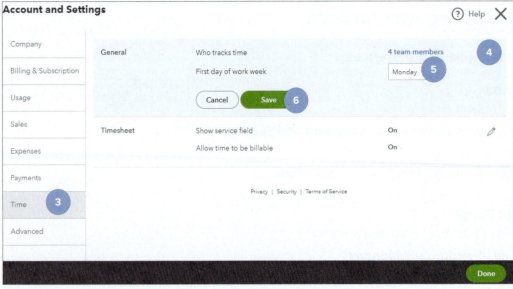

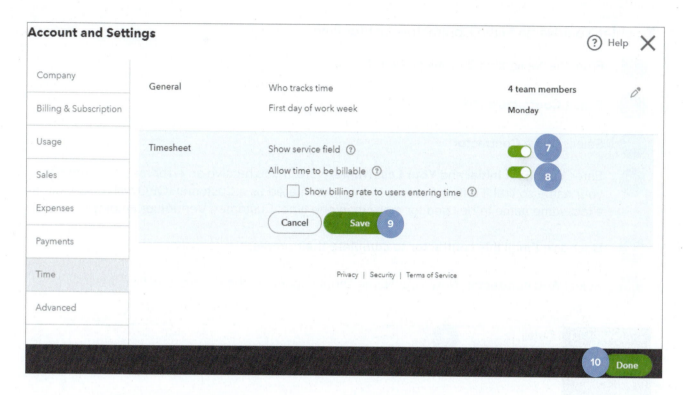

After setting the time-tracking preferences, we are ready to enter time.

ENTER TIME

When employees or contractors use time tracking, the employee or contractor records total time worked and any time that is billable to a specific customer. Time data is then used to:

1. Prepare employee paychecks
2. Prepare contractor payments
3. Invoice customers for billable time

> **Note: At this time, QBO's update to time tracking may have limited functionality of time tracking for Contractors. One workaround to this issue is to enter the contractor as both an employee type and a vendor type. Then use the employee type for time tracking purposes.**

The Enter Time feature can be used to enter the hours worked during the week. If time is billable to a specific customer, this is indicated on the timesheet. Later, billable time can be transferred to a specific customer's invoice.

You decide to earn some extra money running errands for Mookie The Beagle Concierge. To set up time tracking for your name in QBO, we first need to enter your name in the Contractors List and then enter the billable time.

To enter Your Name in the Contractors List for time tracking:

1 From the Navigation Bar, select **Payroll**

2 Select **Contractors** tab

3 Select **Add a Contractor**

4 Enter **Your First Initial** and **Your Last Name**. Note: If you receive an error message, modify your name so that it differs from the name you entered as a Customer. QBO will not permit the exact same name to be used for more than one type: Customer, Vendor, or Employee.

5 **Uncheck: Email this contractor to complete their profile.**

6 Select **Add contractor**. Now Your Name should appear in the Contractors List.

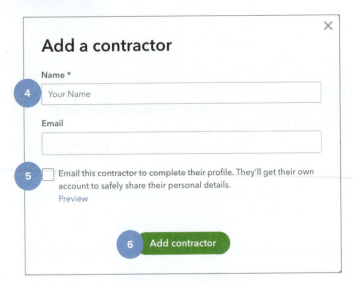

To enter time for time tracking:

1   Select **(+) New icon**

2   From the Employees column, select **Single Time Activity** (or **Time Entry**). (Note: Your Employees column may change from Time Entry to Single Time Activity and Weekly Timesheet.)

If you selected Single Time Activity, complete steps 3 through 11.

If you selected Time Entry, complete steps 12 through 22.

3   If you selected Single Time Activity in Step 2, enter **Date: 01/05/2023**

4   Select **Name: Your Name**

5   Select **Customer/Project: Sandy Copper: Remy**

6   Select **Service: Pet Care Errand**

7   Select **Billable (/hr)**

8   Uncheck **Enter Start and End Times**

9   Enter **Time: 1:00 hour**

10   Description should autofill with **Pet Personal Shopper, 1 hour minimum**

11   Select **Save and close**

If you selected Time Entry in step 2, complete the following steps 12 through 22.

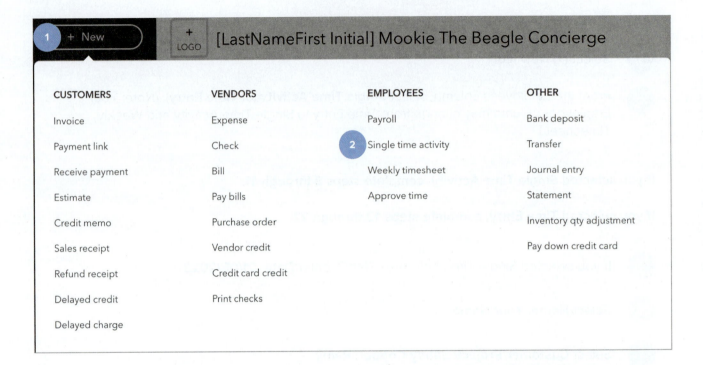

or

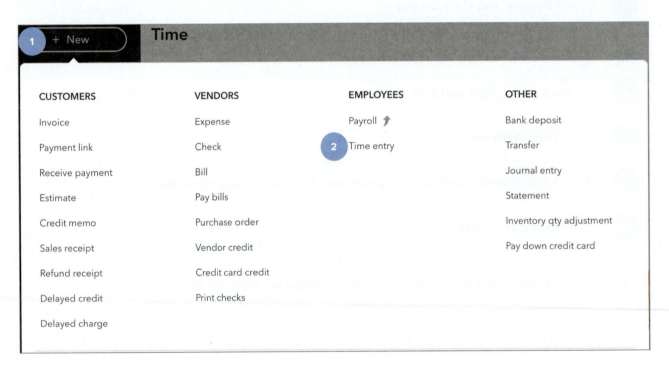

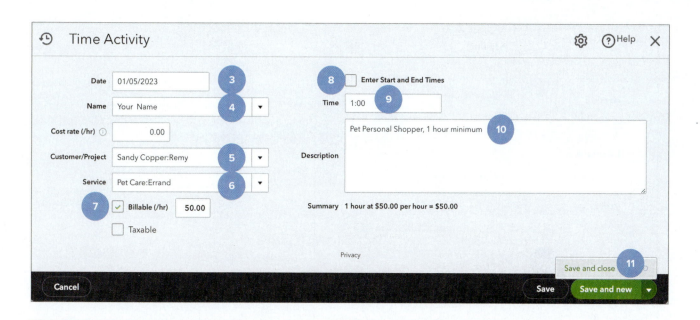

If QBO does not permit you to enter a date, stating it's too far in advance, try clicking on the calendar in the Date field > scroll over to the year needed > select the specific date you need. If you receive an error when entering time, try unclicking the time and click on billable hours to make the time entry.

12   If you selected Time Entry in Step 2, select **Your Name**

13   Select Custom from the drop-down menu. Then use the calendar to select **Date: 01/05/2023**.

14   Select **Add Work Details**

15   **Unselect Enter Start and End Times**

16   Enter **Duration: 1.0**

17   Select **Customer/Project: Sandy Copper: Remy**

18   Select **Service: Pet Care: Errand**

19   Select **Billable (/hr)**

20   Notes should autofill with **Pet Personal Shopper, 1 hour minimum**

21   Select **Done**

22   Select the Save menu arrow, then select **Save and close**

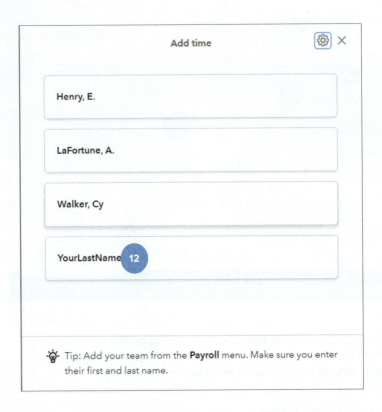

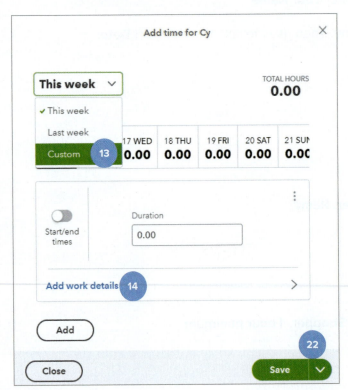

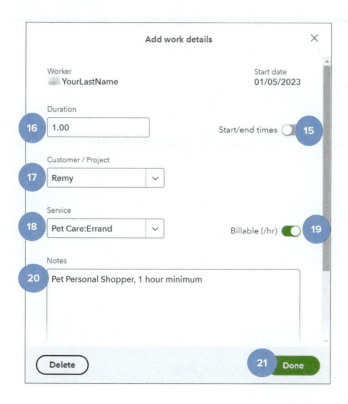

Section 8.6

INVOICE TRACKED TIME

Next, we can transfer billable tracked time to an Invoice to bill a specific customer for the time.

C8.6.1 Invoice with Billable Tracked Time

To create an Invoice with billable tracked time:

1. From the **(+) New icon**, select **Invoice**

2. Select **Customer: Sandy Copper: Remy**

3. Select **Invoice date: 01/05/2023**

4. From the Add to Invoice drawer and the Billable time card, select **Add**

5. Select **Save**

6. Select **More**

7. Select **Transaction journal**. What are the accounts and amounts debited? What are the accounts and amounts credited?

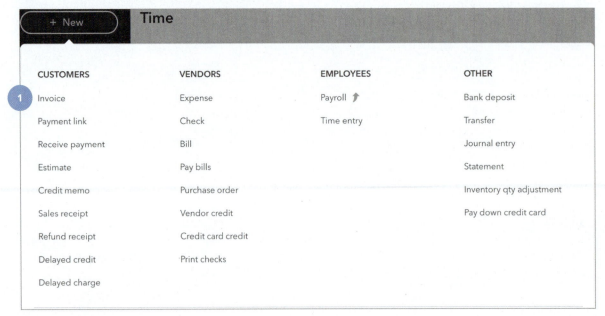

CUSTOMERS	VENDORS	EMPLOYEES	OTHER
Invoice	Expense	Payroll 🕐	Bank deposit
Payment link	Check	Time entry	Transfer
Receive payment	Bill		Journal entry
Estimate	Pay bills		Statement
Credit memo	Purchase order		Inventory qty adjustment
Sales receipt	Vendor credit		Pay down credit card
Refund receipt	Credit card credit		
Delayed credit	Print checks		
Delayed charge			

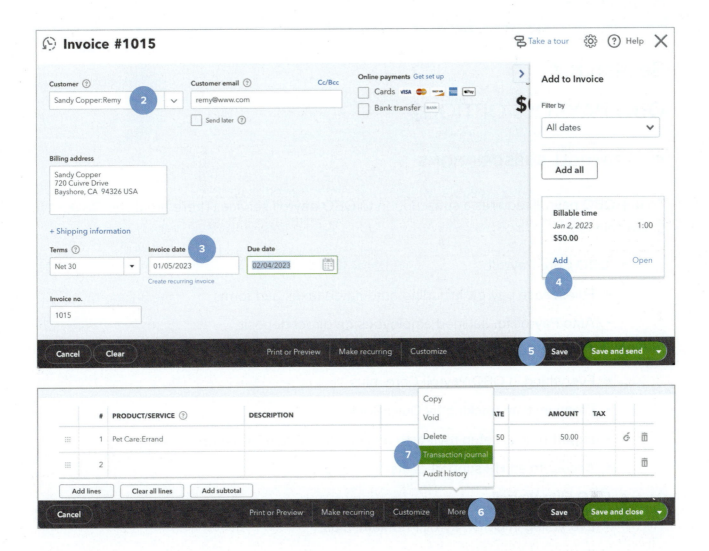

Section 8.7

QBO PAYROLL OPTIONS

QBO PAYROLL SUBSCRIPTIONS

To use QBO payroll requires a subscription to QBO payroll service. There are three QBO payroll plans:

- **QBO Core Payroll**
  - Full-service payroll, including automated taxes and forms
  - Auto Payroll for salaried employees on direct deposit
- **QBO Premium Payroll**
  - Everything in QBO Payroll Core, plus:
  - Premium time tracking by QuickBooks Time
  - Expert payroll setup review to ensure QBO payroll is set up correctly
  - Access to an HR support center
- **QBO Elite Payroll**
  - Everything in QBO Payroll Premium, plus:
  - Track time and projects on the go
  - White glove payroll setup
  - Personal HR Advisor

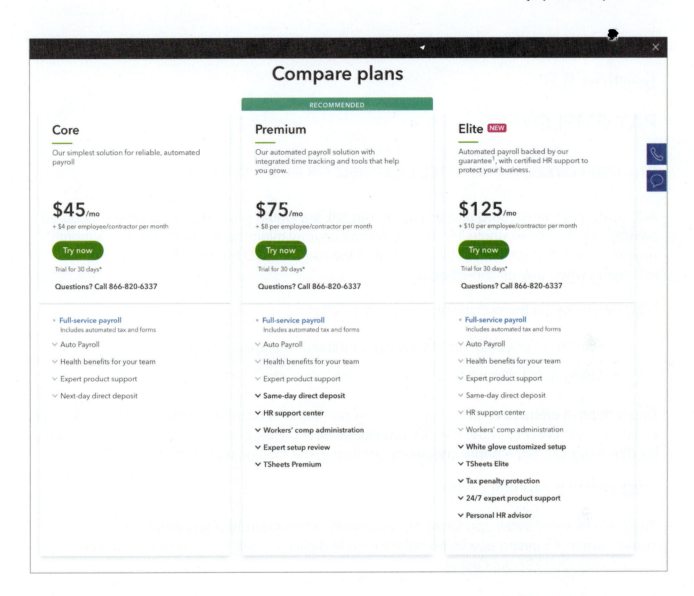

QBO PAYROLL SETUP

QBO payroll is relatively complex to set up and Intuit offers payroll specialists to assist in the payroll setup process. After QBO payroll is set up, it is relatively easy to run payroll.

> **Be advised** that if you select to turn on the QBO payroll trial, it will deactivate the time-tracking feature used to complete the chapter and exercises in this text.

Section 8.8

PAY EMPLOYEES

PAY EMPLOYEES USING DIRECT DEPOSIT OR PRINT CHECKS

After entering time worked and setting up payroll, we would pay employees on a scheduled payroll payday. For example, for weekly payroll payday might be every Friday. For a monthly payroll schedule, payday might be the first of the month. QBO Payroll will send you email reminders when payroll should be run.

QBO Payroll offers the options of:

- Printing checks that are distributed or mailed to employees or

- Using direct deposit to employees' bank accounts

Direct deposit offers several advantages over printing and distributing checks. Direct deposit eliminates the costs of paper checks, envelopes, and postage. Also, security is often better for direct deposit since paper checks can be lost in the mail or subject to theft.

QBO MOBILE PAYROLL APP

The QBO Mobile Payroll app for Apple iPhone/iPad and Android offers employers the convenience of running payroll from their mobile devices. Then the payroll information is synced with QuickBooks Online.

PAY STUB EXAMPLE

The following is an example pay stub, showing:

- Gross pay. Gross pay is the total amount the employee has earned. This can be total salary or total wages earned.

- Deductions. Deductions include payments for benefits such as 401K retirement or health insurance.

- Taxes. Taxes withheld from an employee's paycheck can include federal, state, and local taxes, social security and medicare.

- Net Pay. Net pay is the gross pay less deductions and withholdings.

Collins Paint and Wallpaper Services
123 Main St.
Palo Alto CA 94306

Pay Stub Detail
PAY DATE:06/07/2019
NET PAY:$443.06

Eloisa Catillo
550 Front Boulevard
Menlo Park CA 94025

EMPLOYER
Collins Paint and Wallpaper Services
123 Main St.
Palo Alto CA 94306

PAY PERIOD

Period Beginning	06/01/2019
Period Ending:	06/07/2019
Pay Date:	06/07/2019

EMPLOYEE
Eloisa Catillo
550 Front Boulevard
Menlo Park CA 94025

SS#: ...1111

BENEFITS	Used	Available	NET PAY:		$443.06
Sick	0.00	0.00	Acct#....0000:		$200.00
Vacation	0.00	41.54	Acct#....0000:		$243.06

MEMO:

PAY	Hours	Rate	Current	YTD
Salary	-	-	769.23	1,538.46

DEDUCTIONS	Current	YTD
401K	15.38	30.76
Bright Smile Insurance	40.00	80.00
Good Health Insurance	200.00	400.00

TAXES	Current	YTD
Federal Income Tax	0.00	0.00
Social Security	47.69	95.38
Medicare	11.16	22.31
CA Income Tax	4.25	8.50
CA State Disability Ins	7.69	15.38

SUMMARY	Current	YTD
Total Pay	$769.23	$1,538.46
Taxes	$70.79	$141.57
Deductions	$255.38	$510.76
Net Pay	**$443.06**	

Section 8.9

PAY PAYROLL LIABILITIES

Payroll liabilities include amounts for:

- Federal income taxes withheld from employee paychecks
- State income taxes withheld from employee paychecks
- FICA (Social Security and Medicare, including both the employee and the employer portions)
- Unemployment taxes

Federal income taxes, state income taxes, and the employee portion of FICA are withheld from the employee, and the company has an obligation (liability) to remit these amounts to the appropriate tax agency. The employer share of FICA and unemployment taxes are payroll taxes the employer owes.

QBO Payroll Service offers companies the ability to e-pay payroll liabilities. The company sets up e-pay by selecting which company bank accounts from which to pay the payroll liabilities. The appropriate federal and state agencies are selected to receive the payments. QBO Payroll even sends email reminders when it is time to e-pay the payroll liabilities.

QBO uses a Payroll Tax Center to summarize Payroll Tax Payments and Payroll Tax Filings. QBO keeps track of payroll tax payments that are due to federal, state, and local tax agencies. QBO also tracks payroll tax payments that have already been paid.

To view the Payroll Tax Center:

1 From the Navigation Bar, select **Taxes**

2 Select **Payroll Tax** tab

3 The Payroll Tax Center displays Payroll Tax Payments and Filings. Select **Payments**. Our QBO Payroll is not completely set up. If it was, this screen would list Tax Payments due. When using the QBO Payroll Service, tax payments can be made by simply selecting Create payment for the appropriate tax payment due.

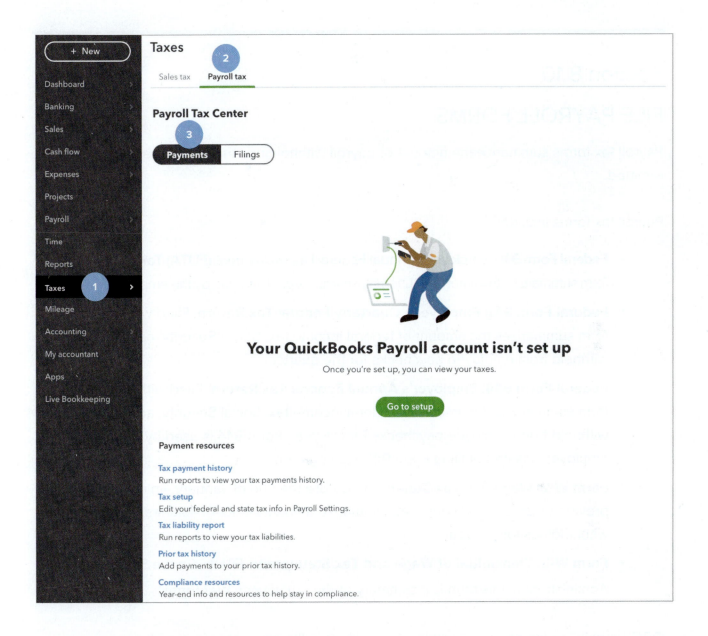

Section 8.10

FILE PAYROLL FORMS

Payroll tax forms summarize the amount of payroll withholdings that have been collected and remitted.

Payroll tax forms include:

- **Federal Form 940: Employer's Annual Federal Unemployment (FUTA) Tax Return.** This form summarizes the amount of unemployment tax paid and due by the employer.

- **Federal Form 941: Employer's Quarterly Federal Tax Return.** Filed with the IRS, this form summarizes the amount of federal income tax, Social Security, and Medicare withheld from employee paychecks for the quarter.

- **Federal Form 944: Employer's Annual Federal Tax Return.** Filed with the IRS, this form summarizes the amount of federal income tax, Social Security, and Medicare withheld from employee paychecks for the year. Form 944 is used by very small employers instead of filing Form 941 each quarter.

- **Form W-2: Wage and Tax Statement.** Before the end of January, an employer must provide W-2s to employees that summarize amounts paid for salaries, wages, and withholdings for the year.

- **Form W-3: Transmittal of Wage and Tax Statements.** Filed with the Social Security Administration, this form is a summary of the employer's W-2 forms.

QBO Payroll Service offers companies the ability to e-file payroll tax forms. The company must set up this feature for e-filing, but once setup is completed with all the appropriate agencies, it simply requires a click of a button to e-file. QBO Payroll Service sends email reminders when it is time to e-file the various payroll forms and sends confirmations once the e-filing has been completed.

QBO Payroll Tax Center to summarizes Payroll Tax Filings, payroll tax forms that must be filed with the appropriate federal, state, and local tax agencies.

To view the Payroll Tax Center:

1 From the Navigation Bar, select **Taxes**

2 Select **Payroll Tax** tab

3 Select **Filings**. If QBO Payroll was completely set up, this would show the payroll tax forms that were due to be filed and had already been filed.

4 View an example of a Form 941, an Employer's Quarterly Federal Tax Return for payroll

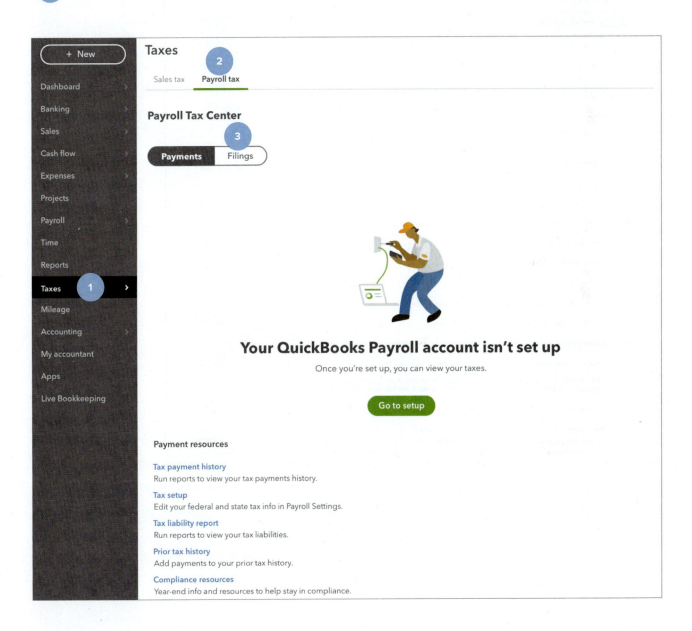

Form **941**
(Rev. January 20)

Employer's QUARTERLY Federal Tax Return
Department of the Treasury — Internal Revenue Service

950117

OMB No. 1545-0029

Employer identification number (EIN) 12-3456788

Name (not your trade name) Collins Paint & Wallpaper Services

Trade name (if any) Collins Paint and Wallpaper Services

Address 123 Main St.
Number   Street   Suite or room number

Palo Alto   CA   94306
City   State ZIP code

Foreign country name   Foreign province/county   Foreign postal code

Report for this Quarter of 2019
(Check one.)

☐ 1: January, February, March

☒ 2: April, May, June

☐ 3: July, August, September

☐ 4: October, November, December

Go to *www.irs.gov/Form941* for instructions and the latest information.

REV 04/26/19 OSP

Read the separate instructions before you complete Form 941. Type or print within the boxes.

Part 1:	Answer these questions for this quarter.

1 Number of employees who received wages, tips, or other compensation for the pay period including: *Mar. 12* (Quarter 1), *June 12* (Quarter 2), *Sept. 12* (Quarter 3), or *Dec. 12* (Quarter 4) **1** | 0

2 Wages, tips, and other compensation . . . . **2** | 3,824.86

3 Federal income tax withheld from wages, tips, and other compensation . . . . . . **3** | 280.72

4 If no wages, tips, and other compensation are subject to social security or Medicare tax ☐ Check and go to line 6.

		Column 1		Column 2
5a	Taxable social security wages . .	4,026.16	× 0.124 =	499.24
5b	Taxable social security tips . . .		× 0.124 =	
5c	Taxable Medicare wages & tips . .	4,026.16	× 0.029 =	116.76
5d	Taxable wages & tips subject to Additional Medicare Tax withholding		× 0.009 =	

5e Add Column 2 from lines 5a, 5b, 5c, and 5d . . . . . . **5e** | 616.00

5f Section 3121(q) Notice and Demand—Tax due on unreported tips (see instructions) . . **5f** |

6 Total taxes before adjustments. Add lines 3, 5e, and 5f . . . . **6** | 896.72

7 Current quarter's adjustment for fractions of cents . . . . **7** |

8 Current quarter's adjustment for sick pay . . . . **8** |

9 Current quarter's adjustments for tips and group-term life insurance . . . . . . **9** |

10 Total taxes after adjustments. Combine lines 6 through 9 . . . . **10** | 896.72

11 Qualified small business payroll tax credit for increasing research activities. Attach Form 8974 **11** |

12 Total taxes after adjustments and credits. Subtract line 11 from line 10 . . . . . **12** | 896.72

13 Total deposits for this quarter, including overpayment applied from a prior quarter and overpayments applied from Form 941-X, 941-X (PR), 944-X, or 944-X (SP) filed in the current quarter **13** |

14 Balance due. If line 12 is more than line 13, enter the difference and see instructions . . . **14** | 896.72

15 Overpayment. If line 13 is more than line 12, enter the difference [ ] Check one: ☐ Apply to next return. ☐ Send a refund.

▶ You MUST complete both pages of Form 941 and SIGN it.   Next ▶

For Privacy Act and Paperwork Reduction Act Notice, see the back of the Payment Voucher. BAA   Form **941** (Rev. 1-2019)

Section 8.11

ACCOUNTING ESSENTIALS
Payroll Liabilities and Payroll Taxes

Accounting Essentials summarize important foundational accounting knowledge you may find useful when using QBO

What are payroll liabilities?

- Payroll liabilities include two types of amounts:

  1. Amounts withheld from employee paychecks that must be paid to third parties
  2. Payroll tax expenses owed by the business

- Payroll liabilities include:

  ‣ Federal income taxes withheld from employee paychecks

  ‣ State income taxes withheld from employee paychecks

  ‣ FICA (Social Security and Medicare, including both the employee and the employer portions)

  ‣ Unemployment taxes

- Federal income taxes, state income taxes, and the employee portion of FICA are withheld from the employee, and the company has an obligation (liability) to remit these amounts to the appropriate tax agency. The employer share of FICA and unemployment taxes are payroll taxes the employer owes.

Payroll Liabilities (Federal)	Withheld from Employee Pay	Payroll Tax Expense Owed by Business
Federal Income Taxes	✓	
FICA (Social Security + Medicare)	✓	✓
Federal Unemployment Tax		✓

What are payroll tax forms?

- Basically, payroll tax forms summarize the amount of payroll withholdings that have been collected and remitted.

- Payroll tax forms include:

  - **Federal Form 940:** Employer's Annual Federal Unemployment (FUTA) Tax Return. This form summarizes the amount of unemployment tax paid and due by the employer.

  - **Federal Form 941:** Employer's Quarterly Federal Tax Return. Filed with the IRS, this form summarizes the amount of federal income tax, Social Security, and Medicare withheld from employee paychecks for the quarter.

  - **Federal Form 944:** Employer's Annual Federal Tax Return. Filed with the IRS, this form summarizes the amount of federal income tax, Social Security, and Medicare withheld from employee paychecks for the year. Form 944 is used by very small employers instead of filing Form 941 each quarter.

  - **Form W-2:** Wage and Tax Statement. Before the end of January, an employer must provide W-2s to employees that summarize amounts paid for salaries, wages, and withholdings for the year.

  - **Form W-3:** Transmittal of Wage and Tax Statements. Filed with the Social Security Administration, this form is a summary of the employer's W-2 forms.

Payroll Liabilities (Federal)	Federal Payroll Tax Form	
	Quarterly	Annual
Federal Income Taxes	941	944
FICA (Social Security + Medicare)	941	944
Federal Unemployment Tax		940

Practice Quiz 8

Q8.1

A company is not required to withhold payroll taxes for:

a. Employees paid by the hour
b. Salaried employees
c. Out-of-state employees
d. Independent contractors

Q8.2

A payment to a stockholder is recorded as a(n):

a. Employee paycheck
b. Vendor payment
c. Distribution
d. None of the above

Q8.3

When using QBO time tracking, you can record:

a. Time billable to a specific vendor
b. Time billable to a specific customer
c. How many shipments of inventory items were received
d. Number of purchase orders from each supplier

Q8.4

A company completes Form _____ to summarize for the IRS the amount of federal income tax, Social Security, and Medicare withheld from employee paychecks for the year.

a. W-3
b. 940
c. 944
d. None of the above

Q8.5

Which one of the following is not a payroll liability?

a. Property taxes
b. Unemployment taxes
c. State income taxes withheld
d. Federal income taxes withheld from employee paychecks

Q8.6

QuickBooks permits you to track employee time using which one of the following:

a. Time Entry

b. Paycheck

c. Contractor List

d. Monthly Timesheet

Q8.7

The employer must match which one of the following taxes paid by an employee?

a. State Income

b. Medicare

c. Federal Income

d. Federal Unemployment

Q8.8

All of the following are payroll liabilities owed to outside agencies except:

a. Net Pay

b. Federal Income taxes

c. State Income taxes

d. Unemployment taxes

Q8.9

The following taxes are reported on Form 941 except:

a. FICA-Medicare (employer and employee)

b. State income taxes withheld from the employee paychecks

c. Federal income taxes withheld from the employee paychecks

d. FICA-Social Security (employer and employee)

Q8.10

Net Pay is equal to:

a. Gross pay minus deductions for federal and state income taxes and unemployment taxes

b. Gross pay minus federal and state income taxes, but not FICA taxes

c. Gross pay plus deductions for FICA taxes and federal and state income taxes

d. Gross pay minus deductions for FICA taxes and federal and state income taxes

Q8.11

QBO Payroll Service can:

a. E-file payroll tax forms

b. E-pay payroll taxes from your company checking account

c. Direct deposit employee paychecks

d. All of the above

Q8.12

Payroll liabilities include the following two types of amounts:

a. Amounts withheld from employees paychecks that must be paid to third parties, such as federal income tax withheld

b. Payroll tax expenses owed by the business, such as unemployment tax

c. Net paycheck amount paid to employees

d. Contractor payments

Exercises 8

> ⚠️ **Due to ongoing changes in QBO Payroll and Time Tracking, your screens and functionality may appear different than the instructions in the following Exercises. If the QBO updates significantly impact your text, the updates to your text can be viewed as follows:**
> 1. Go to www.My-QuickBooksOnline.com > QBO 3e > QBO 3e Updates, or
> 2. If you are using Connect or a digital ebook, you can find updates under **Additional Student Resources (ASR).** If you do not have access to Connect or the ebook, your instructor can provide you with ASR.

E8.1 Employees and Payroll Activities

Match the following activities with the following framework for navigating QBO payroll.

Employees and Payroll Activities

a. Enter Time to track employee time worked to use in processing payroll and billing customers

b. Process Payroll Forms including Forms 940, 941, W-2, and W-3 that must be submitted to governmental agencies

c. Turn on QBO Payroll

d. Pay Employees by selecting employees to pay and creating their paychecks

e. Turn on Time Tracking preference

f. Set up Employees List

g. Pay Payroll Liabilities, such as federal income taxes withheld, state income taxes withheld, FICA (Social Security and Medicare), and unemployment taxes due to governmental agencies

Navigating Employee and Payroll Activities

PAYROLL SETUP

1. _____
2. _____
3. _____

PAYROLL PROCESSING

1. _____
2. _____
3. _____
4. _____

E8.2 Time Tracking and Status

Match the following items with the appropriate status of the individual performing work using time tracking.

Items

- Distributions
- Form W-2
- Paycheck
- Form 1099-MISC
- Owner's Tax Return
- Vendor Payment

Status	QBO Payment	Tax Form
Employee		
Contractor		
Owner		

E8.3 Payroll Liabilities

Place a ✓ in the following appropriate boxes to indicate whether the federal payroll item is paid by the employee or the employer.

Payroll Liabilities (Federal)	Withheld from Employee Pay	Payroll Tax Expense Owed by Business
Federal Income Taxes		
FICA (Social Security + Medicare)		
Federal Unemployment Tax		

E8.4 Time Tracking Preferences

Answer the following questions about the Time Tracking preferences if a company plans to use QBO for time tracking.

1. If a company wants to turn on Time Tracking preferences, use the _____ icon > _____

2. What should be the time-tracking setting for Show Service field?

3. What should be the time-tracking setting for Allow Time to be Billable to Customer?

EM8.5 Time Entry and Time Activities Report

Cy is still working as a full-time professional while launching Mookie The Beagle Concierge and would like a better idea of how many hours he is investing in his new startup. So he uses QBO to track his time spent coding the Mookie The Beagle Concierge app. Complete the following to enter time for Cy.

1. Verify that Service Field on Timesheet is Turned On.
   a. Select **Gear icon > Account and Settings > Time**
   b. **Check Add Service field to time sheets** setting to **On**
   c. **Check Make Time Entry Billable to Customer** setting to **On**
   d. Select **Save > Done**

2. Create Time Entry.
   a. Select **(+) New icon > Time Entry** (or **Single Time Activity**). (Note that your Employees menu may change from Time Entry to Single Time Activity and Weekly Timesheet.)
   b. Select **Name: Cy Walker**
   c. Using Calendar, select **Date: 01/18/2023**
   d. Add **Service: + Add new** > select **Service**. (Note: If your Service field does not provide the option to add a new Product or Service from the Service field, then add the new service specified below, MTB App Development, using the Products and Services List.)
   e. Enter **Product/Service Information Name: MTB App Development**
   f. Select **Category: + Add New**
   g. Enter **New Category Name: Time Tracking**
   h. Select **Save**
   i. Select **I purchase this product/service from a vendor**
   j. Enter **Cost: 0.00**
   k. Enter New **Expense Account: + Add New**
   l. Select **Account Type: Other Expense**
   m. Select **Detail Type: Other Miscellaneous Expense**
   n. Enter **Account Name: Time Tracking**
   o. Select **Save and Close** to close the Account form
   p. Select **Save and close** to close the Product/Service form
   q. Uncheck **Billable (/hr)**
   r. Start Time is 7:00 PM
   s. End Time is 9:00 PM
   t. Given the Start Time and Stop Time, enter **Duration**
   u. What is time worked?
   v. Select **Save**

3. Create Time Entry.
   a. Select **Name: Cy Walker**
   b. Select **Date: 01/19/2023**
   c. If cost rate is displayed, enter **Cost rate (/hr): 0.00**
   d. Select **Service: MTB App Development**
   e. Uncheck **Billable (/hr)**
   f. Start Time is 7:00 PM
   g. End Time is 9:30 PM
   h. Given the Start Time and Stop Time, enter **Duration**
   i. What is time worked?
   j. Select **Save and close**

4. Create Time Activities by Employee Detail Report.

   To view and verify time entered:

   a. Select **Reports > Standard** tab > **Employees (or Payroll) section > Time Activities by Employee Detail**

   b. Select **Time Activity Date: Custom 01/18/2023 to 01/19/2023**

   c. Select **Group by: Employee**

   d. Select **Run Report**

   e. What is the Duration Total for Cy Walker?

EM8.6 Time Entry and Time Activities Report

In addition to using QBO time tracking for tracking his time on MTB Concierge app development, Cy decides to use the time tracking feature to track time he spends on administrative tasks for MTB Concierge. This information might prove useful in assessing whether to hire additional administrative support staff in the future.

1. Create Time Entry.

   a. Select **(+) New icon > Time Entry** (or **Single Time Activity**)

   b. Select **Name: Cy Walker**

   c. Select **Date: 01/20/2023**

   d. If cost rate is displayed, enter **Cost rate (/hr): 0.00**

   e. Add **Service: + Add new** > select **Service**. (Note: If your Service field does not provide the option to add a new Product or Service from the Service field, then add the new service specified below, MTB App Development, using the Products and Services List.)

   f. Enter **Product/Service Information Name: MTB Administrative Services**

   g. Select **Category: Time Tracking**

   h. Select: **I purchase this product/service from a vendor**

   i. Enter **Cost: 0.00**

   j. Select **Expense Account: Time Tracking**

   k. Select **Save and close** to close the Product/Service form

   l. Uncheck **Billable (/hr)**

   m. Start Time is 9:00 PM

   n. End Time is 11:00 PM

   o. Given the Start Time and Stop Time, enter **Duration**

   p. What is time worked?

   q. Select **Save**

2. Create Time Entry.
   a. Select **Name: Cy Walker**
   b. Select **Date: 01/21/2023**
   c. If cost rate is displayed, enter **Cost rate (/hr): 0.00**
   d. Select **Service: MTB Administrative Services**
   e. Uncheck **Billable (/hr)**
   f. Start Time is 8:00 PM
   g. End Time is 11:00 PM
   h. Given the Start Time and Stop Time, enter **Duration**
   i. What is time worked?
   j. Select **Save**

3. Create Time Entry.
   a. Select **Name: Cy Walker**
   b. Select **Date: 01/23/2023**
   c. If cost rate is displayed, enter **Cost rate (/hr): 0.00**
   d. Select **Service: MTB Administrative Services**
   e. Uncheck **Billable (/hr)**
   f. Start Time is 7:00 PM
   g. End Time is 10:00 PM
   h. Given the Start Time and Stop Time, enter **Duration**
   i. What is time worked?
   j. Select **Save**

4. Create Time Entry.
   a. Select **Name: Cy Walker**
   b. Select **Date: 01/24/2023**
   c. If cost rate is displayed, enter **Cost rate (/hr): 0.00**
   d. Select **Service: MTB App Development**
   e. Uncheck **Billable (/hr)**
   f. Start Time is 12:00 PM
   g. End Time is 8:00 PM
   h. Given the Start Time and Stop Time, enter **Duration**
   i. What is time worked?
   j. Select **Save and close**

5. Create Time Activities by Employee Detail Report.
   To view and verify time entered:
   a. Select **Reports** > **Standard** tab > **Employees (or Payroll) section** > **Time Activities by Employee Detail**
   b. Select **Time Activity Date: 01/18/2023 to 01/24/2023**
   c. Select **Group by: Employee**
   d. Select **Run Report**
   e. What is the Duration Total for Cy Walker?
   f. Select **Group by: Product/Service**
   g. Select **Run Report**
   h. What is the Duration Total for MTB Concierge Administrative Services?
   i. What is the Duration Total for MTB Concierge App Development?
   j. What is the Duration Total for Time Tracking?

EM8.7 Time Entry

To streamline billing customers and paying contractors, Cy would like to use the QBO time tracking feature for tracking contractor time. Evan Henry, a vet student and Mookie The Beagle Concierge contractor, volunteers to participate in testing the time tracking feature. Evan Henry will be providing pet care services for Angel Merriman's King Shepherd, Kuno. Angel is tied up in the evenings with an urgent cybersecurity job, so Evan Henry will be stopping by Kuno's home each evening to feed and walk him.

Complete the following time-tracking exercises.

1. Create Time Entry.
   a. Select **Sales** > **Customers** tab > **Angel Merriman** > **New transaction menu** > **Time Activity**
   b. Enter **Date: 01/23/2023**
   c. Select **Name: Evan Henry**
   d. Select **Customer: Angel Merriman: Kuno**
   e. Select **Service: Pet Care: Short Visit**
   f. Check **Billable (/hr) $40.00**
   g. Start Time is 5:00 PM
   h. End Time is 6:00 PM
   i. Given the Start Time and Stop Time, enter **Duration**
   j. What is time worked in hours and minutes?
   k. What is the Total Cost of the time worked?
   l. Select **Save**

EM8.8 Time Entry

Complete the following Time Entry for Evan Henry when he provides services to Angel Merriman's King Shepherd, Kuno. Upon arriving to care for Kuno, Evan found Kuno was distressed by ongoing thunderstorms, so with Angel's approval for the upcharge, Evan extended his visit until Kuno was calm.

1. Create Time Entry.
   a. If needed, select **Sales** > **Customers** tab > **Angel Merriman** > **New transaction menu** > **Time Activity**
   b. Select **Date: 01/24/2023**
   c. Select **Name: Evan Henry**
   d. Select **Customer: Angel Merriman: Kuno**
   e. Select **Service: Pet Care: Medium Visit**
   f. Check **Billable (/hr) $50.00**
   g. Start Time is 5:15 PM
   h. End Time is 7:15 PM
   i. Given the Start Time and Stop Time, enter **Duration**
   j. What is time worked in hours and minutes?
   k. What is the Total Cost of the time worked?
   l. Select **Save**

EM8.9 Time Entry

Complete the following Time Entry for Evan Henry when he provides services to Angel Merriman's King Shepherd, Kuno.

1. Create Time Entry.
   a. If needed, select **Sales** > **Customers** tab > **Angel Merriman** > **New transaction menu** > **Time Activity**
   b. Select **Date: 01/25/2023**
   c. Select **Name: Evan Henry**
   d. Select **Customer: Angel Merriman: Kuno**
   e. Select **Service: Pet Care: Short Visit**
   f. Check **Billable (/hr) $40.00**
   g. Start Time is 5:30 PM
   h. End Time is 6:30 PM
   i. Given the Start Time and Stop Time, enter **Duration**
   j. What is time worked in hours and minutes?
   k. What is the Total Cost of the time worked?
   l. Select **Save and close**

EM8.10 Time Entry and Time Activities Report

Complete the following to add services Evan Henry provided to Angel Merriman's King Shepherd, Kuno, and to create a Time Activities by Employee Detail report.

1. Create Time Entry.
   a. Select **Sales** > **Customers** tab > **Angel Merriman** > **New transaction menu** > **Time Activity**
   b. Select **Date: 01/26/2023**
   c. Select **Name: Evan Henry**
   d. Select **Customer: Angel Merriman: Kuno**
   e. Select **Service: Pet Care: Short Visit**
   f. Check **Billable (/hr) $40.00**
   g. Start Time is 6:00 PM
   h. End Time is 7:00 PM
   i. Given the Start Time and Stop Time, enter **Duration**
   j. What is time worked in hours and minutes?
   k. What is the Total Cost of time worked?
   l. Select **Save and close**

2. Create Time Activities by Employee Detail Report.
   To view and verify time entered:
   a. Select **Reports** > **Standard** tab > **Employees (or Payroll) section** > **Time Activities by Employee Detail**
   b. Select **Time Activity Date: 01/18/2023 to 01/26/2023**
   c. Select **Group by: Employee**
   d. Select **Run Report**
   e. What is the Duration Total for Evan Henry?
   f. What is the Amount Total for Evan Henry?
   g. Select **Group by: Product/Service**
   h. Select **Run Report**
   i. What is the Total for Pet Care Amount?

EM8.11 Invoice and Time Tracking

Using tracked time, complete the following to create an Invoice for services provided to Kuno, Angel Merriman's pet King Shepherd.

1. Create Invoice with Tracked Time.
   a. Select **(+) New icon** > **Invoice**
   b. Select **Customer: Angel Merriman: Kuno**
   c. Select **Invoice Date: 01/29/2023**
   d. From the Add to Invoice drawer on the right side of the screen, select: **Don't group time** > **Add all**
   e. What is the Balance Due on the Invoice?
   f. Select **Save** and leave the Invoice displayed

2. View the Transaction Journal for the Invoice.
   a. From the bottom of the Invoice just prepared, select **More > Transaction Journal**
   b. What are the Account and Amount Debited?
   c. What are the Accounts and Amounts Credited?

Chapter 9

QBO Adjustments

MOOKIE THE BEAGLE™ CONCIERGE

BACKSTORY

Cy Walker realizes that although QuickBooks Online can streamline and perform many accounting tasks automatically, QBO cannot automatically perform some tasks, such as adjusting entries. Cy knows adjusting entries are important because they bring accounts up to date so the correct account balances appear on financial reports.

Cy would like you to learn more about adjusting entries needed to bring Mookie The Beagle™ Concierge accounts up to date at year end. Also, you would like to learn how to streamline entering adjusting entries into QBO using the recurring transactions feature.

Chapter 9

LEARNING OBJECTIVES

Chapter 9 covers adjustments that are required to bring accounts up to date and show the correct account balances on financial reports. Adjustments are typically made at the end of the accounting period so accounts are up to date before year-end reports are prepared.

In Chapter 9, you will learn about the following topics:

- Accounting Cycle
- Trial Balance
- Make Adjusting Entries using QBO
  - ▸ Use the Onscreen Journal to Record Adjusting Entries
  - ▸ Use Recurring Transactions for Adjusting Entries
- Types of Adjusting Entries
  - ▸ Prepaid Items: Related Expense/Asset Accounts
  - ▸ Unearned Items: Related Revenue/Liability Accounts
  - ▸ Accrued Expenses: Related Expense/Liability Accounts
  - ▸ Accrued Revenues: Related Revenue/Asset Accounts
- Adjusted Trial Balance
- Accounting Essentials: Adjustments and Corrections

⚠️ **QBO is updated on an ongoing basis. Updates that affect your text can be viewed as follows:**
1. **Go to www.My-QuickBooksOnline.com > QBO 3e > QBO 3e Updates, or**
2. **If you are using Connect or a digital ebook, you can find updates under Additional Student Resources (ASR). If you do not have access to Connect or the ebook, your instructor can provide you with ASR.**

Section 9.1

 ### QBO SATNAV

QBO SatNav is our satellite navigation for QuickBooks Online, assisting us in navigating QBO

Chapter 9 covers adjustments, which are required to ensure we have reliable QBO Reports.

 **QBO SatNav**

 **QBO Settings**

| Company Settings |
| Chart of Accounts |

 QBO Transactions

| Banking |
| Customers & Sales |
| Vendors & Expenses |
| Employees & Payroll |

 QBO Reports

| Reports |

Section 9.2

ACCOUNTING CYCLE

The accounting cycle is a series of accounting activities that a business performs each accounting period.

> **An accounting period** can be one month, one quarter, or one year.

The accounting cycle usually consists of the following steps.

- **Chart of Accounts.** The Chart of Accounts is a list of all accounts used to accumulate information about assets, liabilities, owners' equity, revenues, and expenses. Create a Chart of Accounts when the business is established and modify the Chart of Accounts as needed over time.
- **Transactions.** During the accounting period, record transactions with customers, vendors, employees, and owners.
- **Trial Balance.** A Trial Balance is also referred to as an unadjusted Trial Balance because it is prepared before adjustments. A Trial Balance lists each account and the account balance at the end of the accounting period. Prepare a Trial Balance to verify that the accounting system is in balance—total debits should equal total credits.
- **Adjustments.** At the end of the accounting period before preparing financial statements, make any adjustments necessary to bring the accounts up to date. Adjustments are entered in the Journal using debits and credits.
- **Adjusted Trial Balance.** Prepare an Adjusted Trial Balance (a Trial Balance after adjustments) to verify that the accounting system still balances. If additional account detail is required, print the general ledger (the collection of all the accounts listing the transactions that affected the accounts).
- **Financial Statements.** Prepare financial statements for external users (Profit and Loss, Balance Sheet, and Statement of Cash Flows). Prepare income tax summary reports and management reports.

This chapter focuses on the adjustments phase of the accounting cycle, but first we are going to prepare a Trial Balance to ensure our account balances are correct.

Section 9.3

TRIAL BALANCE

Before preparing adjusting entries, we want to prepare a Trial Balance. By crosschecking against the Trial Balance below, you can determine if you have the correct account balances.

QBO TRIAL BALANCE CROSSCHECK

C9.3.1 Trial Balance Crosscheck

To crosscheck your QBO Trial Balance:

1. Sign in to your Mookie The Beagle Concierge QBO Company. Using a web browser go to **qbo.intuit.com** > enter **User ID** > enter **Password** > select **Sign in**.

2. Create a Trial Balance by selecting **Reports** on the Navigation Bar > **Standard** tab > in the **For My Accountants** section select **Trial Balance** > select **Date: 01/31/2023**

3. Verify that your QBO account balances are the same as the balances in the following Trial Balance.
   - If your account balances are not the same as the following Trial Balance, proceed to Step 4.
   - If your account balances are the same as the following Trial Balance, proceed to Step 5.

4. If any of your QBO account balances differ from the following Trial Balance, then there must be one or more errors in your accounts. Troubleshoot the discrepancies and update your accounts to the correct balance. See the following Troubleshooting Tips. After updating your accounts to the correct balances, proceed to Step 5.

5. Trial Balance Totals.
   a. What is the amount of Total Debits on the Trial Balance?
   b. What is the amount of Total Credits on the Trial Balance?

6. **Export** the Trial Balance to PDF

7. **Export** the Trial Balance to Excel

TROUBLESHOOTING TIPS

If your QBO account balances differ from the following Trial Balance, try these troubleshooting tips:

- From your Trial Balance report, drill down on any account balances that differ from the following Trial Balance amounts. Review the account for errors.

- Create a Journal report for the period from 01/01/2023 to 01/31/2023. Review the Journal for apparent discrepancies. In the Journal, you can drill down to the source document and correct any errors on the source document, such as a Check or Invoice.

- If necessary, make correcting journal entries as needed to update your accounts to the correct balances. See Chapter 9 Accounting Essentials for more information about correcting entries. To use the Journal to make any necessary correcting entries, select (+) New icon > Journal Entry.

Mookie The Beagle Concierge		
Trial Balance		
As of January 31, 2023		
	Debit	**Credit**
1001 Checking	25,849.30	
1010 Money Market	10,000.00	
1100 Accounts Receivable (A/R)	3,650.66	
1300 Inventory Asset	817.00	
2001 Accounts Payable (A/P)		278.00
2100 VISA Credit Card		788.00
2300 Loan Payable		1,000.00
California Department of Tax and Fee Administration		147.96
3003 Owner's Investment		30,000.00
4100 Billable Expense Income		100.00
4200 Sales		12,470.00
4300 Sales of Product Income		1,784.00
5000 Cost of Goods Sold	671.00	
5001 Advertising & Marketing	1,270.00	
5005 Contractors	1,920.00	
5012 Insurance: Liability Insurance Expense	300.00	
5021 Job Supplies	100.00	
5024 Office Supplies & Software	1,185.00	
5028 Rent & Lease	420.00	
5040 Utilities Expense	385.00	

Section 9.4

ADJUSTING ENTRIES

WHY DO WE MAKE ADJUSTING ENTRIES?

Adjusting entries record adjustments necessary to bring the accounts up to date at the end of an accounting period. We want to make adjusting entries before preparing financial reports so the accounts reflected on the reports are up to date.

HOW DO WE MAKE ADJUSTING ENTRIES?

Adjustments are also called adjusting entries because the way we enter adjustments is by making entries in the Journal. Adjusting entries are entered in the onscreen QBO Journal using debits and credits.

> **The onscreen Journal** using debits and credits to enter transactions is accessed from the **(+) New icon > Other > Journal Entry.**

Some companies use QBO to maintain their financial system throughout the year and then have an accountant prepare the adjusting entries at year end to enter into QBO.

WHEN DO WE MAKE ADJUSTING ENTRIES?

Adjusting entries are dated the last day of the accounting period. Typically, we prepare adjusting entries after we prepare a Trial Balance to verify that our accounts are in balance. The Trial Balance lists all accounts with their debit and credit balances. This permits us to see that our total debits equal our total credits.

To prepare a Trial Balance from the Navigation Bar, select Reports > For My Accountant reports.

Section 9.5

MAKE ADJUSTING ENTRIES USING QBO

USE THE ONSCREEN JOURNAL TO RECORD ADJUSTING ENTRIES

We can use the QBO onscreen Journal to enter adjusting entries.

To do a walk-through of how to make adjusting entries using QBO:

1 Select **(+) New** icon

2 Select **Journal Entry** to access the onscreen Journal

3 Enter **Journal Date: 01/31/2023**

4 Enter **Journal No.: ADJ 0**. QBO will automatically number Journal entries consecutively unless we modify the Journal No. Often we label adjusting entries as ADJ 1, ADJ 2, and so on. Then we can clearly see which Journal entries are adjusting entries. Since this is a test adjusting journal entry, we enter ADJ 0.

5 On Line 1, from the drop-down list of accounts, select the **Account to Debit:**

6 We would enter **Debit Amount**. In this case, enter **1.00** as a placeholder for debit amount.

7 If applicable, we would enter **Description**

8 On Line 2, from the drop-down list of accounts, we would select the **Account to Credit**

9 We would enter **Credit Amount**. In this case, enter **1.00** as a placeholder for credit amount.

10 If applicable, enter **Description**

11 We would enter a **Memo** to describe the adjusting entry and what it records. If we had to make any calculations to determine the adjusting entry amounts, then we could include those calculations in the Memo field. This becomes important if we have to come back later to verify the adjusting entry amounts or when making adjusting entries in later accounting periods.

12 Add **Attachments** that are source documents related to the adjusting entry. For example, for a depreciation adjusting entry, we might attach the depreciation schedule.

13   Leave the Journal Entry window open

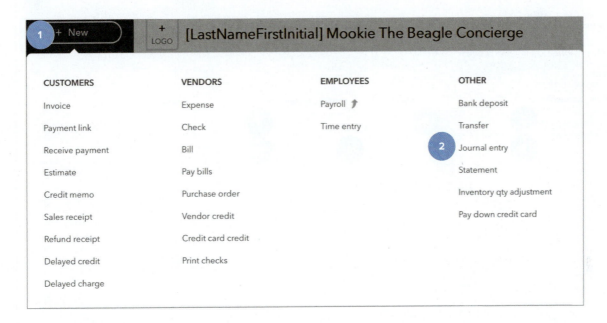

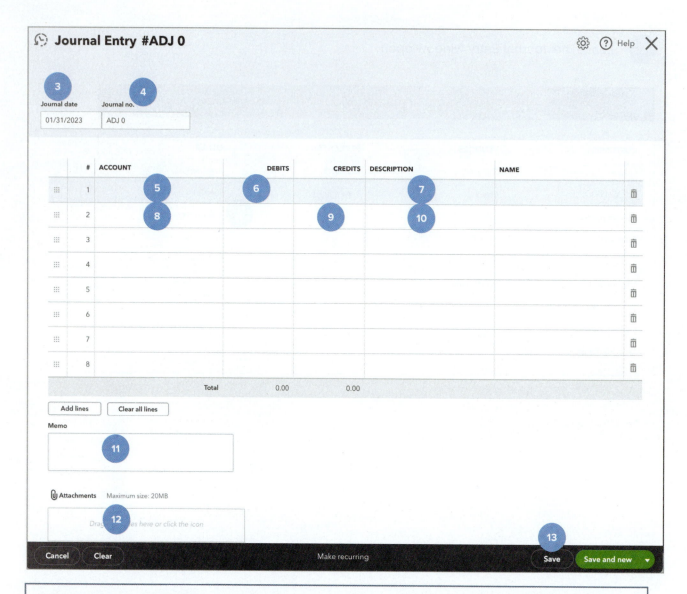

When making journal entries, including adjusting entries, accountants generally list Debits before Credits. Note that QBO may not always list Debits before Credits in journal entries.

USE RECURRING TRANSACTIONS FOR ADJUSTING ENTRIES

To save time, we can save our adjusting entries as recurring transactions.

There are two ways to save adjusting entries as recurring transactions:

1. From the journal screen
2. From the recurring transactions screen

To save an adjusting entry from the journal screen as a recurring transaction:

1 With the previous adjusting entry saved and still open on your screen, select **Make recurring** to save the adjusting entry as a template for a recurring transaction

2 Enter **Template Name: Adjusting Entry**. Since Recurring Transactions are listed alphabetically, we want to name the Templates so they automatically sort in an order that makes it easy for us to find the specific Template we need.

3 Select **Type: Reminder** so we will be reminded to use the Recurring Transaction Template to make the adjusting entry

4 Enter **Remind Days Before The Transaction Date: 3**

5 Enter **Interval: Monthly**

6 Select **On: Day**

7 Select **Date: Last** of every **1** month(s)

8 Enter **Start Date: 01/31/2023**

9 Enter **End: None**. (Note that if we knew we had 5 more years of depreciation to record for a specific asset, for example, we could enter End: After 5 occurrences.)

10 The **Accounts** and **Debits** and **Credits** to be saved for the recurring transaction would appear in this section

11 The **Memo** that we want to appear on the recurring transaction would be entered here. This saves time from re-entering the Memo each time the recurring transaction is used.

12 Normally we would select Save Template. In this case, select **Cancel**. If asked, Do you want to leave without saving?, select **Yes**.

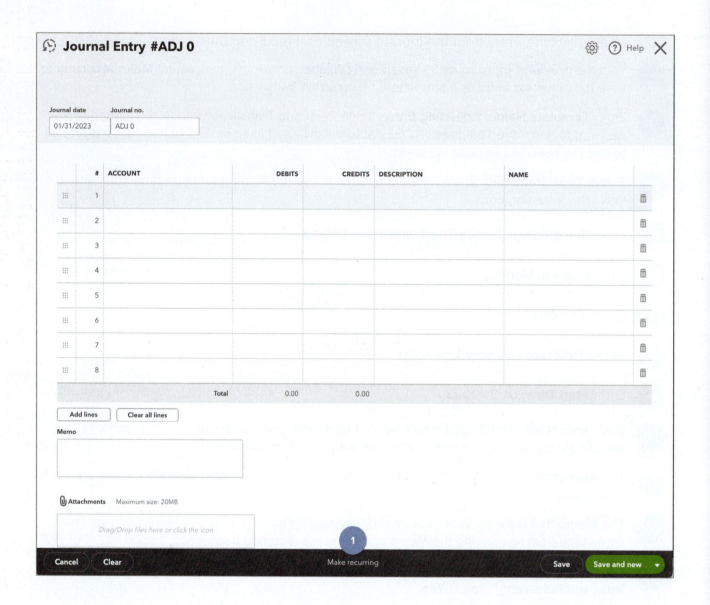

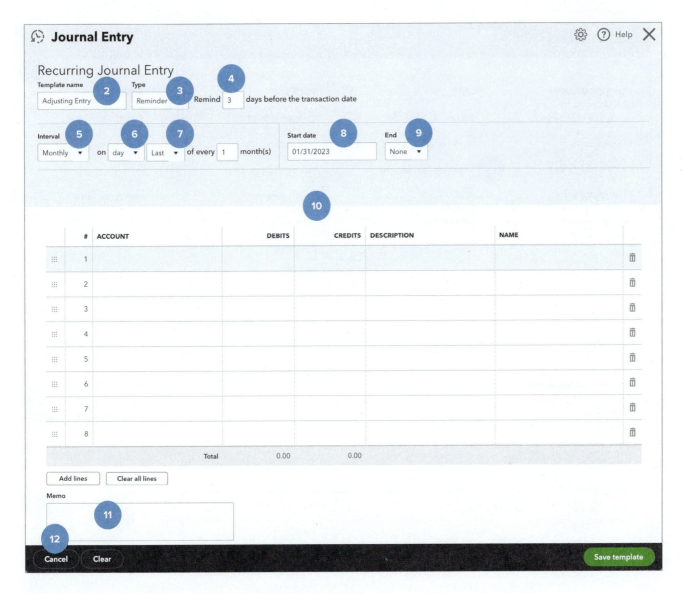

Recurring transactions can be accessed from the Gear icon:

1 Select **Gear** icon

2 Select **Recurring Transactions**

3 Select **New** to add a new recurring transaction

4 Select **Edit** to update the recurring transaction previously entered

5 Select **Use** to use the recurring transaction to enter a new transaction

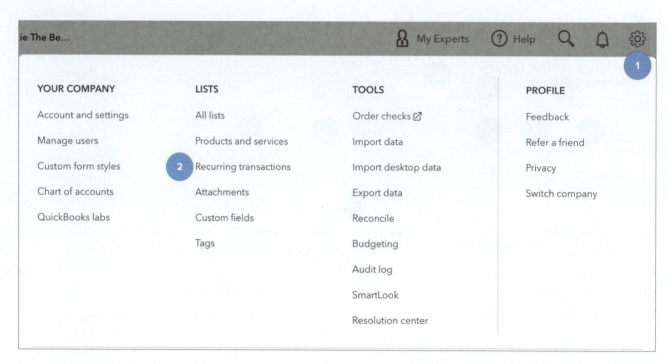

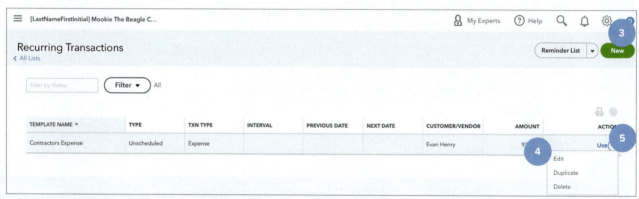

Recurring transactions can be classified as one of three types:

1. Scheduled
2. Unscheduled
3. Reminder

1. **Scheduled Recurring Transactions.** These recurring transaction are scheduled for QBO to automatically enter the transaction on a date we specified. Since we need to update adjusting entry amounts each year, Scheduled is typically not a good option to use for adjusting entry Recurring Transactions.
2. **Unscheduled Recurring Transactions.** Unscheduled transactions will appear in the Recurring Transaction List but QBO will not automatically enter the transaction. Instead, we must go to the Recurring Transaction List and select Use. Although we could use Unscheduled for an adjusting entry Recurring Transaction, this option will not remind us to make the adjusting entry.
3. **Reminder Recurring Transactions.** Recurring Transactions with Reminder option will alert us with a reminder when we should use a recurring transaction to enter a new transaction. Since we need to update the amounts for adjusting entries each month, quarter, or year, select Reminder for adjusting entry Recurring Transactions.

Section 9.6

TYPES OF ADJUSTING ENTRIES

QBO can use the cash or the accrual basis for QBO reports. If we use the accrual basis of accounting to calculate profits, the following four types of adjusting entries may be necessary.

1. **Prepaid items.** Items that are prepaid, such as prepaid insurance or prepaid rent.
2. **Unearned items.** Items that a customer has paid us for, but we have not provided the product or service.
3. **Accrued expenses.** Expenses that are incurred but not yet paid or recorded.
4. **Accrued revenues.** Revenues that have been earned but not yet collected or recorded.

> **The accrual basis of accounting** attempts to match expenses with the revenue (income) they generate. The cash basis records revenues (income) when cash is received and records expenses when cash is paid. The accrual basis attempts to record revenue (income) in the accounting period when it is earned (the product or service is provided) regardless of when the cash is received. The accrual basis attempts to record expenses in the accounting period it is incurred regardless of when the cash is paid.

Typically, an adjusting entry affects:

* A **Profit and Loss account** (Revenue or Expense) and
* A **Balance Sheet account** (Asset or Liability)

Profit and Loss	**Balance Sheet**
$ **Revenue**	▮▤ **Asset**
($) **Expense**	✎ **Liability**

Section 9.7

PREPAID ITEMS: RELATED EXPENSE/ASSET ACCOUNTS

Prepaid items are items that are paid in advance, such as prepaid insurance or prepaid rent. An adjustment may be needed to record the amount of the prepaid item that has not expired at the end of the accounting period. For example, an adjustment may be needed to record the amount of insurance that has not expired as Prepaid Insurance (an asset with future benefit) and the amount of insurance that has expired as Insurance Expense.

Adjusting entries for prepaid items typically affect:

* An **Expense** account and
* An **Asset** account

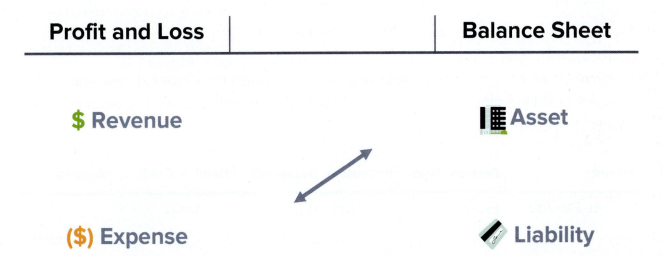

Examples of related Expense and Asset accounts used for prepaid item adjusting entries are as follows.

Prepaid Items	Expense Account	Asset Account
Prepaid Insurance	Insurance Expense	Prepaid Insurance
Prepaid Rent	Rent Expense	Prepaid Rent
Office Supplies	Office Supplies Expense	Office Supplies

Basically we want to make certain that the amounts in the related Expense account (such as Insurance Expense) and Asset account (Prepaid Insurance) are appropriate.

The adjusting entry is a Journal entry recording the amount that needs to be transferred between the two accounts (an Expense account and an Asset account) to show the appropriate balance in each account.

Whether a debit or credit increases or decreases an account depends upon the type of account.

Account Type	Debit	Credit
Assets	Increase	Decrease
Liabilities	Decrease	Increase
Equity	Decrease	Increase
Revenues (Income)	Decrease	Increase
Expenses	Increase	Decrease

For example, if we need to make an adjusting entry to increase Insurance Expense and decrease Prepaid Insurance for $100, we would determine whether to debit or credit the accounts as follows:

Account	Account Type	Increase or Decrease?	Debit or Credit?	Amount
Insurance Expense	Expense	Increase	Debit	$100
Prepaid Insurance	Asset	Decrease	Credit	$100

To enter an adjusting entry for a prepaid item using the QBO Journal:

1 Select **(+) New** icon

2 Select **Journal Entry** to access the onscreen Journal

3 Enter **Journal Date: 01/31/2023**

4 Enter **Journal No.: ADJ 1**

5 On Line 1, from the drop-down list of accounts to debit, select **Account: 5012 Insurance: Liability Insurance Expense (Expense)**

6 Enter **Debit Amount: 100.00**

7 On Line 2, from the drop-down list of accounts to credit, select **Account: 1220 Prepaid Expenses: Insurance (Other Current Assets)**

8 Enter **Credit Amount: 100.00**

9 Enter **Memo: Adjusting entry for prepaid insurance**

10 Normally we would select Save and new, but in this case, select **Cancel**. If asked Do you want to leave without saving?, select **Yes**.

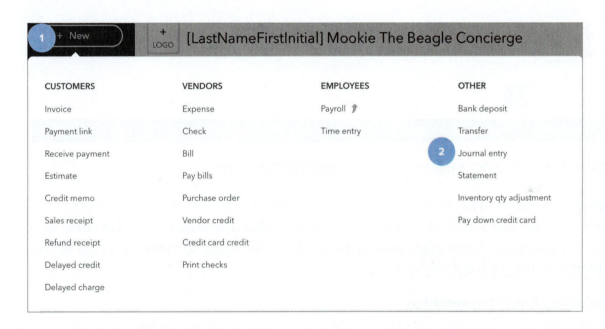

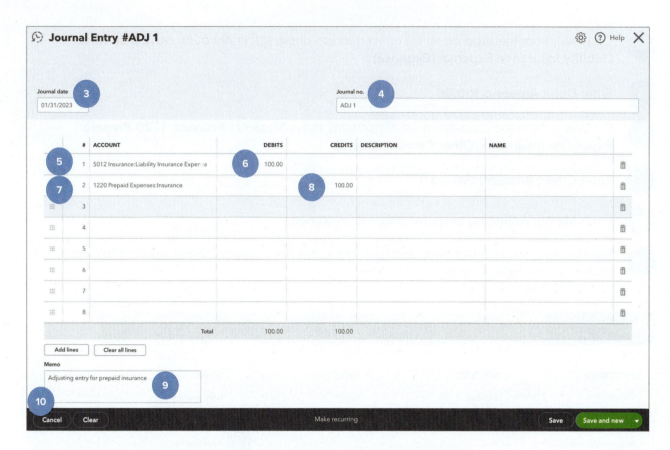

ADJUSTING ENTRY FOR PREPAID ITEMS: DEPRECIATION

Depreciation is a special type of prepaid item involving fixed assets, such as equipment, computers, and cars and trucks. Depreciation is the allocation of a fixed asset's cost over its useful life. For example, a truck might have a useful life of five years so the truck's cost would be allocated over the five-year useful life.

C9.7.1 Adjusting Entry: Depreciation

To record an adjusting entry for depreciation, the two accounts that would be used are:

- Accumulated Depreciation (a Contra-asset account, offsetting an asset account)

- Depreciation Expense (an Expense account)

1 In the adjusting entry to record depreciation, what account would be debited?

2 In the adjusting entry to record depreciation, what account would be credited?

The amount of depreciation to record can be calculated in a number of different ways. For more information about calculating depreciation for tax purposes, go to www.irs.gov.

Section 9.8

UNEARNED ITEMS: RELATED REVENUE/LIABILITY ACCOUNTS

Unearned items consist of revenue that we have not earned. If a customer pays in advance of receiving a service, such as when a customer pays a retainer, our business has an obligation (liability) to either provide the service in the future or return the customer's money. An adjustment may be necessary to bring the revenue account and unearned revenue (liability) account up to date.

Adjusting entries for unearned items typically affect:

* A **Revenue** account and
* A **Liability** account

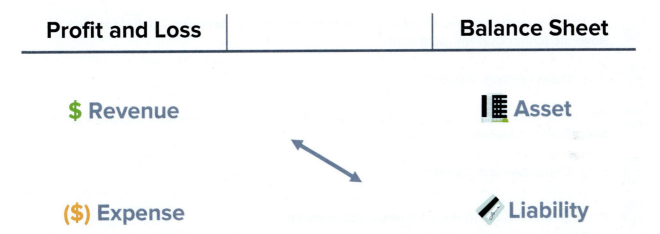

Examples of related Revenue and Liability accounts used for unearned item adjusting entries are as follows.

Unearned Items	Revenue Account	Liability Account
Unearned Rent Revenue	Rent Revenue	Unearned Revenue
App Subscription	App Subscription Revenue	Unearned App Subscription Revenue

The adjusting entry is a Journal entry recording the amount that needs to be transferred between the two accounts, a Revenue account and a Liability account, to show the appropriate balance in each account.

If we need to make an adjusting entry to increase Rent Revenue and decrease Unearned Revenue for $2,000, we would determine whether to debit or credit the accounts as follows:

Account	Account Type	Increase or Decrease?	Debit or Credit?	Amount
Rent Revenue	Revenue	Increase	Credit	$2,000
Unearned Revenue	Liablity	Decrease	Debit	$2,000

To enter an adjusting entry for unearned revenue using the QBO Journal:

1 Select + **New** > **Journal Entry**. Enter **Journal Date: 01/31/2023**.

2 Enter **Journal No.: ADJ 2**

3 On Line 1, from the drop-down list of accounts to debit, select **Account: 2200 Unearned Revenue (Other Current Liabilities)**

4 Enter **Debit Amount: 2,000.00**

5 On Line 2, select credit **Account: + Add New > 4500 Rent Revenue (Other Income > Other Miscellaneous Income)**

6 Enter **Credit Amount: 2,000.00**

7 Enter **Memo: Adjusting entry for unearned revenue**

8 Normally we would select Save and new, but in this case, select **Cancel**. If asked Do you want to leave without saving?, select **Yes**.

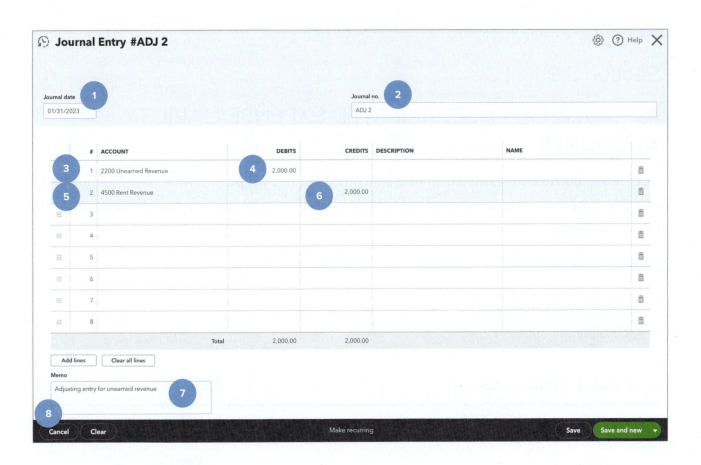

Section 9.9

ACCRUED EXPENSES: RELATED EXPENSE/LIABILITY ACCOUNTS

Accrued expenses are expenses that are incurred but not yet paid or recorded. Examples of accrued expenses include accrued interest expense (interest expense that has been incurred but not yet paid).

Adjusting entries for accrued expenses typically affect:

- An **Expense** account and
- A **Liability** account

Profit and Loss		**Balance Sheet**
$ Revenue		**Asset**
($) Expense	⟷	**Liability**

Examples of related Expense and Liability accounts used for accrued expenses adjusting entries are as follows.

Accrued Expenses	Expense Account	Liability Account
Accrued Interest Incurred	Interest Expense	Interest Payable
Accrued Taxes Payable	Tax Expense	Taxes Payable

The adjusting entry is a Journal entry recording the amount that needs to be transferred between the two accounts, an Expense account and a Liability account, to show the appropriate balance in each account.

If we need to make an adjusting entry to increase Interest Expense and increase Interest Payable for $3,000, we would determine whether to debit or credit the accounts as follows:

Account	Account Type	Increase or Decrease?	Debit or Credit?	Amount
Interest Expense	Expense	Increase	Debit	$3,000
Interest Payable	Liablity	Increase	Credit	$3,000

To enter an adjusting entry for accrued interest expense using the QBO Journal:

1 Select **+ New > Journal Entry**. Enter **Journal Date: 01/31/2023**.

2 Enter **Journal No.: ADJ 3**

3 On Line 1, from the drop-down list of accounts to debit, select **Account: 5020 Interest Paid (Expense)**

4 Enter **Debit Amount: 30.00**

5 On Line 2, select credit **Account: + Add New > 2010 Interest Payable (Other Current Liabilities > Other Current Liablities)**

6 Enter **Credit Amount: 30.00**

7 Enter **Memo: Adjusting entry for accrued interest expense**

8 Normally we would select Save and new, but in this case, select **Cancel**. If asked Do you want to leave without saving?, select **Yes**.

Section 9.10

ACCRUED REVENUES: RELATED REVENUE/ASSET ACCOUNTS

Accrued revenues are revenues that have been earned but not yet collected or recorded. Examples of accrued revenues include interest revenue that has been earned but not yet collected or recorded.

Adjusting entries for accrued revenues typically affect:

* A **Revenue** account and

* An **Asset** account

Profit and Loss		**Balance Sheet**
 $ Revenue	⟷	Asset
($) Expense		 Liability

Examples of related Revenue and Asset accounts used for accrued revenue adjusting entries are as follows.

Accrued Revenues	Revenue Account	Asset Account
Accrued Interest Earned	Interest Revenue	Interest Receivable
Accrued Rent Revenue	Rent Revenue	Rent Receivable

The adjusting entry is a Journal entry recording the amount that needs to be transferred between the two accounts, a Revenue account and an Asset account, to show the appropriate balance in each account.

If we need to make an adjusting entry to increase Interest Revenue and increase Interest Receivable for $4,000, we would determine whether to debit or credit the accounts as follows.

Account	Account Type	Increase or Decrease?	Debit or Credit?	Amount
Interest Revenue	Revenue	Increase	Credit	$4,000
Interest Receivable	Asset	Increase	Debit	$4,000

To enter an adjusting entry for accrued interest revenue using the QBO Journal:

1. Select **+ New > Journal Entry**. Enter **Journal Date: 01/31/2023**.

2. Enter **Journal No.: ADJ 4**

3. On Line 1, from the drop-down list of accounts to debit, select **Account: + Add New > 1110 Interest Receivable (Other Current Assets > Other Current Assets)**

4. Enter **Debit Amount: 40.00**

5. On Line 2, select credit **Account: + Add New > 4600 Interest Revenue (Other Income > Interest Earned)**

6. Enter **Credit Amount: 40.00**

7. Enter **Memo: Adjusting entry for accrued interest revenue**

8. Normally we would select Save and close, but in this case, select **Cancel**. If asked Do you want to leave without saving?, select **Yes**.

9. This completes the chapter activities. If you are ready to proceed to the chapter exercises at this time, leave your browser open with your QBO company displayed. If you will be completing the chapter exercises at a later time, you can close your browser.

Section 9.11

ADJUSTED TRIAL BALANCE

The Adjusted Trial Balance is prepared after adjusting entries are made to view updated account balances and verify that the accounting system still balances.

To view an Adjusted Trial Balance in QBO, simply prepare the Trial Balance report again after adjusting entries have been entered in QBO.

1 From the Navigation Bar, select **Reports**

2 Select **Standard** tab

3 Select **Report Category: For My Accountant**

4 Select **Trial Balance**, then we would complete steps to run the Trial Balance again after adjusting entries are entered.

The Adjusted Trial Balance is discussed further in the next chapter, Chapter 10.

Reports

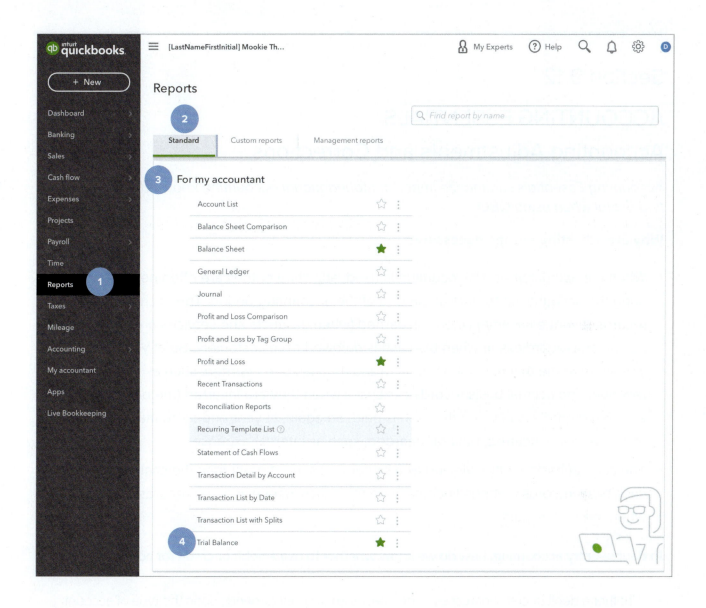

Section 9.12

ACCOUNTING ESSENTIALS
Accounting Adjustments and Corrections

Accounting Essentials summarize important foundational accounting knowledge you may find useful when using QBO

Why are adjusting entries necessary?

- When the accrual basis of accounting is used, adjusting entries are often necessary to bring the accounts up to date at the end of the accounting period. The accrual basis records revenue (income) when it is earned (when products and services are provided to customers) regardless of when the cash is received from customers. So at year end there may be revenue that has not been recorded that has been earned, such as interest revenue. The accrual basis records expenses when they are incurred (the benefits have expired) regardless of when the cash is paid. So again, at year end there may be expenses that have been incurred, but not recorded, such as interest expense.

- The accrual basis is often viewed as a better measure of profit than the cash basis. The cash basis records revenue (income) when the cash is received and records expenses when the cash is paid.

In double-entry accounting, how do we know whether to use a debit or credit for adjusting entries?

- Whether a debit or credit increases or decreases an account depends upon the type of account.

Account Type	Debit	Credit
Assets	Increase	Decrease
Liabilities	Decrease	Increase
Equity	Decrease	Increase
Revenues (Income)	Decrease	Increase
Expenses	Increase	Decrease

What are corrections?

- Corrections, or correcting entries, fix mistakes in the accounting system. Adjusting entries, on the other hand, are not mistakes, but updates that are required to bring accounts to their correct balance as of a certain date.

How do we make a correction using journal entries?

- For example, assume the Cash account should have been debited for $200.00 and the Professional Fees Revenue account credited for $200.00. However, the following incorrect entry was made for $2,000.00 instead of $200.00.

Incorrect Entry	Account	Amount
Debit	Cash	$2,000.00
Credit	Professional Fees Revenue	$2,000.00

- Often the easiest way for us to correct an error is to make two correcting entries in the Journal:

1. **Correcting Entry 1: Eliminate the effect of the incorrect entry by making the opposite journal entry.**

Correcting Entry 1	Account	Amount
Debit	Professional Fees Revenue	$2,000.00
Credit	Cash	$2,000.00

2. **Correcting Entry 2: After eliminating the effect of the incorrect entry, make the correct entry that should have been made initially.**

Correcting Entry 2	Account	Amount
Debit	Cash	$200.00
Credit	Professional Fees Revenue	$200.00

How do we correct errors on saved documents, such as Invoices or Purchase Orders?

- Once a document has been saved, we can use one of three approaches to correct the error:
  1. **Display** the document, correct the error, then save the document again.
  2. **Void** the erroneous document, then create a new document. Voiding keeps a record of the document, but changes the amounts to zero.
  3. **Delete** the erroneous document, then create a new document. Deleting the document erases the document from our system.

- Typically, options 1 or 2 are preferable because we have a better audit trail showing changes.

Practice Quiz 9

Q9.1

QuickBooks Online uses which basis of accounting?

a. Accrual

b. Cash

c. Both a and b

d. Neither a nor b

Q9.2

At the end of an accounting period, adjusting entries are made to:

a. To ensure a profit

b. Bring the accounts up to date

c. Debit or credit the checking account

d. Prove that debits equal credits

Q9.3

Accrued revenues are:

a. Revenues that have been earned, but not collected

b. Payment received in advance of receiving the service

c. Revenues that have been collected, but not yet earned

d. Revenues that have been recorded

Q9.4

Sales are recorded under cash basis accounting when:

a. The goods or services are provided regardless of whether the payment is collected from customers

b. The costs are incurred to earn the revenue

c. The cash is collected from customers

d. The bookkeeper has time to record the transactions

Q9.5

Sales are recorded under accrual basis accounting when:

a. The goods or services are provided regardless of whether the payment is collected from customers

b. The costs are incurred to earn the revenue

c. The actual cash is collected from customers

d. The bookkeeper has time to record the transactions

Q9.6

Adjusting entries are typically made:

a. At the beginning of the accounting period
b. Whenever an error is found and a correction is required
c. At the beginning of each month
d. On the last day of the accounting period

Q9.7

The Journal entry to update the Office Supplies account for office supplies used is which of the following types of adjusting entry?

a. Prepaid item
b. Unearned Revenue
c. Accrued Expense
d. Accrued Revenue
e. Not an adjusting entry

Q9.8

The Journal entry to update the accounts for interest expense incurred but not recorded is which of the following types of adjusting entries?

a. Prepaid item
b. Unearned Revenue
c. Accrued Expense
d. Accrued Revenue
e. Not an adjusting entry

Q9.9

The Journal entry to update the accounts for interest earned but not recorded is which of the following types of adjusting entries?

a. Prepaid item
b. Unearned Revenue
c. Accrued Expense
d. Accrued Revenue
e. Not an adjusting entry

Q9.10

The Journal entry to update the accounts for customer subscriptions that are prepaid but not yet earned is which of the following types of adjusting entries?

a. Prepaid item
b. Unearned Revenue

c. Accrued Expense

d. Accrued Revenue

e. Not an adjusting entry

Q9.11

The Journal entry to update the accounts for prepaid insurance that has expired is which of the following types of adjusting entries?

a. Prepaid item

b. Unearned Revenue

c. Accrued Expense

d. Accrued Revenue

e. Not an adjusting entry

Q9.12

The Journal entry to update the accounts for customer services provided but not yet recorded is which of the following types of adjusting entries?

a. Prepaid item

b. Unearned Revenue

c. Accrued Expense

d. Accrued Revenue

e. Not an adjusting entry

Q9.13

The Journal entry to record payment of cash for office supplies is which of the following types of adjusting entries?

a. Prepaid item

b. Unearned Revenue

c. Accrued Expense

d. Accrued Revenue

e. Not an adjusting entry

Q9.14

The Journal entry to update the accounts for rent expense recorded that has not expired is which of the following types of adjusting entries?

a. Prepaid item

b. Unearned Revenue

c. Accrued Expense

d. Accrued Revenue

e. Not an adjusting entry

Exercises 9

E9.1 Debits and Credits

Enter either Increase or Decrease in the following table to complete it.

- **Increase**
- **Decrease**

Account Type	Debit	Credit
Assets	_____	_____
Liabilities	_____	_____
Equity	_____	_____
Revenues (Income)	_____	_____
Expenses	_____	_____

E9.2 Journal

Identify the labels of the following columns in the QBO Journal.

1 _____

2 _____

3 _____

4 _____

EM9.3 Adjusting Entry Prepaid Insurance

At January 31, 2023 Cy needs to update his accounts before preparing financial statements to review Mookie The Beagle Concierge performance for its first month of operations. Cy has asked for your assistance in preparing the adjusting entries. Mookie The Beagle Concierge will be using the accrual basis of accounting.

In January, Mookie The Beagle Concierge purchased $300 of liability insurance to cover a 3-month period from Phoenix Insurance. So at the end of the accounting period on January 31, 1 month of insurance has expired @ $100 ($300/3 months = $100 per month). The 2 months of unexpired insurance is Prepaid Expenses: Insurance, an asset account with future benefit. Since Mookie The Beagle Concierge recorded the entire $300 as Insurance: Liability Insurance Expense, an adjusting entry is needed to bring accounts up to date at January 31.

QBO CROSSCHECK

Before proceeding, crosscheck your Insurance: Liability Insurance Expense account to verify that it has a balance of $300. (Select Reports > Trial Balance > Report period: 01/31/2023.)

1. Complete the following table.

Account	Account Type	Increase or Decrease?	Debit or Credit?	Amount
Insurance: Liability Insurance Expense	Expense	1. _____	2. _____	3. $_____
Prepaid Expenses: Insurance	Asset	4. _____	5. _____	6. $_____

2. Plan Adjusting Journal Entry.

    a. Complete the following to plan the adjusting journal entry to enter in QBO.

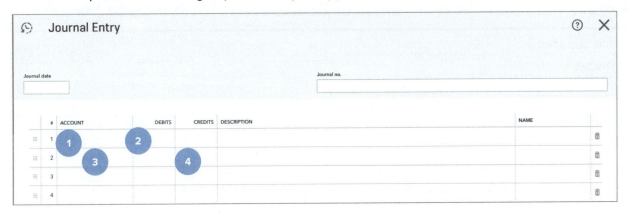

1 _____

2 _____

3 _____

4 _____

3. Enter Adjusting Journal Entry.
    a. Select **(+) New icon > Journal Entry**
    b. Enter the adjusting journal entry in QBO with **Journal Date: January 31, 2023**
    c. Enter **Journal No.: ADJ 1**

EM9.4 Adjusting Entry Supplies

Complete the following adjusting entry for Mookie The Beagle Concierge.

Mookie The Beagle Concierge purchased $1,185 of office supplies during January 2023. At the end of the accounting period on January 31, Mookie The Beagle Concierge still had $685 of unused supplies on hand. The $685 of supplies is an asset with future benefit. Since Mookie The Beagle Concierge recorded the entire $1,185 as Office Supplies & Software (Expenses), an adjusting entry is needed to bring accounts up to date at January 31.

QBO CROSSCHECK

Before proceeding, crosscheck your Office Supplies & Software account to verify that it has a balance of $1,185.

1. Complete the following table.

Account	Account Type	Increase or Decrease?	Debit or Credit?	Amount
Office Supplies & Software	Expense	1. _____	2. _____	3. $_____
Prepaid Expenses: Supplies	Asset	4. _____	5. _____	6. $_____

2. Plan Adjusting Journal Entry.
    a. Complete the following to plan the adjusting journal entry to enter in QBO.

3. Create Adjusting Journal Entry.
   a. Select **(+) New icon** > **Journal Entry**
   b. Enter the adjusting journal entry in QBO with **Journal Date: January 31, 2023**
   c. Enter **Journal No.: ADJ 2**

EM9.5 Adjusting Entry Prepaid Rental

When Mookie The Beagle Concierge started stocking Mookie The Beagle Concierge—branded inventory, Cy rented a centrally located storage locker with digital access. This permits Mookie The Beagle Concierge contractors to access the storage locker for deliveries to customers. Cy has digital surveillance and from his smartphone can electronically permit the contractors access when they arrive at the storage locker. In addition, all inventory has an RFID chip that is automatically read when the contractor exits the storage locker door. This feature improves inventory control in that Cy is immediately notified on his smartphone when any inventory is removed from the storage locker. The storage locker streamlines operations. The only issue is that Cy overlooked recording the storage locker rental in QBO.

Complete the following adjusting entry for Mookie The Beagle Concierge.

In anticipation of stocking Mookie The Beagle Concierge—branded inventory, Cy charged $900 for 6 months storage locker rental from Lynne's Space to Mookie The Beagle Concierge's VISA credit card on January 1, 2023. So at the end of the accounting period on

January 31, Mookie The Beagle Concierge has used 1 month of rent @ $150 ($900/6 months = $150 per month). The unused rent (5 months @ $150 = $750) is Prepaid Expense: Prepaid Rent, an asset account with future benefit.

Since Cy had not recorded anything related to the storage locker rental, an adjusting entry is needed to bring accounts up to date at January 31.

1. Complete the following table.

Account	Account Type	Increase or Decrease?	Debit or Credit?	Amount
Rent & Lease	Expense	1. _____	2. _____	3. $_____
Prepaid Expenses: Rent	Asset	4. _____	5. _____	6. $_____
VISA Credit Card	Liability	7. _____	8. _____	9. $_____

2. Plan Adjusting Journal Entry.
   a. Complete the following to plan the adjusting journal entry to enter in QBO.

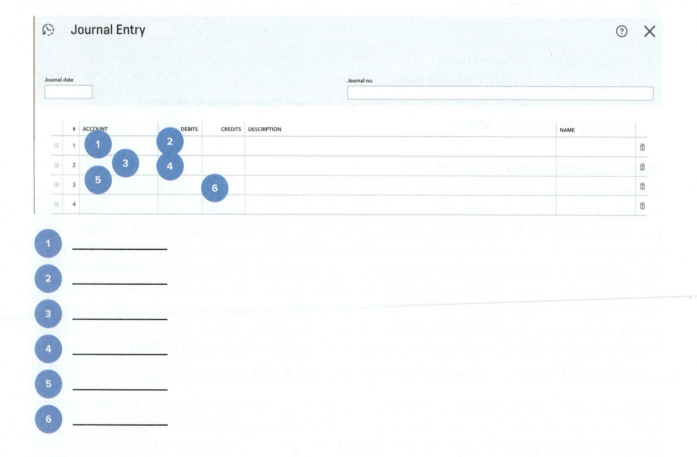

3. Create Adjusting Journal Entry.
    a. Select **(+) New icon > Journal Entry**
    b. Enter the adjusting journal entry in QBO with **Journal Date: January 31, 2023**
    c. Enter **Journal No.: ADJ 3**

EM9.6 Adjusting Entry Unearned Revenue

Complete the following adjusting entry for Mookie The Beagle Concierge.

On January 14, 2023, Angel prepaid $3,200 for pet care services to be provided each Friday for 8 weeks for her King Shepherd, Kuno. Mookie The Beagle Concierge recorded the entire $3,200 as Sales. At the end of the accounting period on January 31, 3 weeks (01/13, 01/20, 01/27) of the pet care services had been provided to Kuno, so 5 weeks of services or $2,000 ($3,200/8 = $400 per week) had not been earned as of the end of January. Since $2,000 has not been earned, the $2,000 is a liability because Mookie The Beagle Concierge has an obligation to provide the pet care service or return the $2,000 to the customer. So an adjusting entry is needed to bring accounts up to date at January 31.

1. Complete the following table.

Account	Account Type	Increase or Decrease?	Debit or Credit?	Amount
Sales	Income	1. _____	2. _____	3. $_____
Unearned Revenue	Liability	4. _____	5. _____	6. $_____

2. Plan Adjusting Journal Entry.
    a. Complete the following to plan the adjusting journal entry to enter in QBO.

1 _____

2 _____

3 _____

4 _____

3. Create Adjusting Journal Entry.
    a. Select **(+) New icon > Journal Entry**
    b. Enter the adjusting journal entry in QBO with **Journal Date: January 31, 2023**
    c. Enter **Journal No.: ADJ 4**

EM9.7 Adjusting Entry Accrued Expenses

Complete the following adjusting entry for Mookie The Beagle Concierge.

Interest on Mookie The Beagle Concierge's Loan Payable to Cy has been incurred, but not recorded or paid. The interest that has been incurred is calculated as principal multiplied by the interest rate multiplied by the time period ($1,000 x 6% x 1/12 = $5.00). Interest Expense of $5.00 must be recorded as an accrued expense and Interest Payable, a liability, recorded for the amount that Mookie The Beagle Concierge is obligated to pay later. So an adjusting entry is needed to bring accounts up to date at January 31.

QBO CROSSCHECK

Before proceeding, crosscheck your Loans Payable account to verify that it has a balance of $1,000.

1. Complete the following table.

Account	Account Type	Increase or Decrease?	Debit or Credit?	Amount
Interest Paid	Expense	1. _____	2. _____	3. $_____
Interest Payable	Liability	4. _____	5. _____	6. $_____

2. Plan Adjusting Journal Entry.

   a. Complete the following to plan the adjusting journal entry to enter in QBO.

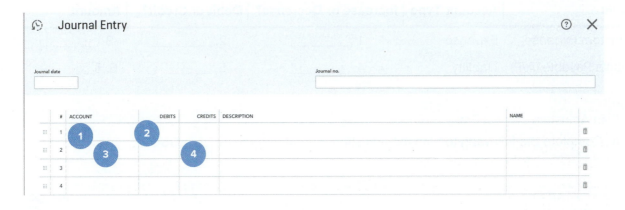

3. Create Adjusting Journal Entry.

   a. Add a new Other Current Liabilities account to the Chart of Accounts: **2010 Interest Payable**

   b. Select **(+) New icon > Journal Entry**

   c. Enter the adjusting journal entry in QBO with **Journal Date: January 31, 2023**

   d. Enter **Journal No.: ADJ 5**

EM9.8 Adjusting Entry Accrued Expenses

Complete the following adjusting entry for Mookie The Beagle Concierge.

During January, Evan Henry, a contractor, provided pet care services to Angel's Kuno for three Fridays in January, totaling 24 hours @ $20 per hour. Cy overlooked recording this contractor expense since Evan had not been paid for these services yet. So at January 31, an adjusting entry is needed to record Contractors Expense that will be paid later. In the future, Cy is hoping that the QBO time tracking will assist in avoiding this type of oversight.

1. Complete the following table.

Account	Account Type	Increase or Decrease?	Debit or Credit?	Amount
Contractors Expense	Expense	1. _____	2. _____	3. _____
Accounts Payable (A/P)	Liability	4. _____	5. _____	6. $_____

2. Plan Adjusting Journal Entry.

    a. Complete the following to plan the adjusting journal entry to enter in QBO.

3. Create Adjusting Journal Entry.

    a. Select **(+) New icon > Journal Entry**

    b. Enter the adjusting journal entry in QBO with **Journal Date: January 31, 2023**. If requested, select **Evan Henry** for the Name field.

    c. Enter **Journal No.: ADJ 6**

EM9.9 Adjusting Entry Accrued Expense

Complete the following adjusting entry for Mookie The Beagle Concierge.

At January 31, Mookie The Beagle Concierge has incurred $330 of accounting services for assistance with QBO. This amount has not been paid nor recorded by Mookie The Beagle Concierge, so an adjusting entry is needed to record the expense incurred.

1. Complete the following table.

Account	Account Type	Increase or Decrease?	Debit or Credit?	Amount
Legal & Professional Services	Expense	1. _____	2. _____	3. $_____
Accounts Payable (A/P)	Liability	4. _____	5. _____	6. $_____

2. Plan Adjusting Journal Entry.
   a. Complete the following to plan the adjusting journal entry to enter in QBO.

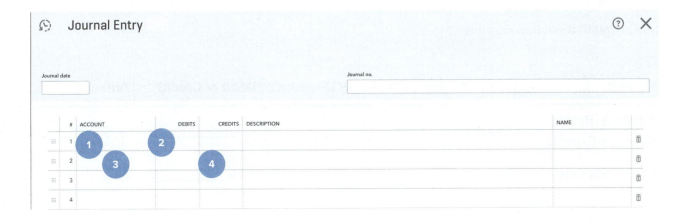

1. _____

2. _____

3. _____

4. _____

3. Create Adjusting Journal Entry.
   a. Select **(+) New icon** > **Journal Entry**.
   b. Enter the adjusting journal entry in QBOwith **Journal Date: January 31, 2023**. If requested, enter **Your First Name Your Last Name** in the Vendor Name field.
   c. Enter **Journal No.: ADJ 7**

EM9.10 Adjusting Entry Renter Insurance

Oops... When cleaning out his jacket pocket, Cy discovers a receipt for renter insurance for the storage locker. The renter insurance was purchased from Phoenix Insurance to provide insurance coverage for the inventory that Cy planned to store in the storage locker. Mookie The Beagle Concierge purchased 1 month of renter insurance coverage for the period January 1 through January 31, 2023. Using the company credit card, Mookie The Beagle Concierge paid $18.00 on January 16, 2023 for the 1 month of insurance coverage.

So at the end of the accounting period on January 31, 1 month of rent had expired at $18.00. Since Mookie The Beagle Concierge had not recorded the transaction, the entire $18.00 should be recorded as Renter Insurance Expense with an adjusting entry to bring accounts up to date at January 31.

1. Complete the following table.

Account	Account Type	Increase or Decrease?	Debit or Credit?	Amount
Insurance: Renter Insurance Expense	Expense	1. _____	2. _____	3. $_____
VISA Credit Card	Liability	4. _____	5. _____	6. $_____

2. Plan Adjusting Journal Entry.

  a. Complete the following to plan the adjusting journal entry to enter in QBO.

1. _____

2. _____

3. _____

4. _____

3. Create Adjusting Journal Entry.

  a. Select **(+) New icon > Journal Entry**

  b. Enter the adjusting journal entry in QBO with **Journal Date: January 31, 2023**

  c. Enter **Journal No.: ADJ 8**

4. How would you save this adjusting entry as a recurring transaction?

5. Make Recommendations on How to Improve Processes.

  Business owners are busy people, juggling multiple items at once. So occasionally accounting items are not recorded due to an oversight. Suggest two ways that Mookie The Beagle Concierge and Cy could improve processes to ensure that all accounting items are recorded in a timely manner.

  a. _____

  b. _____

EM9.11 Journal Report

To review for accuracy the adjusting entries you entered for Mookie The Beagle Concierge, you decide to print a report of the adjusting journal entries. In addition, the adjusting journal entries report may be useful when explaining to Cy your justification for the adjustments.

1. Create Journal Report.
   a. From the Navigation Bar, select **Reports > Standard** tab
   b. Select **Report Category: For My Accountant**
   c. Select **Report: Journal**
   d. Select **Report Period: 01/31/2023 to 01/31/2023**
   e. Notice the Journal report displayed includes transactions dated 01/31/2023 in addition to the adjusting journal entries. To add a filter to display only adjusting journal entries on 01/31/2023, select **Customize**.
   f. Select **Filter**
   g. Check **Transaction Type**
   h. Select **Transaction Type: Journal Entry**
   i. Select **Run report**
   j. Review the adjusting journal entries listed in the report for accuracy

2. Export the Adjusting Journal Entries Report to PDF.
   a. With the Journal report displayed, select the **Export icon**
   b. Select **Export to PDF**
   c. Select **Save as PDF**

3. Export the Adjusting Journal Entries Report to Excel.
   a. With the Journal report displayed, select the **Export icon**
   b. Select **Export to Excel**

EM9.12 Adjusted Trial Balance

Prepare an Adjusted Trial Balance for Mookie The Beagle Concierge after adjusting entries to view updated account balances and verify that the accounting system still balances.

To view an Adjusted Trial Balance in QBO simply run the Trial Balance report again after adjusting entries have been entered in QBO.

1. Create Trial Balance (Adjusted).
   a. From the Navigation Bar, select **Reports > Standard** tab
   b. Select **Report Category: For My Accountant**
   c. Select **Report: Trial Balance**
   d. Select **Date: 01/31/2023**
   e. Select **Run report**

2. What is the amount of Total Debits on the Adjusted Trial Balance?

3. What is the amount of Total Credits on the Adjusted Trial Balance?

4. Export the Adjusted Trial Balance to PDF.
   a. With the Adjusted Trial Balance displayed, select the **Export icon**
   b. Select **Export to PDF**
   c. Select **Save as PDF**

5. Export the Adjust Trial Balance to Excel.
   a. With the Adjusted Trial Balance report displayed, select the **Export icon**
   b. Select **Export to Excel**

Chapter 10

QBO Reports

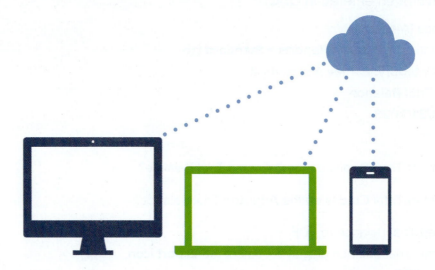

MOOKIE THE BEAGLE™ CONCIERGE

BACKSTORY

After Mookie The Beagle™ Concierge completed its first month in business, Cy Walker realizes that he needs information to assess the financial and operating performance of the business. Also, Cy needs information in order to make sound management decisions going forward. So Cy would like you to learn more about how to create reports using QuickBooks Online and how to use the various QBO reports for better decision making.

Chapter 10

LEARNING OBJECTIVES

Chapter 10 explores some frequently used QBO reports and the reporting process. The objective of financial reports is to provide information to users for decision making. The users of the financial reports include investors, creditors, tax agencies, and management. Different users are focused on different decisions and require different types of reports to provide information related to those decisions. For example, an investor may be deciding whether to invest and a creditor deciding whether to extend credit to a business.

In this chapter, you will learn about the following topics:

- Accounting Cycle
- Adjusted Trial Balance
- Navigating Reports
- Financial Statements
  - Profit and Loss
  - Balance Sheet
  - Statement of Cash Flows
- Management Reports
- Who Owes You Reports
  - Accounts Receivable Aging
- Sales and Customer Reports
  - Income by Customer
  - Sales by Product/Service
  - Physical Inventory Worksheet
- What You Owe Reports
  - Accounts Payable Aging
- Expenses and Vendors Reports
  - Open Purchase Orders
  - Purchases by Vendor Detail
- For My Accountant Reports
  - Journal
  - Audit Log
- Tags

- Accounting Essentials: Financial Reports

Section 10.1

 QBO SATNAV

QBO SatNav is our satellite navigation for QuickBooks Online, assisting us in navigating QBO

Chapter 10 covers QBO Reports, as shown in the following QBO SatNav.

 **QBO SatNav**

 **QBO Settings**

Company Settings
Chart of Accounts

QBO Transactions

Banking
Customers & Sales
Vendors & Expenses
Employees & Payroll

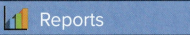 **QBO Reports**

 Reports

Section 10.2

ADJUSTED TRIAL BALANCE

The topic of this chapter is financial reports that are the results or output of the accounting cycle. As discussed in Chapter 9, the accounting cycle is a series of accounting activities that a business performs each accounting period. The accounting cycle usually consists of the following steps.

- **Chart of Accounts.** The Chart of Accounts (Account List) is a list of all accounts used to accumulate information about assets, liabilities, owners' equity, revenues, and expenses.
- **Transactions.** During the accounting period, record transactions with customers, vendors, employees, and owners.
- **Trial Balance.** A Trial Balance is also referred to as an unadjusted Trial Balance because it is prepared before adjustments. A Trial Balance lists each account and the account balance at the end of the accounting period. Prepare a Trial Balance to verify that the accounting system is in balance—total debits should equal total credits.
- **Adjustments.** At the end of the accounting period before preparing financial statements, make any adjustments necessary to bring the accounts up to date. Adjustments are entered in the Journal using debits and credits. (Adjustments were covered in Chapter 9.)
- **Adjusted Trial Balance.** Prepare an Adjusted Trial Balance (a Trial Balance after adjustments) to verify that the accounting system still balances.
- **Financial Reports.** Prepare financial statements (Profit and Loss, Balance Sheet, and Statement of Cash Flows) for external users and internal users. Prepare management reports. Chapter 10 covers financial reports, including financial statements and management reports.

After making adjusting entries and before preparing financial reports, we need to prepare an Adjusted Trial Balance to ensure our accounts are up to date. By crosschecking against the Adjusted Trial Balance below, you can determine if you have the correct account balances.

EXCEL TEMPLATE

For your convenience to complete Chapter 10, an Excel Template is provided with your text to organize your Excel reports. To access the Chapter 10 Excel Template, you have two options:

1. If you are using Connect with your text, the Chapter 10 Excel Template can be downloaded from within Connect.

2. If you are not using Connect, go to www.my-quickbooksonline.com > select QBO 3e > QBO 3e Excel Templates > Download the Chapter 10 Excel Template.

After downloading the Excel Template, select the Instructions sheet in the Excel Template to view the steps to copy your exported Excel reports to the Excel Template.

QBO ADJUSTED TRIAL BALANCE CROSSCHECK

C10.2.1 Adjusted Trial Balance Crosscheck

We can determine if we have the correct account balances by crosschecking against an Adjusted Trial Balance. Update account balances as needed to obtain the correct balances before proceeding to prepare other reports.

To crosscheck your QBO Trial Balance (Adjusted):

1 Sign in to your Mookie The Beagle Concierge QBO Company. Using a web browser go to **qbo.intuit.com** > enter **User ID** > enter **Password** > select **Sign in**.

2 Create a Trial Balance by selecting **Reports** on the Navigation Bar > **Standard** tab > in the **For My Accountants** section select **Trial Balance** > select **Date: 01/31/2023** > select **Active rows/active columns** > select **Accounting Method: Accrual** > **Run report**

3 Verify Account Balances.
Before creating QBO reports, verify that your QBO account balances are the same as the balances in the following Adjusted Trial Balance.
- If your account balances are not the same as the following Adjusted Trial Balance, proceed to Step 4.
- If your account balances are the same as the following Adjusted Trial Balance, proceed to Step 5.

4 Troubleshooting. If any of your QBO account balances differ from the following Adjusted Trial Balance, troubleshoot the discrepancies and update your accounts to the correct balance. See the following Troubleshooting Tips. After updating your accounts to the correct balances, proceed to Step 5.

5 Trial Balance Totals.
   a. What is the amount of Total Debits on the Adjusted Trial Balance?
   b. What is the amount of Total Credits on the Adjusted Trial Balance?

6 **Export** the Adjusted Trial Balance to PDF.

7 **Export** the Adjusted Trial Balance to Excel.
   a. With the Trial Balance (Adjusted) report displayed, select the **Export icon**
   b. Select **Export to Excel**
   c. Download the Excel Template to consolidate your Excel reports for Chapter and Exercises 10. (See the preceding section entitled, Excel Template, for instructions on how to download the template.)
   d. Select the Instructions sheet in the Excel Template. Complete the steps listed in the instructions to copy your Trial Balance (Adjusted) Excel export to the Excel Template.

TROUBLESHOOTING TIPS

If your QBO account balances differ from the following Adjusted Trial Balance, try these troubleshooting tips:

- From your Trial Balance (Adjusted) report, drill down on any account balances that differ from the following Adjusted Trial Balance amounts. Review the account for errors.

- Create a Journal report for the period from 01/01/2023 to 01/31/2023. Review the Journal for apparent discrepancies. In the Journal, you can drill down to the source document and correct any errors on the source document, such as a Check or Invoice.

- If necessary, make correcting journal entries as needed to update your accounts to the correct balances. See Chapter 9 Accounting Essentials for more information about correcting entries. To use the Journal to make any necessary correcting entries, select (+) New icon > Journal Entry.

[LastNameFirst Initial] Mookie The Beagle Concierge

Trial Balance
As of January 31, 2023

	DEBIT	CREDIT
1001 Checking	25,849.30	
1010 Money Market	10,000.00	
1100 Accounts Receivable (A/R)	3,650.66	
1210 Prepaid Expenses:Supplies	685.00	
1220 Prepaid Expenses:Insurance	200.00	
1230 Prepaid Expenses:Rent	750.00	
1300 Inventory Asset	817.00	
1600 Undeposited Funds	0.00	
2001 Accounts Payable (A/P)		1,088.00
2100 VISA Credit Card		1,706.00
2010 Interest Payable		5.00
2200 Unearned Revenue		2,000.00
2300 Loan Payable		1,000.00
California Department of Tax and Fee Ad...		147.96
3001 Opening Balance Equity		0.00
3003 Owner's Investment		30,000.00
4100 Billable Expense Income		100.00
4200 Sales		10,470.00
4300 Sales of Product Income		1,784.00
5000 Cost of Goods Sold	671.00	
5001 Advertising & Marketing	1,270.00	
5005 Contractors	2,400.00	
5011 Insurance:Renter Insurance Expense	18.00	
5012 Insurance:Liability Insurance Expense	100.00	
5020 Interest Paid	5.00	
5021 Job Supplies	100.00	
5022 Legal & Professional Services	330.00	
5024 Office Supplies & Software	500.00	
5028 Rent & Lease	570.00	
5040 Utilities Expense	385.00	

Section 10.3

NAVIGATING REPORTS

Most QBO reports are accessed from the Navigation Bar. Don't be overwhelmed by the number of reports offered by QBO. QBO offers a wide variety of reports to meet the needs of different QBO users. We will explore some of the more frequently used reports in this chapter.

To navigate QBO reports:

1 From the Navigation Bar, select **Dashboard > Business overview** to view a financial dashboard for the company. This dashboard summarizes key financial metrics. The dashboard includes bank account summaries, and charts for expenses, sales, and income. Select **Edit** or **drop-down arrows** to customize the dashboard.

2 From the Navigation Bar, select **Reports**

3 To search for a specific report, in the **Find report by name** field, enter the **report name** and click the magnifying glass

4 Select **Standard** report tab to view QBO reports, grouped by category, such as Favorites, Business Overview, Sales and Customers, and Expenses and Vendors

5 Under Standard report tab, **Favorites** are listed first

6 To list a report in the Favorites category, click the **star** by the report. Then the report is also listed in the Favorites section for easier access. For example, the star by the Balance Sheet is selected, and the Balance Sheet then also appears in the Favorites category.

7 **Business Overview** reports include financial statements, such as Profit and Loss reports, Balance Sheet reports, and Statement of Cash Flows

8 **Who Owes You** reports are used to track amounts that customers owe your business, including Accounts Receivable Aging reports, Collection reports, and Open Invoices

9 **Sales and Customers** reports provide detailed information about customers and sales transactions, including Customers List, Products and Services List, Deposit Detail, Income by Customer, Sales by Customer, and Sales by Product/Service

10 **What You Owe** reports are used to track amounts that your business owes others, including Accounts Payable reports, Unpaid Bills reports, and Vendor Balance reports

11 **Expenses and Vendors** reports provide detailed information about vendors and expenses transactions, including Check Detail report, Expenses by Vendor report, Open Purchase Order Lists, and Vendors List

12   **Sales Tax** reports include reports about Sales Tax Liabilities and Taxable Sales

13   **Employees** reports include the Employees List and Time Activities reports

14   **For My Accountant** reports include the Account List (Chart of Accounts), General Ledger, Journal, and Trial Balance

15   **Payroll** reports are the same reports as the Employees reports, including the Employees List and Time Activities reports

16   Select the **Custom Reports** tab to view saved customized reports. These are reports that you have created, customized, and then saved for reuse. To save a customized report, after preparing the report, select Save Customization.

17   Select the **Management Reports** tab to view management reports that QBO has prepared for you

18   Select the **drop-down arrow** to view report options to Edit, Send, Export as PDF, Export as DOCX, or Copy

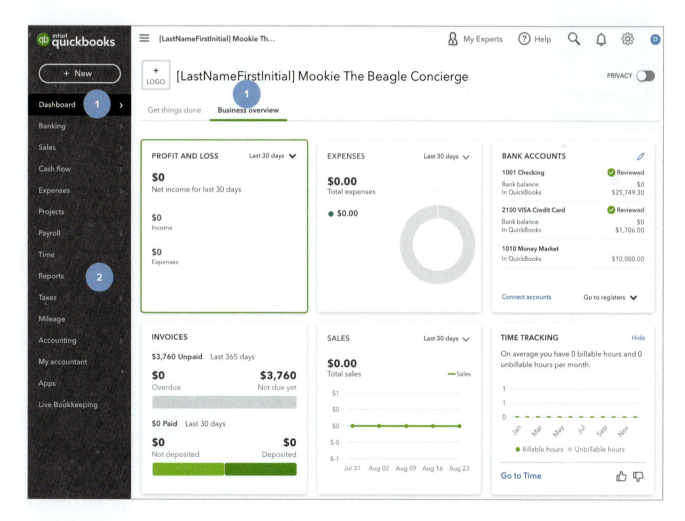

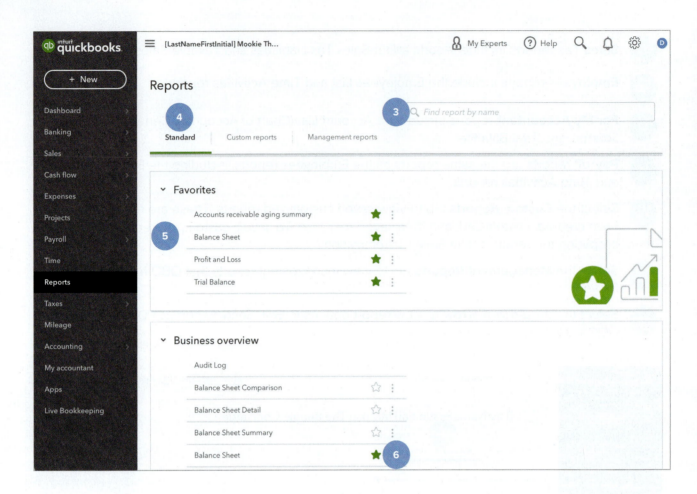

Reports

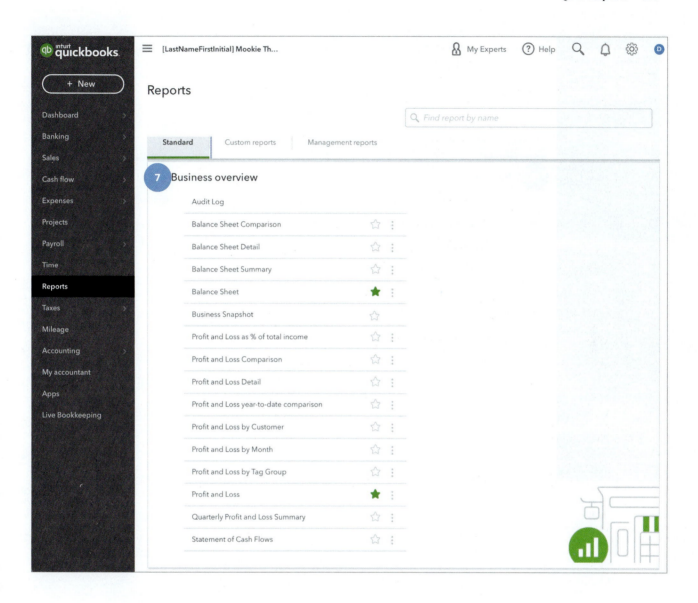

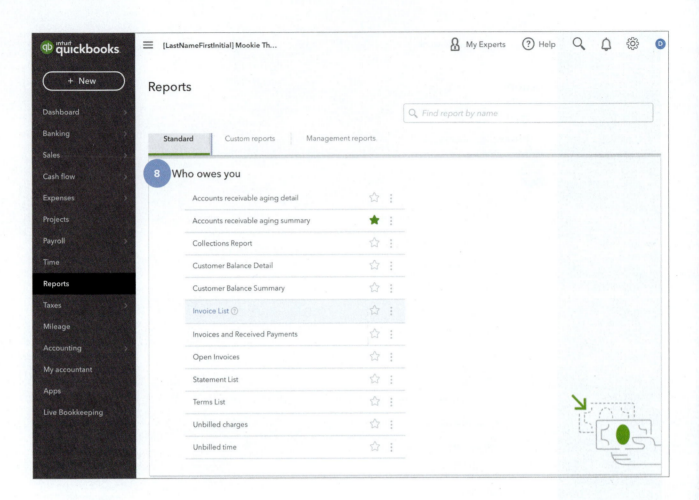

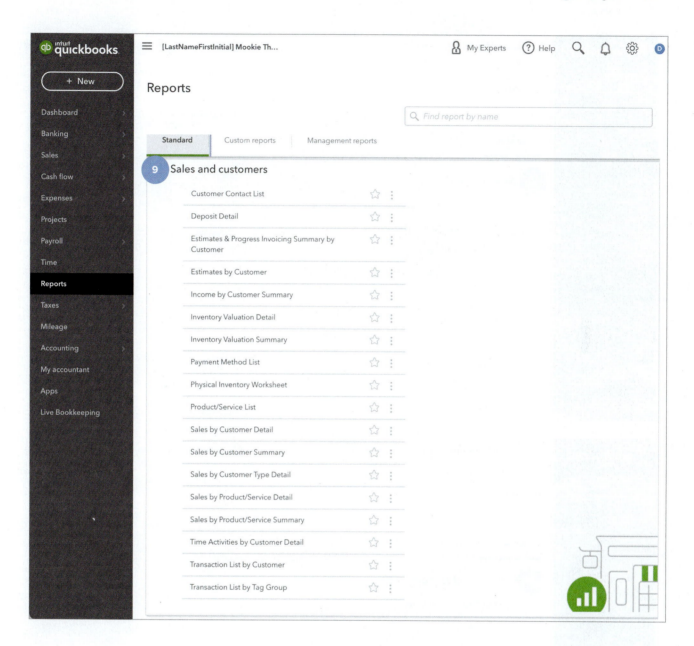

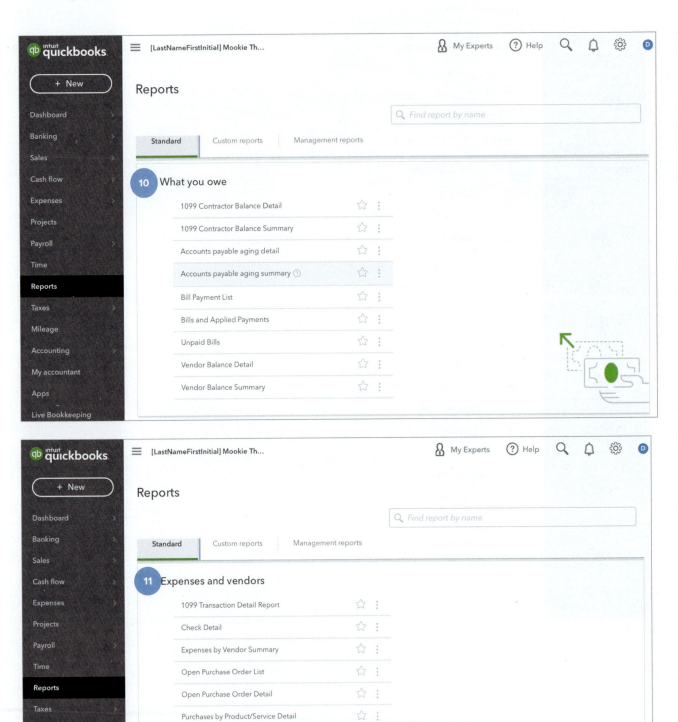

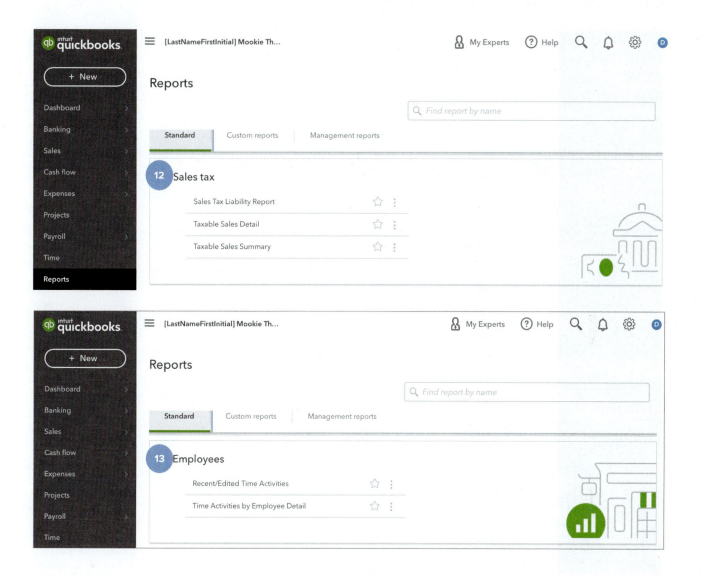

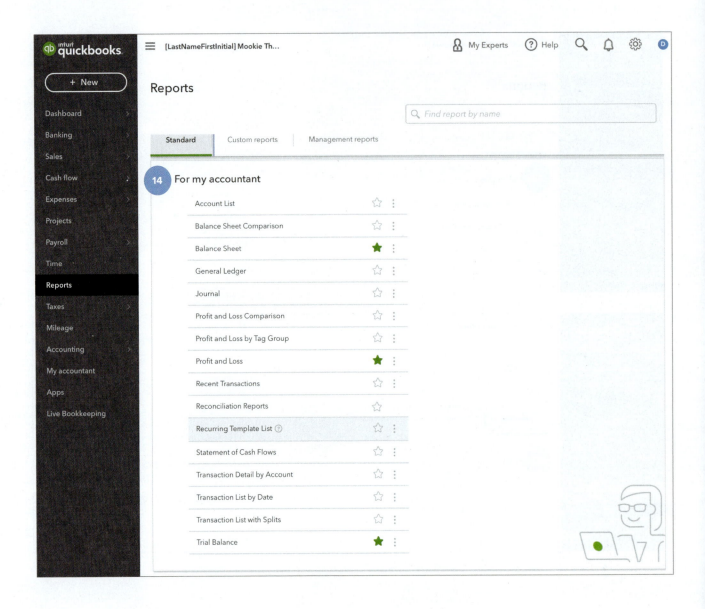

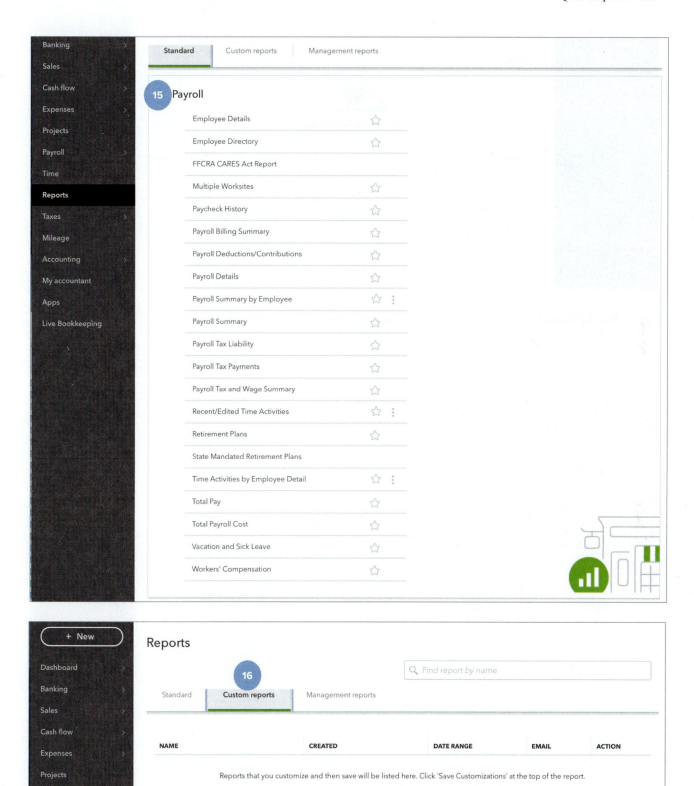

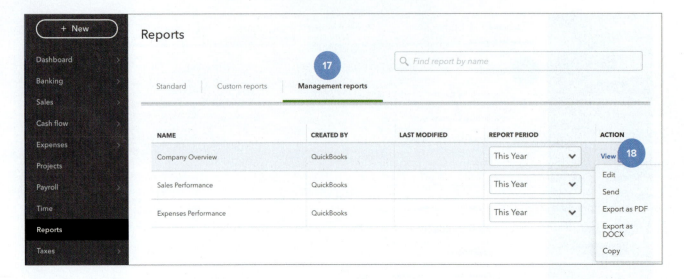

Next, we will explore the process used to prepare QBO financial reports.

Section 10.4

FINANCIAL STATEMENTS

Financial statements are standardized financial reports given to external users, such as bankers and investors. The three main financial statements are the Profit and Loss, Balance Sheet, and Statement of Cash Flows.

> **In general, financial statements** are found under the Standard reports tab > **Business Overview category.**

PROFIT AND LOSS

The Profit and Loss Statement lists sales (sometimes called revenues) and expenses for a specified accounting period. Profit, or net income, can be measured two different ways:

- **Cash basis.** A sale is recorded when cash is collected from the customer. Expenses are recorded when cash is paid.
- **Accrual basis.** Sales are recorded when the good or service is provided regardless of when the cash is collected from the customer. Expenses are recorded when the cost is incurred or expires, even if the expense has not been paid.

QBO permits us to prepare the Profit and Loss Statement using either the accrual or the cash basis. QBO also permits us to prepare Profit and Loss Statements monthly, quarterly, or annually.

To prepare a Profit and Loss Statement using the accrual basis:

1. From the Navigation Bar, select **Reports**

2. Select **Standard** tab

3. Select **Business Overview**

4. Select **Profit and Loss**

5. Select **Customize**

6. Select **Report Period: 01/01/2023 To 01/31/2023**

7 Select **Accounting Method: Accrual**

8 Select **Negative Numbers: (100)**

9 Select **Run report**

10 Select **Save Customization**. Enter **Custom report name: Profit and Loss**. Select **Add new group** > enter **New group name: Financial Statements** > **Add** > **Save**. The customized report will now appear under the Custom Reports tab.

11 Select **Export** icon to display the export options: Export to Excel and Export to PDF

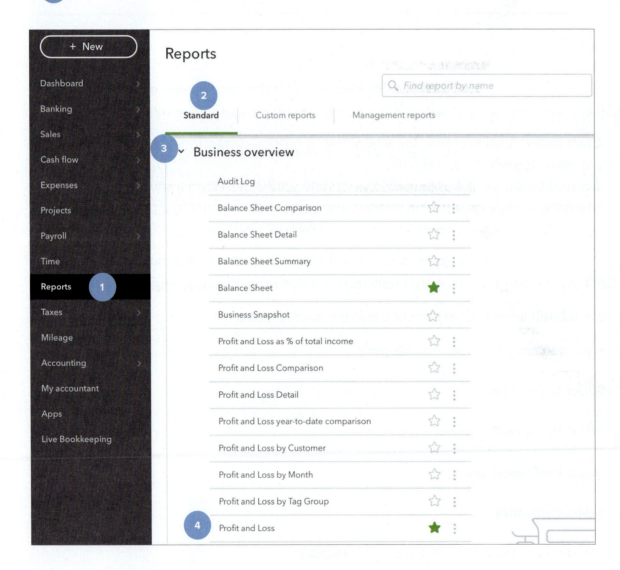

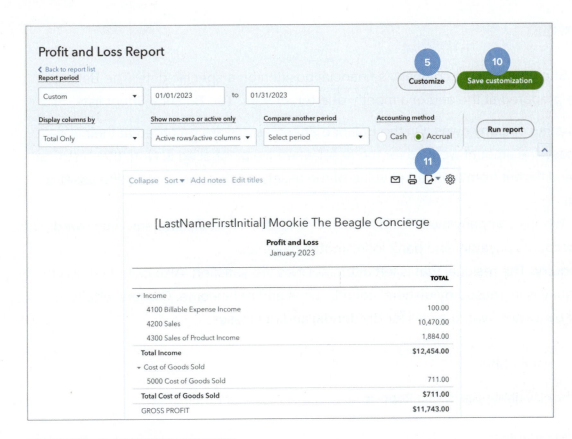

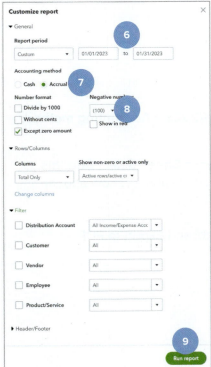

BALANCE SHEET

The Balance Sheet presents a company's financial position on a specific date. The Balance Sheet can be prepared at the end of a month, quarter, or year. The Balance Sheet lists:

1. **Assets**. What a company owns. On the Balance Sheet, assets are recorded at their historical cost, the amount we paid for the asset when we purchased it. Note that historical cost can be different from the market value of the asset, which is the amount the asset is worth now.
2. **Liabilities**. What a company owes. Liabilities are obligations that include amounts owed vendors (accounts payable) and bank loans (notes payable).
3. **Owners' equity.** The residual that is left after liabilities are satisfied. Also called net worth, owners' equity is increased by owners' contributions and net income. Owners' equity is decreased by owners' withdrawals (or dividends) and net losses.

To prepare a Balance Sheet:

1. From the Navigation Bar, select **Reports**

2. Select **Standard** tab

3. Select **Business Overview**

4. Select **Balance Sheet**

5. Enter **Customize** features: **Report Period 01/31/2023 to 01/31/2023 > Accounting method: Accrual > Negative numbers: (100) > Run report**

6. Select **Save Customization**. Enter **Custom report name: Balance Sheet**. Select **Add this report to a group: Financial Statements > Save**. The customized report will now appear under the Custom Reports tab.

7. Select **Export** icon to display the export options: Export to Excel and Export to PDF

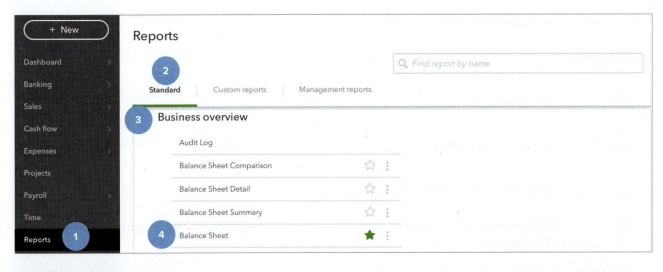

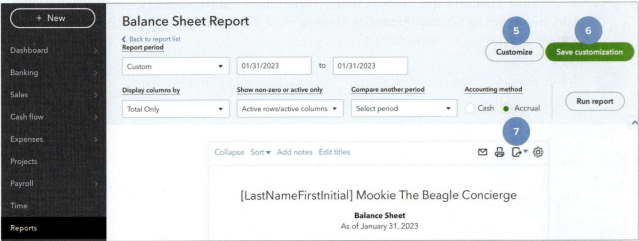

STATEMENT OF CASH FLOWS

The Statement of Cash Flows summarizes cash inflows and cash outflows for a business over a period of time. Cash flows are grouped into three categories:

1. **Cash flows from operating activities.** Cash inflows and outflows related to the company's primary business, such as cash flows from sales and operating expenses.
2. **Cash flows from investing activities.** Cash inflows and outflows related to acquisition and disposal of long-term assets.
3. **Cash flows from financing activities.** Cash inflows and outflows to and from investors and creditors (except for interest payments). Examples include loan principal repayments and investments by owners.

To prepare the Statement of Cash Flows:

1 From the Navigation Bar, select **Reports**

2 Select **Standard** tab

3 Select **Business Overview**

4 Select **Statement of Cash Flows**

5 Enter **Customize** features: **Report Period 01/01/2023 to 01/31/2023 > Negative numbers: (100) > Run report**

6 Select **Save Customization**. Enter **Custom report name: Statement of Cash Flows**. Select **Add this report to a group: Financial Statements > Save**. The customized report will now appear under the Custom Reports tab.

7 Select **Export** icon to display the export options: Export to Excel and Export to PDF

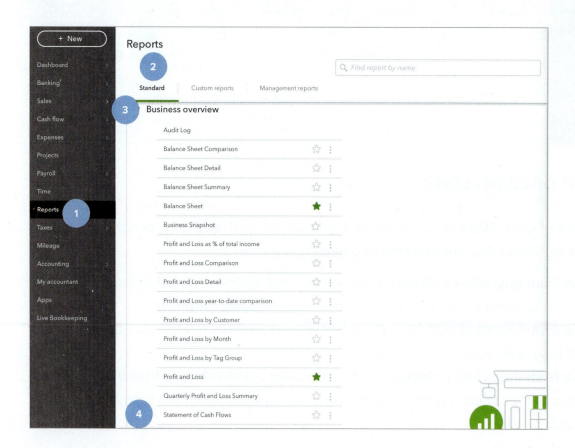

Section 10.5

MANAGEMENT REPORTS

Management reports are prepared as needed to provide management with information for making operating and business decisions. Reports used by management do not have to follow a specified set of rules, such as Generally Accepted Accounting Principles (GAAP) or the Internal Revenue Code.

Management reports include:

1. **Who Owes You reports.** Examples of this category of reports include Accounts Receivable Aging and Open Invoices.
2. **Sales and Customers reports.** This category of reports includes Income by Customer and Sales by Product/Service reports.
3. **What You Owe reports.** Examples of this QBO report category include Accounts Payable Aging and Unpaid Bills.
4. **Expenses and Vendors reports**. This report category includes Open Purchase Orders and Purchases by Product/Service.
5. **For My Accountant reports.** Examples of this type of report include the Trial Balance, Journal, and General Ledger reports. Although the Audit Log appears in the QBO Business Overview report category, typically, it could be considered a report used by an accountant.

> **Although QBO has a Management reports tab that contains bundled reports prepared by QBO, some management reports are included under the Standards reports tab.**

Section 10.6

WHO OWES YOU REPORTS

Who Owes You reports are used to track amounts that customers owe your business. Examples of this type of report includes Accounts Receivable Aging report, Collection reports, and Open Invoices.

ACCOUNTS RECEIVABLE (A/R) AGING

Accounts Receivable reports provide information about which customers owe our business money. When we make a credit sale, our company provides products and services to a customer in exchange for a promise that the customer will pay us later. Sometimes the customer breaks the promise and does not pay. Therefore, a business should have a credit policy to ensure that credit is extended only to customers who are likely to keep their promise and pay their bills.

After credit has been extended, a business needs to track accounts receivable to determine if accounts are being collected in a timely manner.

The Accounts Receivable Aging report provides information useful in tracking accounts receivable by providing information about the age of customer accounts. This report lists the age of accounts receivable balances. In general, the older an account, the less likely the customer will pay the bill. So it is important to monitor the age of accounts receivable and take action to collect old accounts.

To prepare the Accounts Receivable Aging report:

1 From the Navigation Bar, select **Reports**

2 Select **Standard** tab

3 Select **Report Category: Who Owes You**

4 Select **Accounts Receivable Aging Summary**

5 Enter **Customize** features: **Report Period As of: 01/31/2023** > **Negative numbers: (100)** > **Aging method: Report date** > **Days per aging period: 30** > **Number of periods: 4** > **Run report**

6 Select **Save Customization**. Enter **Custom report name: A/R Aging Summary**. Select **Add new group** > enter **New group name: Customer Reports** > **Add** > **Save**. The customized report will now appear under the Custom Reports tab.

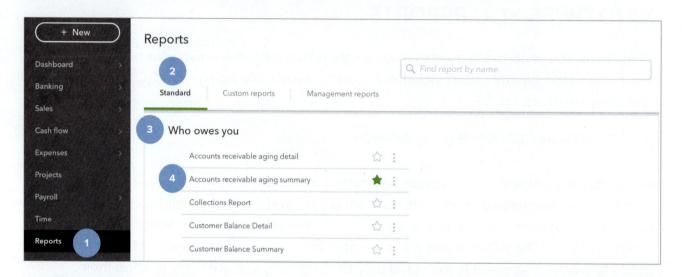

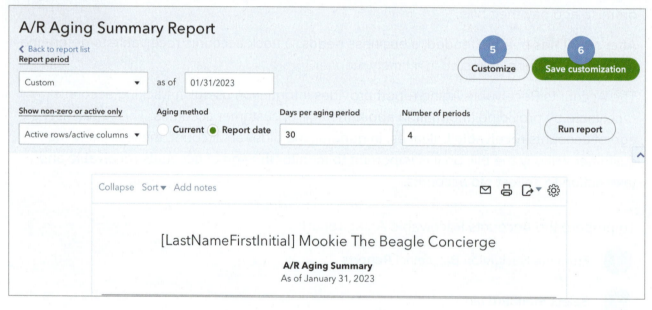

Section 10.7

SALES AND CUSTOMERS REPORTS

Sales and Customers reports provide detailed information about customers and sales transactions, including Customers List, Products and Services List, Deposit Detail, Income by Customer, Sales by Customer, and Sales by Product/Service reports.

INCOME BY CUSTOMER SUMMARY

To improve profitability in the future, a business may evaluate which customers have been profitable in the past. This information permits a business to improve profitability by:

- Increasing business in profitable areas
- Improving performance in unprofitable areas
- Discontinuing unprofitable areas

To determine which customers are generating the most profit for our business, it is necessary to look at both the sales for the customer and associated costs. The Income by Customer Summary can provide insights into which customers are generating the most profit.

SALES BY PRODUCT/SERVICE SUMMARY

The Sales by Product/Service Summary report shows us which products are selling the most and which products are the most profitable. This information is useful for planning which products to order and which services are in demand.

To prepare the Sales by Product/Service Summary report:

1 From the Navigation Bar, select **Reports**

2 Select **Standard** tab

3 Select **Report Category: Sales and Customers**

4 Select **Sales by Product/Service Summary**

5 Enter **Customize** features: **Report Period: 01/01/2023 To 01/31/2023 > Accounting method: Accrual > Negative numbers: (100) > Run report**

6 Select **Save Customization**. Enter **Custom report name: Sales by Product/Service Summary**. Select **Add this report to a group: Customer Reports** > **Save**. The customized report will now appear under the Custom Reports tab.

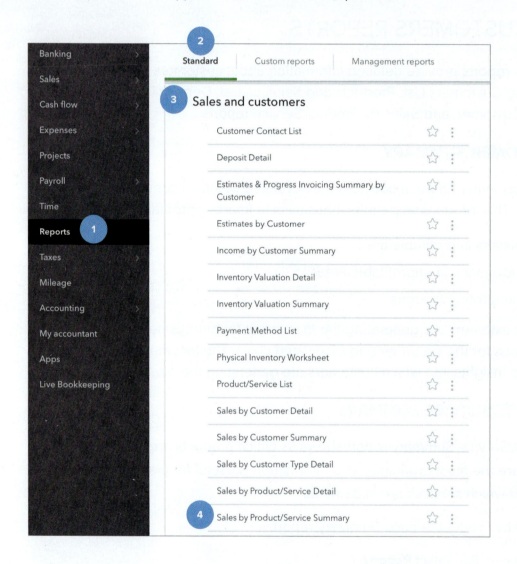

PHYSICAL INVENTORY WORKSHEET

The Physical Inventory Worksheet is used when taking a physical count of inventory. The worksheet lists the quantity on hand per QBO inventory data and provides a blank column in which to enter the quantity counted during a physical inventory count. This worksheet permits us to compare our physical inventory count with our QBO records.

The Physical Inventory Worksheet is found in the Sales and Customers Report Category.

After taking a physical count of inventory and completing the Physical Inventory Worksheet, if we have any unresolved discrepancies, we can use the Inventory Adjustment feature to update our inventory records.

To make an inventory adjustment:

1 Select **Create (+)** icon

2 Select **Inventory Qty Adjustment**

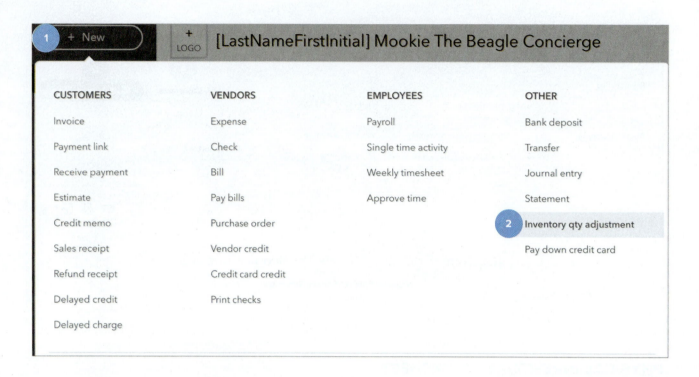

Section 10.8

WHAT YOU OWE REPORTS

What You Owe reports are used to track amounts that your business owes others, including Accounts Payable reports, Unpaid Bills report, and Vendor Balance reports.

ACCOUNTS PAYABLE (A/P) AGING

Accounts payable consists of amounts that our company is obligated to pay in the future. Accounts Payable reports tell us how much we owe vendors and when amounts are due.

The Accounts Payable Aging Summary summarizes accounts payable balances by the age of the account. This report helps to track any past due bills as well as provides information about bills that will be due shortly.

To prepare the Accounts Payable Aging Summary report:

1 From the Navigation Bar, select **Reports**

2 Select **Standard** tab

3 Select **Report Category: What You Owe**

4 Select **Accounts Payable Aging Summary**

5 Enter **Customize** features: **Report Period as of: 01/31/2023** > **Negative numbers: (100)** > **Aging method: Report date** > **Days per aging period: 30** > **Number of periods: 4** > **Run report**

6 Select **Save Customization**. Enter **Custom report name: A/P Aging Summary**. Select **Add new group** > enter **New group name: Vendor Reports** > **Add** > **Save**. The customized report will now appear under the Custom Reports tab.

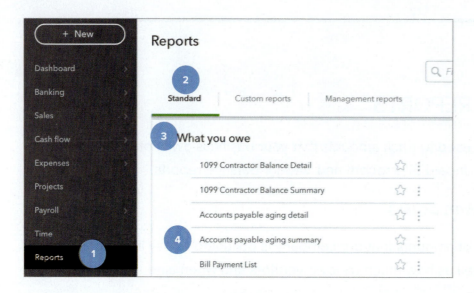

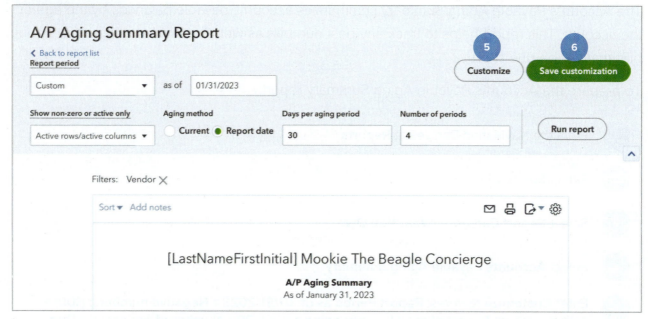

Section 10.9

EXPENSES AND VENDORS REPORTS

Expenses and Vendors reports provide detailed information about vendors and expenses transactions, including Check Detail report, Expenses by Vendor report, Open Purchase Order Lists, and the Vendors List.

OPEN PURCHASE ORDER LIST

Open Purchase Orders are Purchase Orders for items ordered but not yet received. QBO permits us to view all open Purchase Orders or just those for a specific vendor.

PURCHASES BY VENDOR DETAIL

The Purchases by Vendor Detail report lists all purchases, grouped by vendor. This report can be useful in tracking quantities and amounts purchased from vendors to improve purchasing efficiency and cost reductions.

Section 10.10

FOR MY ACCOUNTANT REPORTS

For My Accountant reports include reports used by an accountant in completing various accounting tasks. These reports include the Account List (Chart of Accounts), General Ledger, Journal, and Trial Balance.

JOURNAL

The Journal report lists every transaction entered in our QBO Company in a debit and credit entry form. Even if the transaction was entered using an onscreen form, such as an Invoice, QBO will show the transaction in the Journal as a debit and credit journal entry. The Journal can be useful when tracking down errors. The Journal is also referred to as the Transaction Journal.

To view the Journal report:

1 From the Navigation Bar, select **Reports**

2 Select **Standard** tab

3 Select **Report Category: For My Accountant**

4 Select **Journal**

5 Enter **Customize** features: **Report Period: 01/01/2023 To 01/31/2023 > Negative numbers: (100) > Run report**

6 Select **Save Customization**. Enter **Custom report name: Journal**. Select **Add new group >** enter **New group name: Accountant Reports > Add > Save**. The customized report will now appear under the Custom Reports tab.

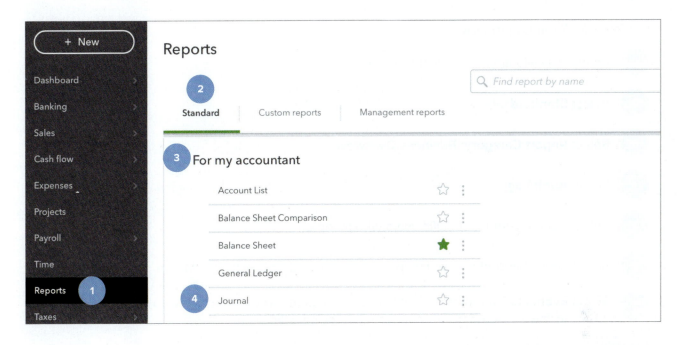

AUDIT LOG

The Audit Log feature of QBO permits us to track all changes (additions, modifications, and deletions) made to our QBO records. When used appropriately, the Audit Log feature improves internal control by tracking any unauthorized changes to accounting records. The owner, manager, or accountant should periodically review the Audit Log for discrepancies or unauthorized changes.

To view the Audit Log in QBO:

1 From the Navigation Bar, select **Reports**

2 Select **Standard** tab

3 Select **Report Category: Business Overview**

4 Select **Audit Log**

5 Select **User** to filter for specific users who made entries

6 Select **Date changed** to filter for specific time periods, such as This Month

7 Select **Events** to filter for entries, such as transactions. Then select View to view the History of the log entry with a record of changes made by specific users.

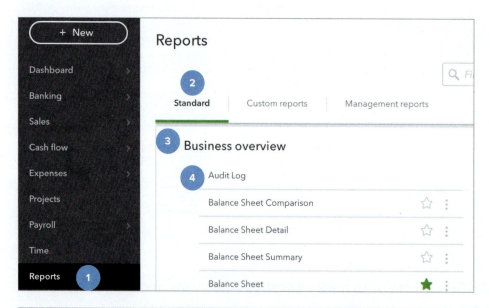

The Audit Log is especially useful if we have more than one QBO user. The Audit Log permits us to determine which user made which changes.

> Although the Audit Log appears in the Business Overview report category in QBO, an Audit Log is a useful tool used by accountants.

> The Audit Log can also be accessed by selecting the Gear icon > Audit Log.

This chapter provided an overview of some frequently used reports. QBO offers many more reports that provide useful information to a business. These additional reports can be accessed from the Reports screen.

Section 10.11

TAGS

Tags are electronic labels. Tags can be customized to fit your business needs and track how you make and spend money.

To understand tags, imagine that you are organizing Mookie's beagle gear for Cy. You have boxes that you sort different items into by type of item. For example, you might have one box for Mookie's leashes, one box for Mookie's coats, and another box for toys. Then you create a label for each box so you can identify the box contents.

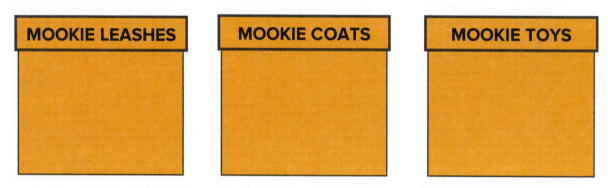

The QBO tags feature is like having an electronic label maker. We can create digital tags or labels for electronic data. For example, for Mookie The Beagle Concierge, we can tag all expenses related to contractors with a contractor tag, or tag revenues by marketing channels to identify which marketing channels are producing the best results. In addition, tags are even better than boxes. We are not limited to one tag for the same data. We can tag the same data in multiple ways.

We can add tags to money in and money out. For example, we can tag transactions, such as:

- Invoices
- Expenses
- Bills

In QBO, we can customize the tags to meet Mookie The Beagle Concierge business needs to gain insights into how Cy can improve the business. Tags can assist in identifying trends swiftly, where changing business conditions and customers require a rapid management response.

CREATE TAG GROUP AND TAGS

Cy Walker would like more insight into which contractors are generating the most revenue for Mookie The Beagle Concierge. First, we need to create a Tag Group for Contractors and then a tag for each contractor.

> **If we compare tags to the Chart of Accounts,** Tag Groups are like Parent accounts and Tags are subaccounts.

To create a Tag Group:

1. Select **Gear** icon

2. Select **Tags**

3. Notice that you can also access Tags from the Navigation Bar, by selecting **Banking > Tags** tab

4. To watch a video about tagging money in, under Get more details about what you earn, select **See how it works**

5. To watch a video about tagging money out, under See a breakdown of what you spend, select **See how it works**

6. Notice the **Tags and Tag Groups** section

7. Select **New down arrow**

8. Select **Tag group**

9. Enter **Group name: Contractors**

10. Select **Tag Group Shade** you would like to identify this Tag Group

11. Select **Save** to save the Tag Group and leave the Create new group drawer open

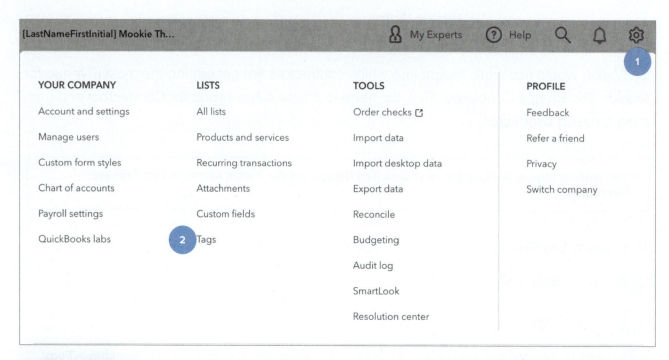

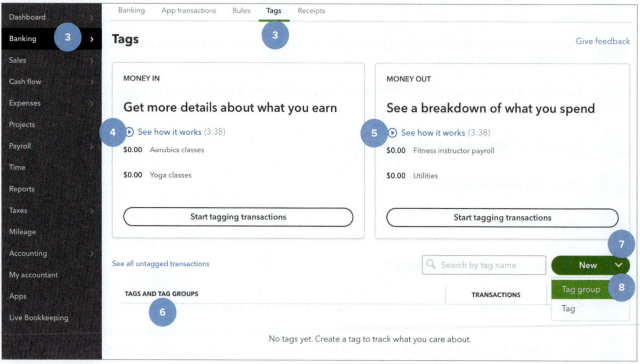

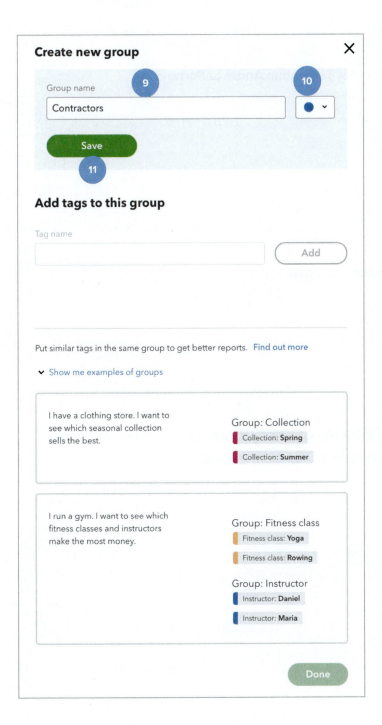

To create tags:

1 In the Add tags to this group section, enter **Tag name: Andre LaFortune**

2 Select **Add**

3 Add **Tag Name: Evan Henry**

4 Add **Tag Name: Your Name**

5 Select **Done**

6 Now in the Tags and Tag Groups section, we have:
- **1 Tag Group: Contractors**
- **3 Tags in the Tag Group:**
  - ‣ **Andre LaFortune**
  - ‣ **Evan Henry**
  - ‣ **Your Name**

Before starting to tag, it's a good idea to think about what you want to measure with tags. Then plan your Tag Groups and Tags before entering them in QBO.

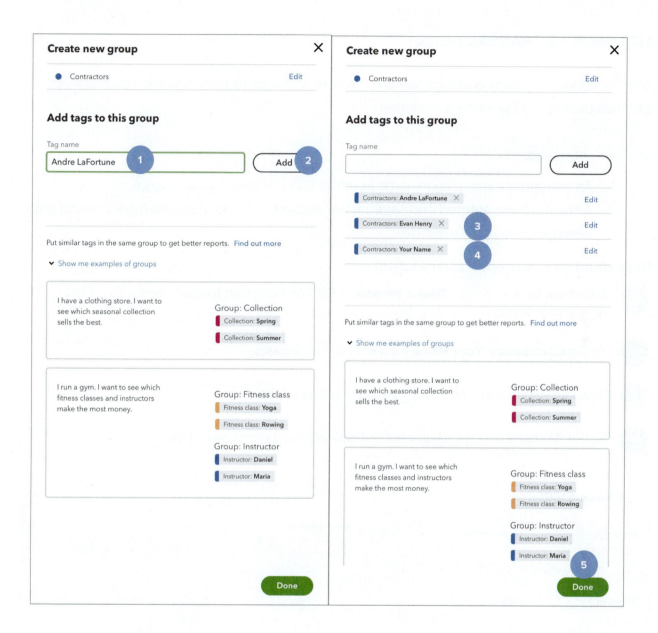

ADD TAGS TO TRANSACTIONS

After creating tag groups and tags, we are ready to add tags to transactions. You can even add multiple tags to the same transaction.

You can enter tags:

1. As you enter a transaction, such as when you are creating an invoice, or
2. After you have entered and saved a transaction, such as after you have created and saved an invoice or expense.

To enter a Tag as you enter a transaction:

1   Select the form, such as **+ New > Invoice**. In the Tag field, start typing to add a Tag. Start typing **Your Name**.

2   Select **Contractors: Your Name** from the list that appears

3   If you wanted to add a new Tag, you would select **+ Add**

4   Select **Cancel**. If asked Do you want to leave without saving?, select **Yes**.

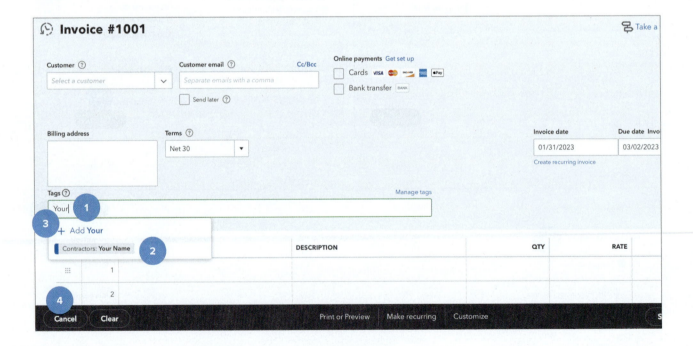

To enter a Tag to a previously entered and saved transaction:

1 From the Navigation Bar, select **Sales > Invoices** tab

2 Select **Invoice No. 1001** from the Invoice list

3 Select **Edit invoice**

4 When Invoice No. 1001 appears, in the Tags field, select **Contractors: Evan Henry**

5 Select **Save and close**

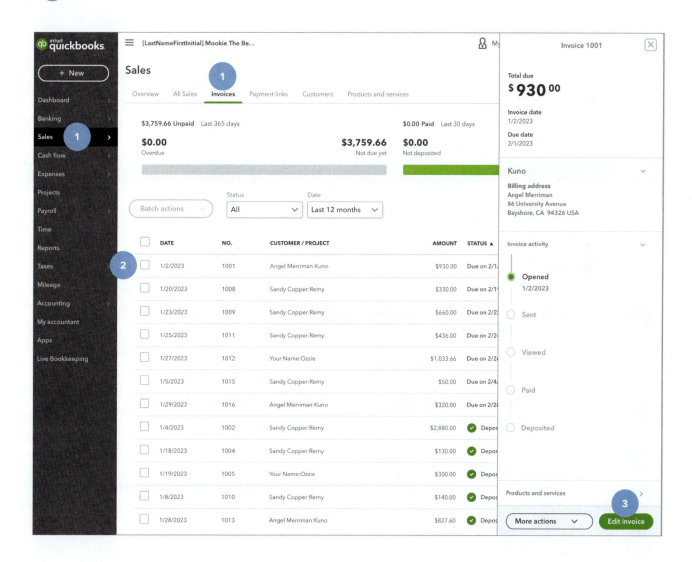

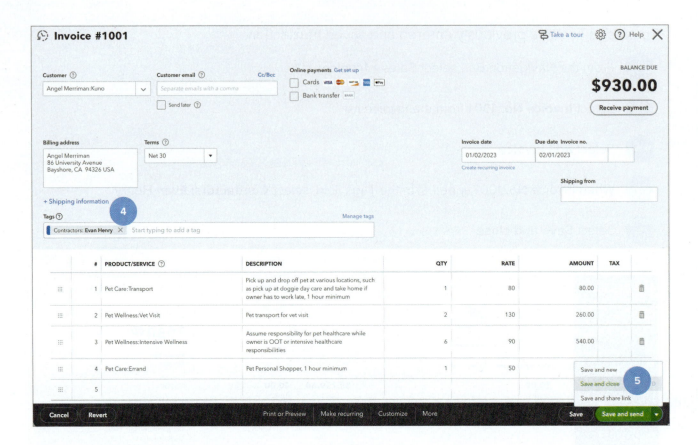

TAGS REPORTS AND INSIGHTS

C10.11.1 Tag Report

To view Tag results:

1 From the Navigation Bar, select **Banking > Tags** tab. You can also access Tags by selecting the Gear icon > Tags.

2 In the Money In section, select **All dates**

3 Notice the Money In tagging results for the Contractor: **Evan Henry**. What is the amount of money brought in that we have tagged Evan Henry?

4 Select **Run report**

5 When the Profit and Loss by Tag Group Report appears, enter **Report Period: 01/01/2023 to 01/31/2023**

6 Select **Run Report**

7 Notice the column titled **Evan Henry**. What is the amount recorded in the 4200 Sales account that we have tagged Evan Henry?

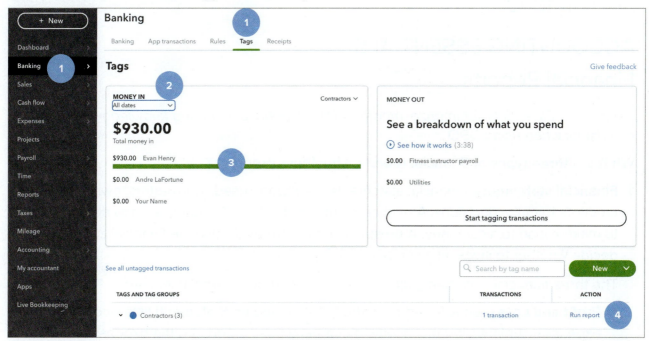

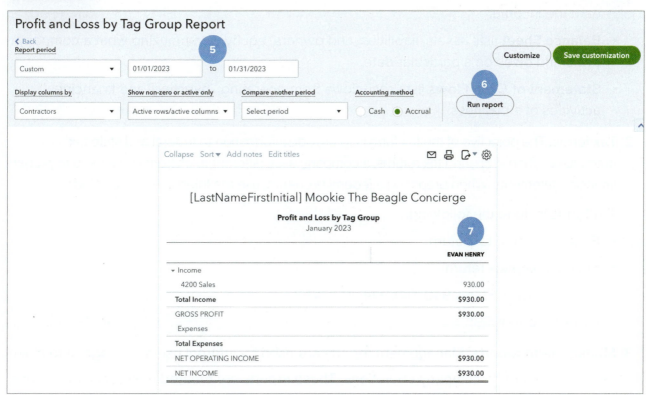

Section 10.12

ACCOUNTING ESSENTIALS
Financial Reports

Accounting Essentials summarize important foundational accounting knowledge you may find useful when using QBO

What are three types of financial reports a business prepares?

1. **Financial statements.** Financial statements are reports used by investors, owners, and creditors to make decisions. A banker might use the financial statements to decide whether to make a loan to a company. A prospective investor might use the financial statements to decide whether to invest in a company.

   The three financial statements most frequently used by external users are:

   • **Profit and Loss** (also referred to as the P & L or Income Statement) lists income and expenses, summarizing the income a company has earned and the expenses incurred to earn the income.

   • **Balance Sheet** lists assets, liabilities, and owners' equity, summarizing what a company *owns* and *owes* on a particular date.

   • **Statement of Cash Flows** lists cash flows from operating, investing, and financing activities of a business.

2. **Tax forms.** The objective of the tax form is to provide information to federal and state tax authorities. When preparing tax returns, a company uses different rules from those used to prepare financial statements. When preparing a federal tax return, use the Internal Revenue Code.

   Tax forms include the following:

   • Federal income tax return

   • State income tax return

   • Federal Payroll Forms 940, 941/944, W-2, W-3

   • Federal Form 1099

3. **Management reports.** Management reports are used by internal users (managers) to make decisions regarding company operations. These reports are created to satisfy a manager's information needs.

Examples of reports that managers use include:

- Cash budget that projects amounts of cash that will be collected and spent in the future. (Note: A Statement of Cash Flows focuses on cash inflows and outflows in the *past*. A Cash Budget focuses on expected cash flows in the *future*.)

- Accounts receivable aging report that lists the age and balance of customer accounts receivable so accounts are collected in a timely manner.

Practice Quiz 10

Q10.1

The physical inventory worksheet is used when:

a. Inventory items are physically placed in the warehouse

b. The computer network goes down

c. Taking a physical count of inventory on hand

d. All of the above

Q10.2

Which one of the following is not a financial statement?

a. Statement of Cash Flows

b. Profit & Loss

c. Trial Balance

d. Balance Sheet

Q10.3

The Chart of Accounts displays:

a. Account Name

b. Type

c. Detail Type

d. All of the above

Q10.4

The Balance Sheet lists:

a. Assets, Revenues, and Owners' Equity

b. Assets, Liabilities, and Owners' Equity

c. Revenues, Expenses, and Net Income

d. Revenues, Liabilities, and Net Income

Q10.5

Which one of the following classifications is not found on the Statement of Cash Flows?

a. Cash Flows from Selling Activities

b. Cash Flows from Financing Activities

c. Cash Flows from Investing Activities

d. Cash Flows from Operating Activities

Q10.6

Which of the following is correct?

a.   Statement of Cash Flows is reported on a particular date

b.   Income Statement is reported on a particular date

c.   Balance Sheet is reported on a particular date

d.   Balance Sheet is reported for a specific time period

Q10.7

QuickBooks Online uses which basis of accounting?

a.   Accrual

b.   Cash

c.   Both a and b

d.   Neither a nor b

Q10.8

The Profit and Loss Statement lists:

a.   Assets, Revenues, and Owners' Equity

b.   Assets, Liabilities, and Owners' Equity

c.   Revenues, Expenses, and Net Income

d.   Revenues, Liabilities, and Net Income

Q10.9

Management reports:

a.   Must follow a set of rules specified by Generally Accepted Accounting Principles

b.   Must follow the rules specified by the Internal Revenue Service

c.   Must follow the rules specified by vendors

d.   Do not have to follow a specified set of rules

Q10.10

Management reports include:

a.   Customer Profitability reports

b.   Accounts Receivable Aging reports

c.   Accounts Payable Aging reports

d.   Inventory reports

e.   All of the above

Q10.11

Which of the following is a Customer report:

a. Accounts Receivable (A/R) Aging
b. Accounts Payable (A/P) Aging
c. Open Purchase Orders
d. None of the above

Q10.12

The Journal:

a. Lists every journal entry made only through the onscreen journal
b. Is also called the Audit Log
c. Lists every transaction entered in QBO through a journal or onscreen form, as a debit and credit entry
d. None the above

Q10.13

The Audit Log tracks:

a. Additions to our QBO records
b. Modifications to our QBO records
c. Deletions to our QBO records
d. All of the above

Q10.14

Which of the following reports can improve internal control by tracking unauthorized changes to accounting records?

a. Cash Budget
b. Cash Forecast
c. Audit Log
d. Journal

Exercises 10

E10.1 Accounting Cycle

Match the following accounting cycle steps with the appropriate description.

Accounting Cycle Descriptions

a. Prepared at the end of the accounting period before preparing financial statements to bring the accounts up to date.

b. Prepared during the accounting period to record exchanges with customers, vendors, employees, and owners.

c. A list of all accounts used to accumulate information about assets, liabilities, owners' equity, revenues, and expenses.

d. Prepared for external users and includes the Profit and Loss, Balance Sheet, and Statement of Cash Flows.

e. Prepared after adjustments to verify that the accounting system still balances.

f. Lists each account and the account balance at the end of the accounting period to verify that the accounting system is in balance—total debits should equal total credits.

Accounting Cycle Steps	Accounting Cycle Descriptions
1. Chart of Accounts	_____
2. Transactions	_____
3. Trial Balance	_____
4. Adjustments	_____
5. Adjusted Trial Balance	_____
6. Financial Statements	_____

EM10.2

For the following accounts on Mookie The Beagle Concierge Trial Balance, identify Account Type and Financial Statement on which it appears.

Account Types

- **Asset**
- **Liability**
- **Equity**
- **Income**
- **Expense**

Financial Statements

- **Balance Sheet**
- **Profit and Loss**

Account	Account Type	Financial Statement
1. Sales		
2. Money Market		
3. Accounts Receivable (A/R)		
4. Rent & Lease		
5. Prepaid Expenses: Supplies		
6. Loan Payable		
7. Inventory Asset		
8. Opening Balance Equity		
9. Utilities Expense		
10. Undeposited Funds		
11. Accounts Payable (A/P)		
12. VISA Credit Card		
13. Prepaid Expenses: Insurance		
14. Interest Payable		
15. Sales of Product Income		
16. Legal & Professional Services		
17. Advertising & Marketing		
18. Insurance: Renters Insurance Expense		

19. Owner's Investment

20. Checking

21. Unearned Revenue

22. Contractors

23. Cost of Goods Sold

24. Office Supplies & Software

25. Utilities Expense

E10.3 Statement of Cash Flows

For each of the following, identify the appropriate classification on the Statement of Cash Flows.

Statement of Cash Flows Classifications

a. Cash Flows from Operating Activities

b. Cash Flows from Investing Activities

c. Cash Flows from Financing Activities

Activity	Statement of Cash Flows Classification
1. Cash flows related to sales	
2. Cash paid to repay a long-term loan	
3. Cash flows related to purchasing inventory to resell	
4. Cash flow from issuance of capital stock	
5. Cash paid to purchase new equipment	
6. Cash from sale of a warehouse	

EXCEL TEMPLATE (EM10.4 Through EM10.10)

For your convenience to complete reports in Chapter 10 and Exercises 10, an Excel Template is provided with your text to organize your Excel reports. If you have not already downloaded the Excel Template, to access it, you have two options:

1. If you are using Connect with your text, the Excel Template can be downloaded from within Connect.
2. If you are not using Connect, go to www.my-quickbooksonline.com > select QBO 3e > QBO 3e Excel Templates > Download the Chapter 10 Excel Template.

After downloading the Excel Template, select the Instructions sheet in the Excel Template to view the steps to copy your exported Excel reports to the Excel Template.

EM10.4 Profit and Loss Statement

Complete the following to prepare a Profit and Loss Statement for Mookie The Beagle Concierge using the custom report you saved in Chapter 10.

1. Create a Profit and Loss Statement.
   a. From the Navigation Bar, select **Reports > Custom reports** tab **> Financial Statements > Profit and Loss**
   b. **Date Range: 01/01/2023 to 01/31/2023**

2. What is the amount of Total Income (Revenue)?

3. What is amount of Total Expenses?

4. What is amount of Net Income?

5. **Export** the Profit and Loss Statement to PDF.

6. **Export** the Profit and Loss Statement to Excel.
   a. With the Profit and Loss report displayed, select the **Export icon**
   b. Select **Export to Excel**
   c. Complete the steps listed in the Instructions sheet of the Excel Template to copy your Profit and Loss Statement Excel export to the Excel Template.

EM10.5 Balance Sheet

Complete the following to prepare a Balance Sheet for Mookie The Beagle Concierge using the custom report you saved in Chapter 10.

1. Create a Balance Sheet.
   a. From the Navigation Bar, select **Reports > Custom reports** tab **> Financial Statements > Balance Sheet**
   b. **Date Range: 01/31/2023 to 01/31/2023**

2. On the Balance Sheet, what are Total Assets?

3. On the Balance Sheet, what are Total Liabilities?

4. **Export** the Balance Sheet to PDF.

5. **Export** the Balance Sheet to Excel.
   a. With the Balance Sheet report displayed, select the **Export icon**
   b. Select **Export to Excel**
   c. Complete the steps listed in the Instructions sheet of the Excel Template to copy your Balance Sheet Excel export to the Excel Template.

EM10.6 Statement of Cash Flows

Complete the following to prepare a Statement of Cash Flows for Mookie The Beagle Concierge using the custom report you saved in Chapter 10.

1. Create a Statement of Cash Flows.
   a. From the Navigation Bar, select **Reports** > **Custom reports** tab > **Financial Statements** > **Statement of Cash Flows**
   b. **Date Range: 01/01/2023 to 01/31/2023**

2. On the Statement of Cash Flows, what is the Net Cash Provided by Operating Activities?

3. On the Statement of Cash Flows, what is the Net Cash Provided by Investing Activities?

4. On the Statement of Cash Flows, what is the Net Cash Provided by Financing Activities?

5. What was Cash at the end of the period?

6. **Export** the Statement of Cash Flows to PDF.

7. **Export** the Statement of Cash Flows to Excel.
   a. With the Statement of Cash Flows report displayed, select the **Export icon**
   b. Select **Export to Excel**
   c. Complete the steps listed in the Instructions sheet of the Excel Template to copy your Statement of Cash Flows Excel export to the Excel Template.

EM10.7 Accounts Receivable (A/R) Aging

Complete the following to prepare an Accounts Receivable (A/R) Aging report for Mookie The Beagle Concierge using the custom report you saved in Chapter 10.

1. Create Accounts Receivable (A/R) Aging Report.
   a. From the Navigation Bar, select **Reports** > **Custom reports** tab > **Customer Reports** > **A/R Aging Summary**
   b. **Date Range: 01/31/2023**

2. On the Accounts Receivable (A/R) Aging Summary, what is the amount of A/R that is Current?

3. On the A/R Aging Summary, what is the amount of A/R that is 1–30 days past due?

4. **Export** the Accounts Receivable (A/R) Aging Summary to PDF.

5. **Export** the Accounts Receivable (A/R) Aging Summary to Excel.
   a. With the Accounts Receivable (A/R) Aging Summary report displayed, select the **Export icon**
   b. Select **Export to Excel**
   c. Complete the steps listed in the Instructions sheet of the Excel Template to copy your Accounts Receivable (A/R) Aging Summary Excel export to the Excel Template.

EM10.8 Accounts Payable (A/P) Aging

Complete the following to prepare an Accounts Payable (A/P) Aging report for Mookie The Beagle Concierge using the custom report you saved in Chapter 10.

1. Create Accounts Payable (A/P) Aging Report.
   a. From the Navigation Bar, select **Reports > Custom reports** tab **> Vendor Reports > A/P Aging Summary**
   b. **Date Range: 01/31/2023**

2. On the Accounts Payable (A/P) Aging Summary Report, what is the amount of A/P that is Current?

3. On the A/P Aging Summary, what is the amount of A/P that is 1–30 days past due?

4. On the A/P Aging Summary, what is the amount of A/P that is 31–60 days past due?

5. **Export** the Accounts Payable (A/P) Aging Summary to PDF.

6. **Export** the Accounts Payable (A/P) Aging Summary to Excel.
   a. With the Accounts Payable (A/P) Aging Summary report displayed, select the **Export icon**
   b. Select **Export to Excel**
   c. Complete the steps listed in the Instructions sheet of the Excel Template to copy your Accounts Payable (A/P) Aging Summary Excel export to the Excel Template.

EM10.9 Sales by Product/Service

Complete the following to prepare a Sales by Product/Service Summary report for Mookie The Beagle Concierge using the custom report you saved in Chapter 10.

1. Create Sales by Product/Service Summary Report.
   a. From the Navigation Bar, select **Reports > Custom reports** tab **> Customer Reports > Sales by Product/Service Summary**
   b. **Date Range: 01/01/2023 to 01/31/2023**

2. On the Sales by Product/Service Summary Report, what is the percentage of sales generated by Pet Wellness Services?

3. On the Sales by Product/Service Summary Report, what is the percentage of sales generated by Pet Care Services?

4. On the Sales by Product/Service Summary Report, what is the percentage of sales generated by Pet Hammock Products?

5. **Export** the Sales by Product/Service Summary to PDF.

6. **Export** the Sales by Product/Service Summary to Excel.
   a. With the Sales by Product/Service Summary report displayed, select the **Export icon**
   b. Select **Export to Excel**
   c. Complete the steps listed in the Instructions sheet of the Excel Template to copy your Accounts Payable (A/P) Aging Summary Excel export to the Excel Template

EM10.10 Tags

Complete the following to prepare a Tags Report for Mookie The Beagle Concierge.

1. Tag Money Out by Contractor.
   a. From the Navigation Bar, select **Reports > Custom reports** tab > **Financial Statements > Profit and Loss**
   b. To drill down, select **the amount displayed for Account: 5005 Contractors**
   c. Add **Tags for the appropriate contractor to each Expense or Bill displayed for Contractors**
   d. **Save** the Expense or Bill. If asked if you want to update the recurring template, select One Time Only.

2. Prepare Tags Report.
   a. From the Navigation Bar, select **Banking > Tags** tab
   b. In the Money Out section, select: **All dates**

3. What is the amount of Money Out for Evan Henry?

4. What is the amount of Money Out for Andre LaFortune?

5. What is the amount of Money Out for Your Name?

Chapter 11

QBO Comprehensive Project

MOOKIE THE BEAGLE™ COACH

BACKSTORY

Cy Walker, founder of Mookie The Beagle™ Concierge, is continually looking for new business opportunities to build on the success of his pet concierge service. So you are not surprised when your smartphone chimes and Cy's text message appears.

> Are you interested in investing in my next enterprise?

> Tell me more.

> MTB Concierge client would like pet etiquette and pet agility training.

> What's the name of the new enterprise?

> Mookie The Beagle Coach.

> Definitely, I'm interested.

Read Yesterday

> Ok, good. Let's talk terms.

Based on client feedback, Cy realizes there is substantial demand for pet training. Busy pet parents often do not have time to train their pets well, but would be happy to invest in concierge pet training to have a well-behaved and content pet.

So Cy is launching a new business, Mookie The Beagle™ Coach, that offers coaching services for pets and pet parents. Pet coaching services begin with the basic commands of sit, stay, leave it, drop it, and heel, then progress to the highest standards of pet etiquette.

Also, Cy would like to offer agility coaching services. Dog agility, a fast-growing dog sport, involves the pet parent directing their pet through an obstacle course with the pet leaping through rings, crawling through tunnels, weaving around poles, and jumping over hurdles. Pet parent and pet communicate through cues and body language signals with the shared activity deepening the bond between pet parent and pet. All of which contributes to a satisfied client and repeat business.

Cy plans to offer the following services for pet manners and agility training:

- Puppy Manners 101
- Pet Manners 101
- Pet Manners 102
- Pet Manners 103
- Pet Agility 101
- Pet Agility 102
- Pet Agility 103

Concierge pet coaching services for pet etiquette will be offered in three different formats:

1. Latchkey services. The concierge trainer goes to the pet's location for training with the trainer and pet only.
2. 1 on 1 pet and pet parent coaching. The concierge trainer works with the pet parent and pet as they learn together.
3. Virtual pet coaching. The concierge trainer works virtually with the pet and pet parent via a virtual app.

Initially, Cy envisions providing agility training services onsite at a customizable agility training course. This represents a substantial initial investment in designing and building the agility course.

In addition to providing pet etiquette and agility training services, Cy realizes there is an opportunity to sell Mookie The Beagle—branded training gear and merchandise. He plans to stock the following inventory with the option to expand inventory offerings in the future.

- Training gear, including treat pouches and training clickers

- Training treats

- Agility equipment for at home training, such as weave poles, tunnels, rings, and hurdles

Cy values your financial and QBO expertise. He asks for your assistance in setting up a new QBO company for Mookie The Beagle Coach to maintain the financial records for this new business endeavor. Mookie The Beagle Coach will be an LLC with S Corporation tax status.

Cy offers you a 20% share of the ownership of the new company for a $2,000 cash investment. You have been saving for an investment opportunity, and after careful consideration, you decide to invest $2,000 for a 20% share. In addition, you ask for an option to purchase another 20% ownership share in the future.

Now that you will be maintaining the financial records and also have an ownership interest, you and Cy agree there needs to be oversight and good internal control with checks and balances to ensure there is no possibility for even the perception of any impropriety. To begin, Cy will review the accounting records each month and two approvals will be required for checks over $1,000.

You emphasize to Cy the importance of ensuring the new business funds are not co-mingled with Cy's personal expenses or expenses from Cy's other business, Mookie The Beagle Concierge. You outline for Cy a plan to maintain the following checking accounts:

- Mookie The Beagle Concierge Checking account
- Mookie The Beagle Coach Checking account
- Cy Walker Personal Checking account

Chapter 11

LEARNING OBJECTIVES

Chapter 11 covers the following QBO topics:

- Set Up New QBO Company
- Lists
  - ▸ Chart of Accounts
  - ▸ Products and Services List
  - ▸ Customers List
  - ▸ Vendors List
  - ▸ Tags
- Transactions
- QBO Crosscheck: Bank and Credit Card Matching
- Adjustments
  - ▸ Trial Balance
  - ▸ Adjusting Entries
  - ▸ Adjusted Trial Balance
- Financial Reports
  - ▸ Financial Statements
    - Profit and Loss
    - Balance Sheet
    - Statement of Cash Flows
  - ▸ Management Reports
    - Accounts Receivable Aging
    - Sales by Product/Service
    - Accounts Payable Aging
  - ▸ For My Accountant Reports
    - Journal
  - ▸ Tag Reports

Section 11.1

 QBO SATNAV

QBO SatNav is our satellite navigation for QuickBooks Online, assisting us in navigating QBO

Chapter 11 covers a comprehensive QBO Company Project, as shown in the following QBO SatNav.

 **QBO SatNav**

 **QBO Settings**

- Company Settings
- Chart of Accounts

 **QBO Transactions**

- Banking
- Customers & Sales
- Vendors & Expenses
- Employees & Payroll

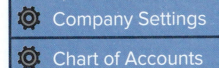 **QBO Reports**

- Reports

Section 11.2

SET UP NEW QBO COMPANY

C11.2.1 Create New QBO Company

Create a new QBO company for Mookie The Beagle™ Coach using the following information.

To obtain your free QBO access, your instructor will need to send you an email invitation. This invite will permit you to create your own QBO company for Mookie The Beagle Coach.

⚠ **Important Note: If you have <u>not</u> received an email invitation from your instructor to create your QBO company for Mookie The Beagle Coach:**
1. **Check your email Spam mailbox to verify that the email was not flagged as Junk mail.**
2. **Contact your instructor to obtain an email invitation. Your instructor must send you the email invitation in order for you to have free access to create a QBO company.**

⚠ **Due to ongoing changes in QBO, the order of steps and exact selections in your QBO company may appear different than the instructions shown in your text. If the QBO updates significantly impact your text, the updates to your text can be viewed as follows:**
- **Go to www.my-quickbooksonline.com > QBO 3e > QBO 3e Updates.**
- **If you are using Connect or a digital ebook, you can find updates under Additional Student Resources (ASR).**

⚠ **Warning: it is important to make the selections as specified. Otherwise, your QBO company may be unusable for completing the remaining instructions.**

Complete the following steps to use the Instructor Invitation for free QBO access:

1 When you receive an email invitation from your instructor to create your own QBO company, select **Accept invitation**. (Note: Intuit recommends using Google Chrome web browser.)

2 To sign into your account, select **Sign In** link. (To create your account, **enter** the requested information in the appropriate fields. Note: If the Create Account screen doesn't appear automatically, select **Need an account? Sign Up**.)
⚠ *Keep a record of your User ID and Password. You will need this later.*

3 Enter your **Email address (User ID)** and your **Password** that you used to set up your Intuit account when you created Mookie The Beagle Concierge QBO Company. (If questions appear appear regarding verification of your identity, select Skip for Now.)

4 When the Welcome! We're glad you're here. screen appears, select **Next**.

5 When the What's your business name? screen appears, enter the name of your business: **[LastNameFirst Initial] Mookie The Beagle Coach**. (Example: KayD Mookie The Beagle Coach.)
⚠ *Remember to include your name before Mookie The Beagle Coach. This will assist your instructor in identifying your QBO file.*

6 Uncheck **I've been using QuickBooks Desktop and want to bring in my data**

7 Select **Next**

8 When the What's your industry? screen appears, leave the field **blank**

9 Select **Skip for now**

10 When the What kind of business is this? screen appears, select **S Corp**

11 Select **Next**. If asked, How does your business make money?, select Provide services and sells products.

12 When the What's your main role? screen appears, select **Bookkeeper or Accountant**.
⚠ *This selection determines your view of QBO and the instructions you will see onscreen. Before proceeding, double check that you have selected Bookkeeper or Accountant.*

13 Select **Next**

14 When the Who works at this business? screen appears, select **Contractors** and **A few partners and owners**

15 Select **Next**

16 When the Link your accounts and see everything in one place screen appears, select **Skip for now**

17 When the What apps do you already use? screen appears, select **Skip for now**

18 When the What is everything you want to set up? screen appears, select:
- **Invoice customers**
- **Track receipts and bills**
- **Pay employees or contractors**
- **Add sales**
- **Enter and pay bills**
- **Track time**
- **Manage inventory**

⚠️ *These selections determine the settings of your QBO company and it may not be possible to change the settings later. Before proceeding, double check that you have made the correct selections.*

19 Select **Next**

20 If the Ready for a free trial of QuickBooks Payroll? screen appears, select **Maybe later**

21 Select **Next**

22 When the screen appears, We're almost ready to dive in!, select **Let's go**

23 Your QBO company for Mookie The Beagle Coach should appear. If a Welcome To QuickBooks! screen appears, select **Take a quick tour** to take a QBO tour.

You have now created a QBO Company for Mookie The Beagle Coach. Later, whenever you need to stop working in your QBO Company, close your browser to log out of the Mookie The Beagle Coach QBO Company. When you are ready to work again, log into QBO using your User ID and Password.

HOW TO SIGN IN TO QBO

After completing the steps to create a QBO company for Mookie The Beagle Coach, the next time we log into QBO, we will complete the following steps:

1   Using a web browser, go to qbo.intuit.com

2   Enter **User ID** (the email address you used to set up your QBO Account)

3   Enter **Password** (the password you used to set up your QBO Account)

4   Select **Sign in**

5   Since Mookie The Beagle Coach is your second QBO company using your QBO account, after you sign in to QBO, you will see the screen: Please select the company you want to open. Select **[LastNameFirstInitial] Mookie The Beagle Coach.**

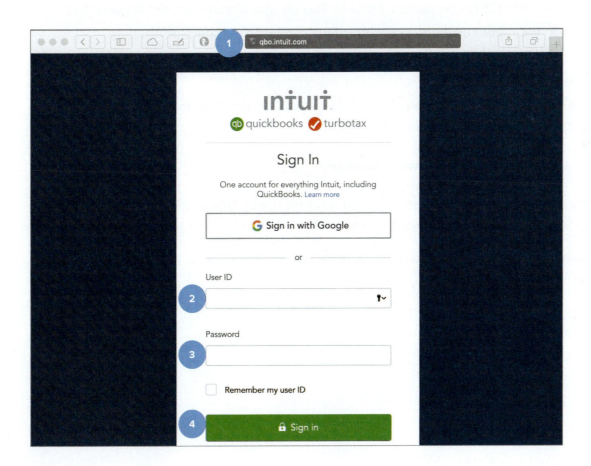

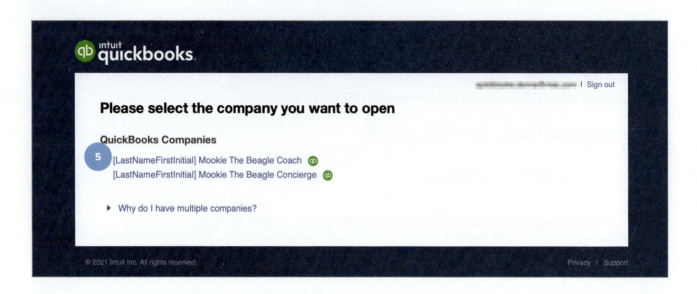

HOW TO SWITCH QBO COMPANIES

Now that you have two QBO companies, Mookie The Beagle Concierge and Mookie The Beagle Coach, in your QBO account, you can switch between companies.

To switch between QBO companies:

1 If you are not already signed into Mookie The Beagle Coach, sign in to the QBO Company, **Mookie The Beagle Coach**. Select the **Gear** icon.

2 Under the Profile column, select **Switch company**

3 When the Please select the company you want to open screen appears, in the QBO Companies section, select the QBO company you want to open

4 If you want to sign out of your QBO account, in the upper right corner of the screen, select **Sign out**

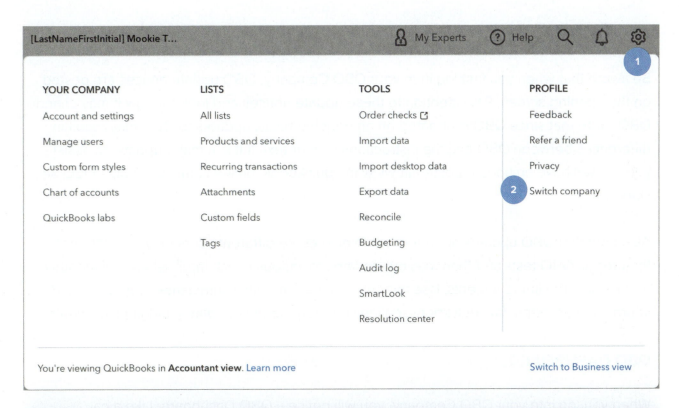

QBO UPDATES

Be aware that when you first log in to your QBO Company, QBO update notices are posted on the opening screen. Pay attention to these update notices and look for how it may change QBO. Note that since QBO is updated on an ongoing basis, updates to QBO may result in differences between QBO and the instructions in your text. If it is a major update, to assist you, we will have an update posted at www.my-quickbooksonline.com > QBO 3e > QBO 3e Updates.

Also note that QBO updates are rolled out in phases, so different users may see different features as QBO tests and then rolls out updates to various users. Intuit releases a monthly update on QBO improvements. Use this link to access monthly summaries of updates and improvements: https://my-quickbooksonline.com/qbo-monthly-updates-and-improvements.

QBO DASHBOARD

When you log into your QBO Company, you will notice a QBO Dashboard. Like a car dashboard, this QBO Dashboard provides a digital overview. We can customize the dashboard to display information to meet our specific business needs and requirements. Note that the dashboard may change over time as Intuit rolls out new QBO updates.

EXCEL TEMPLATE

For your convenience to complete Chapter 11, an Excel Template is provided with your text to organize your Excel reports. To access the Chapter 11 Excel Template, you have two options:
1. If you are using Connect with your text, the Chapter 11 Excel Template can be downloaded from within Connect.
2. If you are not using Connect, go to www.my-quickbooksonline.com > select QBO 3e > QBO 3e Excel Templates > Download the Chapter 11 Excel Template.

After downloading the Excel Template, select the Instructions sheet in the Excel Template to view the steps to copy your exported Excel reports to the Excel Template.

C11.2.2 Company Settings: Company

Select the tax form, Form 1120S (S Corporation), for Mookie The Beagle™ Coach. To select the tax form:

1 Select **Gear** icon > **Account and Settings**

2 Select **Company** tab

3 Select **Company address Edit Pencil** > begin typing the address in the Address field > select **Enter Manually** > enter the following:

- **Street address: 432 Phoenician Way**
- **City: Mountain View**
- **State: California**
- **ZIP Code: 94326**

Select **Save** > verify the address you entered > select **Yes, it's correct** > **Done**

Answer the following questions about Mookie The Beagle Coach Company Settings.

1. What is the Tax Form?
   a. Form 1040
   b. Form 1120
   c. Form 1120S
   d. Form K-1

2. What does the Legal name field display?

C11.2.3 Company Settings: Sales

QBO Sales Settings are preferences related to recording sales using QBO.

1 Select **Gear** icon > **Account and Settings**

2 Select **Sales** tab

Answer the following questions about Mookie The Beagle Coach QBO Sales Settings.

1. What is the setting for Preferred invoice terms?

2. What is the setting for Service Date?

3. What is the setting for Discount?

4. What is the setting for Tags?

5. What is the setting for Show Product/Service column on sales forms?

6. What is the setting for Show SKU column?

7. What is the setting for Track quantity and price/rate?

8. If it does not appear as on, change the Track inventory quantity on hand to **On** > **Save**

C11.2.4 Company Settings: Expenses

QBO Expenses Settings are preferences related to recording expenses using QBO.

1 Select **Gear icon** > **Account and Settings**

2 Select **Expenses** tab

Answer the following questions about Mookie The Beagle Coach QBO Expenses Settings.

1. What is the setting for Show Items table on expense and purchase forms?

2. What is the setting for Show Tags field on expense and purchase forms?

3. What is the setting for Track expenses and items by customer?

4. What is the setting for Make expenses and items billable?

5. Change the setting for Make expenses and items billable to **On**.

6. What is the setting for Use purchase orders?

C11.2.5 Company Settings: Advanced

QBO Advanced Settings are preferences related to advanced items that are not listed under the other preference settings.

1 Select **Gear icon** > **Account and Settings**

2 Select **Advanced** tab

Answer the following questions about Mookie The Beagle Coach QBO Advanced Settings.

1. First month of fiscal year?

2. First month of income tax year?

3. Accounting method?

4. Close the books?

5. Tax form?

6. Enable account numbers?

7. Pre-fill forms with previously entered content?

8. Automatically apply bill payments?

9. Warn if duplicate check number is used?

Section 11.3

CHART OF ACCOUNTS

The Chart of Accounts is a list of all the accounts that a business needs. QBO offers a convenient way to organize and track a company's accounts.

C11.3.1 Display Chart of Accounts

Display the Chart of Accounts for Mookie The Beagle Coach.

1 From the Navigation Bar, select **Accounting**

2 Select **Chart of Accounts** tab

3 If necessary, select **See your Chart of Accounts**

C11.3.2 Account Numbers

Display Account Numbers in the Chart of Accounts for Mookie The Beagle Coach.

1 Select the **Gear** icon to display options

2 Select **Account and Settings**

3 Select **Advanced**

4 For Chart of Accounts, select the **Edit Pencil**, then select **Enable account numbers**

5 Select **Show account numbers**

6 Select **Save**

7 Select **Done** to close Account and Settings

Enter Account Numbers in the Chart of Accounts for Mookie The Beagle Coach. Note that QBO automatically creates a Chart of Accounts. Some of your accounts may differ from the accounts listed here.

1 To display the Chart of Accounts, from the **Navigation Bar** > select **Accounting** > **Chart of Accounts**

2 Asset Account Numbers.
a. From the Chart of Accounts window, select **Edit pencil**.
b. Asset accounts will be numbered in the 1000s. Enter the following accounts numbers for the Asset accounts. If your Chart of Accounts does not display the account, enter the account and the account number into your Chart of Accounts.

- **1500 Uncategorized Asset**
- **1600 Undeposited Funds**

3 Liability Account Numbers.
a. If needed, from the COA window, select **Edit pencil**.
b. Liability accounts will be numbered in the 2000s. Your Chart of Accounts may not display any liability accounts.

4 Equity Account Numbers.
a. If needed, from the COA window, select **Edit pencil**.
b. Equity accounts will be numbered in the 3000s. Enter the following account numbers for the Equity accounts. If your Chart of Accounts does not display the account, enter the account and the account number into your Chart of Accounts.

- **3003 Owner's Investment**
- **3100 Owner's Pay & Personal Expenses**
- **3300 Retained Earnings**

5 Income Account Numbers.
a. If needed, from the COA window, select **Edit pencil**.
b. Income accounts will be numbered in the 4000s. Enter the following account numbers for the Income accounts. If your Chart of Accounts does not display the account, enter the account and the account number into your Chart of Accounts.

- **4100 Billable Expense Income** (Note: If your Chart of Accounts lists more than one Billable Expense Income account, make inactive the extra Billable Expense Income accounts so you have only one active Billable Expense Income account.)
- **4200 Sales**
- **4400 Uncategorized Income**

6 Enter Expense Account Numbers.

a. If needed, from the COA window, select **Edit pencil**.

b. Expense accounts will be numbered in the 5000s. Enter the following account numbers for the Expense accounts. If your Chart of Accounts does not display the account, enter the account and the account number into your Chart of Accounts.

- **5001 Advertising & Marketing**
- **5002 Ask My Accountant**
- **5003 Bank Charges & Fees**
- **5004 Car & Truck**
- **5005 Contractors**
- **5010 Insurance**
- **5020 Interest Paid** (Note: Change Account Title to **Interest Expense**)
- **5021 Job Supplies**
- **5022 Legal & Professional Services**
- **5023 Meals & Entertainment**
- **5024 Office Supplies & Software**
- **5025 Other Business Expenses**
- **5027 Reimbursable Expenses**
- **5028 Rent & Lease**
- **5029 Repairs & Maintenance**
- **5030 Taxes & Licenses**
- **5031 Travel**
- **5032 Uncategorized Expense**
- **5040 Utilities Expense**

C11.3.3 Add Accounts

Complete the following steps to add Asset accounts to Mookie The Beagle Coach Chart of Accounts.

> QBO is continually rolling out new features, so it is possible your Chart of Accounts may not appear the same as your text. If your COA doesn't have the following accounts, add them to your COA as follows.

To add accounts to the COA, from the Navigation Bar, select **Accounting** > **New**.

1   Add Checking Account.
- a. Select **Account Type: Bank**
- b. Select **Detail Type:** _____
- c. Enter **Name: Checking**
- d. Enter **Number: 1001**
- e. Leave **Description blank**
- f. Leave **Is sub-account unchecked**
- g. Select **Save and New**

2   Add Accounts Receivable Account.
- a. Select **Account Type:** _____
- b. Select **Detail Type:** _____
- c. Enter **Name: Accounts Receivable (A/R)**
- d. Enter **Number: 1100**
- e. Leave **Description blank**
- f. Leave **Is sub-account unchecked**
- g. Select **Save and New**

3   Add Prepaid Expenses Account.
- a. Select **Account Type: Other Current Assets**
- b. Select **Detail Type:** _____
- c. Enter **Name: Prepaid Expenses**
- d. Enter **Number: 1200**
- e. Leave **Description blank**
- f. Leave **Is sub-account unchecked**
- g. Select **Save and Close**

4 Add Accounts Payable Account.

a. Select **Account Type:** _____

b. Select **Detail Type:** _____

c. Enter **Name: Accounts Payable (A/P)**

d. Enter **Number: 2001**

e. Leave **Description blank**

f. Leave **Is sub-account unchecked**

g. Select **Save and New**

5 Add VISA Credit Card Account.

a. Select **Account Type:** _____

b. Select **Detail Type:** _____

c. Enter **Name: VISA Credit Card**

d. Enter **Number: 2100**

e. Leave **Description blank**

f. Leave **Is sub-account unchecked**

g. Select **Save and New**

6 Add Unearned Revenue Account.

a. Select **Account Type:** _____

b. Select **Detail Type: Other Current Liabilities**

c. Enter **Name: Unearned Revenue**

d. Enter **Number: 2200**

e. Leave **Description blank**

f. Leave **Is sub-account unchecked**

g. Select **Save and New**

7 Add Owner Distributions Account.

a. Select **Account Type: Equity**

b. Select **Detail Type:** _____

c. Enter **Name: Owner Distributions**

d. Enter **Number: 3200**

e. Leave **Description blank**

f. Leave **Is sub-account unchecked**

g. Select **Save and Close**

C11.3.4 Add Subaccounts

Complete the following to add subaccounts to Mookie The Beagle Coach Chart of Accounts.

> **QBO is continually** rolling out new features, so it is possible your Chart of Accounts may not appear the same as your text.

To add subaccounts to the COA, from the Navigation Bar, select **Accounting > New**.

1 After verifying your COA has a Prepaid Expenses account, add the subaccount: Prepaid Expenses: Supplies.
   a. Select **Account Type: Other Current Assets**
   b. Select **Detail Type: _____**
   c. Enter **Name: Supplies**
   d. Enter **Number: 1210**
   e. Leave **Description blank**
   f. Check: **Is sub-account**
   g. Enter **Parent Account: Prepaid Expenses**
   h. Select **Save and New**

2 Add Subaccount: Prepaid Expenses: Insurance.
   a. Select **Account Type: _____**
   b. Select **Detail Type: _____**
   c. Enter **Name: Insurance**
   d. Enter **Number: 1220**
   e. Leave **Description blank**
   f. Check: **Is sub-account**
   g. Enter **Parent Account: Prepaid Expenses**
   h. Select **Save and New**

3 Add Subaccount: Prepaid Expenses: Rent.
   a. Select **Account Type: _____**
   b. Select **Detail Type: _____**
   c. Enter **Name: Rent**
   d. Enter **Number: 1230**
   e. Leave **Description blank**
   f. Check: **Is sub-account**
   g. Enter **Parent Account: Prepaid Expenses**
   h. Select **Save and New**

4 After verifying your COA has an Insurance (Expenses) account, add the subaccount: Insurance: Renter Insurance Expense.

   a. Select **Account Type: _____**

   b. Select **Detail Type: _____**

   c. Enter **Name: Renter Insurance Expense**

   d. Enter **Number: 5011**

   e. Leave **Description blank**

   f. Check: **Is sub-account**

   g. Enter **Parent Account: Insurance** (Expenses)

   h. Select **Save and New**

5 Add Subaccount: Insurance: Liability Insurance Expense.

   a. Select **Account Type: _____**

   b. Select **Detail Type: _____**

   c. Enter **Name: Liability Insurance Expense**

   d. Enter **Number: 5012**

   e. Leave **Description blank**

   f. Check: **Is sub-account**

   g. Enter **Parent Account: Insurance** (Expenses)

   h. Select **Save and Close**

C11.3.5 Create Chart of Accounts Report

Create a Chart of Accounts report for Mookie The Beagle Coach as follows:

1 From the Navigation Bar, select **Accounting** to display the COA

2 To run the COA report, from the Chart of Accounts window, select **Run report**

3 To view more detail about a specific account in the COA, from the Chart of Accounts window, select **View register** for the specific account. A register shows every transaction for an account with the running balance.

4 **Export** the Chart of Accounts to PDF

5 **Export** the Chart of Accounts to Excel. Complete the steps listed in the Instructions sheet of the Excel Template to copy your Chart of Accounts Excel export to the Excel Template.

C11.3.6 Account Types

The following accounts are from Mookie The Beagle Coach's Chart of Accounts. For each account, identify Account Type and Financial Statement on which it appears.

Account Types

- **Asset**
- **Liability**
- **Equity**
- **Income**
- **Expense**

Financial Statements

- **Balance Sheet**
- **Profit and Loss**

Account	Account Type	Financial Statement
1. Sales		
2. Checking		
3. Accounts Receivable (A/R)		
4. Rent & Lease		
5. Prepaid Expenses		
6. Prepaid Expenses: Supplies		
7. Office Supplies & Software		
8. Prepaid Expenses: Insurance		
9. Insurance: Liability Insurance Expense		
10. Undeposited Funds		
11. Accounts Payable (A/P)		
12. VISA Credit Card		
13. Prepaid Insurance: Rent		
14. Interest Expense		
15. Contractors		
16. Legal & Professional Services		
17. Advertising & Marketing		
18. Meals & Entertainment		

19. Retained Earnings

20. Owner's Investment

21. Owner Distributions

22. Inventory

23. Utilities

C.11.3.7 Align the COA with the Tax Return

Typically when customizing the Chart of Accounts for a business, we want to verify that the accounts on the Chart of Accounts correspond to expenses shown on the tax return the business files.

Mookie The Beagle Coach, an S Corporation, files the following IRS Form 1120S for its business operations.

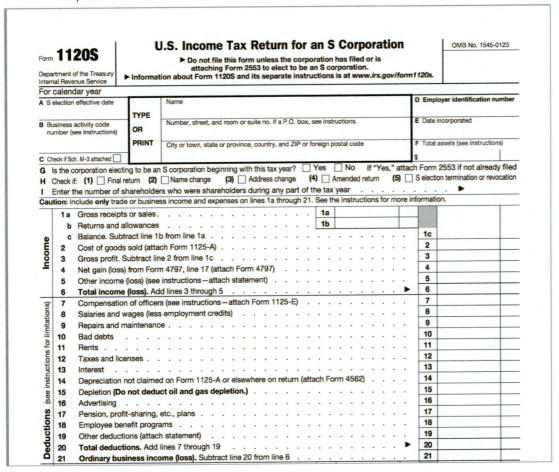

For the following accounts from Mookie The Beagle Coach QBO COA, identify the corresponding Line number on Form 1120S.

QBO COA	IRS Form 1120S
1. Rents	Form 1120S Line _____
2. Advertising	Form 1120S Line _____
3. Repairs and maintenance	Form 1120S Line _____
4. Interest	Form 1120S Line _____
5. Bad debts	Form 1120S Line _____
6. Taxes and licenses	Form 1120S Line _____

Section 11.4

PRODUCTS AND SERVICES LIST

The Products and Services List collects information about the products and services that a company buys from vendors and/or sells to customers. The Products and Services List saves time, permitting us to store information that we will reuse, so we do not have to repeatedly re-enter the same information about products and services.

We can create a QBO Products and Services List with the following information Cy summarized about the services Mookie The Beagle Coach will be providing clients. None of the services are subject to sales tax. Products sold to customers are subject to a 9% sales tax.

C11.4.1 Enter Services in Products and Services List

To enter the services into the Products and Services List:

 Select **Navigation Bar > Sales > Products and Services** tab > **Add a product or service > Service**. Use the Income account: **4200 Sales.**

 Enter the following Services Items.

CATEGORY	NAME	TYPE	DESCRIPTION	SALES PRICE
Puppy Manners 101	Puppy Manners 101 Latchkey	Service	Essentials Puppy Etiquette Latchkey services with concierge trainer onsite with pet only	$300
Puppy Manners 101	Puppy Manners 101 1 on 1	Service	Essentials Puppy Etiquette 1:1 services with concierge trainer working with pet parent and pet	$300
Puppy Manners 101	Puppy Manners 101 Virtual	Service	Essentials Puppy Etiquette Virtual with concierge trainer working with pet and pet parent via virtual app	$300
Pet Manners 101	Pet Manners 101 Latchkey	Service	Essentials Pet Etiquette Latchkey services with concierge trainer onsite with pet only	$400
Pet Manners 101	Pet Manners 101 1 on 1	Service	Essentials Pet Etiquette 1:1 services with concierge trainer working with pet parent and pet	$400
Pet Manners 101	Pet Manners 101 Virtual	Service	Essentials Pet Etiquette Virtual with concierge trainer working with pet and pet parent via virtual app	$400

Pet Manners 102	Pet Manners 102 Latchkey	Service	Intermediate Pet Etiquette Latchkey services with concierge trainer onsite with pet only	$500
Pet Manners 102	Pet Manners 102 1 on 1	Service	Intermediate Pet Etiquette 1:1 services with concierge trainer working with pet parent and pet	$500
Pet Manners 102	Pet Manners 102 Virtual	Service	Intermediate Pet Etiquette Virtual with concierge trainer working with pet and pet parent via virtual app	$500
Pet Manners 103	Pet Manners 103 Latchkey	Service	Advanced Pet Etiquette Latchkey services with concierge trainer onsite with pet only	$600
Pet Manners 103	Pet Manners 103 1 on 1	Service	Advanced Pet Etiquette 1:1 services with concierge trainer working with pet parent and pet	$600
Pet Manners 103	Pet Manners 103 Virtual	Service	Advanced Pet Etiquette Virtual with concierge trainer working with pet and pet parent via virtual app	$600
Pet Agility	Pet Agility 101	Service	Essentials Pet Agility Training	$700
Pet Agility	Pet Agility 102	Service	Intermediate Pet Agility Training	$800
Pet Agility	Pet Agility 103	Service	Advanced Pet Agility Training	$900

3 Export the Products and Services List to PDF. From the Products and Services screen, select **More > Run Report > Export icon > Export to PDF > Export to Excel**.

C11.4.2 Enter Products in Products and Services List

To enter products into the Products and Services List:

1 Select **Navigation Bar > Sales > Products and Services** tab **> New > Inventory**

2 Enter the following Product Items.
Note that since the cost of the inventory items are expected to change, only the sale price and not the cost will be entered into the Products and Services List. The cost will be entered at the time the inventory items are purchased for resale.
Use the following for Inventory items:

- **Inventory asset account: Inventory Asset**

- **Income account: Sales of Product Income**

- **Expense account: Cost of Goods Sold**

- **Initial quantity on hand: 0**

- **As of date: 02/01/2023. Note: If you receive an error message when saving, try re-entering the date.**

CATEGORY	NAME	TYPE	DESCRIPTION	SALES PRICE
Training Gear	Treat Pouches	Inventory	Dog Treat Training Pouch	$50
Training Gear	Training Clickers	Inventory	Dog Training Clicker	$10
Training Treats	Training Treats Small	Inventory	Dog Training Treats, Small size	$20
Training Treats	Training Treats Large	Inventory	Dog Training Treats, Large size	$30
Agility Equipment	Weave Poles	Inventory	Agility Dog Training Weave Poles	$54
Agility Equipment	Tunnel	Inventory	Agility Dog Training Tunnel	$42
Agility Equipment	Ring	Inventory	Agility Dog Training Ring	$36
Agility Equipment	Hurdle	Inventory	Agility Dog Training Hurdle	$22
Agility Equipment	Essentials Agility Set	Inventory	Essentials Agility Set including weave poles, hurdle and ring	$127
Agility Equipment	Advanced Agility Set	Inventory	Advanced Agility Set including weave poles, hurdles, ring and tunnel	$270

 Export the Products and Services List to PDF. From the Products and Services screen, select **More** > **Run Report** > **Export icon** > **Export to PDF** > **Export to Excel**.

C11.4.3 Products and Services List

Answer the following questions about Mookie The Beagle Coach Product and Services List.

1. How many Services are listed in MTB Coach Products and Services List?

2. How many Products (Inventory Items) are listed in MTB Coach Products and Services List?

3. How many categories of Services are listed in MTB Coach Products and Services List?

4. How many categories of Inventory are listed in MTB Coach Products and Services List?

C11.4.4 Update Chart of Accounts

After we add at least one inventory item to the Products and Services List, QBO should automatically add some additional accounts to our Chart of Accounts. Examples of such accounts include: Inventory Asset, Sales of Product Income, Cost of Goods Sold, and Purchases. We can easily identify the added accounts since they do not display account numbers.

To enter account numbers for the new accounts in the Chart of Accounts for Mookie The Beagle Coach:

1. Display the Chart of Accounts by selecting **Navigation Bar > Accounting > Chart of Accounts**

2. Enter Inventory Asset Account Number.
   a. From the Chart of Accounts window, select **Edit pencil**.
   b. Enter the account number into your Chart of Accounts.
   - **1300 Inventory Asset**

3. Enter Sales of Product Income Account Number.
   a. If needed, from the Chart of Accounts window, select **Edit pencil**.
   b. Enter the account number into your Chart of Accounts.
   - **4300 Sales of Product Income**

4. Enter Sales of Product Income Account Number.
   a. If needed, from the Chart of Accounts window, select **Edit pencil**.
   b. Enter the account number into your Chart of Accounts.
   - **5000 Cost of Goods Sold**

5. Enter Sales of Product Income Account Number.
   a. If needed, from the Chart of Accounts window, select **Edit pencil**.
   b. Enter the account number into your Chart of Accounts.
   - **5050 Purchases**

Section 11.5

CUSTOMERS LIST

Cy Walker has been marketing and promoting the new business, Mookie The Beagle Coach. As a result of his efforts, clients are signing up for both pet etiquette and pet agility training services.

- Ozzie, your curly apricot Goldendoodle and delightful bundle of playful joy, loves every person he meets. But sometimes Ozzie's unexpected affectionate exuberance can leave people off balance. So you sign Ozzie up for Puppy Manners 101 in the 1 on 1 format to polish his pet etiquette. Also, Ozzie is scheduled for Pet Agility 101 as a beneficial outlet for his playful energy.

- Maggie, a smart, willful, beautiful cream Havanese, is scheduled for Pet Manners 101, 102, and 103 by her pet parent, Sherry Byran. With poise and grace of a ballerina, Maggie is a natural for agility training. So Sherry has scheduled Maggie for intensive agility training in Pet Agility 101, 102, and 103. In addition, Maggie is a potential contender for participating in upcoming agility competitions, which would increase the visibility of Mookie The Beagle Coach as a successful agility training program.

- Remy, the Rescue Dog, recently adopted by Sandy Copper, is scheduled for Pet Manners 101. Sandy also signed Remy up for Pet Agility 101 and 102 because agility training appears to be a good fit with Remy's athletic ability and an outlet for her high energy level.

- Kuno, a mischievous black and tan King Shepherd, has been signed up for Pet Manners 101 by his pet parent, Angel Merriman. Kuno's easy athleticism makes him a perfect fit for agility training, so Angel signed him up for Pet Agility 101, 102, and 103.

- Tito, a rescue Scottish Border Terrier mix, is already surprisingly well mannered, but MJ Monet, his pet parent, would like him to complete Pet Manners 101 and Pet Agility 101. MJ thinks it would be fun, strengthen their pet/pet parent bond, and build Tito's confidence.

C11.5.1 Create Customers List

Use the following information to create a Customers List with Projects for Mookie The Beagle Coach.

To add a customer, select **Navigation Bar** > **Sales** > **Customers** tab > **New customer**.

To add a project for a customer, from the Customer screen, select **Add Project**.

Customer First Name	Customer Last Name	Project	Address	Mobile
[Enter Your First Name]	[Enter Your Last Name]	Ozzie	[Enter Address]	[Enter Phone]
Sherry	Byran	Maggie	222 Mure Drive Bayshore, CA 94326 USA	415-555-2222
Sandy	Copper	Remy	720 Cuivre Drive Bayshore, CA 94326 USA	415-555-4320
Angel	Merriman	Kuno	623 Thorsmork Road Bayshore, CA 94326 USA	415-555-7579
MJ	Monet	Tito	999 Artiste Way Bayshore, CA 94326 USA	415-555-9999

C11.5.2 Export Customers List

Export the Customers List by selecting **Reports** > **Customer Contact List** > Export to **PDF** > Export to **Excel**.

Section 11.6

VENDORS LIST

The Vendors List collects information about vendors that can be reused for transactions with vendors. Again, this saves us time from re-entering the vendor information we need to enter a vendor transaction. Instead, we can simply select the Vendor name and then the rest of the Vendor information in the Vendors List will auto-populate in the appropriate form fields.

C11.6.1 Create Vendors List

Using the following information, create a Vendors List for Mookie The Beagle Coach.

Vendor/Display Name	First Name	Vendor ID	Address	Phone
Merriman Cybersecuirty	Angel	37-3571656	623 Thorsmork Road Bayshore, CA 94326 USA	415-555-7579
Joseph Leasing	Joseph	37-1726354	13 Appleton Drive Bayshore, CA 94326 USA	415-555-0412
Bichotte Supplies	Bichotte	37-1599517	810 Francais Drive Bayshore, CA 94326 USA	415-555-4567
Toronto LLC	Tor		416 Wellington Drive Bayshore, CA 94326 USA	415-555-5377
Carole Media Design	Carole	234-56-7891	100 Bonhomme Avenue Bayshore, CA 94326 USA	415-555-8686
Luminesse Link	Luminesse		22 Beach Street Bayshore, CA 94326 USA	415-555-2222
Evan Henry	Evan	123-45-6789 Track 1099	99 Andrea Street Bayshore, CA 94326 USA	415-555-0301

C11.6.2 Export Vendors List

Export the Vendors List by selecting **Reports** > **Vendor Contact List** > Export to **PDF** > Export to **Excel**.

Section 11.7

TAGS

After you demonstrated how Cy could use QBO Tags for Mookie The Beagle Concierge, Cy would like you to set up tags for Mookie The Beagle Coach.

Before creating tags, you and Cy discuss what you want to measure with tags. This permits you to plan your Tag Groups and Tags before entering them in QBO.

Cy would like a quick, easy way to see which pets are bringing in the most money. He asks if you could set up tags for each pet and then run reports for him to see which pets are generating the most in sales. Although every pet is important, Cy knows that the additional information could be useful in how to continually improve client services.

Furthermore, Cy would like to learn more about how clients find Mookie The Beagle Coach. So he would like you to set up tags for marketing channels that reached and influenced the client to try Mookie The Beagle Coach. This could permit Cy to focus resources on the most effective marketing channels that not only reach the targeted clients, but also influence the client's decision making to give Mookie The Beagle Coach a try. It's not enough for the marketing channel to reach potential clients. The marketing channel must be able to influence the client's decision to try Mookie The Beagle Coach.

We would have two Tag Groups:

- Pets
- Marketing Channel

For the Tag Group, Pets, we can enter the pet names as tags for pets that have already been entered in the Customer/Project List. Going forward, when new pets are added to the Customer/Project List, the workflow process would be to add a tag for the new pet at the time it is entered into the Customer/Project List.

For the Tag Group, Marketing Channels, we can add the following tags:

- Social Media Instagram
- Internet Ad
- Friends & Family
- Pet Store
- Vet Office
- Other

To gather the Marketing Channel information, Cy would like to collect the information about how the client learned of Mookie The Beagle Coach when they complete their online data collection form to sign up for services.

C11.7.1 Create Tags Groups

To create the Tag Groups:

1   From the Navigation Bar, select **Banking > Tags** tab or from select the **Gear icon > Tags**

2   Select **New down arrow**

3   Select **Tag group**

4   Enter **Group name: Pets**

5   Select **Tag Group Shade** you would like to identify this Tag Group

6   Select **Save** to save the Tag Group > **Done**

7   Select **New down arrow**

8   Select **Tag group**

9   Enter **Group name: Marketing Channel**

10   Select **Tag Group Shade** you would like to identify this Tag Group

11   Select **Save** to save the Tag Group > **Done**

C11.7.2 Create Tags

To create tags for the Pets Tag Group:

1   Select the **down arrow for the Pets Tag Group > Add tag** > enter **Tag name: Kuno** > select **Save**

2   Add **Tag Names for each of the pets you entered as Projects linked to a Customer in the Customer List in Section 11.5**

To create tags for the Marketing Channel Tag Group:

1 For the Marketing Channel Tag Group, add **Tag name: Social Media Instagram**

2 Add **Tag Name: Internet Ad**

3 Add **Tag Name: Friends & Family**

4 Add **Tag Name: Pet Store**

5 Add **Tag Name: Vet Office**

6 Add **Tag Name: Other**

C11.7.3 Tags

Answer the following questions about Mookie The Beagle Coach QBO Tags.

1. How many Tag Groups does Mookie The Beagle Coach have?

2. How many Tags are in the Marketing Channel Tag Group?

3. How many Tags are in the Pets Tag Group?

Section 11.8

TRANSACTIONS

C11.8.1 Transactions Week 1

Record the following transactions for Mookie The Beagle Coach for week 1 of operations from February 1 through February 7, 2023.

- The sales tax rate for products sold is 9%.
- All customer invoices for pet coaching services are due on receipt.
- Enter appropriate Tags for Pets on Invoices.
- Enter Tags for Marketing Channels as indicated in following transaction information.
- To streamline transaction entry, use recurring transactions as appropriate.

Date	Transaction
1 02/01/2023	Cy Walker invests $8,000 and you invest $2,000 in Mookie The Beagle Coach as owners of the LLC S Corporation for an 80/20 split in ownership. Both amounts are paid by e-check and the funds deposited into the company Checking account using one bank deposit.
	For the Received From field, **add Cy Walker** and **Your First Initial Last Name** as Employees. (Note: We use Employees because there is no Type for Other or Owners.)
	Save the Deposit. Reopen the Deposit > from the lower Menu Bar, select **More > Transaction Journal**.
	a. What are the Accounts and Amounts Debited?
	b. What are the Accounts and Amounts Credited?
2 02/01/2023	Pay $1,000 rent for February to Joseph Leasing by e-check. To record, select + **New > Expense > 5028 Rent & Lease (Expenses)**.
	Save the transaction > select **More > Transaction Journal**.
	a. What are the Accounts and Amounts Debited?
	b. What are the Accounts and Amounts Credited?
3 02/01/2023	Pay Phoenix Insurance $600 for 6 months of liability insurance using the company VISA credit card. **Add** Phoenix Insurance as a new Vendor. Record full amount as **Liability Insurance Expense**.
	a. What are the Accounts and Amounts Debited?
	b. What are the Accounts and Amounts Credited?

4 02/02/2023 Purchase 4 Advanced Agility Training sets from Toronto LLC, terms net 30, for a wholesale price of $100.00 each to build 2 agility training courses indoors and 2 agility training courses outdoors in the leased facilities for onsite agility training services. Cy provides the labor to build out the agility training courses. Record the cost as Supplies since it is will be used in the operations and not resold to customers and the amount is not large enough nor long-lived enough to result in a depreciable asset.

Enter as a **Purchase Order**. Then enter **Bill** and **add Purchase Order to the Bill**.

a. What are the Accounts and Amounts Debited?
b. What are the Accounts and Amounts Credited?

5 02/02/2023 Purchase technology and cybersecurity services for $500 on account, terms net 30, from Merriman Cybersecurity. Record as Legal & Professional Services (Expense). Select **+ New > Bill > Legal & Professional Services (Expenses)**.

a. What are the Accounts and Amounts Debited?
b. What are the Accounts and Amounts Credited?

6 02/03/2023 Purchased technology supplies for $342 on account from Merriman Cybersecurity. Use the **Office Supplies & Software (Expenses)** account.

a. What are the Accounts and Amounts Debited?
b. What are the Accounts and Amounts Credited?

7 02/03/2023 Purchased office supplies for $110 with a VISA credit card from Bichotte Supplies. Use the **Office Supplies & Software (Expenses)** account.

a. What are the Accounts and Amounts Debited?
b. What are the Accounts and Amounts Credited?

8 02/05/2023 You schedule Ozzie for Puppy Manners 101: Latchkey training and his onsite Pet Agility 101 training. To record, select **+ New > Invoice**. Terms: Due on receipt. Enter Tag for Pets. Omit Tags for Marketing Channels.

a. What are the Accounts and Amounts Debited?
b. What are the Accounts and Amounts Credited?

9 02/6/2023 You pay by credit card for Ozzie's Puppy Manners 101: Latchkey training and Pet Agility 101 training. Deposit to Checking.

a. What are the Accounts and Amounts Debited?
b. What are the Accounts and Amounts Credited?

10 02/07/2023   Mookie The Beagle Coach purchases the following inventory from Toronto LLC, terms net 30, for resale to customers. Enter as a **Purchase Order**. Then enter **Bill** and **add Purchase Order to the Bill**.

Note: When entering Vendor: Toronto LLC into Bill, the Bill will autofill with prior bill information. Delete the prior bill information before adding the new PO dated 02/07/2023.

- 8 Dog Treat Training Pouches at a cost of $10 each
- 8 Dog Training Clickers at a cost of $2 each
- 8 Dog Training Treats, Small size at a cost of $5 each
- 8 Dog Training Treats, Large size at a cost of $8 each

a. What are the Accounts and Amounts Debited?
b. What are the Accounts and Amounts Credited?

C11.8.2 Transactions Week 2

Record the following transactions for Mookie The Beagle Coach for week 2 of operations from February 8 through February 14, 2023.

	Date	Transaction
1	02/08/2023	Pay Luminesse Link $70 by VISA credit card for the month of February Internet services. Use **Utilities (Expenses)** account.

    a. What are the Accounts and Amounts Debited?
    b. What are the Accounts and Amounts Credited?

	Date	Transaction
2	02/08/2023	Sherry Byran schedules Maggie for Pet Manners 101: 1 on 1 and Pet Agility 101 training. On the Invoice, enter Tags for Pet and Tags for Marketing Channel: Social Media Instagram. Terms: Due on receipt.

    a. What are the Accounts and Amounts Debited?
    b. What are the Accounts and Amounts Credited?

	Date	Transaction
3	02/09/2023	Clients approach Cy with requests to rent the onsite agility training course for a fee to practice agility training between lessons. Cy thinks it's an opportunity to gain additional revenue from the facilities when they are not in use for agility training classes. So he creates an online scheduling website for client rental, charging $50 per hour.

Sherry Byran rents the agility training course for 1 hour for Maggie. On the Invoice, enter **Product/Service > + Add New > Service: Agility Course Rental > Category: Agility Course Rental > Sales price: $50.00.** Terms: Due on receipt. Enter Tags for Pet and Tags for Marketing Channel: Social Media Instagram.

    a. What are the Accounts and Amounts Debited?
    b. What are the Accounts and Amounts Credited?

	Date	Transaction
4	02/10/2023	Sherry Byran pays by credit card for Invoices dated 02/08/2023 and 02/09/2023. Deposit to Checking.

    a. What are the Accounts and Amounts Debited?
    b. What are the Accounts and Amounts Credited?

	Date	Transaction
5	02/12/2023	Purchased technology supplies for $86 on account from Merriman Cybersecurity. Use the **Office Supplies & Software (Expenses)** account.

    a. What are the Accounts and Amounts Debited?
    b. What are the Accounts and Amounts Credited?

6 02/12/2023 Sandy Copper schedules Remy for Pet Manners 101: Virtual training. On the Invoice, enter Tags for Pet and Tags for Marketing Channel: Friends & Family. Terms: Due on receipt.

    a. What are the Accounts and Amounts Debited?
    b. What are the Accounts and Amounts Credited?

7 02/13/2023 **1. Set up Sales Tax.**
    a. From the Navigation Bar, select **Taxes** > **Use Automatic Sales Tax**
    b. Verify **Business Address** for **Mookie The Beagle Coach** > select **Next**
    c. Do you need to collect sales tax outside of California? Select **No** > **Next**
    d. Select **Create Invoice** from the Automatic Sales Tax is All Set Up window
    2. Create Invoice.
    a. If the Invoice does not automatically appear on your screen, select **(+) New** > **Invoice**
    b. Select **Customer: Sandy Copper: Remy**
    c. Select **Invoice Date: 02/13/2023**
    d. Enter Tags: **Pet Tag: Remy** > **Marketing Channel Tag: Friends & Family**
    e. Select Item Details Line 1: **Product/Service: Dog Treat Training Pouch**
    f. Enter **QTY: 1**
    g. **Rate** and **Amount** fields should autofill
    h. Check **Tax**
    i. Select Item Details Line 2: **Product/Service: Dog Training Clicker**
    j. Enter **QTY: 1**
    k. **Rate** and **Amount** fields should autofill
    l. Check **Tax**
    m. Select Item Details Line 3: **Product/Service: Dog Training Treats, Small**
    n. Enter **QTY: 2**
    o. **Rate** and **Amount** fields should autofill
    p. Check **Tax**
    q. Select **Sales Tax Rate** > select **Add rate** > select **Single** > enter **Name: Sales Tax** > select **Agency: California Department of Tax and Fee Administration** > enter **Rate: 9%** > select **Save**.
    r. Select **Save** and leave the Invoice displayed
    3. View the Transaction Journal for the Invoice.
    a. From the bottom of the Invoice, select **More** > **Transaction Journal**
    b. What are the Accounts and Amounts Debited?
    c. What are the Accounts and Amounts Credited?

8 02/14/2023 Sandy Copper pays by e-check for Invoices dated: 02/12/2023 and 02/13/2023. Deposit to Checking.

    a. What are the Accounts and Amounts Debited?
    b. What are the Accounts and Amounts Credited?

9   02/14/2023   Paid Phoenix Insurance $50 for February renters insurance using company VISA credit card. Record as Renter Insurance Expense.

       a. What are the Accounts and Amounts Debited?
       b. What are the Accounts and Amounts Credited?

10   02/14/2023   Evan Henry is the contractor providing the training services to clients as needed. Record **Contractors (Expenses)** for 30 hours for the first two weeks at $20 per hour, paid by check using the QBO Expenses form.

       a. What are the Accounts and Amounts Debited?
       b. What are the Accounts and Amounts Credited?

Copyright 2023 © McGraw Hill LLC. All rights reserved. No reproduction or distribution without the prior written consent of McGraw Hill LLC.

C11.8.3 Transactions Week 3

Record the following transactions for Mookie The Beagle Coach for week 3 of operations from February 15 through February 21, 2023.

Date	Transaction
1 02/15/2023	Because Ozzie enjoys agility training, you sign him up for the next agility training course, Pet Agility 102, and purchase the following training gear subject to a 9% sales tax. Enter Pet Tags on the Invoice. • 1 Dog Treat Training Pouch • 1 Dog Training Clicker • 1 Dog Training Treats, Large size a. What are the Accounts and Amounts Debited? b. What are the Accounts and Amounts Credited?
2 02/15/2023	You pay by credit card for the Invoice dated 02/15/2023 for Ozzie's Pet Agility 102 training and training gear. Deposit to Checking account. a. What are the Accounts and Amounts Debited? b. What are the Accounts and Amounts Credited?
3 02/16/2023	Purchased the following inventory for resale to customers from Toronto LLC, terms net 30. Record **PO** first, then **add PO to Bill**. (Note: The Bill will autofill with the prior bill information. Delete the prior bill information before adding the new PO to the bill.) • 2 Essentials Agility Sets at a cost of $30 each • 1 Advanced Agility Set at a cost of $100 each • 2 Tunnels at a cost of $13 each • 2 Weave Poles at a cost of $18 each a. What are the Accounts and Amounts Debited? b. What are the Accounts and Amounts Credited?
4 02/17/2023	You sign Ozzie up for his next agility training course, Pet Agility 103. In addition, you purchase more training treats and an essentials agility set so that you can set up an agility training course at home for Ozzie to practice. Both the treats and agility set are subject to 9% sales tax. On the Invoice, enter Pet Tags. • Pet Agility 103 • 2 Dog Training Treats, Large size • Essentials Agility Set a. What are the Accounts and Amounts Debited? b. What are the Accounts and Amounts Credited?

5 02/19/2023 You pay by credit card for the Invoice dated 02/17/2023 for Ozzie's Pet Agility 103 training, treats, and Essentials Agility Set. Deposit to Checking account.

a. What are the Accounts and Amounts Debited?
b. What are the Accounts and Amounts Credited?

6 02/19/2023 Prepare the Invoice and Receive Payment for the following items that Sherry Byran purchased for Maggie by credit card. Add 9% sales tax to products. Enter Tags.

- Pet Manners 102: 1 on 1
- Pet Agility 102
- 1 Advanced Agility Set
- 1 Dog Treat Training Pouch
- 1 Dog Training Clicker
- 2 Dog Training Treats, Small size

a. For the Invoice, what are the Accounts and Amounts Debited?
b. For the Invoice, what are the Accounts and Amounts Credited?

7 02/19/2023 Prepare the Invoice and Receive Payment for Sandy Copper's purchase of Remy's Pet Agility 101 training by credit card. Enter Tags.

a. For the Invoice, what are the Accounts and Amounts Debited?
b. For the Invoice, what are the Accounts and Amounts Credited?

8 02/20/2023 Prepare the Invoice and Receive Payment for Angel Merriman's purchase of the following items for Kuno, with payment by credit card. Add 9% sales tax to products. Enter Pet Tags and Marketing Channel Tag: Friends & Family.

- Pet Manners 101: 1 on 1
- Pet Agility 101
- 1 Essentials Agility Set
- 1 Dog Treat Training Pouch
- 1 Dog Training Clicker
- 1 Dog Training Treats, Large size

a. For the Invoice, what are the Accounts and Amounts Debited?
b. For the Invoice, what are the Accounts and Amounts Credited?

9 02/21/2023 Prepare the Invoice and Receive Payment for MJ Monet's purchase by e-check for Tito's Pet Manners 101: 1 on 1 training. Enter Pet Tags and Marketing Channel Tag: Pet Store.

a. For the Invoice, what are the Accounts and Amounts Debited?
b. For the Invoice, what are the Accounts and Amounts Credited?

02/21/2023   Angel Merriman rents the agility training course for 2 hours for Kuno. Prepare the Invoice and Receive Payment with a credit card. Enter Tags.

a. For the Invoice, what are the Accounts and Amounts Debited?
b. For the Invoice, what are the Accounts and Amounts Credited?

C11.8.4 Transactions Week 4

Record the following transactions for Mookie The Beagle Coach for week 4 of operations from February 22 through February 28, 2023.

	Date	Transaction
1	02/22/2023	Prepare the Invoice and Receive Payment for Sherry Byran's purchase for Maggie of the following items with payment by credit card. Enter Tags. • Pet Manners 103: 1 on 1 • Pet Agility 103 a. For the Invoice, what are the Accounts and Amounts Debited? b. For the Invoice, what are the Accounts and Amounts Credited?
2	02/22/2023	Prepare the Invoice and Receive Payment for Sandy Copper's purchase of the following items for Remy, with payment by e-check. Add 9% sales tax to products. Enter Tags. • Pet Agility 102 • 1 Weave Poles a. For the Invoice, what are the Accounts and Amounts Debited? b. For the Invoice, what are the Accounts and Amounts Credited?
3	02/23/2023	Prepare the Invoice and Receive Payment for MJ Monet's purchase of the following items for Tito, with payment by e-check. Enter Tags. • Pet Agility 101 • 1 Weave Poles • 1 Tunnel a. For the Invoice, what are the Accounts and Amounts Debited? b. For the Invoice, what are the Accounts and Amounts Credited?
4	02/23/2023	Prepare the Invoice and Receive Payment for Angel Merriman's purchase of Kuno's Pet Agility 102 training, with payment by credit card. Enter Tags. a. For the Invoice, what are the Accounts and Amounts Debited? b. For the Invoice, what are the Accounts and Amounts Credited?
5	02/24/2023	Paid Toronto LLC by check for agility training sets purchased on 02/02/2023. a. What are the Accounts and Amounts Debited? b. What are the Accounts and Amounts Credited?

6   02/26/2023   Purchased the following inventory for resale to customers from Toronto LLC, terms net 30. Record **PO** and then **add PO to Bill**.

- 1 Essentials Agility Sets at a cost of $30 each
- 1 Advanced Agility Set at a cost of $100 each
- 1 Tunnels at a cost of $13 each
- 1 Weave Poles at a cost of $18 each
- 5 Dog Training Treats, Small size at a cost of $5 each
- 5 Dog Training Treats, Large size at a cost of $8 each

a. What are the Accounts and Amounts Debited?
b. What are the Accounts and Amounts Credited?

7   02/27/2023   Prepare the Invoice for Sherry Byran rental of the agility training course for 1 hour for Maggie's practice. Enter Tags.

a. What are the Accounts and Amounts Debited?
b. What are the Accounts and Amounts Credited?

8   02/27/2023   Prepare the Invoice for Angel Merriman's purchase of Kuno's Pet Agility 103 training. Enter Tags.

a. For the Invoice, what are the Accounts and Amounts Debited?
b. For the Invoice, what are the Accounts and Amounts Credited?

9   02/28/2023   Evan Henry is the contractor providing the training services to clients as needed. Record Contractors Expense for 33 hours for the last two weeks of the month at $20 per hour, paid by check using the QBO Expense form.

a. What are the Accounts and Amounts Debited?
b. What are the Accounts and Amounts Credited?

Section 11.9

QBO CROSSCHECK: BANK AND CREDIT CARD MATCHING

The QBO Matching feature streamlines tracking bank and credit card transactions. We can enter transactions into QBO, connect to our bank accounts, and then match our entered QBO transactions with the transactions the bank indicates we have. Matching bank transactions we have entered into QBO with transactions that the bank shows is the ultimate QBO crosscheck. We can check the QBO transaction we entered with what the bank or credit card company shows.

If we are unable to connect a bank or credit card account to QBO, we can still use the matching feature with a workaround. We can download the bank transactions into a csv file. Then we load the bank or credit card transactions into QBO to match against the transactions we entered into QBO.

Mookie The Beagle Coach is unable to connect QBO to its bank and credit card companies, so you will need to use the following process to matching your QBO transactions against what the bank and credit card companies show.

1 Enter transactions into QBO. (You completed this step in Section 11.8.)

2 Download banking transactions from the bank and credit card transactions from the credit card company in csv file format. (The csv files have already been prepared for you.)

3 Load the csv files with downloaded transactions into QBO. (Instructions in C11.9.1.2 for Checking and C11.9.2.2 for Credit Card.)

After loading your bank and credit card transactions, match loaded bank and credit card transactions to transactions previously entered in QBO. (Instructions in C11.9.1.3 for Checking and C11.9.2.3 for Credit Card.)

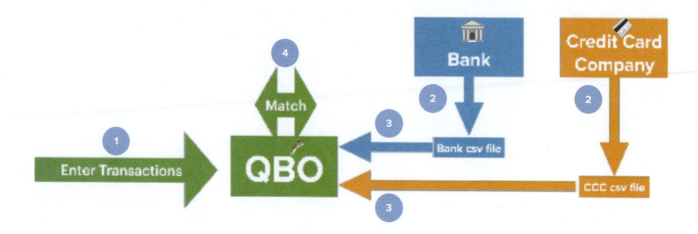

C11.9.1 Match Bank Transactions Checking

Mookie The Beagle Coach has downloaded the following Checking account transactions in spreadsheet form (csv file). We need to load these bank transactions into QBO and then match them against QBO transactions previously entered in Section 11.8.

CHECKING				
Type	**Trans Date**	**Post Date**	**Description**	**Amount**
Expense	02/24/2023	02/26/2023	TORONTO LLC	-400.00
Deposit	02/23/2023	02/25/2023	ANGEL MERRIMAN	800.00
Deposit	02/23/2023	02/25/2023	MJ MONET	804.64
Deposit	02/22/2023	02/23/2023	SANDY COPPER	858.86
Deposit	02/22/2023	02/23/2023	SHERRY BYRAN	1500.00
Deposit	02/21/2023	02/23/2023	ANGEL MERRIMAN	100.00
Deposit	02/21/2023	02/22/2023	MJ MONET	400.00
Deposit	02/20/2023	02/22/2023	ANGEL MERRIMAN	1336.53
Deposit	02/19/2023	02/21/2023	SANDY COPPER	700.00
Deposit	02/19/2023	02/21/2023	SHERRY BYRAN	1703.30
Deposit	02/19/2023	02/21/2023	YOUR NAME	1103.83
Deposit	02/15/2023	02/17/2023	YOUR NAME	898.10
Expense	02/14/2023	02/15/2023	EVAN HENRY	-600.00
Deposit	02/14/2023	02/15/2023	SANDY COPPER	509.00
Deposit	02/10/2023	02/11/2023	SHERRY BYRAN	1150.00
Deposit	02/06/2023	02/08/2023	YOUR NAME	1000.00
Expense	02/01/2023	02/03/2023	JOSEPH LEASING	-1000.00
Deposit	02/01/2023	02/02/2023	CY WALKER + YOUR NAME	10000.00

1. First, download the csv file containing the checking information from the bank.
   - If you are using Connect, select the link for the data file: **QBO 3E C11.9.1 Checking.csv**.
   - If you are not using Connect, go to **www.my-quickbooksonline.com** > select **QBO 3e** > select **QBO 3e Data Files** > download **QBO 3E C11.9.1 Checking.csv**.

2. Load Checking Account Transactions into QBO.
   a. From the Navigation Bar, select **Banking** > **Banking** tab
   b. Select **Upload transactions**
   c. Select **Drag and drop or select files** to select the file to upload > select **File: QBO 3E C11.9.1 Checking.csv** > **Continue**
   d. Select **QuickBooks Account: 1001 Checking** > **Continue**
   e. Select **Is the first row in your file a header? Yes**
   f. Select **How many columns show amounts? One column**
   g. Select **What's the date format used in your file? MM/dd/yyyy**
   h. Select **Date: Column 2: Trans Date**
   i. Select **Description: Column 4 Description**
   j. Select **Amount: Column 5 Amount**
   k. Select **Continue**
   l. Select **The transactions to import: Select All** > **Continue**
   m. When asked, Do you want to import now?, select **Yes**
   n. When Import completed appears, select **Done**
   o. How many transactions were imported?

3. Complete a Checking Account Bank Match.
   a. From the Navigation Bar, select **Banking**
   b. How many open items appear on the Checking card at the top of the screen?
   c. What is the dollar amount displayed for the 1001 Checking in QuickBooks?
   d. Select **Match** for all Matching items
   e. Now how many open items appear on the Checking card at the top of the screen?

C11.9.2 Match Bank Transactions Credit Card

Mookie The Beagle Coach has the following transactions for its VISA Credit Card in spreadsheet form that have not yet been uploaded into QBO. You need to upload the credit card transactions into QBO and then match them to QBO transactions previously entered in Section 11.8.

VISA CREDIT CARD

Type	Trans Date	Post Date	Description	Amount
Expense	02/14/2023	02/16/2023	PHOENIX INSURANCE	-50.00
Expense	02/08/2023	02/09/2023	LUMINESSE LINK	-70.00
Expense	02/03/2023	02/05/2023	BICHOTTE SUPPLIES	-110.00
Expense	02/01/2023	02/03/2023	PHOENIX INSURANCE	-600.00

1. First, download the csv file containing the credit card transaction information from the credit card company.
   - If you are using Connect, select the link for the data file: **QBO 3E EC11.9.2.6 Credit Card.csv**.
   - If you are not using Connect, go to **www.my-quickbooksonline.com** > select **QBO 3e** > **QBO 3e Data Files** > download **QBO 3E C11.9.2 Credit Card.csv**.

2. Load Credit Card Account Transactions into QBO.
   a. From the Navigation Bar, select **Banking > Banking** tab
   b. Select the Link account drop-down arrow > select **Upload from file**
   c. Select **Drag and drop or select files** to select the file to upload > select **File: QBO 3E C11.9.2 Credit Card.csv > Continue**
   d. Select **QuickBooks Account: 2100 VISA Credit Card > Continue**
   e. Select **Is the first row in your file a header? Yes**
   f. Select **How many columns show amounts? One column**
   g. Select **What's the date format used in your file? MM/dd/yyyy**
   h. Select **Date: Column 2: Trans Date**
   i. Select **Description: Column 4 Description**
   j. Select **Amount: Column 5 Amount**
   k. Select **Continue**
   l. Select **The transactions to import: Select All > Continue**
   m. When asked, Do you want to import now?, select **Yes**
   n. When Import completed appears, select **Done**
   o. How many transactions were imported?

3. Complete a Credit Card Account Bank Match.
   a. From the Navigation Bar, select **Banking**
   b. How many open items appear on the VISA Credit Card at the top of the screen?
   c. What is the dollar amount displayed for the 2100 VISA Credit Card in QuickBooks?
   d. Select **Match** for all Matching items
   e. Now how many open items appear on the VISA Credit Card at the top of the screen?

Section 11.10

ADJUSTMENTS

Adjustments are one of the steps in the accounting cycle. As discussed in Chapters 9 and 10, the accounting cycle usually consists of the following steps.

- **Chart of Accounts.** The Chart of Accounts (Account List) is a list of all accounts used to accumulate information about assets, liabilities, owners' equity, revenues, and expenses.
- **Transactions.** During the accounting period, record transactions with customers, vendors, employees, and owners.
- **Trial Balance.** A Trial Balance is also referred to as an unadjusted Trial Balance because it is prepared before adjustments. A Trial Balance lists each account and the account balance at the end of the accounting period. Prepare a Trial Balance to verify that the accounting system is in balance—total debits should equal total credits.
- **Adjustments.** At the end of the accounting period before preparing financial statements, make any adjustments necessary to bring the accounts up to date. Adjustments are entered in the Journal using debits and credits.
- **Adjusted Trial Balance.** Prepare an Adjusted Trial Balance (a Trial Balance after adjustments) to verify that the accounting system still balances.
- **Financial Reports.** Prepare financial statements (Profit and Loss, Balance Sheet, and Statement of Cash Flows) for external users and internal users. Prepare management reports.

For Mookie The Beagle Coach, we have prepared the Chart of Accounts and entered Transactions. Next, we need to create a Trial Balance, make Adjusting Entries, create an Adjusted Trial Balance, and then prepare Financial Reports for Mookie The Beagle Coach.

TRIAL BALANCE

The purpose of the Trial Balance is to verify that our accounting system balances (debits equal credits) before we enter adjusting entries.

C11.10.1 Trial Balance

Complete the following to prepare a Trial Balance for Mookie The Beagle Coach.

1 From the Navigation Bar, select **Reports**

2 Select **Standard** report tab

3 Select **Report Category: For My Accountant**

4 Select **Trial Balance** and complete steps to run the Trial Balance at **02/28/2023**

5 Export the Trial Balance to **PDF**. Export the Trial Balance to **Excel**.

Answer the following questions about Mookie The Beagle Coach Trial Balance.

1. What is the amount of Total Debits?

2. What is amount of Total Credits?

3. What is balance in the 5024 Office Supplies & Software account?

4. What is balance in the 5012 Insurance: Liability Insurance Expense account?

ADJUSTING ENTRIES

Adjusting entries are required to bring the accounts up to date to reflect the correct account balances before we prepare financial reports.

If we use the accrual basis of accounting to calculate profits, the following four types of adjusting entries may be necessary.
1. **Prepaid items.** Items that are prepaid, such as prepaid insurance or prepaid rent.
2. **Unearned items.** Items that a customer has paid us for, but we have not provided the product or service.
3. **Accrued expenses.** Expenses that are incurred but not yet paid or recorded.
4. **Accrued revenues.** Revenues that have been earned but not yet collected or recorded.

For more detailed information about adjusting entries, see Chapter 9.

C11.10.2 Adjusting Entries
Make adjusting entries for Mookie The Beagle Coach at February 28, 2023, using the following information.

1. **ADJ1:** One month of liability insurance has expired as of February 28, 2023.

2. **ADJ2:** A count of office supplies revealed $400 of supplies on hand at February 28, 2023.

3. **ADJ3:** On 02/27/2023 Mookie The Beagle Coach invoiced Angel Merriman $900 and recorded sales of $900 for an agility training class for Kuno that will not occur until March. Because we are using the accrual basis, at February 28, 2023, the $900 amount should be recorded as Unearned Revenue since it will not be earned until the month of March.

To enter an adjusting entry using the QBO Journal:

1 Select **(+) New** icon

2 Select **Journal Entry** to access the onscreen Journal

3 Enter **Journal Date: 02/28/2023**

4 Enter **Journal No.: ADJ 1**

5 On Line 1, from the drop-down list of accounts to debit, select **Account to Debit**

6 Enter **Debit Amount**

7 On Line 2, from the drop-down list of accounts to credit, select **Account to Credit**

8 Enter **Credit Amount**

9 Enter **Memo**

10 Select **Save and new**

Answer the following questions about Mookie The Beagle Coach Adjusting Entries.

1. a. For Adjusting Entry 1, what are the Account and Amount for Debits?

    b. For Adjusting Entry 1, what are the account and amount for Credits?

2. a. For Adjusting Entry 2, what are the account and amount for Debits?

    b. For Adjusting Entry 2, what are the account and amount for Credits?

3. a. For Adjusting Entry 3, what are the account and amount for Debits?

    b. For Adjusting Entry 3, what are the account and amount for Credits?

ADJUSTED TRIAL BALANCE

The Adjusted Trial Balance is a trial balance that is prepared after adjusting entries have been made. The purpose of the Adjusted Trial Balance is to verify that our accounting system still balances after adjustments. In addition, it permits us to review the adjusted account balances to crosscheck that our adjusting entries had the desired effect on the account balances.

C11.10.3 Adjusted Trial Balance

To view an Adjusted Trial Balance in QBO simply run the Trial Balance report again after adjusting entries have been entered in QBO.

1 From the Navigation Bar, select **Reports**

2 Select **Standard** report tab

3 Select **Report Category: For My Accountant**

4 Select **Trial Balance** and complete steps to run the Trial Balance again at **02/28/2023** after adjusting entries are entered

5 Export the Trial Balance (Adjusted) to **PDF**. Export the Trial Balance (Adjusted) to **Excel**.

1. What is the amount of Total Debits?

2. What is amount of Total Credits?

3. What is balance in the Liability Insurance Expense account?

4. What is the balance in the Unearned Revenue (Liability) account?

5. What is the balance in the Office Supplies & Software (Expenses) account?

6. What is the balance in the Prepaid Expenses: Supplies (Asset) account?

Section 11.11

FINANCIAL STATEMENTS

Prepare financial statements for Mookie The Beagle Coach.

PROFIT AND LOSS STATEMENT

The Profit & Loss Statement (also called the Income Statement) lists income earned and expenses incurred to generate income. Summarizing the amount of profit or loss a company has earned, the Profit & Loss Statement is one of the primary financial statements given to bankers and investors.

Profit, or net income, can be measured in two different ways:

- **Cash basis.** A sale is recorded when cash is collected from the customer. Expenses are recorded when cash is paid.
- **Accrual basis.** Sales are recorded when the good or service is provided regardless of when the cash is collected from the customer. Expenses are recorded when the cost is incurred or expires, even if the expense has not been paid.

QBO permits us to prepare the Profit and Loss Statement using either the accrual or the cash basis. QBO also permits us to prepare Profit and Loss Statements monthly, quarterly, or annually.

C11.11.1 Profit and Loss

Complete the following to prepare a Profit and Loss Statement for Mookie The Beagle Coach.

1 From the Navigation Bar, select **Reports** > **Standard** tab > **Business Overview** > **Profit and Loss**

2 Select **Date Range: 02/01/2023 to 02/28/2023**

3 Select **Active rows/active columns**

4 Select **Accounting Method: Accrual**

5 Select **Run report**

6 Export the Profit and Loss Statement to **PDF**

7 Export the Profit and Loss Statement to **Excel**. Complete the steps listed in the Instructions sheet of the Excel Template to copy your Profit and Loss Statement Excel export to the Excel Template.

Answer the following questions about Mookie The Beagle Coach Profit and Loss Statement.

1. What is the amount of Total Income (Revenue)?

2. What is amount of Total Expenses?

3. What is amount of Net Income?

BALANCE SHEET

The Balance Sheet is the financial statement that summarizes the financial position of a business. Listing assets, liabilities, and equity, the Balance Sheet reveals what a company owns and what it owes.

C11.11.2 Balance Sheet

Complete the following to prepare a Balance Sheet for Mookie The Beagle Coach.

1 From the Navigation Bar, select **Reports** > **Standard** tab > **Business Overview** > **Balance Sheet**

2 Select **Date Range: 02/28/2023**

3 Select **Run report**

4 Export the Balance Sheet to **PDF**

5 Export the Balance Sheet to **Excel**. Complete the steps listed in the Instructions sheet of the Excel Template to copy your Balance Sheet Excel export to the Excel Template.

Answer the following questions about Mookie The Beagle Coach Balance Sheet.

1. On the Balance Sheet, what are Total Assets?

2. On the Balance Sheet, what are Total Liabilities?

3. On the Balance Sheet, what is the balance of the company's VISA credit card account?

STATEMENT OF CASH FLOWS

The Statement of Cash Flows summarizes a company's cash inflows and cash outflows. The cash flows are grouped by activity:

- Cash flows from operating activities. Cash flows related to the operations of the business—providing goods and services to customers.

- Cash flows from investing activities. Cash flows that result from investing (buying and selling) long-term assets, such as investments and property.

- Cash flows from financing activities. Cash flows that result from borrowing or repaying principal on debt or from transactions with owners.

C11.11.3 Statement of Cash Flows

Complete the following to prepare a Statement of Cash Flows for Mookie The Beagle Coach.

1. From the Navigation Bar, select **Reports** > **Standard** tab > **Business Overview** > **Statement of Cash Flows**

2. Select **Date Range: 02/01/2023 To 02/28/2023**

3. Select **Run report**

4. Export the Statement of Cash Flows to **PDF**

5. Export the Statement of Cash Flows to **Excel**. Complete the steps listed in the Instructions sheet of the Excel Template to copy your Statement of Cash Flows Excel export to the Excel Template.

Answer the following questions about Mookie The Beagle Coach Statement of Cash Flows.

1. On the Statement of Cash Flows, what is the Net Cash Provided by Operating Activities?

2. On the Statement of Cash Flows, what is the Net Cash Provided by Investing Activities?

3. On the Statement of Cash Flows, what is the Net Cash Provided by Financing Activities?

4. What was Cash at the end of the period?

Section 11.12

MANAGEMENT REPORTS

Management reports are prepared as needed to provide management with information for making operating and business decisions.

ACCOUNTS RECEIVABLE AGING

The Accounts Receivable Aging report provides information useful in tracking accounts receivable by providing information about the age of customer accounts. This report lists the age of accounts receivable balances.

C11.12.1 Accounts Receivable Aging

Complete the following to prepare the Accounts Receivable Aging report:

1. From the Navigation Bar, select **Reports**

2. Select **Standard** tab

3. Select **Report Category: Who Owes You**

4. Select **Accounts Receivable Aging Summary**

5. Enter **Customize** features: **Report Period As of: 02/28/2023 > Negative numbers: (100) > Aging method: Report date > Days per aging period: 30 > Number of periods: 4 > Run report**

6. Select **Save Customization**. Enter **Custom report name: A/R Aging Summary**. Select **Add new group** > enter **New group name: Management Reports > Add > Save**. The customized report will now appear under the Custom Reports tab.

7. Export the Accounts Receivable Aging Summary report to **PDF**

8. Export the Accounts Receivable Aging Summary to **Excel**. Complete the steps listed in the Instructions sheet of the Excel Template to copy your Accounts Receivable Aging Summary Excel export to the Excel Template.

Answer the following questions about Mookie The Beagle Coach Accounts Receivable Aging Summary report.

1. On the Accounts Receivable Aging Summary Report, what is the amount of accounts aged 1–30 days?

2. On the Accounts Receivable Aging Summary Report, what is the amount of accounts aged 31–60 days?

3. On the Accounts Receivable Aging Summary Report, what is the amount of accounts aged 91 days and over?

SALES BY PRODUCT/SERVICE

The Sales by Product/Service Summary report shows us which products are selling the most and which products are the most profitable. This information is useful for planning which products to order and which services are in demand.

C11.12.2 Sales by Product/Service
Complete the following to prepare the Sales by Product/Service Summary report for Mookie The Beagle Coach:

1 From the Navigation Bar, select **Reports**

2 Select **Standard** tab

3 Select **Report Category: Sales and Customers**

4 Select **Sales by Product/Service Summary**

5 Enter **Customize** features: **Report Period: 02/01/2023 To 02/28/2023 > Accounting method: Accrual > Negative numbers: (100) > Run report**

6 Select **Save Customization**. Enter **Custom report name: Sales by Product/Service Summary**. Select **Add this report to a group: Management Reports > Save**. The customized report will now appear under the Custom Reports tab.

7 Export the Sales by Product/Service report to **PDF**

8 Export the Sales by Product/Service report to **Excel**. Complete the steps listed in the Instructions sheet of the Excel Template to copy your Sales by Product/Service Excel export to the Excel Template.

Answer the following questions about Mookie The Beagle Coach Sales by Product/Service Summary report.

1. On the Sales by Product/Service Summary Report, what is the percentage (rounded to 2 decimal places) of sales generated by Pet Agility Training Services?

2. On the Sales by Product/Service Summary Report, what is the percentage of sales generated by all Pet Manners Training Services?

3. On the Sales by Product/Service Summary Report, what is the percentage of sales generated by sales of products?

ACCOUNTS PAYABLE AGING

The Accounts Payable Aging Summary summarizes accounts payable balances by the age of the account.

C11.12.3 Accounts Payable Aging
Complete the following to prepare the Accounts Payable Aging Summary report for Mookie The Beagle Coach.

1 From the Navigation Bar, select **Reports**

2 Select **Standard** tab

3 Select **Report Category: What You Owe**

4 Select **Accounts Payable Aging Summary**

5 Enter **Customize** features: **Report Period as of: 02/28/2023 > Negative numbers: (100) > Aging method: Report date > Days per aging period: 30 > Number of periods: 4 > Run report**

6 Select **Save Customization**. Enter **Custom report name: A/P Aging Summary**. Select **Add this report to a group: Management Reports > Save**. The customized report will now appear under the Custom Reports tab.

7 Export the Accounts Payable Aging Summary report to **PDF**

8 Export the Accounts Payable Aging Summary report to **Excel**. Complete the steps listed in the Instructions sheet of the Excel Template to copy your Accounts Payable Aging Summary Excel export to the Excel Template.

Answer the following questions about Mookie The Beagle Coach Accounts Payable Aging Summary report.

1. On the Accounts Payable (A/P) Aging Summary Report, what is the amount of A/P that is Current?

2. On the A/P Aging Summary, what is the amount of A/P that is 1–30 days past due?

3. On the A/P Aging Summary, what is the amount of A/P that is 31–60 days past due?

Section 11.13

MY ACCOUNTANT REPORTS

My Accountant reports include reports used by an accountant in completing various accounting tasks. These reports include the Account List (Chart of Accounts), General Ledger, Journal, and Trial Balance.

JOURNAL

The Journal report lists every transaction entered in our QBO Company in debit and credit entry form. Even if the transaction was entered using an onscreen form, such as an Invoice, QBO will show the transaction in the Journal as a debit and credit journal entry. The Journal can be useful when tracking down errors.

C11.13.1 Journal

To view the Journal report:

1 From the Navigation Bar, select **Reports**

2 Select **Standard** tab

3 Select **Report Category: For My Accountant**

4 Select **Journal**

5 Enter **Customize** features: **Report Period: 02/28/2023 To 02/28/2023** > **Negative numbers: (100)** > **Run report**.

6 Select **Save Customization**. Enter **Custom report name: Journal**. Select **Add new group** > enter **New group name: Accountant Reports** > **Add** > **Save**. The customized report will now appear under the Custom Reports tab.

7 Export the Journal to **PDF**

8 Export the Journal to **Excel**. Complete the steps listed in the Instructions sheet of the Excel Template to copy your Journal export to the Excel Template.

Answer the following questions about Mookie The Beagle Coach Journal.

1. What are Total Debits?

2. What are Total Credits?

3. How many journal entries appear in the Journal for the date 02/28/2023?

Section 11.14

TAG REPORTS

By adding customized tags to transactions for money in and money out, we can gain valuable insights into how we bring in money and how we spend money.

To gain insight into which clients are bringing in the most money and how the client learned about Mookie The Beagle Coach, we are using two different Tag Groups:

- Pets

- Marketing Channel

C11.14.1 Tag Results

Complete the following to view Tag results:

1 From the Navigation Bar, select **Banking** > **Tags** tab or select the **Gear** icon > **Tags**

2 In the Money In section, select **All dates**

Answer the following questions about Mookie The Beagle Coach Tag results.

1. In the Money In tagging results section for Pets, which Pet brought in the **largest** amount of money?

2. How much money does pet client, Kuno, bring in?

3. In the Money In tagging results section for Marketing Channel, which Marketing Channel brought in the **largest** amount of money?

4. How much money does the Pet Store Marketing Channel bring in?

C11.14.2 Tag Report

Complete the following to view Tag reports:

1 From the Tags and Tag Groups section, for the Tag Group Marketing Channel, select **Run report**

2 When the Profit and Loss by Tag Group Report appears, enter **Report Period: 02/01/2023 to 02/28/2023**

3 Select **Run Report**

4 Export the Marketing Channels Tag report to **PDF**

5 Export the Marketing Channels Tag report to **Excel**. Complete the steps listed in the Instructions sheet of the Excel Template to copy your export to the Excel Template.

6 From the Tags and Tag Groups section, for the Tag Group Pets, select **Run report**

7 When the Profit and Loss by Tag Group Report appears, enter **Report Period: 02/01/2023 to 02/28/2023**

8 Select **Run Report**

9 Export the Pets Tag report to **PDF**

10 Export the Pets Tag report to **Excel**. Complete the steps listed in the Instructions sheet of the Excel Template to copy your export to the Excel Template.

Answer the following questions about Mookie The Beagle Coach Tag reports.

1. What is the amount recorded for Total Income that we have tagged Friends & Family?

2. What is the amount recorded for Total Income that we have tagged Maggie?

3. What is the amount recorded for Total Income that we have tagged Ozzie?

QBO Apps: Mac, Windows, and Mobile

QBO MAC OR WINDOWS APP

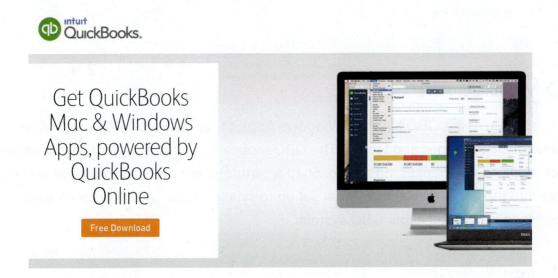

Whether using a Mac or Windows-based desktop or laptop, we can access QuickBooks Online using a browser and the Internet. In addition, QuickBooks Online also offers the option to download and install a QBO Mac App or a QBO Windows App on our desktop or laptop. The Mac and Windows Apps provide additional features. First, we must determine whether we will use the App with Mac or Windows. Then download either the QBO Mac App or the QBO Windows App to our desktop or laptop. After installing the App, use our QBO Company sign in.

The QBO Mac and Windows Apps provide a blended approach. We can still access our QBO company from anywhere, anytime through a browser. In addition, if we have the desktop QBO Mac or Windows App installed, we have additional features available, including a menu bar (similar to the QuickBooks Desktop version), the functionality to open multiple windows at the same time, and the ability to enter QBO data without an active Internet connection. Later, when you establish an Internet connection, the data will sync with QBO in the cloud. The QBO Mac and Windows Apps are available free with a QBO subscription.

Open multiple windows at the same time

- Drag and drop them anywhere, even across screens and side by side
- Switch quickly between multiple tasks
- Save time with automatic refresh of open windows

QBO MOBILE APP

In addition to the QBO Mac and Windows Apps, there is also a QBO Mobile App available for smartphones and tablets. The QBO mobile app permits us to add transactions, such as credit card expenses, on the go. Snap a picture of our credit card receipt and input the data into the QBO mobile app. When set up to sync with our QBO, the credit card expense then is updated in our QBO system.

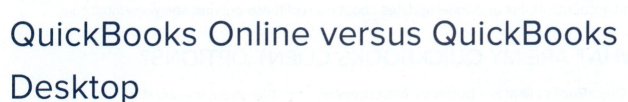

QuickBooks Online versus QuickBooks Desktop

ASK MY ACCOUNTANT: WHICH QUICKBOOKS SHOULD I USE?

To meet different QuickBooks users' needs, Intuit offers several different versions of QuickBooks. If we are advising different clients on the best fit between their needs and QuickBooks version, then a general knowledge of the different types of QuickBooks available becomes vital to provide sound client advice.

In general, QuickBooks versions can be divided into two broad categories:

- **QuickBooks Client.** Businesses and organizations that use QuickBooks to maintain their accounting and financial records.
- **QuickBooks Accountant.** Accountants who provide accounting and financial services to multiple clients who use QuickBooks.

Since QuickBooks offers several different options (summarized in the following table), QuickBooks users often turn to their accountants for recommendations about which QuickBooks to use. The QuickBooks version that the client uses dictates which QuickBooks version the client's accountant must use. As the accountant making recommendations, we need to consider not only how the recommendation affects our client, but also how the recommendation will impact our client services.

	QuickBooks Online (QBO)	**QuickBooks Desktop (QBDT)**
Client	• QuickBooks Online (QBO) Simple Start • QuickBooks Online (QBO) Essentials • QuickBooks Online (QBO+) Plus • QuickBooks Online (QBO) Advanced	• QuickBooks Desktop (QBDT) Pro • QuickBooks Desktop (QBDT) Premier • QuickBooks Enterprise
Accountant	• QuickBooks Online Accountant (QBOA)	• QuickBooks Desktop Accountant (QBDTA)

Although features and functionality of QuickBooks options can be expected to change over time, the following sections summarize information about some of the QuickBooks options for clients and accountants. For additional updates about each of these options, see www.Intuit.com.

WHAT ARE MY QUICKBOOKS CLIENT OPTIONS?

A QuickBooks client is a business, entrepreneur, or not-for-profit organization that uses QuickBooks to maintain accounting and financial records for that entity. A QuickBooks client has two basic options:

- QuickBooks Desktop (QBDT)
- QuickBooks Online (QBO)

If the QuickBooks client selects the QuickBooks Desktop option, then there are several additional choices to consider that are summarized next.

QUICKBOOKS DESKTOP (QBDT)

QuickBooks Desktop software can be installed on the hard drive of desktop computers, laptops, or servers controlled by the client. If QuickBooks is installed on a network, it can be accessed by multiple QuickBooks users. QuickBooks Desktop can also be hosted in the cloud by Intuit authorized providers. QuickBooks Desktop software can be purchased using three different approaches:

1. Software Download. Since new desktop computers and laptops increasingly do not have CD drives, users can purchase a QuickBooks software key code and download the QuickBooks software using an Internet browser.
2. Subscription. Instead of purchasing QuickBooks software, the user can choose to pay a monthly subscription fee to use the software. The QuickBooks software is still downloaded to the desktop computer or laptop, but when the user decides to stop paying the monthly fee, the user's access to the QuickBooks software is blocked.

In general, QuickBooks Desktop offers several advantages including:

- Additional features and functionality not offered by QuickBooks Online
- User control over desktop computer access and security
- User control over backups and access to backup data files
- Portability of backup and portable QuickBooks files
- Navigation features to streamline use, such as the Home Page with flowcharts

- Intuit offers the following different editions of the QuickBooks Desktop software to meet specific user needs, including:
  - QuickBooks Pro
  - QuickBooks Premier
  - QuickBooks Enterprise

QuickBooks Desktop Pro is a good option for small businesses that do not require industry-specific features because it is less expensive.

QuickBooks Desktop Premier offers more advanced features than QuickBooks Pro and permits you to customize QuickBooks by selecting a version with industry-specific features. QuickBooks Premier has different industry versions from which you can choose including the following.

- Contractor
- Manufacturing and Wholesale
- Nonprofit
- Professional Services
- Retailers
- General Business

QuickBooks Enterprise is designed for mid-size companies that have outgrown QuickBooks Premier. QuickBooks Enterprise can be used to track inventory at multiple locations and consolidate reports from multiple companies.

QUICKBOOKS ONLINE (QBO)

Accessed using a browser and the Internet, with QuickBooks Online, there is no need to install software on a computer hard drive or local server. (See Appendix A for the QBO App that can be installed on a computer to enhance the features of QBO.) The main advantage to QuickBooks Online is its anytime, anywhere use, as long as Internet access is available. Factors to consider when using QuickBooks Online include:

- Internet connection needs to be a secure connection with data in transit encrypted. Using an open WiFi at a café or a hotel when traveling to access QuickBooks Online, while convenient, places data in transit at risk. Our login, password, and confidential financial data could be viewed by others.

- Fewer features and functionality than QuickBooks Desktop with features that will continue to change as QuickBooks Online is dynamically updated.
- The convenience of dynamic updates that occur automatically without needing to download and install.
- Loss of control over when updates occur, which may result in the need to learn new updates at unplanned times.
- Backups are performed automatically by Intuit.
- QBO Mobile app that makes it easier to stay up to date while on the go.

WHAT ARE MY QUICKBOOKS ACCOUNTANT OPTIONS?

Designed for accountants serving multiple clients, Intuit offers two QuickBooks Accountant options:

- QuickBooks Desktop Accountant (QBDTA)
- QuickBooks Online Accountant (QBOA)

Which option the accountant chooses is typically dictated by client use because QuickBooks Desktop files, in general, are not compatible with QuickBooks Online. For example, if all the accounting firm's clients use QuickBooks Desktop software, then the accounting firm would use QuickBooks Desktop Accountant version. If the clients use QuickBooks Online, then the accountant needs to use QuickBooks Online Accountant. Some accounting firms have clients using QuickBooks Desktop versions and other clients using QuickBooks Online, so those accounting firms must use both QuickBooks Desktop Accountant and QuickBooks Online Accountant to be able to work with both types of clients.

QUICKBOOKS DESKTOP ACCOUNTANT (QBDTA)

QuickBooks Desktop Accountant is the software used with Kay's *Computer Accounting with QuickBooks* text. Like QuickBooks Desktop software, QuickBooks Desktop Accountant is installed on the hard drive of desktop computers, laptops, or network servers. The QuickBooks Desktop Accountant edition permits the accountant to toggle between different desktop user editions of QuickBooks. This permits the accountant to view whatever edition of QuickBooks (QuickBooks Pro, QuickBooks Premier, and so on) that a particular client uses.

For more information about using QuickBooks Desktop, see Kay's *Computer Accounting with QuickBooks* at www.My-QuickBooks.com.

How Can Our Accounting Firm Streamline Our QuickBooks Desktop Consulting?

Which QuickBooks version our clients use affects our consulting services operations. Some accounting firms relate nightmarish stories about clients using an array of QuickBooks Desktop software from the 2010 edition and every year to the present edition. This approach to QuickBooks consulting requires the accounting firm to maintain all the various versions of the client software and track which clients use which versions. This can become a logistical nightmare for an accounting firm since it must have not only all the QuickBooks editions operational but also staff trained on the multiple versions.

Other accounting firms take a more streamlined, proactive approach when working with multiple clients that use QuickBooks. These firms recommend to clients which QuickBooks edition to use based on the best fit for the client while still keeping it manageable for the firm. Some accountants move all their clients to the next edition of QuickBooks at the same time. For example, after the 2022 QuickBooks edition is released, the accounting firm thoroughly tests the new edition, and then the firm moves all clients to QuickBooks 2022 on January 1, 2022. This approach permits the accounting firm to test the new software for possible issues, install updates, and create workarounds before moving clients to the new edition. Since many clients are on a calendar year starting January 1, this timeline permits a nice cutoff. Also, this approach streamlines firm operations since now all clients and the firm are in sync, using the same version of QuickBooks.

This proactive approach requires the accounting firm to communicate clearly with clients, working as a team with clients to prepare and transition them to the new version. Firms that use this proactive approach often state that it requires time and effort to do so, but much less time than trying to maintain multiple versions of QuickBooks for multiple clients. If clients start moving to the new edition as soon as it is released, clients may encounter unexpected issues that the accounting firm has not had time to thoroughly investigate and resolve. Some firms even provide training for clients as they transition them to the new version, summarizing differences and new features to proactively prepare clients for what to expect. This can minimize client errors in working with the new version and save the firm from unexpected disruptions and surprises.

QUICKBOOKS ONLINE ACCOUNTANT (QBOA)

QuickBooks Online Accountant is designed for accounting firms that provide services to multiple clients who use QuickBooks Online. QuickBooks Online Accountant is accessed using the Internet and a browser and permits the accountant to collaborate with several different clients, viewing their QuickBooks Online company files. At this time QuickBooks Online Accountant does not use the Home Page navigational feature. In addition, there are fewer features and functionality with the QuickBooks Online Accountant version than the QuickBooks Desktop Accountant version.

QBOA offers more features than QBO for clients. For example, QBOA has Adjusted Trial Balance and Adjusting Journal Entry features. In addition, there are other Accountant Tools in QBOA.

The main advantage to QuickBooks Online Accountant is the anytime, anywhere access when an Internet connection is available. Of course, since the accountant is responsible for maintaining the confidentiality of client financial data, the Internet connection needs to be a secure connection with data in transit encrypted. Using an open WiFi connection risks data in transit (such as login, password, and confidential client financial data) being viewed by others. Since accounting firms have a responsibility to maintain client data confidentiality and security, this is a serious concern.

For more information about QuickBooks Online, go to www.my-quickbooksonline.com.

QBO Certification

QBO CERTIFICATION TYPES

In general, QuickBooks Online versions can be divided into two broad categories:

- **QuickBooks Online Client.** Businesses and organizations that use QuickBooks Online to maintain their accounting and financial records.
- **QuickBooks Online Accountant.** Accountants who provide accounting and financial services to multiple clients who use QuickBooks Online.

Corresponding to this, there are two basic levels of QBO Certification Exams:

- **QuickBooks Online User Certification Exam.**
- **QuickBooks Online Accountant Certification Exam.**

The *Computer Accounting with QuickBooks Online* text provides you with a good starting point for preparing for QBO certification. The next step is to decide which QBO Certification you wish to pursue.

Note that the QBO Certification information is subject to change.

QUICKBOOKS ONLINE USER CERTIFICATION

QBO User Certification focuses on the user (client) perspective. This is the perspective of the client using QuickBooks Online to maintain its accounting and financial records.

The following table summarizes the seven QBO User Exam Objectives. Note that exam coverage is subject to change and this is not an exhaustive list of exam topics.

QBO User Exam Objective	Topics Include...
1. QBO Setup and Maintenance	• Setting up a QBO Company • How to import lists • How to modify elements after setup • How to navigate QBO
2. List Management	• The lists used in QBO and what type of information is tracked on each, such as Chart of Accounts, Customers List, Vendors List, and Products and Services List • How to manage lists, including adding, editing, and removing list entries • How to merge list entries
3. Sales/Money In	• How to set up a Product or Service • How to set up Customers • How to record sales using Sales Receipts with no A/R workflow • How to record sales using Invoice with A/R workflow • Know when to Sales Receipts or Invoice • How to invoice for billable expenses • How to record a customer credit
4. Purchases/Money Out	• How to set up a Product or Service • How to set up Vendors • How to record Purchase Order workflow • How to Enter Bills and Pay Bills (A/P) • How to enter Checks • How to record Credit Card transactions • How to record Debit Card transactions • How to void and delete checks • How to use Vendor reports to determine amount owed and when payment is due
5. Basic Accounting	• Identify the basic financial statements and understand their format and meaning • Understand the difference between cash and accrual reporting • How to enter a Journal entry • How to use the Audit Log to identify changes made by a specific user
6. Reports	• How to customize a report • How to export reports
7. Customization/Saving Time	• How to create recurring transactions • Know the time-saving benefits of QuickBook Online

The QBO User Certification is offered through www.certiport.com. If you decide to move forward with QBO User Certification, consider the following approach:

- Learn QBO. Your *Computer Accounting with QuickBooks Online* text provides an excellent starting point and solid foundation for learning QBO.
- Prep for QBO Certification. Review the QBO User Exam objectives and use the QBO Certification Study Guide that can be found at www.certiport.com.
- QBO Certification Exam Practice. Try the QBO Practice tests. See www.certiport.com for more information.
- Take and Pass QBO Certification Exam. Go to www.certiport.com for more information about how to sign up for the QBO User Certification Exam.

Note that there is a fee for taking the QBO User Certification offered through www.certiport.com.

QUICKBOOKS ONLINE ACCOUNTANT CERTIFICATION

The QuickBooks Online Accountant Certification exam includes many topics that are focused on the accountant perspective using QuickBooks Online Accountant. For example, topics covered have an emphasis on accountants using QuickBooks Online for clients, such as onboarding new clients. Note that at this time, it appears you can complete the QBOA Certification without incurring additional fees to take the QBOA certification exam.

There are three different QBO Accountant Certifications:

- QBO Accountant Certification
- QBO Accountant Advanced Certification
- New—QBO Payroll Certification

Topics covered in the QBO Accountant Certification exam include topics focused on accountants who use QBO for clients. For example, topics include:

- Setting up clients
- Supporting small business clients
- Banking and Tools
- Reports
- Managing your work
- Preparing clients' books
- QuickBooks solutions for clients

The QBO Accountant Certification Exam is in multiple-choice format. Although time will vary, on average it takes about 3 to 4 hours to complete the QBO Accountant Certification Exam, but you do not have to take all 8 sections at one sitting. You have 3 attempts to pass a section, requiring 80% to pass each section. You only need to re-take sections not passed instead of the entire exam.

After obtaining your QBO Accountant Certification, each year you must complete a QBO Recertification Exam to maintain your QBO Certification. July 31 of each year is the recertification date for QBO Recertification. Shorter than the QBO Certification Exam, the QBO Recertification Exam is an abbreviated exam, covering new features of QBO that were introduced during the past year.

Your *Computer Accounting with QuickBooks Online* text is your launchpad to prepare for QBO Certification. If you are interested in QBO Certification, after completing the assignments in your text using QBO+, consider the following steps to pursue your QBO Certification.

1. Sign up for QuickBooks Online Accountant (QBO Accountant). (Note: This is a different version of QBO than the version you used with your text.) **Visit http://bit.ly/proadvisor_free > select Sign up (or Sign up for free) > set up your free account.**

2. **Sign into your QBO Accountant account at qbo.intuit.com.** (Note: If you used the same email address for both QBO+ and QBO Accountant then QuickBooks Online may consolidate your company logins into one login screen.)

3. Select **ProAdvisor** on the left Navigation Bar. Sign up to be a ProAdvisor. (Note: You must be signed up as ProAdvisor before taking the QBO certification exam.)

4. In QBO Accountant, select **ProAdvisor tab > Training** tab

5. To train for certification, select: **Self-paced** to view training modules

6. When you are prepared, select **Take Exam.** Review the exam instructions.

7. Click **Start Section w**hen you are ready to being taking the QBO Certification Exam. Good luck!

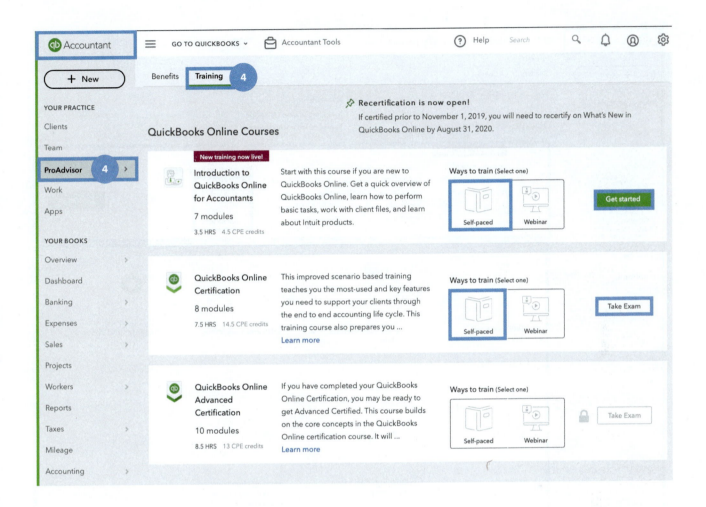

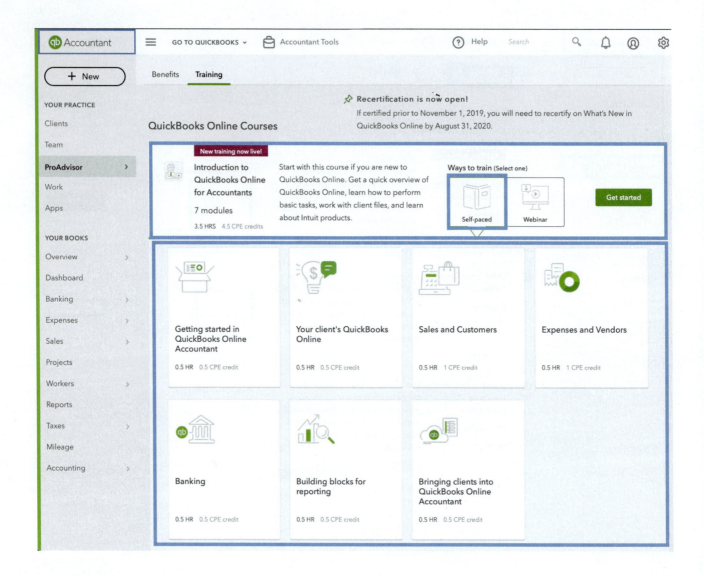

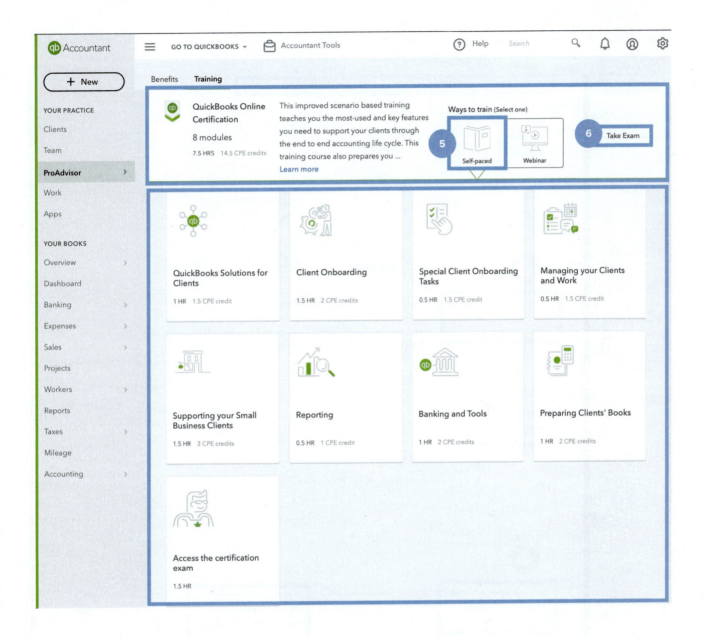

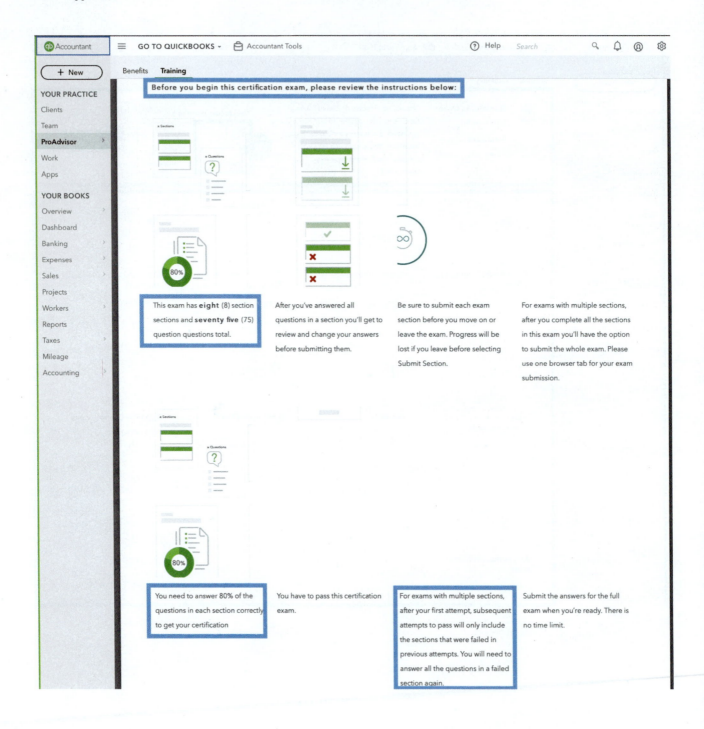

Before you begin this certification exam, please review the instructions below:

This exam has **eight** (8) section sections and **seventy five** (75) question questions total.

After you've answered all questions in a section you'll get to review and change your answers before submitting them.

Be sure to submit each exam section before you move on or leave the exam. Progress will be lost if you leave before selecting Submit Section.

For exams with multiple sections, after you complete all the sections in this exam you'll have the option to submit the whole exam. Please use one browser tab for your exam submission.

You need to answer 80% of the questions in each section correctly to get your certification

You have to pass this certification exam.

For exams with multiple sections, after your first attempt, subsequent attempts to pass will only include the sections that were failed in previous attempts. You will need to answer all the questions in a failed section again.

Submit the answers for the full exam when you're ready. There is no time limit.

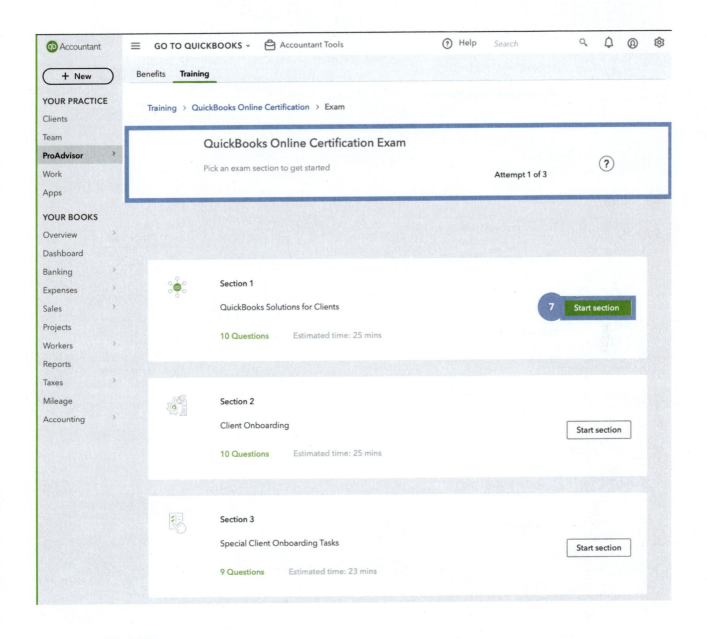

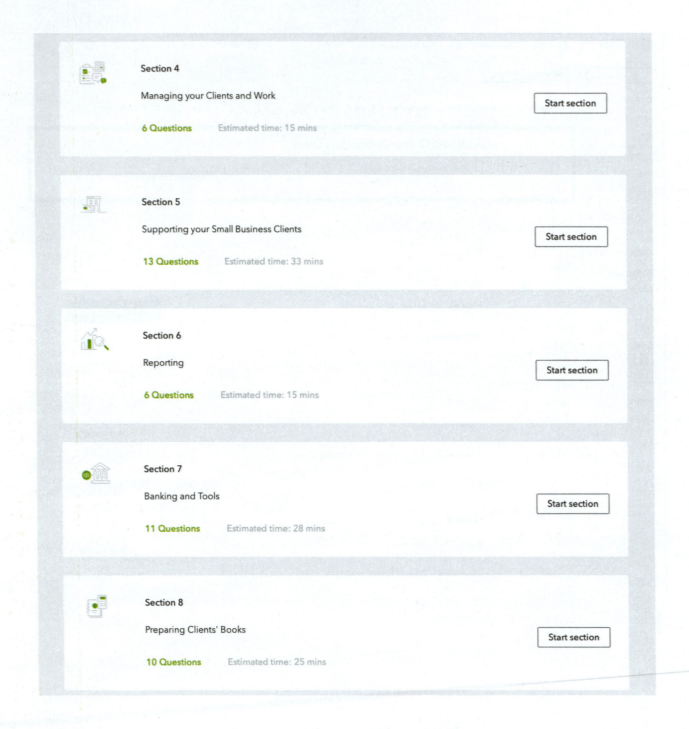

Section 4

Managing your Clients and Work

Start section

6 Questions   Estimated time: 15 mins

Section 5

Supporting your Small Business Clients

Start section

13 Questions   Estimated time: 33 mins

Section 6

Reporting

Start section

6 Questions   Estimated time: 15 mins

Section 7

Banking and Tools

Start section

11 Questions   Estimated time: 28 mins

Section 8

Preparing Clients' Books

Start section

10 Questions   Estimated time: 25 mins

QBO Troubleshooting

This appendix summarizes resources to assist you with QBO Troubleshooting (QT) including:

- QBO Help
- QBO Text Updates
- QBO Troubleshooting (QT) Best Practices
- QBO Troubleshooting Techniques and Tools

QBO Help

To use the QBO Help feature:

1 Select the **? Help** icon

2 Enter the question

3 Select **Search**

4 For additional assistance, select **Contact us** and search for the question

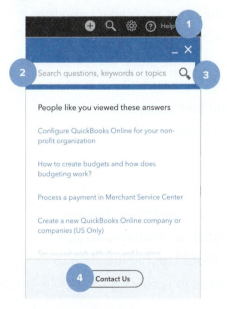

QBO Updates

QBO is updated on an ongoing basis. So some features on your screen may be slightly different from those shown in your text due to new, dynamic QBO updates.

To check for QBO updates that affect your text:

1 Go to www.my-quickbooksonline.com > QBO 3e > QBO 3e Updates, or

2 If you are using Connect or a digital ebook, go to Additional Student Resources (ASR). If you do not have access to Connect or the ebook, your instruction can provide you with ASR.

QBO TROUBLESHOOTING (QT) BEST PRACTICES

QBO Troubleshooting (QT) Best Practices can increase your chances of success at troubleshooting QBO. Develop your QuickBooks Troubleshooting (QT) skills by trying some of these best practices.

TROUBLESHOOTING MINDSET

One of the most important factors in determining troubleshooting success is adopting a **Troubleshooting Mindset**. Focus on shifting your mindset from a Dependent Mindset to a Troubleshooting Mindset.

- Dependent Mindset. This is a typical mindset, a mindset of being dependent on someone else, such as an instructor, to solve problems for you.
- Troubleshooting Mindset. Tap into a mindset that if you put in the effort, you can resolve the issue. Be willing to be resilient. If the first thing you try doesn't work, what else can you try? A troubleshooting mindset is valuable to entrepreneurs and employers because often they encounter new issues that no one else has encountered before. Sometimes there is no one else to turn to for solving an issue. Start believing in yourself and your ability to troubleshoot. With practice, your confidence and troubleshooting skills will improve.

TROUBLESHOOTING PROCESS

QBO Troubleshooting (QT) Process, like any business process, can be thought of as a blueprint that depicts pathways of related activities to reach a goal as efficiently as possible. A QT Best Practice is to use a structured, process approach to QBO Troubleshooting to streamline the troubleshooting process and increase effectiveness in resolving issues.

Typically, a troubleshooting process can be divided into two stages:

1. Identify the issue.
2. Fix the issue.

Consider the following example of a QT Process, summarized in the following QBO Troubleshooting Process Map, that you can customize to create your own QT process.

1. Identify the issue and isolate whether it is an accounting/financial issue or a QBO technology issue that is causing the problem.

2. If you have an accounting error in your QBO company file:
   - Isolate and identify the specific accounting issue. For example, is your trial balance not in balance. What is causing the imbalance? Trace back through the related accounts to identify discrepancies.
   - Review Accounting Essentials for the related chapter(s).
   - Try displaying the Journal report to track the error. Sometimes it is easier to see the error when viewing the associated journal entries, such as a missed bill payment or customer payment received.
   - Try reviewing your Audit Log to review transactions to track down the accounting error.
   - See Chapter 9, Accounting Essentials, Accounting Adjustments and Corrections, to learn more about how to correct accounting errors.
   - Conduct additional research as needed to resolve the accounting issue.
   - Finally, if unable to resolve the issue on your own, contact your instructor for assistance, detailing the issue and actions steps you completed. (See www.my-quickbooksonline.com > QBO Troubleshooting link, for a QT form that you can use to complete and send to your instructor.)

3. If you are experiencing a QBO issue:
   - Isolate and identify the QuickBooks issue.
   - Review related QBO Chapter and Section.
   - Verify QBO tasks and instruction steps were completed correctly.
   - Check out Updates for your *Computer Accounting with QuickBooks Online* edition at www.my-quickbooksonline.com > QBO 3e > QBO 3e Updates. If you are using Connect with your text, see Connect for any additional updates. Note that posted updates include text updates and QBO application updates that affect your text.
   - Use QBO Help to research the issue. If you receive a specific error code, search for that code.

- Finally, if unable to resolve the issue on your own, contact your instructor for assistance, detailing the issue and actions steps you completed. (See www.my-quickbooksonline.com > QBO Troubleshooting link, for a QT form that you can use to complete and send to your instructor.)

For more QuickBooks Troubleshooting Best Practices, go to www.my-quickbooksonline.com > QBO Troubleshooting link.

QBO TROUBLESHOOTING PROCESS MAP		
	1 Identify Issue and Isolate whether an Accounting Issue or a QBO Issue	
2 Accounting Issue? ↓ Isolate and Identify Specific Accounting Issue ↓ Review Accounting Essentials ↓ Create Journal Report to Track Error or Review Audit Log ↓ See Chapter 9, Accounting Essentials, to Learn How to Correct Accounting Errors ↓ If Not Resolved, Conduct Additional Research ↓ Finally, Contact Your Instructor using QT Form Online		**3** QBO Issue? ↓ Isolate and Identify QBO Issue ↓ Review Relevant QBO Chapter and Section ↓ Verify QBO Tasks Were Completed Correctly ↓ Check out Updates for Your QBO Text Online ↓ If Not Resolved, Conduct Additional Research Using: • QBO Help • QBO Community ↓ Finally, Contact Your Instructor Using QT Form Online

TROUBLESHOOTING INCENTIVIZE

Incentivize yourself when troubleshooting. What does this mean? Sometimes we count on others to provide us with incentives to motivate us to take action and succeed at a task. But that may be an unrealistic expectation. Sometimes no one notices when we undertake a challenging task and succeed. So we need to incentivize ourselves. Reward ourselves. For example, when you encounter a QBO issue, such as a QBO update you were not expecting, you might incentive yourself by telling yourself that instead of becoming frustrated (although that would be normal) or expecting someone else to solve the problem for you (sometimes that would be nice...but unrealistic), you dive in to resolve the issue and after you resolve the issue, reward your efforts. Maybe watch a movie that you've been wanting to see or reward yourself with a snack that you adore. Reward yourself to incentivize yourself to troubleshoot successfully.

QBO TROUBLESHOOTING TECHNIQUES AND TOOLS

QBO troubleshooting techniques and tools can be used as needed as part of the troubleshooting process. In addition to QBO Help that was discussed earlier in Appendix D, other techniques and tools that can assist in troubleshooting include:

- Journal
- Audit Log
- QBO Search
- Autofill Issues
- Connected Bank and Credit Card Account Matches
- Void and Delete
- Correcting Entries
- Test Drive QBO
- Browser Troubleshooting

JOURNAL

The Journal can be a valuable troubleshooting tool for QBO. When transactions are entered in QBO using onscreen forms, such as Invoices, behind the screen, QBO converts the transactions into journal entries with debits and credits. When isolating accounting errors, reviewing the Journal for a specific date range can provide useful insights into missing or incorrect data.

For more information how to use the Journal, see Chapters 9 and 10.

AUDIT LOG

One of the best troubleshooting tools that QBO offers is the Audit Log. The Audit Log provides a chronological listing of all the items and transactions entered into QBO, including date and user name. The Audit Log provides a behind-the-scenes view of what has happened in a QBO company.

For more information about how to use the Audit Log, see Chapter 10.

QBO SEARCH

When troubleshooting, QBO Search can be a useful tool. For example, if we know our system is off by an amount of $72, then we use QBO Search to search on that dollar amount. The search results might show us that we have two transactions entered for $72, instead of just one. Then we can select the transactions returned in the search results, and fix the issue by deleting the duplicate transaction.

AUTOFILL ISSUES

QBO features an autofill option, where certain fields in forms are automatically filled using information from a prior transactions. For example, the date may be autofilled based on the date used on the previously entered transaction. Another example is after a vendor is selected on an Expense form, QBO will autofill the accounts or categories on the current Expense form based upon the accounts or categories used on the prior Expense form completed for that specific vendor.

The autofill feature is intended to save time. However, sometimes the automatically filled fields are not correct. This is a frequent way that errors can inadvertently enter the financial system. A good practice is to always check and crosscheck the autofilled dates and fields on a form. When searching for an error in the financial system, autofilled fields can be reviewed to verify accuracy.

CONNECTED BANK AND CREDIT CARD ACCOUNT MATCHES

QBO offers the option of connecting bank and credit card accounts to QBO. After the bank or credit card account is connected, then the bank or credit card transactions are automatically downloaded into QBO. The process of matching the downloaded transactions to the transactions entered into QBO provides a check and crosscheck opportunity. If an amount is entered incorrectly, then the transaction will not show as a possible match. Reviewing the transactions in the bank or credit card accounting for discrepancies with the downloaded transactions can prove to be useful in identifying errors.

VOID AND DELETE

After isolating an accounting error, the next step is determining how to fix it. Depending upon the type of accounting error, sometimes you can void or delete a transaction to correct the discrepancy. If after reviewing the error, voiding or deleting the transaction will resolve the issue, complete the following steps.

- To void a transaction, display on the screen the QBO form, such as an invoice or expense. From the bottom menu, select Void.
- To delete a transaction, display on the screen the QBO form, such as an invoice or expense. From the bottom menu, select Delete.

CORRECTING ENTRIES

When voiding or deleting the transaction is not option to fix an accounting error, sometimes we need to resort to using the Journal to fix an accounting issue.

A Journal entry to fix an accounting error is called a correcting entry. To make sure that in attempting to fix an error, we don't enter another error, the two-entry approach is often the best approach. The first entry reverses the incorrect entry. The second entry makes the correct entry. See Chapter 9, Accounting Essentials, Accounting Adjustments and Corrections, for examples of how to correct accounting errors using Journal entries.

TEST DRIVE QBO

If you want to test out a troubleshooting fix, consider using the test drive company before trying it in your QBO company project. The test drive company resets every time it is reopened so you can't break it. This permits you to try out a troubleshooting fix, such correcting entries or voiding a transaction, before entering it into your QBO company.

Access QBO Sample Company

To access the QBO Test Drive Company, complete the following steps.

1   Open a web browser. (Note: Intuit recommends using Google Chrome.)

2   Go to the Sample Company at https://qbo.intuit.com/redir/testdrive

3   Follow onscreen instructions for security verification. If a message about cookies or blocking pop-up windows appears, follow the onscreen instructions.

> **Note: Although the Test Drive Company link should work, if for some reason the previous link for the Test Drive Company doesn't work with your browser, using Google search, type in "qbo.intuit.com Sample Company". Select the link to Test Drive Sample Company.**

Craig's Design and Landscaping Services, the QBO Sample Company, should appear on your screen.

QBO Sample Company Reset

While you are using the Craig's Design and Landscaping Services Sample Company, the information you enter will be saved. *After you close* the Sample Company, automatically all the settings and data are reset to the original data and settings before you entered your work. The Sample Company repopulates with its original data. If you are using the Sample Company to explore and practice with QBO, the reset will permit you to start over each time you enter the Sample Company.

The Sample Company default setting is to log out after one (1) hour of inactivity. Since the Sample Company then repopulates with the original data automatically, you will lose any work you entered. Therefore, it is important to plan accordingly so that you can complete all activities needed before closing the Sample Company.

To increase the amount of time from one (1) hour to three (3) hours before the log out for inactivity occurs:

1   From Craig's Design and Landscaping Services QBO Sample Company, select the **Gear** icon

2   Under Your Company section, select **Account and Settings**

3   Select **Advanced**

4   Select **Other preferences**

5   For the option Sign me out if inactive for, click on **1 hour**

6   From the drop-down menu, select **3 hours**

7   Select **Save**

8   Select **Done**

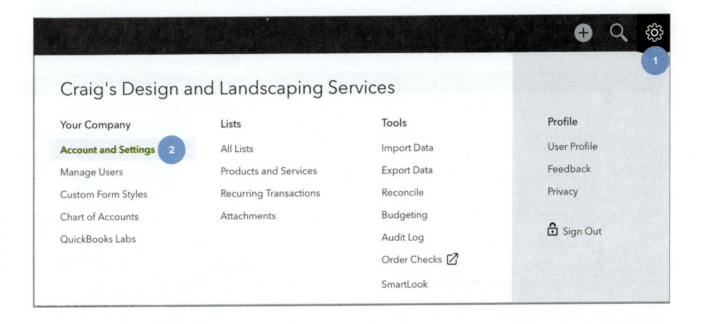

Craig's Design and Landscaping Services

Your Company	Lists	Tools	Profile
Account and Settings	All Lists	Import Data	User Profile
Manage Users	Products and Services	Export Data	Feedback
Custom Form Styles	Recurring Transactions	Reconcile	Privacy
Chart of Accounts	Attachments	Budgeting	
QuickBooks Labs		Audit Log	🔓 Sign Out
		Order Checks ⬈	
		SmartLook	

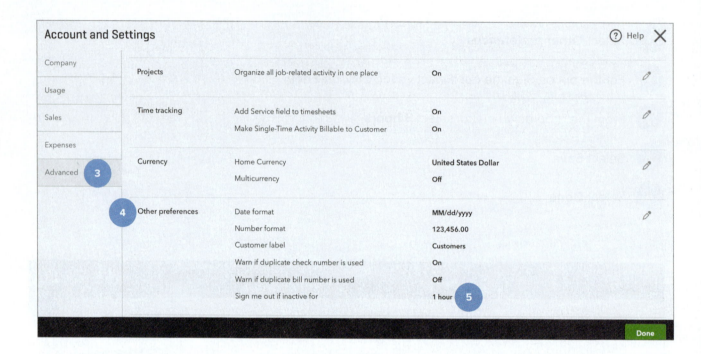

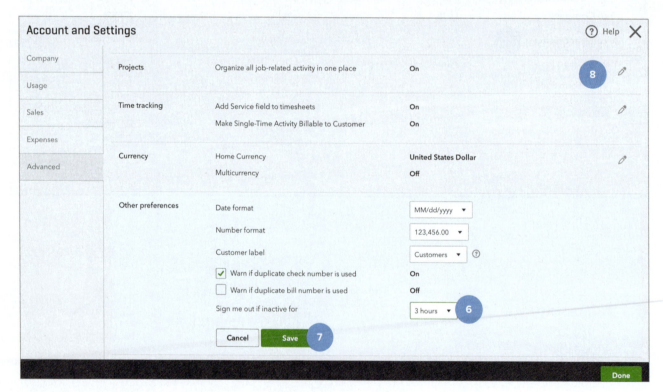

⚠️ **The Sample Company** will reset each time it is reopened. This allows you to explore and practice QBO without concern about carrying forward errors. However, since your data is not saved, you will want to make certain to allow enough time to complete activities before closing the Sample Company. Otherwise, you will lose the work you have entered when you reopen the Sample Company. Furthermore, when instructed to close the browser to reset the Sample Company, it is important to follow the instructions precisely and close and reopen the browser as instructed.

BROWSER TROUBLESHOOTING

Chrome Browser

Intuit recommends Google Chrome browser for use with QBO. If you are using a different type of browser and receiving error messages, try switching to using a Chrome browser.

Clearing Cookies and Cache

If you receive an error message when using Chrome to access your QBO company, try clearing Cookies and Cache as follows:

1. From the upper right of the Chrome browser, select the **3 dots**

2. Select **More tools**

3. Select **Clear browsing data**

4. Select Time range: **All time**

5. Select **Cookies and other site data**

6. Select **Cached images and files**

7. Select **Clear data**

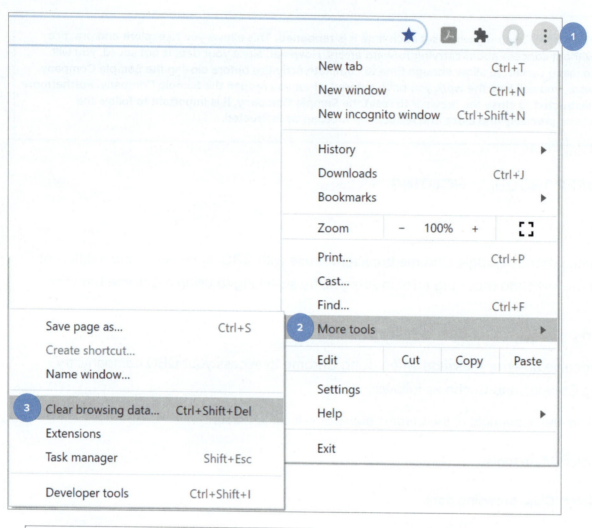

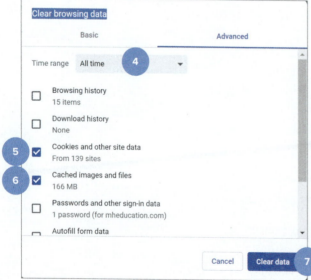

Multiple Browser Windows

When working in QBO, sometimes it is more convenient to have more than one QBO window open. This permits you to compare amounts from screen to screen instead of clicking back and forth, back and forth in the same QBO window.

For example to have two QBO company windows open at the same time:

1. **Log in** to your QBO Company using Google Chrome browser

2. In the browser, **right-click** the **QBO browser tab** to display a pop-up menu

3. From the pop-up menu, select **Duplicate**

Now you should have two tabs open with two windows for the same QBO company.

Index